# Birds
## of the
# British Isles
## & Europe

# Birds
## of the
# British Isles
## & Europe

**John Gooders**

*Birds of the British Isles & Europe*
was conceived, edited and
designed by
Team Media Limited, London

Copyright © Team Media Ltd

Published by
SILVERDALE BOOKS in 2001
an imprint of Bookmart Ltd
Registered Number 2372865
Trading as Bookmart Limited
Desford Road
Enderby
Leicester LE9 5AD

Illustrations front cover,
Frank Hecker, back cover
Ardea / Richard Vaughan
(top), Windrush Photos /
D. M. Cotteridge (bottom)

A CIP catalogue record for this
book is available from the
British Library.

ISBN 1 85605 622 8

Printed and bound in Germany

**Birds of Europe Team**
**Project Editor** Alice Bell
**Editors** Marian Broderick,
Rupert Matthews
**Art Editors** Christopher
Howson, Colin Goody,
Duncan Paré
**Picture Researcher**
Veneta Bullen
**Consultant Editor**
Jonathan Elphick

**Illustrators** Norman Arlott,
Stephen Lings, Richard Orr,
Sarah Smith, Stuart Lufford,
Andrew Robinson

**Cartographer** Patrick Mulrey

**Team Media**
**Publishing Manager**
Hal Robinson
**Managing Editor**
Elizabeth Tatham
**Editorial Director**
Louise Tucker
**Art Directors** Eddie Poulton,
Paul Wilkinson

# CONTENTS

No matter where we live, we tend to take our surroundings for granted. In Europe, we are encompassed by a rich natural environment, which often goes unnoticed. This environment is home to many wonderful plants and animals, including a large variety of birds, which are the subject of this book.

The European avifauna is rich both in species and numbers, and in *Birds of Europe* we seek to understand how this avifauna evolved and how birds relate to the diverse range of habitats found in what often seems such an overcrowded landscape. While much of Europe's wildlife has been eliminated as a result of human action, many birds have adapted to the changes humans have wrought on the landscape and have managed to survive.

In seeking to understand birds, we start with their evolution and the study of birds through history. Moving on to explore the physical structure of birds and their adaptations to flight – the very essence of their existence – we delve further into their lifestyles and examine their structural adaptations to feeding and reproduction. We explore what motivates migration, but while we marvel at the prodigious journeys made by some birds, such as the Arctic Tern and the Turnstone, we also examine the way in which those that don't migrate, such as the fabulous Great Grey Owl and Hawk Owl, manage to survive the harshest of winters.

Birds are creatures of habit and the variety of European species is closely linked to the landscape of our continent. *Birds of Europe* picks out the range of habitats found in Europe and explores how different birds have adapted to particular lifestyles, places or landforms where they can live successfully. Some species, such as the stream-loving Dipper, are highly specialized, while others, such as Common Kestrel and Starling, are extremely flexible and can live in the town or the countryside. The majority of birds are less specialized, but also less generalized, and have favoured habitats in which they are mostly, but not invariably, found.

Understanding how birds function and where they prefer to live is not only worthwhile in itself, but is also an extraordinarily useful aid in finding and identifying the various species, and provides a key to the species section that comprises the largest section of this book.

*Birds of Europe* is essentially a practical book designed to link bird to birdwatcher. With guidance on birdwatching as a field art, and an assessment of bird conservation, a description of the birds found in Europe, from the Atlantic to the Russian Urals, is then given. Each species is described and illustrated, facilitating not only identification, but also supplying information on where and how the bird lives. We have not accorded full treatment to rare vagrant species, or to those that occur only in remote corners of the region, but such species are noted on pages 280–281, in the list of accidental and marginal species. Eagle-eyed critics may, therefore, notice that birds such as the Crested Coot, White-rumped Swift and Little Button-quail, which may live in southernmost Spain, or the Cinereous Bunting of the easternmost Greek islands, are not included. What is important, however, is that all the regular European birds that anyone could reasonably encounter are here to be enjoyed and understood. For this book is not just a field guide. It is a book that can be read, used for reference, or dipped into by anyone with even the slightest interest in this great, colourful and diverse group of animals that live alongside us in Europe.

Arctic Tern
(first winter)

Great Grey Owl

Avocet

Turnstone

# THE ANCESTRY AND EVOLUTION OF BIRDS

Life on planet Earth is in a state of continuous flux, a process of adaptation to circumstances generally referred to as evolution.

The paths of evolution can be traced by comparing the characteristics of present-day living things with the fossil remains of earlier organisms. Fossils are formed by a process in which the bodies of organisms are preserved in silt and mud, which then turn into sedimentary rock over millions of years; when the rock erodes, the organisms' fossilized remains are left behind.

*Archaeopteryx feather found in Germany in 1860*

The large, heavy bones of animals such as dinosaurs and mammoths have frequently been fossilized. Many of the fossils have become fragmented, but occasionally a complete fossil skeleton has been found, providing us with a picture of an animal that may have been extinct for millions of years.

The evolutionary development of birds is far more difficult to trace because their remains have not fossilized well – many of their hollow bones and lightweight feathers

| Million years ago | | | | | | |
|---|---|---|---|---|---|---|
| **450** | **400** | **350** | **300** | **250** | **200** | |
| Land plant spores (c440) | Jawed fish (c425) | Wingless insects (c385) | Sharks (c375) | Winged insects (c310) | Conifers (c298) | Therapsids (c270) | Oysters (c225) | Early mammals (c208) | Birds (c150) |

| Period | Silurian | Devonian | Carboniferous | Permian | Triassic | Jurassic |
|---|---|---|---|---|---|---|
| Era | | Paleozoic | | | | |

have disintegrated or been washed away – so that far fewer bird fossils have been preserved. The fossil evidence that we do have, however, suggests that birds originated between 200 and 150 million years ago and were descended from reptiles. It is thought that over millions of years the scales of reptiles became extended and flexible to form feathers. What remains a matter of speculation is *why* feathers evolved and whether the ancestors of birds were ground-dwelling animals that escaped danger by making longer and longer leaps, or tree-dwellers that glided farther and farther by making certain adaptations. However, we do know that these creatures gradually became more effective fliers by a process of weight reduction, in which feathers, hollow bones, fast digestion and egg-laying all played a part.

### Early Fossil Discoveries

The earliest known birdlike fossil was found in 1861 in a limestone quarry in Bavaria, Germany. In 1860 a single feather had been uncovered; in the following year came the

Archaeopteryx (above) may not have been the first birdlike creature, but it is the first feathered bird of which we have evidence. It had claws at the bend of each wing that may have helped it to climb, rather

as the modern-day Hoatzin climbs through its waterside treetop habitat in northern South America. Though Archaeopteryx could undoubtedly fly, it was probably not capable of much more than extended glides, and spent most of its life climbing trees in search of food.

From the age of the limestone in which the fossil was found, it was estimated that Archaeopteryx (above) was 140 million years old. It was crow-sized, with strong

teeth, and had a long, bony tail. But for the fact that it was covered with feathers and could probably fly, it might easily have been dismissed as a reptile.

| | | | | | | Present |
|---|---|---|---|---|---|---|
| 125 | 100 | 75 | 50 | 25 | 5 | |
| Placental mammals (c135) | Diatoms (c106) | Early grasses (c72) | Primates (c60) / Grasses (c57) / Mammals diversify / Rodents (c47) / Early anthropoids | | Homo erectus (humans) (c1.5) | |
| | | Cretaceous | | Tertiary | | |
| Mesozoic | | | | Cenozoic | | |

Archaeopteryx, reconstructed from fossil remains

discovery of a feathered skeleton. The fossils were examined and named *Archaeopteryx lithographica* by the German palaeontologist Hermann von Meyer, who, from analyzing the limestone, accorded them an age of about 140 million years. *Archaeopteryx* was probably not the first birdlike creature, but it shares certain characteristics with modern birds, notably feathers and a 'U'-shaped wishbone, and it could probably fly short distances. It also displays reptilian features, such as teeth and a long, bony tail, and seems to provide us with a link in the evolutionary pathway between reptiles and birds.

For the Cretaceous period, between 140 and 70 million years ago, only about ten more bird species have been found, providing little evidence about the development of birds during this time. However, some of those fossils bear a stronger resemblance to modern bird species than *Archaeopteryx* does.

**Birds in the Tertiary Period**

Although only a few bird fossils have been found dating from between 140 and 70 million years ago, many more have been discovered for the Tertiary period, between about 65 and 3 million years ago. Many birds from this period have clear affinities with modern-day species. *Prophaeton* bears a strong resemblance to a tropicbird – indeed its name, meaning 'pre-tropicbird', implies a familial relationship. Among bird fossils from the later Tertiary period (about 25 to 12 million years ago), many have been found to resemble modern birds so closely that we can be far more certain that they are related. These birds include the early ancestors of birds such as swallows, palm swifts, vultures, storks and secretarybirds. Although the early species are now extinct, they share many features with their present-day descendants.

The vast majority of prehistoric birds for which fossils have been found date from between about 12 million and 10,000 years ago. During this period, there seems to have been a tendency towards gigantism. Some species may have become larger in order to conserve energy in cold climates or to be less vulnerable to predators. Even today, birds such as the Ostrich and the long-winged albatross still exist. Other large birds became extinct relatively recently. The Dodo, for example, a huge,

**BIRD EVOLUTION ACROSS THE CONTINENTS**
*Tracing bird evolution is complicated by the fact that the continents have shifted over millions of years. We cannot be sure whether similarities between birds on different continents exist because the birds are related, or as a result of convergent evolution. This occurs when animals living far apart, but in similar conditions, come to resemble one another.*

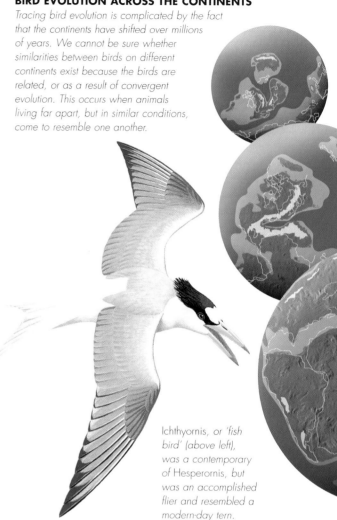

*Ichthyornis, or 'fish bird' (above left), was a contemporary of Hesperornis, but was an accomplished flier and resembled a modern-day tern.*

*Halcyornis (left) existed during the Tertiary period, between 65 and 3 million years ago. It could fly, and had many characteristics in common with a modern-day kingfisher.*

flightless, pigeonlike bird, lived in Mauritius and died out in about 1600. It is the written account of the extinction of the Dodo – one of the first descriptions of its type – that marks the beginning of modern ornithology.

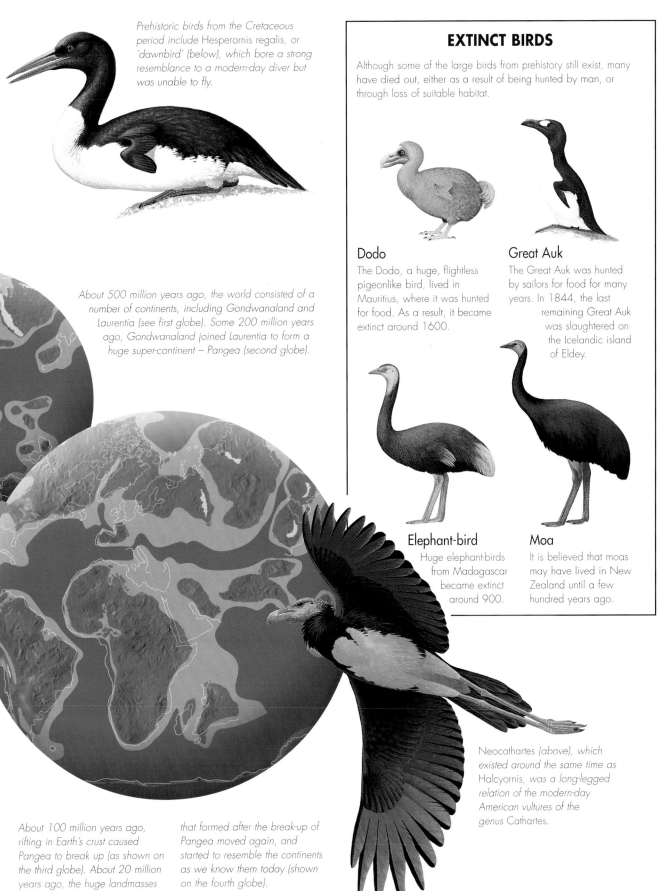

*Prehistoric birds from the Cretaceous period include Hesperornis regalis, or 'dawnbird' (below), which bore a strong resemblance to a modern-day diver but was unable to fly.*

*About 500 million years ago, the world consisted of a number of continents, including Gondwanaland and Laurentia (see first globe). Some 200 million years ago, Gondwanaland joined Laurentia to form a huge super-continent – Pangea (second globe).*

## EXTINCT BIRDS

Although some of the large birds from prehistory still exist, many have died out, either as a result of being hunted by man, or through loss of suitable habitat.

### Dodo

The Dodo, a huge, flightless pigeonlike bird, lived in Mauritius, where it was hunted for food. As a result, it became extinct around 1600.

### Great Auk

The Great Auk was hunted by sailors for food for many years. In 1844, the last remaining Great Auk was slaughtered on the Icelandic island of Eldey.

### Elephant-bird

Huge elephant-birds from Madagascar became extinct around 900.

### Moa

It is believed that moas may have lived in New Zealand until a few hundred years ago.

*About 100 million years ago, rifting in Earth's crust caused Pangea to break up (as shown on the third globe). About 20 million years ago, the huge landmasses that formed after the break-up of Pangea moved again, and started to resemble the continents as we know them today (shown on the fourth globe).*

*Neocathartes (above), which existed around the same time as Halcyornis, was a long-legged relation of the modern-day American vultures of the genus Cathartes.*

# THE HISTORY OF ORNITHOLOGY

Illustration of a Goshawk, from Willoughby and Ray's *Ornithologia,* published in 1676

**M**ost of the bird species we know today have been in existence for the last 10,000 years. However, few people recorded their sightings, described birds, or accurately named them until comparatively recently.

The Greek philosopher Aristotle (*c*384–322 BC) was perhaps the first person to record his observations of birds. He described the comings and goings of birds in about 350 BC, and speculated about the seasonal journeys of White Storks that swirled in great flocks over his native Greece.

The first written evidence of British birds occurs in literature, especially in poems written between 600 and 700, which refer to about 16 different species. By 1600, the number of birds that had been recorded had grown to 150. Since 1600, many more birds have been discovered in Europe and the rest of the world, and following the introduction of a classification system by the Swedish naturalist Carolus Linnaeus in 1758 (see page 14), they have also been properly named and classified.

## Early Books on Birds

Ornithology, the study of birds, was first recognized as a science in the seventeenth century. The British naturalist John Ray spent his entire life travelling and recording details of bird habitats, distribution, behaviour and seasonality, often accompanied by Francis Willoughby. Ray and Willoughby journeyed to Holland, France, Germany, Austria and as far as Italy in their search for avian understanding. Their great illustrated work, *Ornithologia,* first published in 1676, can be regarded as the world's first serious bird book.

During the eighteenth century, the English naturalist Gilbert White developed ornithology further by recording detailed bird behaviour in his nature diaries, many of which were later illustrated with woodcuts and engravings by Thomas Bewick. By the early nineteenth century, several more books about birds had been published, including *Birds of America* (1836) by the American artist and naturalist John James Audubon, whose colourful images created a sensation. Most books, however, were written by gentlemen who were often also hunters and collectors. Armed with shotguns and backed by private incomes, these collectors travelled the world in their search for the new, the rare and the unusual, recording the details of their finds in notebooks.

## The Growth of Birdwatching

Towards the middle of the twentieth century, fashions changed and birdwatching became more popular than bird hunting. Changing ideas and a new awareness of the concept of conservation soon led to the passing of laws for the purpose of protecting birds. The growth of birdwatching was further aided by the publication in 1936 of a field guide to the birds of North America, written by Roger Tory Peterson, which provided a tool for identifying birds. A version published for the European market in 1954 marked the start of the European birdwatching boom that has continued to the present day.

*During the eighteenth century, the naturalist and watercolourist Eleazar Albin made engravings of birds like the Crested Tit, shown on the left. These were published in his Natural History of Birds in 1731.*

## BIRD COLLECTING

One of the most famous collectors was E.T. Booth of the gin-making family. Booth, shown here leaning against a walking stick in which his gun is concealed, amassed one of the great collections of British birds. While other collectors bought, traded and swapped specimens, Booth collected all his specimens himself, so the provenance of each bird is recorded. The collection is now housed in a museum that bears his name in Brighton on the south coast of England. Case upon case of stuffed specimens line the walls of this purpose-built establishment.

*These cigarette cards (left), produced in 1915 as a result of a new craze in collecting, also mark the start of the growth of birdwatching. The birds, from left to right, are the Linnet, Swift, Siskin and Corn Bunting.*

*The Woodcock (left) was painted in 1787 by the watercolourist Sydenham Edwards, who was a member of the Linnean Society. He was a protégé of William Curtis, who founded a botanical magazine.*

# NAMING AND CLASSIFYING BIRDS

The Eagle Owl, a member of the *Strigidae* family, which has 23 subspecies

The naming and classification of birds can be said to have started with the work of the Swedish naturalist Carl Von Linné (1707–78).

Using Latin, the scientific language of his time, Von Linné, known as Linnaeus, set out the principles of classifying animals and plants by their similarities of form.

The Linnaean system can be most easily understood if it is regarded as a two-dimensional pyramid. At the top of the pyramid is the single item 'Life on Earth'. The living world is then divided into self-contained 'classes', such as reptiles, plants, insects, mammals, birds, and so on. Each class is divided into orders, then families, subfamilies, genera, and species.

## The Binomial System

Each species is given a two-part (binomial) name, which has a Latin basis. The first part of this name relates to the type of bird or genus, and is known as the generic part. The second part of the name is known as the specific name and relates to the unique characteristics of each particular species. For example, while the first part of the Ruff's name, *Philomachus*, relates to the bird's physical appearance, the second part of its name, *pugnax*, reflects its combative nuptial displays. Where different populations of the same species are separated geographically, they are given a third part to their scientific name, which is known as the trinomial. For example, Dunlin that breed in Britain and Holland are called *Calidris alpina schinzii*, whereas those that breed in the rest of Europe, are named *Calidris alpina alpina*. By convention, generic, specific and trinomial names are written in italics.

Linnaeus first introduced the binomial system in the tenth edition of his book *Systema Natura* (1758), and it remains the basis of modern systematics and ornithology. It

## CAROLUS LINNAEUS

Linnaeus was responsible for introducing the scientific classification system of plants and animals that we still use today. He was born in Rashult, Sweden, as Carl Von Linné, but later Latinized his name. He chose to study medicine rather than follow his father into the Church, but his passion for botany soon led him to an intensive exploration of Lapland, during which he walked hundreds of miles collecting plant specimens. Linnaeus took a position as curator of a large botanic garden in Amsterdam, but later returned to Sweden as Professor of Botany at Uppsala University, where he spent the rest of his life.

established the means by which each distinct species is named and its relationship to other animals is explained. Since Linnaeus' day, systematists have included internal structure and behaviour, as well as physical appearance, as criteria of classification. This inclusive approach, while changing the detail, has not altered the basic structure of Linnaeus' original system. Even the very latest techniques of classification, which use DNA analysis, still follow the Linnaean system of classifying a bird according to family, genus and species.

## CLASSIFICATION OF THE TAWNY OWL

**Name** Tawny Owl *Strix aluco sylvatica*
**Class** *Aves* (all birds)
**Order** *Strigiformes* (owls as opposed to other birds)
**Family** *Strigidae* (a specific group of owls)
**Subfamily** *Striginae* (a subgroup of owls within family *Strigidae*)
**Genus** *Strix* (owls within subfamily *Striginae*)

**Species** *aluco* (denotes Tawny Owl within genus *Strix*)
**Subspecies** *sylvatica* (separates birds found in Europe from 12 other subspecies found in Asia)

**Close relatives** Ural Owl *Strix uralensis*
Great Grey Owl *Strix nebulosa*

There are only three owl species within the genus Strix found in Europe. From the front, moving in a clockwise direction, they are: the Tawny Owl Strix aluco, the Great Grey Owl Strix nebulosa, and the Ural Owl Strix uralensis.

# HOW BIRDS WORK

Common Swift

**B**irds are highly evolved, extremely diverse creatures, with physical and behavioural characteristics that equip them for a unique way of life. Most of the world's birds, and all European birds, can fly, and understanding how they are adapted to flight is crucial to understanding how they work. The need to be highly mobile has dictated how birds have evolved and, specifically, how their external and internal structure has developed.

Although for many birds flight provides the most important means for survival, other adaptations are also crucial to their existence. The shape of a bird's bill, for example, is ideally suited to the food it eats, while a bird's feet are suited to its lifestyle and the habitat in which it lives. Birds have also developed complex courtship rituals and breeding routines to ensure the propagation of their genes. The following section explores how a bird's physical structure and its behaviour enable it to have the best chance of survival.

*The Barn Owl (above) glides silently on soft-margined wings in search of prey. Its ultra-sensitive powers of hearing enable it to hunt by night.*

*The supreme agility of birds is captured as this Hoopoe hovers with food for its mate (right). It fulfils this courtship ritual by coordinating all parts of its body.*

Balancing on one leg, a Shoveler (above) stretches its wing. This duck's most obvious physical adaptations to its environment are its huge, shovel-shaped bill, from which its name is derived, and its large, webbed feet that function as powerful paddles for swimming.

The majestic Golden Eagle (right), is a highly successful hunting machine. It uses its broad, powerful wings to glide through the air in search of prey, its sharply taloned feet to grasp its victims, and its large, hooked bill to tear its food apart. The Golden Eagle also has very good eyesight to help it spot quarry from great distances.

While some birds may have many different mates in a lifetime, Mute Swans (left) mate for life. They only seek another mate if their existing partner dies.

Brent Geese fly across the moonlit sky on migration (right). The ability to migrate enables them to breed in the far north of Europe, where food is abundant for their young, and to spend the winter farther south.

The linings of Swallow chicks' mouths (below) are bright yellow as an adaptation to attract their parents' attention and encourage their parents to feed them. Combined with their begging cries, these are powerful signals that their parents find very difficult to ignore.

The Kingfisher (left), a prodigious angler, can catch up to 20 fish a day. It dives like a dart into the water, with wings held back, and then emerges with a fish tightly grasped in its strong bill.

A ferocious battle occurs between two male Mallards (right), probably over a female. Male Mallards will vigorously defend the female from other males for a short time after mating to protect the paternity of their young, and to ensure the propagation of their genes.

**B**irds are fascinating and beautiful animals, found in huge variety throughout the world.

The Curlew's bill is adapted for use in mud

In total, there are more than 9,000 bird species in existence. They survive in almost every habitat – from the highest mountains and the most barren of deserts, from the largest oceans or most hostile icecaps, to cities, parks and gardens. Most birds can fly, although some have abandoned flight and have developed greater swimming and running abilities instead, and most are covered with feathers, although in some instances feathers have lost their typical structure and now resemble mammalian hair. Birds vary in size and weight – from the Ostrich, at a height of 2m (6ft) and weighing 100kg (220lb), to the Cuban Bee Hummingbird, measuring about 60mm (2½in) and weighing less than 2g (1½oz).

Most of a bird's internal organs are similar to those found in other animals, but birds are specially built to save weight, and their digestive system is remarkably fast. Many birds eject the indigestible parts of their food, such as bones and shells, from the mouth in the form of pellets (see box, page 31).

**A Diversity of Adaptations**

The skeletons of birds resemble those of the reptiles from which they evolved, but their different means of locomotion are clearly reflected. Because birds fly using their front limbs and walk on their hind legs, they have developed a strong shoulder girdle that gives support in flight, and a strong pelvic girdle that provides support on the ground.

The variety of bird bills and feet illustrates the diversity of the bird kingdom. Bills vary according to food preference, and are adapted for use in grasping, tearing, hacking, spearing and cracking. The more exaggerated the bill, the greater the degree of specialization. Feet are also adapted to habitat and feeding methods.

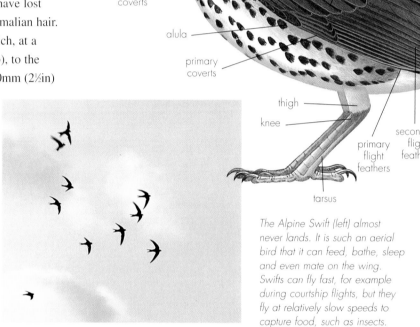

**EXTERNAL FEATURES**

crown
ear-coverts
nape
mantle
scapulars
greater coverts
tertials
upper mandible
lower mandible
throat
breast
median coverts
alula
primary coverts
thigh
knee
secon-
flig
feath
primary flight feathers
tarsus

*The Alpine Swift (left) almost never lands. It is such an aerial bird that it can feed, bathe, sleep and even mate on the wing. Swifts can fly fast, for example during courtship flights, but they fly at relatively slow speeds to capture food, such as insects.*

*The feathers of the Bee-eater (left) exhibit myriad colours: blue, brownish red, yellow and green, and its beak is specially adapted for eating insects.*

*The Great Bustard (left), a huge, turkeylike bird, is the heaviest flying bird in Europe. The male bird can weigh up to 18kg (40lb). During courtship, the male inflates his throat pouch into a large balloon and appears to turn his feathers inside out to produce a brilliant white ball, visible at long range.*

*While the Bee Hummingbird is the smallest bird in the world, the Goldcrest (below), measuring about 9cm (3½in) in length, is the smallest European bird. The Goldcrest feeds entirely on insects and migrates from Scandinavia during the winter in search of food.*

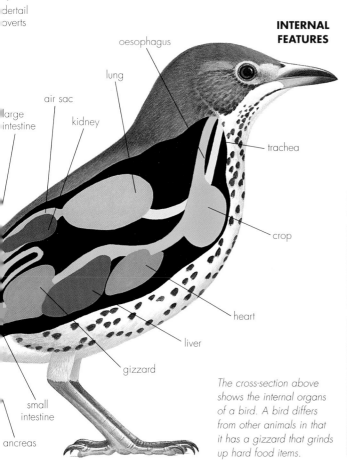

uppertail coverts

tail

dertail overts

**INTERNAL FEATURES**

oesophagus

lung

air sac

large intestine

kidney

trachea

crop

heart

liver

gizzard

small intestine

ancreas

*The cross-section above shows the internal organs of a bird. A bird differs from other animals in that it has a gizzard that grinds up hard food items.*

# ADAPTATIONS TO FLIGHT

**P**erhaps the greatest attraction of birdwatching is observing birds in flight.

Birds are among the most mobile of all animals: those that can fly are able to escape from predators, migrate for the cold winter months and gain access to foods that other animals cannot reach. This incredible mobility has been achieved by the sustained evolution of most birds into streamlined, lightweight animals.

*Blue Tit in flight*

Most small birds have highly refined skeletons. The main bones of their wings, legs and skulls are not solid, but have a 'honeycomb' structure for maximum strength and minimum weight. Bird feathers, particularly the major flight feathers of the wing, are also designed for strength and lightness. The heaviest part of many small birds is the two well-developed sets of breast muscles that power flight. The outer muscle produces the downbeat (power stroke) of the wing, while the smaller inner muscle drives the wing back for the upbeat (see box, page 23).

## Body Systems

The internal structure of birds, and their metabolism and behaviour, are also designed for maximum efficiency during flight. Their rapid digestive system maintains a high metabolic rate, which provides them with the energy they need to fly. They lay eggs rather than give birth to live young because carrying young during pregnancy would hinder flight (see box, page 23). Their respiratory apparatus, which includes powerful lungs, a large heart and an efficient circulatory system, provides maximum oxygen and energy during flight. Flight is further assisted by a large number of air sacs connected to the lungs, which function like bellows, driving air in and out through the lungs. Flight at high altitudes, where oxygen is scarce, is made possible by the 'honeycomb' structure of the bones, which provides extra space for the storage of oxygen reserves.

When birds have plentiful food or live in a predator-free habitat, they may dispense with flight. Flightless birds, including the Ostrich and the penguins of the southern oceans, have evolved according to their needs. Swimming, for example, is crucial to the survival of penguins, while flying is not. They therefore have rigid flippers, which help them to pursue their prey in water, instead of wings.

*Although bird bones (below) are light, the whole skeleton is quite rigid and many bones are fused. In this way, they form a strong frame that supports the bird while it is on the ground, and also during flight.*

**THE SKELETON OF A FLYING BIRD**

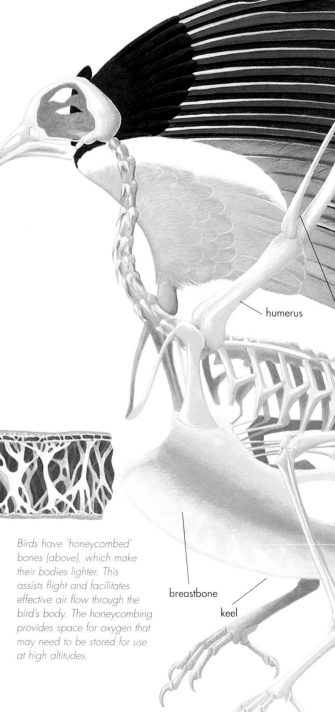

humerus

breastbone

keel

*Birds have 'honeycombed' bones (above), which make their bodies lighter. This assists flight and facilitates effective air flow through the bird's body. The honeycombing provides space for oxygen that may need to be stored for use at high altitudes.*

*Birds' legs (right) are thin in order to save weight, and their feet are angled so that it is easier for them to land and cling to precarious perches.*

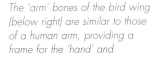

*The 'arm' bones of the bird wing (below right) are similar to those of a human arm, providing a frame for the 'hand' and 'fingers' of the wing. Together these support the wing feathers, which comprise the primary and secondary feathers.*

outer 'fingers'

primary flight feathers (primaries)

secondary flight feathers (secondaries)

*A bird's 'forearm' (or ulna) extends from the 'upper arm' (the humerus), as shown on the left. The ulna has two 'fingers', from which the primary feathers grow. These primaries, of which most small birds have about 11, are the power-house of flight.*

## WHY BIRDS LAY EGGS

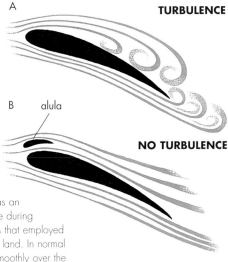

The way that birds reproduce is by laying eggs. This is an important adaptation to flight. The average small warbler, for example, weighs about 7g (¼oz) and usually lays a clutch of four or five eggs. An average clutch of this size also has a combined weight of about 7g (¼oz). If the warbler were to carry these eggs inside its body during pregnancy, its ability to fly would be hindered, or it might not be able to fly at all. By producing a single egg at a time, and then placing each egg in a well-hidden nest, the female is able to go about her everyday life efficiently. Although incubating the eggs outside the body (and feeding the young when they hatch) may be time-consuming, laying eggs is a highly efficient weight-saving strategy specifically geared to flight.

## THE MUSCLES OF FLIGHT

inner flight muscle

outer flight muscle

breastbone

keel

The breastbone, or sternum, of flying birds has a deep, prominent ridge called a keel at its base. The major inner and outer flight muscles are attached to the keel, as shown in this cross-section. The outer flight muscle is always larger than the inner flight muscle because it powers the downstroke of the wing which lifts the bird and propels it forward. In addition to providing a base for these muscles, the breastbone also protects the heart and lungs.

## THE ALULA

A

TURBULENCE

At the bend of a bird's wing is a small bunch of three or four stiff feathers, called the alula, which grow from the outer 'finger'. Though small, these feathers are crucial to all flying birds because they act as an 'anti-stalling' device during slow flight, such as that employed when coming in to land. In normal flight, air passes smoothly over the wing, creating lift. In slower flight, this smoothness turns to turbulence (as shown in diagram A above) and it is then that the alula is raised (as shown in diagram B

B    alula

NO TURBULENCE

above), turning the uneven air flow back into a smooth flow. As a bird hovers in the air, the alula can usually be seen jutting from the bend of its wing.

23

**F**eathers are a bird's most important adaptation to flight. It is thought that they evolved from the scales of birds' reptilian ancestors, the scales becoming longer and lighter over millions of years.

Feathers grow from keratin – the same material that forms the hair and fingernails of humans. The growth process of a feather begins when the outer skin cells of a bird's epidermis die and are filled with keratin. A feather is formed when a mass of keratin pulp sticks together.

*Contour feather from a Golden Plover*

It is thought that ants could play an important role in ridding some birds of parasites. Here, a Jay (above) has picked up ants in its bill and placed them among its feathers. The formic acid that the ants produce destroys or dislodges any parasites that may be living on the bird.

### The Functions of Feathers

Most of the average bird's feathers cover its body. Some, such as the primary feathers used for flight, perform one function. Others, such as contour feathers, perform a variety of functions. One of the functions of contour feathers is to act as insulation – they can be fluffed up by the bird at night and during the winter to trap air and prevent heat loss. In many species, these feathers also act as camouflage and help birds to recognize one another. Some species have brightly coloured contour feathers year-round, often with boldly patterned plumage, while others adopt distinctive plumage only for the short periods of the year during which they breed. For example, the male Ruff's contour feathers are a dull colour for most of the year to assist camouflage, but during the spring he sacrifices camouflage for the opportunity to reproduce by growing colourful tufts on his head and breast which he uses during territorial and mating displays.

Feather care is crucial to a bird's health and ability to fly. All birds spend lengthy periods of each day preening their plumage in order to keep their feathers in prime condition. Nevertheless, feathers are damaged during nesting and by everyday activities, such as searching for food. A wing or tail feather is so important that, if it is broken off, a replacement will quickly grow.

Birds replace their feathers at least once a year, new replacing old over a few weeks or months, depending on the species. Most birds moult at the end of the breeding season, when their feathers have been damaged by contact with the nest. Crucial feathers, such as wing feathers, are moulted one or two at a time, so that the bird will always be able to fly. Ducks, geese and swans, however, moult all their wing feathers at once and lose the ability to fly for a short period.

Feathers grow from a single mass of keratin pulp inside a sheath. The tufts of the feather gradually emerge from the sheath, pushing upwards to form the main vane (below, left to right). The sheath drops off when the feather has grown.

main vane

sheath

The primary, or flight, feathers are joined to the 'hand' of the wing. A large number of barbs grows from the central shaft. These barbs branch out and together make up the main surface of the feather, which is also known as the vane. In the photograph on the right the feather has been magnified in order to show the alignment of the barbs.

*Although birds repair their feathers by preening, they may also wash them (above). When bathing, a bird usually sits in shallow water and rapidly beats its wings to shower itself.*

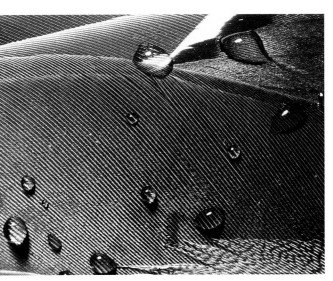

*A strong, flexible shaft (or rachis) runs along the centre of the feather.*

*Barbs grow from the shaft and make up the vane, the feather's smooth surface.*

## FEATHER TYPES

There are many different types of feather, including primary, secondary, contour, down, tail, covert, axiliary, tertial and scapular. Some examples are illustrated below.

Primary feathers are the major flight feathers. They overlap and are usually narrower on one side than the other help to produce lift on the downbeat during flight.

Secondary flight feathers are closer to a bird's body than primary feathers.

Contour feathers (left) provide insulation and assist in camouflage and recognition.

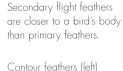

Down feathers (right), which lack barbules, are found close to the skin and help to provide insulation.

Tail feathers, or rectrices, are very strong. They are used for steering and help to produce lift when a bird is flying.

*Almost all birds have a well-developed gland that secretes oil, which is situated at the base of the tail (above). The oil is applied to the feathers during preening in order to waterproof the plumage and prevent it from becoming waterlogged. This is especially important for swimming birds, such as ducks – as the phrase, 'water off a duck's back' acknowledges.*

*From each barb, a number of barbules grow. These, in turn, support many hooklike barbicels that link the whole feather structure together like Velcro. When birds preen their feathers, they run their bill along the barbules, realigning the barbicel hooks. A microscopic photograph of a feather, such as the one shown on the left, clearly illustrate the hooklike shape of the barbicels.*

**B**ills are highly functional structures that have evolved to suit each particular bird's lifestyle. They are used largely for feeding, but also for activities such as preening and nest-building.

The Hawfinch's strong, thick bill

Bills vary in shape and size – from the huge bills of the pelicans, with their fish-trapping pouches, to the tiny, insect-snatching bills of the warblers, and the flesh-tearing bills of the eagles. Birds of prey are unusual in that they catch their prey with their sharply taloned feet. Prey is then killed and torn apart by a strong, hooked bill. The longer and more powerful the bill, the larger the prey that can be dispatched and butchered.

While raptors concentrate on large prey items, other species, such as the surface-feeding ducks, filter a wealth of tiny food particles from water or mud with their sievelike bills. Species such as the Shoveler, with its extra-large spatulate bill, may spend an hour or more feeding continuously at a single spot. Flamingos are also filter feeders, but their extremely long legs and necks enable them to feed in deeper water than ducks.

## The Specialized Bills of the Waders

Perhaps the greatest variety of special-purpose bills can be found among the waders. The long bills of the Curlew, Black-tailed Godwit and Snipe are probes evolved to catch prey hidden in soft mud. The shorter and finer bill of the Common Sandpiper is more like a pair of tweezers, perfectly suited to picking small food items from water margins. The short, stubby bill of the Turnstone is, as its name implies, adapted to turning stones to capture whatever lurks beneath. The Avocet's slender, upturned bill is swept from side to side over the mud surface to locate prey hidden in shallow water. Despite its name, the Oystercatcher uses its stout, orange bill to feed primarily on mussels. Oystercatchers can be divided into two distinct types – the 'prisers' and the 'bashers'. Prisers ease the mussel shell apart to sever the muscle holding the mollusc's shell together, while bashers use their blunter-tipped bills to hammer the shell apart.

*The Spoonbill (left) usually feeds on small crustaceans and aquatic insects. It passes its long, flat bill through muddy water, and the sensitive nerve endings lining the bill enable it to recognize the vibrations from its prey. Once the prey has been located, it quickly snaps its bill shut around it. The tip of the bill also filters the Spoonbill's food.*

# BILL TYPES

Most birds are adapted for survival in a particular habitat. This adaptation is apparent in the type of bill they have, which also indicates the food type to which the bird is suited. Even within the same family, such as the finch family shown below, bills vary according to specific diets and feeding methods.

## BILLS OF THE FINCH FAMILY

### Hawfinch
The thick, triangular bill of the Hawfinch is adapted to crushing the hardest seeds, such as cherry stones.

### Chaffinch
The smaller and more pointed bill of the Chaffinch enables it to scavenge seeds that have fallen on the ground.

### Bullfinch
Smaller than the Hawfinch's bill, the Bullfinch's bill is designed to split and roll seeds from husks.

### Goldfinch
The thinnest bill of the finch family belongs to the Goldfinch. It uses it like tweezers to pick out seeds from thistles.

## OTHER BILL TYPES

### Griffon Vulture
With its sharp, hooked bill, the Griffon Vulture is adapted to tearing flesh.

### Crossbill
The crossed bill is specifically adapted to opening pine and fir cones and extracting the seeds.

### Avocet
The side-to-side motion of the Avocet's long, upcurved bill enables it to catch shrimps and worms close to the water's surface.

### Blackcap Warbler
The short, fine, pointed bill of the warbler is suitable for picking insects from vegetation.

### Purple Gallinule
A very large, red bill is used by the Purple Gallinule to dig out roots and strip off seeds from aquatic plants.

### Spoonbill
The long, sensitive bill of the Spoonbill is able to pick up the vibrations of its prey in muddy water.

### Curlew
The long, curved bill of the Curlew is a sensitive probe used to detect worms and other marine creatures hidden in deep mud.

*The Goshawk (top) uses its strong, hooked bill to tear the flesh of its prey into pieces. It feeds mainly on rabbits, pigeons and squirrels. In contrast, the unique structure of the Crossbill's beak (above) is specially adapted to opening pine and fir cones. The off-centre, crossed mandibles hook into the cone scales, prising them apart.*

**M**ost birds have feet with three toes pointing forwards on each and one pointing backwards, which equips them for perching and walking. Birds that do a lot of walking, such as larks and pipits, have longer claws than those that spend most of their time perching. Birds that spend much of their time swimming, such as ducks, usually have webbed feet. Webbing binds three toes together, producing feet that function as paddles. Diving ducks use their large, webbed feet as a means of propulsion under water, in contrast to the similarly web-footed auks, which use their wings. Grebes have feet with lobes lining each toe to serve the same purpose. Pelicans and cormorants also spend much of their time afloat, but have webbing linking all four toes, which act as take-off paddles as they jump, feet together, across the water's surface to heave their great bulk into the air. In contrast, the waders have long toes, rather than webbing, which help to spread their weight. Some species have partial webbing and these are known as semipalmated (or partly webbed).

**Birds of Prey**

Birds of prey are unusual in that they capture their prey with their feet. Some species have two toes pointing forwards and two pointing backwards, forming an effective killing weapon. There are sharp talons on their long, powerful toes. The Osprey, which captures fish by diving feet-first into the water, has a unique series of tiny spines on the sole of each toe to prevent the escape of slippery prey.

In general, the more aerial a bird's lifestyle, the smaller and weaker its legs and feet. Conversely, specialist feeders with long legs and strong feet, such as owls and woodpeckers, are seldom strong fliers. Woodpeckers have feet with two toes pointing forwards and two backwards, ideal for clinging to and climbing trees. When excavating a nest hole, or hacking bark, they use their strong tail feathers in combination with their two feet as a tripod, creating a firm base for their energetic activities.

*The Great Spotted Woodpecker (above) pecks very rapidly at tree bark to make a nest hole or to find insects. Its feet and stiff tail feathers support its body.*

*The Puffin (left) has strong, webbed feet that it uses principally for swimming and walking. A Puffin also uses its feet to help steer it when flying, particularly when coming in to land, and to excavate its burrow, which tends to be located in soft earth at or near a cliff top.*

*The Goshawk (below) uses its strong claws to capture prey. It then rips the prey apart using its hooked bill.*

# TYPES OF FEET

Like bills, bird feet have evolved in huge variety to fit in with each bird's lifestyle. Birds have big feet or small feet, webbed feet or sharply taloned feet, four toes, three toes or even two toes. Some have feet with long claws, some have short claws, while others have such weak feet that they simply act as something on which to rest. Some birds use their feet to help them steer during flight and to brake before landing.

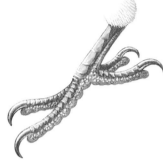

## Great Crested Grebe

Grebes have semi-webbed feet, with flaps of skin attached to either side of each toe. They use their feet rather like propellers, to swim fast.

## Ringed Plover

The long, thin toes of plovers are ideal for wading. Often, when feeding in very muddy areas, the Ringed Plover shakes its foot rapidly to disturb invertebrates, which then float to the surface, where the Plover can snap them up.

## Green Woodpecker

Feet with two forward- and two backward-pointing toes are suitable for clinging to, and climbing up, trees and act as an effective stand for woodpeckers.

## Cormorant

All four toes connected by webbing make an efficient paddle for cormorants. Webbing also distributes the bird's weight more evenly, preventing it from sinking in mud.

## Yellow Wagtail

A walking/perching foot enables wagtails to walk on grassland or at the edge of a river, catching small insects.

## Garden Warbler

The three forward-pointing toes and one backward-pointing toe allow a warbler to remain upright when clinging to a branch.

## Swift

Four tiny forward-pointing toes with sharp claws are suitable for clinging to rough surfaces, but upright perching is virtually impossible for swifts.

## Jacana

Although several European birds have long toes, none match those of the tropical jacanas, or lilytrotters. These birds have four long, thin toes to distribute their weight evenly. This enables them to walk over floating vegetation.

**B**irds have such a high rate of metabolism that they must spend most of their lives eating. They need to eat enough to maintain their high body temperature, and to produce enough energy for activities such as flight.

Bee-eater feeding on flying insects

Birds have evolved to exploit most of the food sources that exist, as the range of bills exhibited in the bird kingdom, adapted to different food types, illustrates. While some birds, such as finches and sparrows, feed predominantly on seeds and nuts, others, such as tits and swifts, feed on insects. Fish are eaten by birds like kingfishers, divers and grebes, but many fish-eaters also feed on crustaceans and other aquatic animals. Birds of prey, including eagles, vultures, hawks, harriers and owls, are carnivorous and feed on small animals, rodents, reptiles and other birds. A few birds of prey eat the decaying flesh of other dead animals, and some birds, especially those living in cities, survive by scavenging on rubbish.

## Semi-specialized and Specialized Feeders

In Europe, where climatic conditions vary considerably between summer and winter, certain plants and insects are not available all year round. Many European birds are, therefore, semi-specialized feeders or opportunist feeders, and they migrate as the seasons change to take advantage of the best feeding conditions available. Warblers, for example, which feed largely on insects, visit northern Europe during the summer, when insects are plentiful. The longer hours of daylight give them time to build their nests, lay and incubate their eggs, and rear their young. Before the winter arrives in Europe, they fly 8000 km (5000 miles) or more, to warmer climates where they can enjoy another insect-rich summer.

In contrast, many of the world's birds are highly specialized feeders, especially those that live in the tropics, and rely on the year-round availability of a specific food. Some of the New World hummingbirds, for example, feed on the nectar of a single species of flower throughout the whole year.

Birds establish themselves evenly throughout a territory for many reasons, including avoiding competition for food. Birds such as the waders, for example, have developed very specific feeding techniques that allow the various species access to different food sources in the same area.

*A Kingfisher (above) emerges from the water with a fish in its strong bill, after diving head first into the water.*

Snipe

Turnstone

*The Turnstone searches for molluscs and crustaceans by turning over stones and seaweed.*

*The Snipe probes the mud rapidly for worms, molluscs and crustaceans.*

A male Greenfinch (left) brings food to the female during the breeding season. Courtship feeding is an important bonding ritual for some birds, and takes place after pairing. The main advantage of this type of feeding is that the female is supplied with the extra food and nourishment she needs during the time she is producing, laying and incubating her eggs.

The stout, triangular bill of the Puffin (below) is slightly hooked and has spikes that enable it to grasp its slippery prey.

A great variety of feeding techniques is exhibited by waders, which feed along the seashore and at shallow inland waters. As shown below, the variable shapes and lengths of their bills enable them to extract food from the mud in different ways and at different levels. By doing this, they avoid direct competition for food.

## BIRD PELLETS

Birds lack teeth, so many swallow their food whole. They then eject the hard, indigestible parts of their food from their mouths in the form of pellets, an amalgam of undigested items. The shape of a bird pellet offers important clues about the bird which produced it. The large pellets shown on the left are owl pellets. They are usually dropped by the owl below a nest or roosting site.

## INSIDE A BIRD PELLET

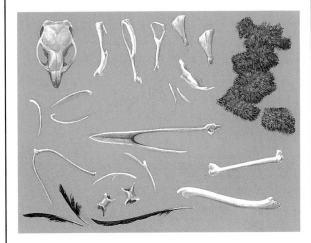

By opening a bird pellet, it is possible to discover what the bird has eaten. In the case of owls, which may swallow a rat or mouse whole, a large pellet made up of bones and fur is ejected. The pellet may also contain feathers made of protein that cannot be digested. The pellets of birds of prey sometimes contain the complete skulls and limbs of rodents and the bones of smaller birds. Seabirds may eject a pellet consisting mainly of fish bones, while other birds may eject insect remains, or seed cases.

Curlew

Redshank

Avocet

The Curlew probes deep into the muddy water for its food, which includes molluscs, crabs and worms.

The Redshank probes quite close to the surface to collect molluscs, shrimps and worms.

The Avocet sweeps its bill from side to side over the surface of the water, filtering out tiny insects and shrimps.

# COURTSHIP, BREEDING AND NESTING

Warbler nest

**I**t is important for a bird to establish a territory as a place to build its nest, breed, and rear its young, safe from interference by other members of the same species.

Territories are claimed in spring and are then 'advertised' to attract a mate, and defended, often by singing. Despite the lyricism with which poets have treated bird song, singing is in fact aggressive. It clearly says, 'This is my territory – keep out'.

Courtship and pair formation, in preparation for breeding, often involve elaborate rituals. Cranes, for example, dance and yelp together on their chosen marsh. Great Crested Grebes perform an aquatic *pas de deux* that involves displaying their nuptial plumes and presenting nest material to each other. Some birds gather at a courtship site, known as a lekking ground, where they display throughout the summer. Females visit, mate, and then usually perform the nesting duties by themselves.

*The courtship dance of the Great Crested Grebe (left) takes place on water and involves both the male and the female. They begin by swimming apart, but keeping in contact by calling. Then they turn back to face each other and, with their long necks extended and their beaks often full of water plants, they shake their heads in a 'weed dance'.*

*Male Ruff (below) gather at traditional lekking grounds in May and June in their splendid summer plumage. Tufts and ruffs in various colours adorn their heads and they joust in mock combat for pride of place and dominance. Each male bird establishes his own area, known as a 'residence'. Females visit the lek and select a mate, usually the most dominant male. A male Ruff may mate with more than one female in a short space of time.*

## Nests and Eggs

Nests vary considerably in shape and size – some birds, such as the Ringed Plover, merely scrape out a shallow hole in the ground, while others, like the Penduline Tit, create quite elaborate structures. Many birds construct a simple cup in a bush or tree. The number of eggs varies, too: while a bird like the Guillemot may lay only one egg, the Grey Partridge can lay as many as 15. Each batch of eggs is known as a clutch, and a bird may lay more than one clutch each season.

The eggs of many small birds are laid at daily intervals until the clutch is complete. They are then incubated by the female alone, by both parents sharing in varying degrees or, in some cases, by the male alone.

Hatching, for most birds, occurs after about a fortnight. Small birds usually hatch naked, blind and helpless, and are totally dependent on their parent. The young of ground-nesting birds hatch covered in down and can walk and feed themselves within about an hour.

During the breeding season, male Black Grouse (above) are usually seen in groups at courtship sites, known as lekking grounds, in the early morning or evening. They compete for patches of ground, where they perform elaborate displays, lifting their tails to reveal the white feathers on the underside. These displays are watched by the female birds, and the males that control the central areas of the lekking ground usually attract the greatest number of females. Lekking grounds may contain anywhere between about 10 and 150, or even more, male birds.

The Long-tailed Tit creates an attractive, round, pouch-like nest using moss, spider's silk, and lichen (above). It then lines the nest, which may be in a thorn bush or tree, with up to 2,000 feathers, which help to provide insulation. This complex nest may take three weeks to build, and is expanded as the young grow.

The Cuckoo chick (above) is exhibiting behaviour known as 'brood parasitism'. After mating, the female Cuckoo finds the unattended nest of a small songbird in which to lay her egg. The Cuckoo chick hatches after about ten days, before the other eggs in its foster parents' nest. It then throws the other, legitimate, eggs, or chicks, out of the nest. In this way, the Cuckoo chick is able to consume food destined for many mouths.

An old hat hung on a nail (above) is the perfect shape for a Wren's nest. The male Wren builds the nest and then sings to attract a mate. The female inspects the nest and, if it is suitable, she lines it with leaves and moss and lays her eggs. When they hatch she brings food to her young. Some males build several nests and may attract more than one mate, but others are monogamous and will help to raise the young of one female.

# ROOSTING

**B**irds need to sleep regularly, and most do so at night. They usually find a sheltered spot, safe from the wind and rain, in which to roost, and tuck their heads under their wings.

Birds roost throughout the year, even during the breeding season, and a female may roost on her nest while incubating her young. In some species the male bird helps with this task, but

*While asleep, the Long-tailed Tit tucks its head under its wing*

when the male bird is not involved with incubating the eggs, he may find his own roosting site elsewhere, or join other birds in a communal roost.

**Roosting Sites**

The most important criterion in selecting a roosting site is safety, especially from predators, and birds gain more protection when they roost in groups. Gathering in large groups helps the birds to maintain body temperature, especially during the winter. Birds, such as the Greenfinch and the Blackbird for example, often gather together to roost in dense, evergreen bushes. Wrens will often cram together inside a nestbox; as many as 63 have

been discovered roosting inside a single nestbox. Swallows and Sand Martins crowd in vast numbers among reeds surrounded by water. However, there are birds that break the rule and do not roost in large numbers. Some birds, ranging from owls and other birds of prey, to woodpeckers and tits, roost solitarily, while others roost in small groups.

Although warmth and safety are the primary benefits of roosting in groups, the habit also provides an ideal opportunity for birds to exchange information about feeding grounds. After roosting at night, Starling flocks set out in the early morning to fly more than 10km (6 miles) to places where they fed the previous day. Although the largest roosts are in the countryside, many city centres are used, perhaps because of the extra warmth generated by large conurbations and built-up areas.

34

Some birds gather in huge flocks to roost. The high-tide roosts of waders, for example, are very dramatic, with masses of Oystercatchers, Redshank, Dunlin and Knot crammed cheek by jowl on an isolated rock or island, safe from predators and disturbance. They are sometimes so tightly packed that late arrivals may have to land on the backs of other birds. The arriving flocks of waders often perform spectacular aerial displays prior to settling. Once again, they seem to gather for safety, although this may not

deter a predatory falcon, such as a Merlin or Peregrine, from circling above, looking for a suitable meal.

While most birds hunt for food during the day and rest during the night, nocturnal birds hunt at night and sleep by day. The Nightjar, for example, is a nocturnal species which roosts during the day by sitting on twigs in its heath and scrubland habitat, where it is effectively camouflaged.

**Raptors and Owls**

Birds of prey do not need to seek safety from many predators, but, like other birds, they do need to sleep. They usually roost alone, but may congregate for warmth at suitable roosts during the winter. Long-eared Owls, for example, form winter roosts and Short-eared Owls may gather in roosts up to a hundred strong.

# ROOSTING OF STARLINGS

Perhaps the most dramatic of all communal roosts are those of the Starling. In fact, during the early days of radar, watchers searching their screens for incoming enemy aircraft were amazed to see small dots that spread out into large circles, sometimes over 10 km (6 miles) in diameter, like the ripples created by a stone dropped into still water. The watchers originally referred to these dots as 'Angels', but further investigation revealed that they were flocks of Starlings dispersing from their communal roosts in the early morning.

An autumn roost of Starlings may number more than a million birds, crowded together for warmth and safety. Before settling down for the night, they arrive, flock after flock, to a pre-roost gathering ground. Here they often perform dramatic flights, with tens of thousands of birds rising together to create huge swirling masses in the air. These performances may last half an hour or more as new flocks arrive and settle. Eventually, a swirling mass of birds dives towards the roost to take cover, usually followed directly by other large flocks.

Starlings on their way to their roosting sites (left) are a common sight in both cities and rural areas, sometimes blackening the sky as they converge on their roosts in their thousands (above). Starlings are gregarious and roost in loosely formed groups, often returning to the same roosting site.

Oystercatchers and Knot arrive at a winter roost (left). The Knot are grey with a pale wingbar, while the Oystercatchers are black with a white underside. Both species fly long distances to winter among the rich feeding grounds offered by the ice-free estuaries of western Europe.

Common Cranes (below) usually fly to their roosting sites in a chevron, or V-shaped, formation. Many species fly in these formations, which are an energy-saving device: the wings of each bird create an 'upwash' of air, which prevents 'drag' for the bird flying behind it.

As a member of a nocturnal species, the Long-eared Owl (above) usually sleeps during the day. It finds a suitable roosting site on a tree branch or tree stump, and sits very still and upright so that it is camouflaged against the tree and will be left undisturbed. Long-eared Owls form communal roosts during the winter, gathering together to protect themselves from the cold.

birds such as woodpeckers and finches, for example, fly with a very distinctive bounding motion, taking pauses with their wings folded between bouts of flapping.

## Flying techniques

Most birds utilize a form of flapping flight, in which the wings are beaten to produce propulsion, but a wide variety of species are incapable of sustaining such energetic activity over long periods. Many birds of prey, for instance,

*In preparation for landing, the Blue Tit holds its feet forwards, reaching out for its landing site (below). The feathers of the tail and wing are spread out wide to slow the bird down.*

**T**he ability to fly is perhaps the single most important feature of birds. Flight enables the individual bird to move from one source of food to another – often to reach foods unavailable to competitors – or to collect nest-building materials.

Although all European birds can fly, there is huge variation in the type of flight they are able to make and the distances they can travel. Wing shape is important in determining the characteristics of flight. For example, swifts have long, pointed, crescent-shaped wings that cut through the air and reduce drag, enabling them to fly with a minimum of effort. Some swifts are so aerial that they sleep and mate on the wing, landing only to nest. In sharp contrast, broad, rounded wings enable the Red Grouse to make short flights to escape danger and to change direction quickly, although it usually walks about its territory.

## Long and short flights

While some birds travel thousands of kilometres, others may move less than one kilometre (half a mile) from their birth site during the whole of their lives. The Arctic Tern travels more than 30,000 kilometres (18,640 miles) a year on migration alone, while the Red Grouse is probably incapable of flying a single kilometre without stopping.

The majority of birds are able to fly well enough to migrate, with good acceleration to avoid predation. Some

have a soaring and gliding technique that utilizes columns of warm air, known as thermals, rising over the land. By using this rising air, they are able to make lengthy migrational journeys with minimal expenditure of energy. However, thermals do not occur over the sea, presenting an obstacle for migrating European birds of prey that need to cross the Mediterranean. Species such as the Honey Buzzard, Booted and Short-toed Eagles therefore make the shortest possible sea crossings, at Gibraltar and the Turkish Bosphorus.

*The Mute Swan (above) is one of the largest European birds. It heaves its body into the air across the water by flapping its wings vigorously and literally running over the water's surface. When it moults, the Mute Swan loses the power of flight for a short time.*

*The Red Kite (right), like many birds of prey, glides smoothly on rising air, using its tail as a rudder to change direction. The Red Kite is an endangered bird that has been recently reintroduced into England and Scotland. As a result of a protection scheme in Wales, the native population there has increased to more than a hundred pairs.*

The great oceanic travellers, such as the shearwaters, and their non-European relatives the albatrosses, do not rely on thermals to sustain lengthy flights, but on air moving over water. When a wave or sea swell moves, it displaces the air in its path upwards. It is on this moving air that these great oceanic travellers depend. During a period of dead calm, however, albatrosses, in particular, are unable to fly and have to wait for rough weather. European shearwaters may be less dependent on wave power, but their mode of flight is, in essence, the same.

## WING TYPES

Wing shape, as shown below, directly determines the flight characteristics of an individual species.

### Black Grouse

Short, square-shaped wings enable the Black Grouse to take off rapidly for fast, short flights.

### Common Swift

Long, crescent-shaped wings allow the Swift to be an expert at gliding.

### Sparrowhawk

Blunt, rounded wings, beaten rapidly, enable the Sparrowhawk to change direction quickly.

### Kestrel

Long, pointed wings enable the Kestrel to hover in the air while searching for its prey.

### Golden Eagle

Long, broad wings make the Golden Eagle a superb soarer and glider.

### Manx Shearwater

Long, stiff wings enable the Manx Shearwater to soar on air currents above the sea.

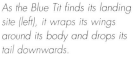

*As the Blue Tit finds its landing site (left), it wraps its wings around its body and drops its tail downwards.*

37

# MIGRATION

Brent Goose
on migration

**B**irds may migrate thousands of kilometres from one place to another at set times of the year. How and why they do this has long intrigued ornithologists.

The dangers of migrating are considerable, so the advantages must be great to make the journey worthwhile. Most birds that migrate breed in an area where food is plentiful in the summer, then spend the winter in another area. A few tropical species migrate to avoid dry or wet seasons. In fact, the birds' very survival may depend on migration.

**Breeding Grounds**

In spring, migrant birds arrive on their breeding grounds. Few birds can survive the frost and snow in the far north, but in the brief summer months there are plenty of seeds, berries and insects on which to feast. There is enough food for birds to raise their young and to build up the reserves of fat needed to sustain them on long flights. As autumn arrives, the birds migrate to warmer areas where food can be found throughout the winter.

As the seasons in the Northern Hemisphere are the reverse of those in the Southern Hemisphere, many birds migrate from one hemisphere to the other to enjoy a permanent summer.

The most widely travelled of all birds is the Arctic Tern, which covers about 15,000km (9300 miles), between breeding and wintering grounds.

Birds can build up sufficient fat reserves for up to four days of continuous flight; the Sedge Warbler, for instance, may double its weight to 20 grams (¾oz). Most birds need periodic stops for feeding. For this reason, some migrating birds follow routes known as flyways. Two flyways lead from Europe to Africa, one across the Strait of Gibraltar, the other across the narrow sea crossing at the Bosphorus. North America has a flyway along both the eastern and western coasts and a third down the Mississippi valley.

*In autumn, Sand Martins (above) leave their European breeding grounds to winter in tropical Africa. They are shown here gathering on wires prior to migration. Sand Martins usually return to their northern breeding grounds as early as March, often to the same site year after year. The recent decline in the Sand Martin population is thought to be due to the prolonged drought in the Sahelian wetlands, which stretch across the southern margin of the Sahara.*

*The longest migration journeys of all are made by the Arctic Tern (left), which in a year covers a distance of about 30,000km (18,640 miles), or about twice the annual mileage of an average car.*

## Partial Migrants and Irruptions

Partial migration refers to the fact that some individuals within a bird population migrate while others remain resident year-round. Thrushes in northern Europe are typical partial migrants; each year some individuals migrate to areas around the Mediterranean Sea while others stay put. Bird that do not migrate at all are known as resident birds.

A few species make long journeys in massive numbers, but are not migrating. Gulls may gather on remote cliffs to breed then, in a movement known as dispersal, fly off to find food for the rest of the year. More mysterious are the irruptions that occur when large numbers of birds leave their usual range for distant lands. The Waxwings of northern Europe, for instance, move south and west in large numbers every four or five years.

## MYTHS OF MIGRATION

During the eighteenth century, the English naturalist Gilbert White (1720–93) regularly watched Swallows disappearing among the reeds that lined his local Hampshire ponds on late summer and autumn evenings. As these birds subsequently disappeared for the winter, White, along with other naturalists of the time, presumed that they must hibernate at the bottom of the ponds. Such an idea may seem incredible to us, but to the eighteenth-century naturalist, the idea that these tiny birds could fly 10,000km (6250 miles) to South Africa, was even more incredible. We now know that Swallows gather among reeds only to roost, before they set off on their great journeys.

### Key to Migration Routes

 White Storks

 Brent Geese

 Common Terns

*The globe (left) shows the migration routes of three different species, each of which follows a different migration route between their breeding grounds and winter homes. White Storks, shown in purple, follow migration routes from Europe to central Africa. Common Terns, shown in yellow, are divided into two groups; those terns starting their journey in western Europe follow the coastline to reach West Africa, while terns departing from eastern Europe fly directly southward then turn west to avoid the Sahara desert, and so reach West Africa. Brent Geese, shown in red, breed in three different areas in the far north of Europe and then travel southward for the winter. These separate populations move to different wintering grounds and seldom mix with each other. One group travels from Greenland to Northern Ireland, another from Spitzbergen (an arctic Norwegian island) to Northumberland, England, and the last group journeys from the arctic island of Novaya Zemlya (off the north coast of Russia) to reach Holland and southeast England.*

The first attempts at understanding bird migration began in Denmark in the 1890s with bird ringing. The practice spread rapidly and today thousands of birds are ringed each year.

Marking birds with numbered rings, and the subsequent recovery of the rings, allows scientists to track the lifespan and movements of individual birds. By amassing details of a large number of recoveries, it has proved possible to identify the destinations of many migratory birds. For example, while Swallows from Britain spend the winter in South Africa, Swallows from Germany winter in the Congo. But ringing could not explain why migrations began nor how the birds found their way.

It has long been known that caged birds become restless as migration time approaches. They perch facing in the direction they should fly and flap around more frequently, but this behaviour ceases as the migrations come to an end. It would appear that day length, which varies with the seasons, triggers such behaviour, although in the wild a lack of food may prompt birds to begin their migration early.

### Key to Ringing Sites

Northern Wheatear

Spotted Flycatcher

*The map (right) shows the migrations of two summer visitors to Europe – the Spotted Flycatcher and the Northern Wheatear – as revealed by ringing results. The Spotted Flycatcher shows a clear migrational divide in Central Europe: some birds head southwest in autumn, others southeast. The Northern Wheatear has colonized both eastward and westward to reach North America. All Northern Wheatears migrate to winter in Africa, crossing the Atlantic eastward and the whole of Siberia westward to do so. This creates a migrational divide in Africa similar to that of the Spotted Flycatcher in Europe.*

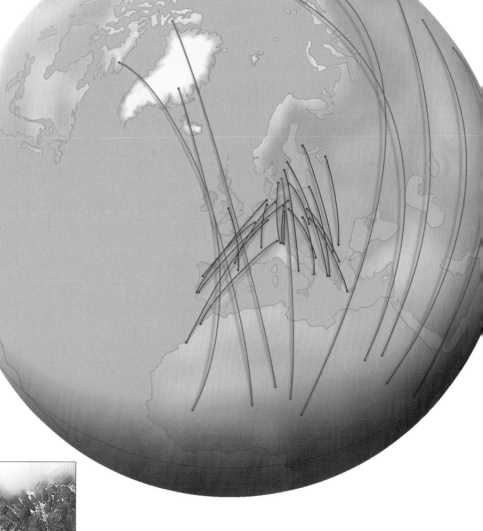

*Migrating birds must fly vast distances and overcome great natural obstacles. Demoiselle Cranes (left), like most migrating birds, do not usually fly at very high altitudes. However, in their migrations eastwards, they have to cross the high mountains of Central Asia and may then fly up to 5000 metres (16,500ft).*

## Attaching the Ring

*Bird rings, like this Spur-winged Plover's ring (left) are made of strong metal alloy. As the close up of a Great Tit (above) shows, the ring is attached around the tarsus, or lower part of the leg. Rings come in many different sizes (above right). A coded number is printed on the ring, which will identify the bird when it is retrapped at another location. The ring also carries the address to which it should be returned. The recoveries of birds that are ringed are monitored by various national ringing schemes*

*throughout Europe and the rest of the world. Studies are also being made using large, coloured plastic rings, or collars, so that birds can be identified from a distance, by using binoculars or a telescope.*

## Bird Ringing

*The advent of large-scale cooperative ringing between countries in recent years has dramatically increased the percentage of birds that are ringed, retrapped and then released. It is now possible to assess the distances birds have flown and the season at which the flight was made. This information is obtained by comparing the ringing and recovery sites, as shown by the ringing and recoveries marked on the globe (left).*

## Star Navigation

The German scientist Franz Sauer, working in the 1950s, believed that birds navigated by the stars. To test his theory, he released a group of Blackcaps inside a planetarium. They flew in the correct direction for their normal migration, but when the star pattern was altered they flew true to the stars they could see, even though this was now the wrong direction. Similar experiments with daytime fliers showed that the sun was controlling the direction of flight.

Other scientists believe that birds use the Earth's magnetic field to navigate. The Robin is known to have tiny lumps of magnetite, a magnetic iron compound, in its head, and it is thought that these may allow the bird to detect magnetic fields through which it passes. It has also been suggested that the sense of smell helps birds to find their way, and that birds remember the angle and direction of the sun in the sky over their destination – an idea supported by the fact that young birds on their first migration are more easily confused than older birds.

While there may be a degree of truth in all such explanations, the fact that migrating birds do get lost during bad weather indicates that viewing the sky (either the stars at night or the sun during the day) must play a large part in the way they navigate.

## Radar Technology

As interest in bird migrations has increased, the technology to study them has developed. Radar devices can distinguish a flock of birds from a light aircraft. These show that birds flying south from Europe move in great waves, with flocks advancing in parallel on a very wide front, giving the lie to the idea that birds follow narrowly defined routes.

# BIRD HABITATS

Water Rail

**B**irds are found in every type of habitat in Europe and throughout the rest of the world, from the most remote mountain ranges to the open ocean and even the centres of large cities. A habitat must provide a bird with food, a suitable nesting site and adequate cover from predators and harsh weather. While some birds are able to live in a range of different habitats, others may have much more specific requirements. The suitability of a habitat may also change with the seasons, and many birds migrate to find more favourable conditions at certain times of year.

For each of the ten habitats covered in this section, a list is provided containing the species that are most likely to be found there. Habitats also appear in the species section as a category within each species entry, to inform the birdwatcher where they are most likely to see each of the 423 bird species.

The Feral Pigeon is one of the most successful inhabitants of towns and cities. It can drink from fountains without raising its head, (above), nest in the crevices of buildings and under bridges, and feed on human refuse.

Guillemots (right) live at sea for most of the year. They visit the land only to breed in large, noisy colonies. They nest on the ledges of sea cliffs, close to sources of food and well away from predators.

As a bird of deciduous woodland, the Great Spotted Woodpecker (right) looks to trees for all its needs. It excavates a hole in a tree for its nest and marks its territory by drumming on a dead branch with rapid blows of the bill. The bird searches decaying wood for the insects and larvae on which it feeds, and it plucks caterpillars from leaves for its chicks.

The Red-legged Partridge (below) inhabits open areas of ground on heaths and farmland. By living on open land, it is able to spot predators from a great distance and is also well camouflaged against its habitat as an extra precaution. Its ground nest is well hidden by low vegetation.

The Ptarmigan (above) blends into this winter landscape so well that it could almost be mistaken for a snow-covered boulder. As the Ptarmigan is a bird of open country, it is important that it merges with its surroundings at different times of year. Its plumage moults from greyish brown in summer to pure white in winter.

A Great Crested Grebe (left) tends to its nest among dense aquatic vegetation. Grebes find conditions perfect for nesting around lakes and reservoirs, but spend the winter on larger fresh waters and around sea coasts.

The Spoonbill (right) is specially adapted to living around estuaries and reed marshes. Its spoon-shaped bill enables it to feed on a variety of food found in both fresh and salt water, and it builds its nest among reedbeds.

Most often found alongside rushing streams, the Grey Wagtail (above) is sometimes seen beside weirs and ditches in suburban areas during the winter months. However, the bird's need for woodland in which to hunt caterpillars to feed its young restricts its range to the countryside during the breeding season.

Some lakes and other water habitats become quite crowded, as they provide a suitable winter home for many species. Whooper Swans, and Canada and Greylag Geese (left) gather on lowland lakes close to open grasslands on which they graze as dusk approaches. Other birds are attracted to waters where aquatic plants grow, or which have broad, muddy margins.

45

# WHERE BIRDS LIVE

White Stork
nesting on top
of a chimney

**T**he landscapes found in Europe were created by latitude, altitude and climate. These areas can be divided into broad habitats in which birds live.

These habitats include mountains and tundra, moorland, coniferous and deciduous forests, mixed forests, Mediterranean scrub, desert and built-up areas around towns and cities. Aquatic habitats, which are more difficult to show in map form, include freshwater lakes, rivers and streams, estuaries and saltmarshes, coasts, cliffs and islands. A relatively small geographical area may contain a variety of habitats, providing a home for a number of different bird species.

*Starlings (above) are widespread residents in Europe, adaptable enough to find their nesting and*
*roosting sites in the relative safety of high-rise buildings in European towns and cities.*

## Habitat

Birds are creatures of habitat as well as of habit. Many have very specific requirements in terms of feeding or nesting sites, which may be found only in certain areas. Crossbills and Capercaillies, for example, cannot exist without conifer trees, while terns and grebes are confined to aquatic habitats. In contrast, the Starling is just as happy in towns and cities as it is in the countryside, providing it can find a suitable nesting or roosting site.

The range of habitat preferences between birds that are closely related helps to prevent competition between species. Among the warblers, for example, the Willow Warbler can

live in woods or tree-covered heaths, while its relative the Chiffchaff is confined chiefly to woodland, and the Wood Warbler is even more specialized, requiring mature woods with a dense canopy and scanty undergrowth.

## The European Environment

The natural environment of Europe has been changed so much as a result of human intervention that we now have only a patchwork of habitats into which birds must somehow fit. Large areas of temperate Europe were once covered by deciduous forests, but today only remnants exist. The warm shores of the Mediterranean were previously clothed in evergreen woodlands that have now almost vanished. Rivers that meandered across their flood plains, leaving oxbow lakes and marshes in their wake, have now been drained and straightened. The loss of such habitats has caused the populations of many bird species to decline. However, only one European bird has become extinct since records began. This was the Great Auk and it died out because it was hunted, not because its habitat was destroyed.

*Spoonbills (above) need to live in aquatic habitats, such as coastal lagoons, estuaries and shallow marshes. They form breeding colonies close to the water, usually among reedbeds, where*
*they build their nests. The Spoonbill's long, spatulate beak is adapted for sweeping the water for food. Such highly specialized species are most vulnerable to habitat changes.*

The photograph (left) taken from space, shows a view of Europe at night. In contrast to the map below, which shows the ranges in vegetation, this photograph shows the location of cities and major conurbations. As the cities grow and encroach on the countryside, the natural habitats of many birds are destroyed. However, some species, such as the pigeon, have been able to adapt and now lead a successful life in towns and cities.

The natural habitat of Alpine Choughs (above) is mainly high in the mountains. These crows usually congregate in groups. They are easy to identify by their yellow bills and red legs.

Key
- Tundra
- Mountainous
- Moorland
- Coniferous Forest
- Deciduous Forest
- Mediterranean
- Shrubland
- Desert

One of the most widely distributed members of the woodpecker family in Europe is the Great Spotted Woodpecker (left). Despite differences in climate, it can live in any woodland habitat with mature coniferous or deciduous trees. The Great Spotted Woodpecker can thrive not only in extensive areas of woodland, but also in well-timbered farmland, gardens and parks. It avoids competition with other species of woodpeckers by feeding mainly near the tops of trees and among the smaller branches.

The map (above) shows the major variations in vegetation found in Europe. These areas have been formed by the underlying soil characteristics combined with different climatic factors. Europe has a wide range of bird species that are suited to the many habitats across the area. For instance, Steller's Eider winters in Arctic waters especially in Varanger Fjord, Norway, while the Wallcreeper is a bird of the high mountains, especially the Spanish Pyrenees. Many birds migrate to find the ideal habitat at different times of the year.

European habitats have changed greatly over recent years, indeed few other parts of the world have been so modified by human intervention. The effects of changes in areas of vegetation on bird populations have been extremely complex. Sometimes the same change has been of benefit to some bird species and a disaster for others. For example, species of deciduous forests have declined in number owing to tree felling, but the new open areas have meant that many grassland species, such as the larks, have increased.

47

The Corsican Nuthatch is found only in Corsica

**T**he distribution of a particular bird species is best defined as the geographical area in which all of the members of that species are found throughout the world.

Some bird species, such as the Barn Owl, have a very widespread distribution and are found all over the world, while others such as the Corsican Nuthatch, found only in Corsica, have a much more restricted distribution.

Assessing the distribution of birds is complicated by the fact that a species will not always occupy the habitat to which it seems ideally suited. There is, for example, plenty of habitat suited to the Great Grey Shrike in Britain, but it has never bred there.

On an individual level, a bird has a particular range throughout the year. Although some birds are resident, found in the same area all year round, others make migrations and therefore have two ranges each year – one in the summer and another in the winter. Showing areas where birds breed in map form provides a picture of their range for part of the year. If we add to it their winter range a much clearer picture emerges. While some birds are summer visitors to Europe, others are winter visitors, and yet others are resident all year round, in some areas at least.

**Distribution Maps**

In Europe for example, the map for the Swallow is simple. These birds breed throughout the continent but are absent from Iceland, the mountains and the far north of Scandinavia. In winter, they do not normally occur at all in Europe. The map for Bewick's Swan shows only a winter distribution and is similarly straightforward. In contrast, the map for the Meadow Pipit is a complex affair, showing that this species breeds in the north, but winters in the south and west. Over most of Europe, the Meadow Pipit is a partial migrant (some individuals stay resident all year and others migrate), although in Scandinavia it is a summer visitor only, while in southern Europe it is a winter visitor only.

Birds are confined by their range, but their ranges are not necessarily fixed and may expand or contract for a variety of reasons. The Collared Dove, for example, has spread, within living memory, from the Balkans right across Europe and now breeds from Norway to Portugal. The range of a particular species is affected by the availability of food and suitable nesting sites in its chosen habitat.

*Bird populations are never static. They increase or decrease in numbers from one year to the next. In many cases, species change their ranges as a result. The Collared Dove (above), for example, has extended its range from the Balkans (Greece, Romania, Bulgaria and nearby lands) north to Norway. On its way, it colonized Britain, where it arrived during the 1950s. It is now one of the most successful European land birds.*

*The Ruddy Duck (above) was introduced from North America to England in the twentieth century. The species multiplied and spread through southern Britain to the adjacent continent, and eventually to Spain.*

*Unfortunately, it has now started to interbreed with the White-headed Duck of southern Europe, endangering the existence of this rare bird. During the breeding season, the bill of the male Ruddy Duck turns bright blue.*

*Over the last century, the Gannet (above) has extended its range from one or two isolated colonies on remote islands, to 50 or 60 colonies around the North Sea and Atlantic coasts. The success of this colonization is thought to be due in part to food waste, in the form of fish, deposited by deep-sea fishing trawlers.*

# MIGRATION TACTICS OF THE ROBIN AND THE MEADOW PIPIT

**DISTRIBUTION OF THE MEADOW PIPIT**

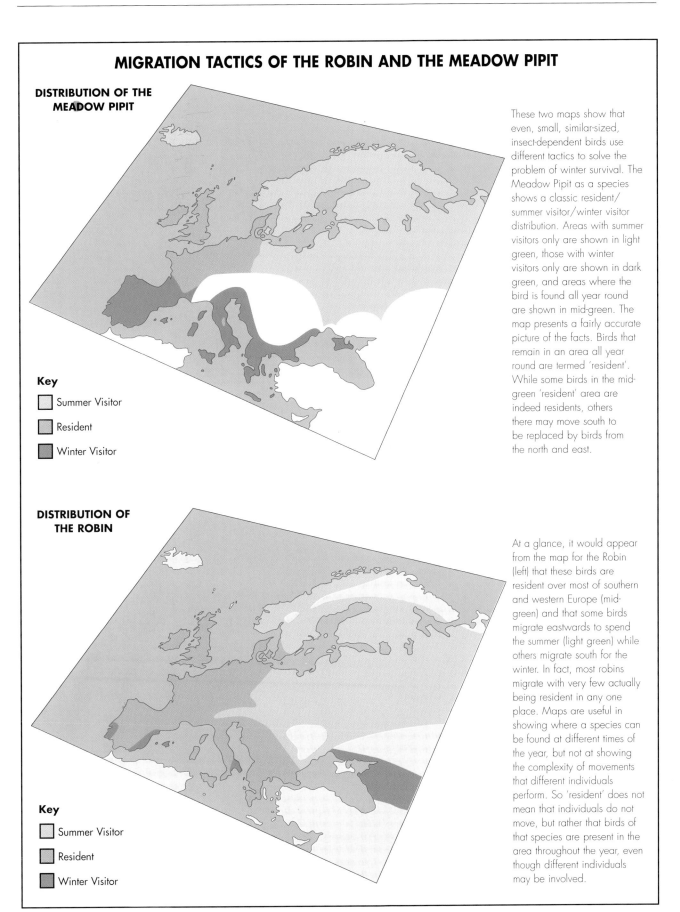

**Key**

☐ Summer Visitor

☐ Resident

☐ Winter Visitor

These two maps show that even, small, similar-sized, insect-dependent birds use different tactics to solve the problem of winter survival. The Meadow Pipit as a species shows a classic resident/summer visitor/winter visitor distribution. Areas with summer visitors only are shown in light green, those with winter visitors only are shown in dark green, and areas where the bird is found all year round are shown in mid-green. The map presents a fairly accurate picture of the facts. Birds that remain in an area all year round are termed 'resident'. While some birds in the mid-green 'resident' area are indeed residents, others there may move south to be replaced by birds from the north and east.

**DISTRIBUTION OF THE ROBIN**

**Key**

☐ Summer Visitor

☐ Resident

☐ Winter Visitor

At a glance, it would appear from the map for the Robin (left) that these birds are resident over most of southern and western Europe (mid-green) and that some birds migrate eastwards to spend the summer (light green) while others migrate south for the winter. In fact, most robins migrate with very few actually being resident in any one place. Maps are useful in showing where a species can be found at different times of the year, but not at showing the complexity of movements that different individuals perform. So 'resident' does not mean that individuals do not move, but rather that birds of that species are present in the area throughout the year, even though different individuals may be involved.

Black
Woodpecker

Natural European woodlands can be divided into three main groups: deciduous forests, evergreen forests and coniferous forests. Each supports its own unique array of bird species.

European deciduous woodlands provide breeding habitats for migrant birds such as warblers, flycatchers and pipits, which live alongside resident tits, woodpeckers, nuthatches and finches. Some species, such as Brambling and Chaffinch, are not summer, but winter, visitors to deciduous woods, where they search among the leaves of the forest floor for fallen seeds. Deciduous trees also provide perfect nesting conditions for a mixed population of birds of prey, such as the resident European Sparrowhawk and Goshawk, and the migratory Honey Buzzard and Lesser Spotted Eagle. But this habitat is rapidly disappearing as huge areas of deciduous forest have been felled to provide timber and agricultural land. In addition, the evergreen forests of southern Europe

European Nuthatch

have almost all been destroyed by deliberate felling to make way for olive groves and grazing land. Where small patches still remain, they provide an ideal habitat for species such as the Great Spotted Woodpecker and Hawfinch.

*A juvenile Eurasian Jay (above) stretches forward to beg some food from its parent. Jays are able to exploit a great range of foods, so they are widespread. They are found in deciduous and conifer woods, as well as in wooded farmland and in parks.*

**Great Northern Forests**

Coniferous forests, with trees such as spruce, larch and pine, can be found in a broad swathe across northern Europe, from Scotland through Scandinavia to northern Russia. They are also found in harsh conditions on mountain slopes from the Pyrenees to the Carpathians.

Great
Grey Owl

Conifer trees have survived because they are one of the few crops that will grow in the far north and among high mountains. They grow on poor soil and are able to endure the harshest winter conditions, while retaining most of their leaves and providing a year-round food supply for a variety of bird species. However, they are usually felled early for timber and seldom reach maturity.

Some birds, such as Black Grouse, feed on conifer leaves and seeds, while others feed by scouring the

Woodcock

*The Capercaillie (above) is a specialist in its choice of woodland habitat. It is confined to conifer forests and is found in Scandinavia, Central Europe and the Pyrenees. In spring, the male makes a loud, hollow clicking sound to mark his territory.*

Golden Oriole

forest for insects and spiders, even during the winter. Birds of prey also manage to survive throughout the year, and the northern coniferous forests of Europe are home to a wonderful selection of owls.

Wood Warbler

With the arrival of summer, the conifer woods are suddenly alive with birds that have wintered in milder climates. Warblers and flycatchers flourish on the insect life during the longer days and many respond by laying more eggs than birds living farther south. Conifer forests in the mountain regions of southern Europe provide similar conditions for birds. In winter, many birds are able to make short flights to the valleys nearby, rather than migrate vast distances.

Pied Flycatcher

Crested Tit

## Mixed Forests

In some areas, coniferous and deciduous trees may co-exist naturally, or as a result of human planting. These mixed forests suit a variety of bird species, among them the Black Woodpecker, which finds its food among conifers and excavates its nest holes in deciduous trees. Chaffinch and Bonelli's Warbler also thrive in mixed forests, and the Goshawk nests in both coniferous and deciduous trees.

*The Woodcock (above) is an unusual member of the wader family in that it prefers to live in damp woodland, rather than in an aquatic habitat. It is a nocturnal bird that feeds on worms and insect larvae, locating its food by probing the forest floor and leaf litter with its long, sensitive bill.*

## Birds of Woodland

| | |
|---|---|
| Black Stork | *Ciconia nigra* |
| Honey Buzzard | *Pernis apivorus* |
| Goshawk | *Accipiter gentillis* |
| European Sparrowhawk | *A. nisus* |
| Levant Sparrowhawk | *A. brevipes* |
| Common Buzzard | *Buteo buteo* |
| Lesser Spotted Eagle | *Aquila pomarina* |
| Booted Eagle | *Hieraaetus pennatus* |
| Black Grouse | *Tetrao tetrix* |
| Capercaillie | *T. urogallus* |
| Woodcock | *Scolopax rusticola* |
| Scops Owl | *Otus scops* |
| Hawk Owl | *Surnia ulula* |
| Tawny Owl | *Strix aluco* |
| Ural Owl | *S. uralensis* |
| Great Grey Owl | *S. nebulosa* |
| Long-eared Owl | *Asio otus* |
| Great Spotted Woodpecker | *Dendrocopos major* |
| Middle Spotted Woodpecker | *D. medius* |
| Lesser Spotted Woodpecker | *D. minor* |
| Black Woodpecker | *Dryocopus martius* |
| Wood Lark | *Lullula arborea* |
| Tree Pipit | *Anthus trivialis* |
| Song Thrush | *Turdus philomelos* |
| Garden Warbler | *Sylvia borin* |
| Blackcap | *S. atricapilla* |
| Nightingale | *Luscinia megarhynchos* |
| Bonelli's Warbler | *Phylloscopus bonelli* |
| Wood Warbler | *P. sibilatrix* |
| Chiffchaff | *P. collybita* |
| Greenish Warbler | *P. trochiloides* |
| Goldcrest | *Regulus regulus* |
| Firecrest | *R. ignicapillus* |
| Spotted Flycatcher | *Muscicapa striata* |
| Collared Flycatcher | *Ficedula albicollis* |
| Semi-collared Flycatcher | *F. semitorquata* |
| Pied Flycatcher | *F. hypoleuca* |
| Willow Tit | *Parus montanus* |
| Siberian Tit | *P. cinctus* |
| Crested Tit | *P. cristatus* |
| Coal Tit | *P. ater* |
| Blue Tit | *P. caeruleus* |
| Great Tit | *P. major* |
| European Nuthatch | *Sitta europaea* |
| Common Treecreeper | *Certhia familiaris* |
| Short-toed Treecreeper | *C. brachydactyla* |
| Eurasian Jay | *Garrulus glandarius* |
| Siberian Jay | *Perisoreus infaustus* |
| Magpie | *Pica pica* |
| Golden Oriole | *Oriolus oriolus* |
| Nutcracker | *Nucifraga caryocatactes* |
| Chaffinch | *Fringilla coelebs* |
| Brambling | *F. montifringilla* |
| Common Redpoll | *Carduelis flammea* |
| Common Crossbill | *Loxia curvirostra* |
| Parrot Crossbill | *L. pytyopsittacus* |
| Two-barred Crossbill | *L. leucoptera* |
| Hawfinch | *Coccothraustes coccothraustes* |

# TUNDRA, MOUNTAINS AND MOORLAND

Lammergeier

**A**long with the permanently ice-covered Arctic and Antarctic zones, mountains and tundra regions are among the most inhospitable places on Earth. Temperatures often fall below freezing, and may remain so week after week.

It is, therefore, not surprising that most birds abandon such habitats during the winter, when conditions are severe. However, in the summer, the days are much longer in high altitudes, allowing more time for plants to grow and birds to feed, so many birds return to breed in these areas.

## Feeding Grounds in the Tundra

The European tundra begins in the far north of Scandinavia, and extends eastwards across Russia to the Urals. The ground remains frozen in the winter, but in the late spring the upper layer of the soil thaws, creating ideal conditions for dwarf plants and lichens to grow and insects to hatch. These offer great feeding opportunities for birds such as geese, ducks, cranes, waders, terns and skuas.

In many tundra areas, the ground remains unfrozen for only a few weeks, and birds must rush to fit in their breeding cycle before the ice returns. As a result, some tundra breeders have evolved quite complex breeding routines. Little Stints, for example, perform their courtship and form pairs before

they reach their breeding grounds, timing their arrival to coincide exactly with the thawing of the ground, on which they then build their nests. The female lays her eggs at once and then flies off to recover and, perhaps, to find another mate. The male Little Stint incubates the eggs for about three weeks and cares for the young until they can fly. By then, the female may be thousands of kilometres away on her way to winter quarters. The whole breeding cycle takes just six weeks.

Peregrine Falcon

With such a short breeding season, things can easily go wrong. A cold snap in late summer, for example, will kill off the insects on which some birds rely to build up their fat reserves before migrating, wiping out an entire year's young.

## High Mountain Lands

Many mountain areas are very similar in landscape to the tundra, but are found at lower latitudes. The mountainous landscape high above the coniferous forests is made up of stones and lichens and is inhabited by few animals in winter, but is utilized by many during the summer. Mountainous areas that lie south of the Arctic Circle do not enjoy 24 hours of daylight, as parts of the tundra do in

Golden Eagle

*Alpine Choughs (above) live at high altitude in southern Europe for most of the year and feed by digging in the ground for insects. They sometimes descend to a lower altitude when weather conditions are particularly severe. The Alpine Chough has a yellow bill, in contrast to the orange bill of the Chough.*

Ptarmigan

*The Lammergeier (left) is a rare and endangered species, resident in only a few mountain ranges in southern Europe. It makes its nests high up on steep cliffs, and may return year after year to the same nest site. The Lammergeier soars at great heights in search of its food.*

*A resident bird in the tundra of Scandinavia and northern Russia, the Willow Grouse (right) has distinct summer and winter plumage. During the summer, its body is a reddish brown colour with white wings, and in winter almost all its plumage is white. In this way, the Willow Grouse adapts to the changing environment and is superbly camouflaged all year round.*

summer, and the variations in temperature within a single day can be extreme. These variations are too severe for many bird species, but Ptarmigan, Dotterel, Northern Wheatear and Citril Finch all cope very well. Other species find mountains attractive because they offer secluded, safe nesting sites and unique feeding opportunities. Mountain areas are also perfect for eagles, and most European vultures nest among mountains, including the remnant populations of the great Lammergeier.

Dotterel

## Moorland

Usually found on the lower slopes of mountains, moorland is made up of peat bogs interspersed with heather, coarse grass, bracken and moss. As a result of poor conditions for agriculture, many of these areas have been left relatively untouched by people. However, a recent surge in the use of peat in gardens has led to many of these areas being disturbed. Where they do still exist, these heather-clad wetlands are the haunt of Red or Willow Grouse, Meadow Pipit and Hen Harrier.

Merlin

## Birds of Tundra, Mountains and Moorland

| | |
|---|---|
| Lammergeier | *Gypaetus barbatus* |
| Egyptian Vulture | *Neophron percnopterus* |
| Griffon Vulture | *Gyps fulvus* |
| Black Vulture | *Aegypius monachus* |
| Rough-legged Buzzard | *Buteo lagopus* |
| Golden Eagle | *Aquila chrysaetos* |
| Bonelli's Eagle | *Hieraaetus fasciatus* |
| Merlin | *Falco columbarius* |
| Peregrine Falcon | *F. peregrinus* |
| Willow (Red) Grouse | *Lagopus lagopus* |
| Ptarmigan | *L. mutus* |
| Dotterel | *Charadrius morinellus* |
| European Golden Plover | *Pluvialis apricaria* |
| Little Stint | *Calidris minuta* |
| Eagle Owl | *Bubo bubo* |
| Alpine Swift | *Apus melba* |
| Shore Lark | *Eremophila alpestris* |
| Water Pipit | *Anthus spinoletta* |
| Meadow Pipit | *A. pratensis* |
| Alpine Accentor | *Prunella collaris* |
| Black Wheatear | *Oenanthe leucura* |
| Northern Wheatear | *O. oenanthe* |
| Rock Thrush | *Monticola saxatilis* |
| Blue Rock Thrush | *M. solitarius* |
| Ring Ousel | *Turdus torquata* |
| Western Rock Nuthatch | *Sitta neumayer* |
| Wallcreeper | *Tichodroma muraria* |
| Alpine Chough | *Pyrrhocorax graculus* |
| Jackdaw | *Corvus monedula* |
| Citril Finch | *Serinus citrinella* |
| Linnet | *Carduelis cannabina* |
| Snow Finch | *Montifringilla nivalis* |

Sky Lark

**H**abitats such as heaths and scrubland are usually found in areas of uncultivated land made up of sandy, stony soils covered by low scrub, gorse and heather. This type of vegetation occurs in regions where soil is poor and where a moderate temperature is combined with low rainfall.

There are heaths in northern and western Europe, for example, in Dorset in southern England, in the Maastricht region of southern Holland and along the north German plains. These northern heaths have grasses and well-cropped green turf, with a growth of stunted willows, birches, gorse and heather.

Hobby

Heaths and scrubland also occur farther south, throughout the Mediterranean coastal regions, where the areas of drier scrubland are known as *maquis*. In contrast to the northern heaths, these dry, stony southern landscapes are covered with dwarf prickly vegetation, evergreen shrubs and bushes. Rainfall drains directly into the soil, washing many nutrients away, so growing conditions are extremely harsh. Many of these areas were covered with evergreen forests, but wholesale clearance has meant that only the most thorny shrubs have survived.

**Rare Habitats**

Both northern and southern heaths provide habitats that are seldom found elsewhere, with conditions suitable for a

Dartford Warbler

variety of bird species. A typical northern heath is home to Meadow Pipit, Stonechat and Whinchat, Sky Lark, Red-backed and Great Grey Shrikes, and to one of Europe's few resident warblers, the Dartford Warbler. Although several birds of prey use heaths as their hunting grounds, the Hobby is a heathland specialist, cruising the open skies to hunt large insects and, later in the summer, swallows and martins.

While at first the southern heaths, or *maquis,* may seem to be almost free of birds, they provide an ideal habitat for the *Sylvia* warblers, one of Europe's most rare and delightful groups of birds. Dartford, Spectacled and Marmora's Warblers have a distinctly western distribution, with the latter confined to a few Mediterranean islands. Rüppell's

Warbler has an eastern distribution, while Orphean, Subalpine and Sardinian Warblers are widespread throughout the Mediterranean region. Rüppell's Warbler has a decided preference for uniform, low scrub, while the Orphean Warbler makes its home among tall bushes of at least 2–3m (6–10ft) in height. The Subalpine Warbler prefers rocky outcrops among dwarf vegetation, but Sardinian and Marmora's Warblers often occur virtually side by side.

Nightjars are among the best camouflaged of all European birds and are ideally suited to heaths and scrubland. Indeed, they are so well hidden when they nest among dead leaves and broken stumps that they no longer need to produce camouflaged eggs, producing pure white ones instead.

Heaths and scrubland are also home to more wide-ranging birds, such as the Common Cuckoo, European Sparrowhawk and Linnet, but it is the birds that are specifically adapted to these areas, such as warblers and Red-backed Shrikes, that are the greatest attraction to birdwatchers.

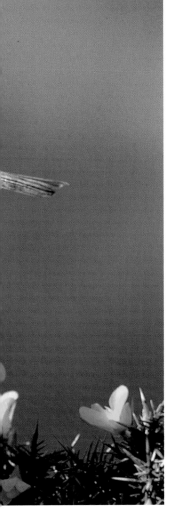

The Whinchat (above) is an inhabitant of heaths and scrubland which spends the summer in western Europe and migrates to Africa for the winter. It builds its nest at the base of hedgerows and bushes.

The Stonechat (left) makes use of its heathland habitat in many ways. It uses various shrubs and branches as posts from which to keep a look-out for its food, and to keep guard over its territory. It also requires low, dry vegetation for its nest, which it usually builds at the base of a gorse bush.

The Linnet (below) prefers to live on heaths, but it can also survive in open farmland. Its bill is small and is ideally suited to feeding on small soft seeds.

## Birds of Heaths and Scrubland

| | |
|---|---|
| Montagu's Harrier | Circus pygargus |
| European Sparrowhawk | Accipiter nisus |
| Short-toed Eagle | Circaetus gallicus |
| Hobby | Falco subbuteo |
| Chukar Partridge | Alectoris chukar |
| Red-legged Partridge | A. rufa |
| Great Spotted Cuckoo | Clamator glandarius |
| Common Cuckoo | Cuculus canorus |
| Short-eared Owl | Asio flammeus |
| European Nightjar | Caprimulgus europaeus |
| Red-necked Nightjar | C. ruficollis |
| Hoopoe | Upupa epops |
| Short-toed Lark | Calandrella brachydactyla |
| Lesser Short-toed Lark | C. rufescens |
| Crested Lark | Galerida cristata |
| Thekla Lark | G. theklae |
| Wood Lark | Lullula arborea |
| Sky Lark | Alauda arvensis |
| Tawny Pipit | Anthus campestris |
| Tree Pipit | A. trivialis |
| Meadow Pipit | A. pratensis |
| Thrush Nightingale | Luscinia luscinia |
| Nightingale | L. megarhynchos |
| Common Redstart | Phoenicurus phoenicurus |
| Whinchat | Saxicola rubetra |
| Stonechat | S. torquata |
| Black-eared Wheatear | Oenanthe hispanica |
| Pied Wheatear | O. pleschanka |
| Northern Wheatear | O. oenanthe |
| Isabelline Wheatear | O. isabellina |
| Icterine Warbler | Hippolais icterina |
| Melodious Warbler | H. polyglotta |
| Marmora's Warbler | Sylvia sarda |
| Dartford Warbler | S. undata |
| Spectacled Warbler | S. conspicillata |
| Subalpine Warbler | S. cantillans |
| Sardinian Warbler | S. melanocephala |
| Orphean Warbler | S. hortensis |
| Rüppell's Warbler | Sylvia rueppellii |
| Lesser Whitethroat | S. curruca |
| Common Whitethroat | S. communis |
| Willow Warbler | Phylloscopus trochilus |
| Red-backed Shrike | Lanius collurio |
| Woodchat Shrike | L. senator |
| Great Grey Shrike | L. excubitor |
| Linnet | Carduelis cannabina |

The preferred habitat of the Hobby (right) is heaths or open agricultural land with isolated copses or shelter belts. It has wings almost as long proportionally as those of the Swift, giving it the ability to fly extremely gracefully and fast. The Hobby, which is the smallest European falcon, feeds on small birds, bats and insects.

# FRESHWATER LAKES

Crane

**I**nland fresh waters, including lakes, ponds, man-made reservoirs and gravel pits, have their own special character and birdlife.

The suitability of a lake as a bird habitat depends on its altitude: large, shallow lowland lakes can provide a superb home for a great range of species, while lakes found on gently sloping land may be home to just a few terns or waders. Deeper lakes, set high in mountain regions, are much less suitable for birds, due to a lack of food and nesting sites.

### Lakeland Plenty

Lowland reservoirs and gravel pits are usually sited near large cities. Over time, the natural

Great Reed Warbler

*Bewick's Swan (above) is the smallest European swan. It breeds in the open tundra regions of the Arctic and then moves southwards during the winter to the lowland lakes, ponds and reservoirs of northwestern Europe. Swans have long necks and can reach for their food underwater.*

*The Grey Heron (below) is the most widespread of the herons found in Europe. It lives in wetlands, nesting in nearby trees, and can survive in either freshwater or saltwater habitats. The Grey Heron's diet consists largely of fish, but it will eat frogs and small water birds as well.*

*The Great Crested Grebe (above) lives on freshwater lakes, ponds and rivers. Grebes build their nests on a bed of reeds and add extra material to make sure the*

*nest rises well above the water. Both the male and female birds take turns to incubate the eggs, and when the nest is unattended, the nest lining hides the eggs.*

margins of these man-made environments become covered with lush vegetation and form rich bird habitats.

Whether natural or man-made, the reedy margins of lakes come alive in summer, with warblers producing their croaking and reeling songs, while harriers drift overhead, hoping to surprise and catch a Moorhen or a Common Coot. Although the main habitat of the Hobby is among heaths and scrubland, they may gather around lowland lake areas in spring to

Little Ringed Plover

## Birds of Freshwater Lakes

| | |
|---|---|
| Red-throated Diver | *Gavia stellata* |
| Black-throated Diver | *G. arctica* |
| Little Grebe | *Tachybaptus ruficollis* |
| Great Crested Grebe | *Podiceps cristatus* |
| Little Egret | *Egretta garzetta* |
| Great White Egret | *E. alba* |
| Grey Heron | *Ardea cinerea* |
| Bewick's Swan | *Cygnus columbianus* |
| Mute Swan | *C. olor* |
| Canada Goose | *Branta canadensis* |
| Mallard Duck | *Anas platyrhynchos* |
| Pintail | *A. acuta* |
| Shoveler | *A. clypeata* |
| Common Pochard | *Aythya ferina* |
| Tufted Duck | *A. fuligula* |
| Ferruginous Duck | *A. nyroca* |
| Goldeneye | *Bucephala clangula* |
| Osprey | *Pandion haliaetus* |
| Hobby | *Falco subbuteo* |
| Moorhen | *Gallinula chloropus* |
| Common Coot | *Fulica atra* |
| Crane | *Grus grus* |
| Little Ringed Plover | *Charadrius dubius* |
| Ringed Plover | *C. hiaticula* |
| Common Tern | *Sterna hirundo* |
| Arctic Tern | *S. paradisaea* |
| Common Kingfisher | *Alcedo atthis* |
| Swallow | *Hirundo rustica* |
| House Martin | *Delichon urbica* |
| Bluethroat | *Luscinia svecica* |
| Fan-tailed Warbler | *Cisticola juncidis* |
| Grasshopper Warbler | *Locustella naevia* |
| River Warbler | *L. fluviatilis* |
| Savi's Warbler | *L. luscinioides* |
| Aquatic Warbler | *Acrocephalus paludicola* |
| Sedge Warbler | *A. schoenobaenus* |
| Marsh Warbler | *A. palustris* |
| Blyth's Reed Warbler | *A. dumetorum* |
| Great Reed Warbler | *A. arundinaceus* |

feed on the dragonflies that have recently hatched. Groups of Little and Great White Egrets may also be present, patiently stalking the shallow waters for food. An Osprey may hover over the water before plunging feet first in pursuit of fish.

In winter, lowland freshwaters offer safe roosting sites to many wildfowl and a rich source of food to others. Even concrete reservoirs, though lacking food, can hold thousands of roosting ducks and gulls, while lakes near feeding grounds act as a roost for geese.

### Food For All

Although there may be many different birds feeding on a lake, few of them are in direct competition for food. Shoveler and Mallard ducks, for example, feed on plants along the shores, while Pintails and swans upend to reach vegetation as much as a metre (3ft) below the surface. Coot, Goldeneye and other diving water birds reach deeper water plants.

Osprey

Small ponds, too, may provide food and shelter for species such as Moorhen, Coot and Little Grebe, and their muddy margins are a source of nest-building material for House Martins and Swallows. A reedy corner may allow a Sedge Warbler or Tufted Duck to rear young. Ponds also attract a wide variety of migrant birds that may pause for a few hours or even for several days to break their journeys.

Lakes and ponds are under threat throughout the world. They have a natural tendency to silt up and turn into marshy pasture. More damaging is the drainage that forms part of many agricultural schemes and lowers the water table. Run-off of fertilizers and pesticides can also accumulate in lakes and seriously affect the birds living there.

Mute Swan

# LOWLAND MARSHES AND DELTAS

**C**oastal marshes and deltas have always held an irresistible attraction for birdwatchers, as they are one of the richest of all bird habitats and are home to a large variety of species.

Little Bittern

Lowland marshes exist along many European coastlines and are often protected by beaches and sea walls and in some instances, breaches of these walls allow sea water in to create salty lagoons. In other areas, the flow of fresh water remains untainted, allowing shallow marshes with a strong growth of vegetation similar to that found near lakes to form.

## River Marshes

Marshland exists along the lower reaches of many European rivers, where sea walls act to confine the river, creating a kaleidoscope of small fields drained by a network of dykes. Winter rains flood these areas, which often remain water-logged for months. In northern, temperate Europe, such flooded land is a winter home to geese, wild swans and duck, and a summer breeding ground to Lapwing, Common Redshank, Black-tailed Godwit and Ruff. Where river walls have collapsed and been left unrepaired, extensive marshes have been

Little Egret

Whiskered Tern

created, many of which have now been incorporated into nature reserves. These areas have been so successful as bird habitats that, in several parts of Europe, active management of schemes to create such floods and marshes has been encouraged and subsidized by governments. In some

Penduline Tit

The preferred habitat of the Avocet (above) is among muddy lagoons. During courtship, Avocet pairs establish their own territory in which to lay their eggs, close to a good feeding area with plenty of food for their young.

As its name suggests, the Black-winged Stilt (left), an inhabitant of lowland marshes, has extremely long legs, the longest of any bird in relation to its body size. Its legs enable it to search for its food in deeper water than other waders can.

The young Black-winged Stilt (above) has a shorter bill and legs than the adult, but both grow rapidly. The young stilt is sandy coloured, rather than black and white, which helps to hide it from predators.

Little Crake

*Cormorants and White Pelicans (above) are both suited to the conditions provided by lowland marshland habitats. Cormorants, (the black birds shown above), can live in either fresh- or salt-water habitats, and they dive for fish. The White Pelican prefers to live around deltas or near large lakes, where the reeds from which it builds its nest are plentiful. Pelicans also feed on fish, which they scoop up using their huge, pouched bills.*

areas of Britain, Germany, Holland and France such sites are being scraped out to form shallow lagoons dotted with small islands, which are perfect breeding sites for Avocets and several species of tern.

**Deltas**

Deltas are formed where rivers enter the sea and silt and debris are not washed away. In Europe, deltas have been created at the mouths of the Guadalquivir in Spain, the Rhône in France, and the Danube in Romania. These European deltas are home to many bird species.

Spoonbill

However, in spite of conservation schemes, many of these areas face growing threats. In Spain, parts of the Guadalquivir delta have been converted into rice fields that, although suitable for the Whiskered Tern, are unsuitable for many other species which prefer undrained marshes.

The Camargue, in the Rhône delta, has become a popular holiday destination, with new houses and developments disturbing the unique birdlife.

Romania's Danube delta remains undeveloped, although there is a reed-harvesting industry in this area that destroys hundreds of hectares every year.

Lesser Spotted Eagle

Grey Heron

**R**ivers begin as a trickle of water, which joins with other trickles to form a stream, and then with other streams to become a river. At all stages along their journey to the sea, rivers provide habitats for a variety of birds.

Rivers are often still pools or drainage ditches at their origins, providing a simple bathing or drinking site for the birds of the surrounding landscape. Once they become flowing streams, however, they begin to have a life of their own.

**White-water Birds**

Fast-flowing water, tumbling over stones and among rocks, is home to a few highly specialized birds otherwise found only near weirs and locks. The Dipper can literally walk along a stream bed under water, and is at home among the ferocious rapids. It is such a highly specialized little bird, confined to fast-moving streams, that its territory may be several kilometres long, but only a few metres wide. This fast-flowing river habitat is also shared by Grey Wagtails and, in summer, by Common Sandpipers. Harlequin Ducks are also at home among fast-flowing waters, although in Europe they are confined to Iceland. These buoyant swimmers and expert divers are able to use every eddy, backwash and undercurrent to swim where swimming would seem impossible. In winter, when Icelandic rivers are frozen, these ducks move to the coast to feed among the crashing waves alongside sea cliffs.

House Martin

**Slower Rivers**

Farther downstream, where gently-flowing water alternates with tumbling torrents, Common Kingfishers appear. Although Europe is home to only one member of this large and diverse family of birds, the brilliantly coloured Common Kingfisher is a jewel within the kingfisher family. The breeding grounds of Goosander and Red-breasted Merganser, two of Europe's sawbill ducks, are found even farther downstream, where rivers widen.

Where turbulent mountain streams enter the lowlands they often deposit shingle and gravel in extensive banks. Birds such as Oystercatchers and Common Sandpipers, which are more often associated with stony

Red-breasted Merganser

The Common Kingfisher (above) is most likely to live near slow-flowing, unpolluted water full of fish, since the adult bird needs 10–20 fish each day. During courtship, the male bird will often bring an offering of fish to the female.

Living alongside fast-flowing rivers and streams, the Grey Wagtail (below) often perches on rocks or trees above the water, waiting for passing insects. A ledge on the river bank forms the ideal site for its nest, which it lines with leaves, moss and grass.

## Birds of Rivers and Streams

| | |
|---|---|
| Little Grebe | *Tachybaptus ruficollis* |
| Little Egret | *Egretta garzetta* |
| Grey Heron | *Ardea cinerea* |
| Purple Heron | *A. purpurea* |
| Harlequin Duck | *Histrionicus histrionicus* |
| Red-breasted Merganser | *Mergus serrator* |
| Goosander | *M. merganser* |
| Moorhen | *Gallinula chloropus* |
| Common Coot | *Fulica atra* |
| Oystercatcher | *Haematopus ostralegus* |
| Common Sandpiper | *Actitis hypoleucos* |
| Common Tern | *Sterna hirundo* |
| Common Kingfisher | *Alcedo atthis* |
| Sand Martin | *Riparia riparia* |
| Grey Wagtail | *Motacilla cincerea* |
| Dipper | *Cinclus cinclus* |
| Rufous Scrub-robin | *Cercotrichas galactotes* |
| Reed Warbler | *Acrocephalus scirpaceus* |
| Penduline Tit | *Remiz pendulinus* |

*The Dipper (above) lives along fast-flowing shallow streams or rivers. It dives into the water and actually walks along the stream bed, under water up to 1m (3ft) deep, collecting food such as aquatic insects.*

*The Common Sandpiper also lives near fast-flowing streams and rivers. In contrast to the Dipper, which dives under water, the Common Sandpiper feeds by picking insects from the surface of the water, or from rocks and mud.*

Moorhen

coastal areas and marshes, find suitable breeding conditions here. Where rivers widen and flow slowly, they offer opportunities to a wider collection of birds. Common Coots, Moorhens, Little Grebes, and Purple and Grey Herons all find food in these rich waters. Bankside willows provide safe nesting sites for these and other species, such as the Penduline Tit.

### River Beds

Many south European rivers, fed by melting snow, become raging torrents during the spring. In summer, however, they may dry out to form a wilderness which attracts a few rather specialized birds. Nightjars, for example, may find bare, sandy areas, which have a strong resemblance to the sparse heaths they prefer, and Rufous Scrub-robins find perfect nesting conditions among the oleanders.

It is unfortunate that many of these dried-out rivers have also become dumping grounds for human refuse, including debris such as concrete and bricks and chemical waste, which threatens this habitat and the birdlife it supports.

Black-winged
Stilt

**T**ides rise and fall twice each day along the shores and estuaries of northern and western Europe and with them they bring plankton, which is left behind as the tide recedes. This wealth of plant and animal life is food for hosts of crustaceans, molluscs and worms that live in the land between the tides, making this habitat a rich feeding ground for birds.

The most specialized estuary and foreshore birds are the waders which, in winter, descend on the feeding grounds in tens, or even hundreds, of thousands. Even though food is plentiful, the varying lengths and shapes of their bills, together with their different feeding techniques, enable different species of wader to avoid competition for food.

Avocet

## Probing For Food

Long-billed Curlews and godwits probe deep into the mud and sand in search of worms. Curlews, with their slender down-turned bills, are among the most distinctive waders. When they catch a small crab, they delicately remove the legs before swallowing the creature. Dunlin, the most common and widespread of European waders, probe nonstop, like sewing machines, along the softer mudflats. Common Redshanks and Greenshanks dig for molluscs near the surface, while Avocets sweep their graceful bills from side to side near the mud surface. Knot are among the most numerous waders, but while they are common on some estuaries, they may be completely absent from others. Where they do occur, they form spectacular flocks in flight and at their high-tide roosts.

## Shoreline Birds

Geese and ducks are frequently present in large flocks around estuaries, although most species use the lonely shores only as safe roosting sites. Brent Geese feed on seaweed called eelgrass, but this is disappearing and being replaced by an introduced American weed, so they now usually feed on nearby grasslands. They do, however, still return to the estuary to find roosting sites.

Many species of duck feed along the shoreline, but while some wade

Caspian
Tern

*Bar-tailed Godwits (above), spend the winter around western European coasts. In summer they acquire a reddish breeding plumage and then fly to Siberian peat bogs to nest.*

*A flock of Knot (right) is spending the winter in the shallow waters of a European estuary before returning to its Arctic breeding grounds. The Knot, a medium-sized wader, takes its name from its habitual cry of 'knot, knot'.*

## Birds of Estuaries and Foreshores

| | |
|---|---|
| Red-necked Grebe | *Podiceps grisegena* |
| Slavonian Grebe | *P. auritus* |
| Cormorant | *Phalacrocorax carbo* |
| Pink-footed Goose | *Anser brachyrhynchus* |
| Barnacle Goose | *Branta leucopsis* |
| Brent Goose | *B. bernicla* |
| Common Shelduck | *Tadorna tadorna* |
| Pintail | *Anas acuta* |
| Scaup | *Aythya marila* |
| Long-tailed Duck | *Clangula hyemalis* |
| Osprey | *Pandion haliaetus* |
| Oystercatcher | *Haematopus ostralegus* |
| Black-winged Stilt | *Himantopus himantopus* |
| Avocet | *Recurvirostra avosetta* |
| Ringed Plover | *Charadruis hiaticula* |
| Kentish Plover | *C. alexandrinus* |
| Grey Plover | *Pluvialis squatarola* |
| Knot | *Calidris canutus* |
| Sanderling | *C. alba* |
| Little Stint | *C. minuta* |
| Dunlin | *C. alpina* |
| Bar-tailed Godwit | *Limosa lapponica* |
| Curlew | *Numenius arquata* |
| Whimbrel | *N. Phaeopus* |
| Common Redshank | *Tringa totanus* |
| Greenshank | *T. nebularia* |
| Terek Sandpiper | *Xenus cinereus* |
| Turnstone | *Arenaria interpres* |
| Mediterranean Gull | *Larus melanocephalus* |
| Little Gull | *L. minutus* |
| Black-headed Gull | *L. ridibundus* |
| Audouin's Gull | *L. audouinii* |
| · Common Gull | *L. canus* |
| Lesser Black-backed Gull | *L. fuscus* |
| Herring Gull | *L. argentatus* |
| Yellow-legged Gull | *L. cachinnans* |
| Great Black-backed Gull | *L. marinus* |
| Iceland Gull | *L. glaucoides* |
| Glaucous Gull | *L. hyperboreus* |
| Caspian Tern | *Sterna caspia* |

*The group of Brent Geese (above) belongs to the dark-bellied subspecies* bernicla, *which winters on the southern coasts of the North Sea and spends the summer in Siberia. The subspecies* hrota *has a paler belly and winters along the Atlantic coasts before spending the summer in Greenland and Spitzbergen.*

*Flocks of Oystercatchers on tidal estuaries and beaches can be huge – up to 5000 in some cases. The birds scatter to feed at low tide, but as high tide approaches they gather in vast roosts just above the tidemark.*

through the mud banks, others dive into the incoming tide. Turnstones live up to their name, turning over stones to search for food. More dramatic is the Oystercatcher, which uses its bill to stab into mussels and other shellfish.

Such a variety of life does not go unnoticed by predators and most estuaries are a winter home to a Peregrine or two. With so many birds to choose from, the living is easy for this falcon. When a Peregrine dives into a flock of waders, the spectacle of every bird on the estuary in the air at the same time is magnificent.

Herring Gull

# COASTS, CLIFFS AND ISLANDS

Manx Shearwater

F or most birds that live there, coasts simply offer convenient places to lay their eggs and rear their young. It is the sea around the coasts that provides a variety of food in rich abundance.

Europe supports relatively few truly oceanic bird species compared with land near the great oceans of the Southern Hemisphere. European cliffs and offshore islands are home to large numbers of Fulmars, storm-petrels and shearwaters, but only eight individual species are represented. Two other species appear regularly on migration and several more may do so, but they are either rare or difficult to locate.

Gannets and Guillemots breed on coastal cliffs. The single egg laid on a narrow cliff ledge by Guillemots is a pointed shape that spins rather than rolls when knocked, which means that there are few accidental egg losses. A colony of Gannets can easily be counted as the birds sit a bill-length apart. The Gannetries of Europe have been regularly counted, providing one of the most accurate censuses of any population of wild animals. Numbers have more than doubled since the 1950s, and it is thought that the increase in

Razorbill

Common Scoter

*Arctic Terns (above) breed around the shores of the northern oceans. These aggressive birds are fiercely protective of their breeding territory and nests.*

*Although Puffins (right) spend the winter at sea, in spring they congregate in breeding colonies on islands and cliffs that are safe from predators.*

European Storm-petrel

## Nesting Grounds

The cliffs and coasts of Europe do, however, provide a breeding and nesting ground for many species of coastal birds. Vast colonies of auks congregate to breed around the Atlantic and North Sea coasts. Guillemots and Puffins, Razorbills and Kittiwakes, Gannets and Fulmars cling to the most precipitous of cliff faces, or wheel in vast flocks over remote islands. Herring Gulls and Great Black-backed Gulls, Black-headed Gulls, and Sandwich, Common, Arctic, Little and Roseate Terns all nest along the more remote shorelines, hunting close to the shore. Eiders and other robust diving ducks may also nest in colonies on offshore islands and promontories.

*The Kittiwake (right) spends most of its life at sea but it finds perfect nesting sites on cliff ledges along the coast. Kittiwakes nest in colonies and the thousands of nests in a colony are built from seaweed and are balanced on very narrow ledges.*

Arctic Skua

numbers of Gannets has resulted because these birds have learned to scavenge waste from deep-sea trawlers.

Other birds, such as auks, have been in serious decline as a result of the increasing pollution of the sea and changing patterns of fish shoals owing to climatic conditions. Intensive fishing in recent years has led to a steady decline in fish populations, upon which coastal birds depend. With the exception of birds like the Gannet and Fulmar, it is perhaps only a matter of time before there is also a decline among many seabirds.

Common Eider

## Birds of Coasts, Cliffs and Islands

| | |
|---|---|
| Red-throated Diver | *Gavis stellata* |
| Black-throated Diver | *G. arctica* |
| Great Northern Diver | *G. immer* |
| Great Crested Grebe | *Podiceps cristatus* |
| Red-necked Grebe | *P. grisegena* |
| Slavonian Grebe | *P. auritus* |
| Fulmar | *Fulmarus glacialis* |
| Cory's Shearwater | *Calonectris diomedea* |
| Manx Shearwater | *Puffinus puffinus* |
| Balearic Shearwater | *P. mauretanicus* |
| Levantine Shearwater | *P. yelkouan* |
| European Storm-petrel | *Hydrobates pelagicus* |
| Leach's Storm-petrel | *Oceanodroma leucorhoa* |
| Gannet | *Morus bassanus* |
| Cormorant | *Phalacrocorax carbo* |
| Shag | *P. aristotelis* |
| Common Eider | *Somateria mollissima* |
| King Eider | *S. spectabilis* |
| Common Scoter | *Melanitta nigra* |
| Velvet Scoter | *M. fusca* |
| White-tailed Eagle | *Haliaeetus albicilla* |
| Eleonora's Falcon | *Falco eleonorae* |
| Peregrine Falcon | *F. peregrinus* |
| Pomarine Skua | *Stercorarius pomarinus* |
| Arctic Skua | *S. parasiticus* |
| Long-tailed Skua | *S. longicaudus* |
| Great Skua | *S. skua* |
| Black-headed Gull | *Larus ridibundus* |
| Herring Gull | *L. argentatus* |
| Yellow-legged Gull | *L. cachinnans* |
| Great Black-backed Gull | *L. marinus* |
| Kittiwake | *Rissa tridactyla* |
| Sandwich Tern | *Sterna. sandvicensis* |
| Common Tern | *S. hirundo* |
| Arctic Tern | *S. paradisaea* |
| Roseate Tern | *S. dougallii* |
| Little Tern | *S. albifrons* |
| Common Guillemot | *Uria aalge* |
| Razorbill | *Alca torda* |
| Black Guillemot | *Cepphus grylle* |
| Little Auk | *Alle alle* |
| Puffin | *Fratercula arctica* |

*Sandwich Terns (right), which nest in dense colonies on low-lying islands, are summer visitors to the shores of Europe. They spend the rest of their lives at sea, usually within sight of land, where they dive expertly in search of small fish and sand eels.*

Fulmar

Tawny Owl

The artificial environment of the city or town would seem unlikely to offer much to birds, but several adaptable species have not only survived, but actually flourished, among the steel and concrete of modern European conurbations.

The Industrial Revolution in the late eighteenth and nineteenth centuries led to an increase in the population of Europe and to an extraordinary concentration of people in towns and cities. The House Sparrow was one of the first birds to take advantage of urban habitats. During the nineteenth and early twentieth centuries, it fed on grain intended for horses that was spilt in streets and near stables.

White Storks (above) build a huge nest with twigs and branches balanced on the top of a telegraph pole, or on an old house or church. They often return to the same nest year after year.

Today, modern methods of transport have seriously reduced the population of this opportunist little bird and, in some areas, the House Sparrow is now regarded as an endangered species. Perhaps the most typical town bird is the pigeon, whose cooing call and fluttering flight is familiar to town and city dwellers. Pigeons have evolved from the domestic pigeon, descended from the wild Rock Dove. In summer, pigeons may fly out from cities and towns to feed in the countryside, but in winter they depend on whatever scraps they can scavenge from pavements and roads.

Blue Tit

Lesser Kestrel

### New Arrivals

Services provided in cities, such as water supply and sewage treatment, along with waste left on rubbish tips, all provide living opportunities for birds. Black-headed Gulls, which were virtually unknown in urban areas 100 years ago, are now regular winter visitors to many large towns

Black Kite

The Herring Gull (left) is adaptable enough to live in towns, as well as around the coasts and in open countryside near the sea. Although the traditional sites for their breeding colonies are on cliffs, Herring Gulls will also use the rooftops and chimneys of the buildings in seaside towns.

*Great Tits will fearlessly take advantage of human activity. They prefer to nest in a space with a small entrance, and as well as taking readily to nestboxes, they have been known to nest in all types of hollow spaces, including traffic lights (above). Great Tits are among the most common birds at birdtables, and they often drive other birds away from tasty morsels.*

Jackdaw

Common Swift

and cities. They feed on rubbish tips, and on playing fields and spend the nights in safety on water reservoirs on the outskirts of towns and cities.

The Black Redstart's colonization of Britain in the 1940s was due largely to the derelict sites created as a result of wartime bombing. As these areas were rebuilt during the post-war period, these handsome birds moved on to gasworks, railway sidings and other empty sites.

Common Starlings use the inexhaustible supply of nest holes among city buildings. They also use town centres as winter roosts, flying out each morning to rural feeding grounds up to 10km (6 miles) away. As many as a million birds may be found in one roost (see page 35).

## Birds of Cities and Towns

| | |
|---|---|
| White Stork | *Ciconia ciconia* |
| Black Kite | *Milvus migrans* |
| Lesser Kestrel | *Falco naumanni* |
| Common Kestrel | *F. tinnunculus* |
| Peregrine Falcon | *F. peregrinus* |
| Blackheaded Gull | *Larus ridibundus* |
| Herring Gull | *L. argentatus* |
| Rock Dove (Feral Pigeon) | *Columba livia* |
| Tawny Owl | *Strix aluco* |
| Common Swift | *Apus apus* |
| House Martin | *Delichon urbica* |
| Robin | *Erithacus rubecula* |
| Black Redstart | *Phoenicurus ochruros* |
| Blackbird | *Turdus merula* |
| Great Tit | *Parus major* |
| Common Starling | *Sturnus vulgaris* |
| House Sparrow | *Passer domesticus* |
| Chaffinch | *Fringilla coelebs* |
| Greenfinch | *Carduelis chloris* |

### Urban Nesting Sites

Common Swifts and House Martins, Kestrels and Lesser Kestrels, and even Tawny Owls and Peregrine Falcons, have all taken to breeding on buildings in towns and cities. In the case of the Swifts and House Martins, which were formerly confined to caves and cliffs, the populations of both species have experienced an extraordinary boom with increased urbanization. They are able to treat the buildings of towns and cities as the artificial equivalent of their natural habitat. Kestrels and Tawny Owls have also adapted to city life, switching from a diet of small mammals to one dominated by House Sparrows and other urban birds.

### Garden Birds

The parks and gardens found in European towns and cities also offer opportunities to birds. Blackbirds, Robins, Black Redstarts, Chaffinches, Greenfinches and Great Tits all live alongside humans, where open spaces and greenery survive.

However, the typical city or town remains inhospitable to the majority of birds, and provides suitable habitat only for those species that are adaptable. This is why migrating birds may be more obvious over a city than in the open countryside. The movements of, say, Lapwings at the end of July are a feature of cities, but they pass unnoticed over the surrounding countryside where they may be seen at any time of year. Even the movements of small night migrants, such as warblers and flycatchers, can be more easily distinguished in urban areas than among woods and hedgerows.

# FARMLAND AND VILLAGES

**F**armland and the land surrounding villages has changed dramatically over the last 50 years, as a result of the modernization of farming techniques. This has had a significant effect on the bird populations that once found a home there.

All over Europe, vast areas of natural vegetation have disappeared as people have sought to earn a living from the land. The hedgerows, wooded copses and methods of cultivation used by early farmers created new opportunities for birds. In recent years, however, conservationists have become concerned about the threat to birdlife posed by the destruction of hedgerows to create vast fields suitable for the mechanical farming techniques of single-crop agriculture.

Cattle Egret

Wryneck

## Barn Owl

The appropriately named Barn Owl has suffered as a result of the destruction of old farm barns, which have been replaced by modern farm buildings. Many barn lofts have now been destroyed. Easy access to nest sites – and the Owl's survival in many areas – now depends on the provision by enlightened farmers of nestboxes in the eaves of new buildings. But the nesting Barn Owl is intolerant of disturbance and may shun even the most inviting nestbox because of noise and human activity. In addition, old hedgerow trees, whose hollows provided natural nesting sites, are being felled, further reducing owl populations. Equally and perhaps even more important, the modern farmer has reduced the uncultivated corners of fields that provide the Barn Owl with its perfect hunting grounds. Without hunting grounds, the provision of nest sites seems quite pointless.

Swallow

## Modern Farming Methods

Farm stock, especially chickens and pigs, are now often fed on prepared foods and kept permanently housed rather than allowed to search for food outside among grassy weeds. In addition, repeated cutting of grass for silage has replaced haymaking, and this has reduced the availability of seeds and destroyed the nests

White Stork

*Farmland areas, and land at the edge of villages, with plenty of rough grasses, hedges and banks, are the habitat of the Barn Owl (above). The Barn Owl does not build a nest, but lays its eggs on the bare boards of a loft in barns, or in other old bulidings.*

*The vegetation of traditional farmland provides a perfect home for the Grey Partridge (right), but their populations have reduced as a result of the destruction of the hedgerows in which they build their nests.*

of many ground-dwelling birds.
As a result, the numbers of seed-
eating birds have fallen. In particular,
the Corn Crake has suffered, largely
because of increased mechanization,
and is extinct over much of Europe.

Calandra Lark

## Conservation Projects

Various projects introduced by governments and
conservation bodies have gone some way towards rectifying
this situation, but many species remain seriously endangered.
An unexpected result of successful conservation has been the
spread of Marsh Harriers to cereal fields during the past 20
years. Formerly confined to large reedbeds, which remain
their preferred habitat, these raptors have taken to the large
single-crop fields of wheat, barley and oats as substitutes

for reeds. The nests of Marsh Harriers are prone
to loss of eggs and chicks during harvest
time, but enough young survive to
sustain numbers. The birds that
make farmland their home are
found in greatest numbers in
areas where traditional small-scale
farming techniques have survived.

Rook

## Bird-Friendly Villages

Villages in many parts of Europe have become more bird-
friendly. Many birds may find nesting opportunities in
village buildings while commuting to find food
in the surrounding countryside. In addition, the
contemporary passion for gardens with berry-bearing
shrubs, fruit trees and ponds, as well as gardens made
specially to attract birds, provides a wealth of new
feeding and nesting opportunities for many species,
such as Pied Wagtails.

*The Sky Lark (above) benefited
from forest clearance, as it
favours an open countryside
habitat. However, it has declined
massively due to modern drill-
seeding techniques and chemical
seed dressings. Sky Larks feed
on the ground and are
severely affected in
the winter if the
ground is
frozen.*

Corn Bunting

# BIRDS AND PEOPLE

Rüppell's Warbler

**B**irds preceded humankind on the Earth by some 145 million years, so humans have always lived alongside them. Although people have long been fascinated by their beauty and agility, and particularly their ability to fly, the relationship between humans and birds has not always been positive. We have hunted them for food and for sport, and have polluted and destroyed many of their habitats.

The study of birds in recent times has led to a greater awareness of how they work and why they are dependent on certain foods and habitats, which has highlighted the need for conservation. It has also encouraged a growth in the popularity of birdwatching, bird photography and bird gardening.

The following section provides an introduction to birdwatching by giving advice on how to identify birds, and on how and where to watch them. It also assesses the value of conservation in maintaining bird populations.

*Great Tits feed on fat balls in winter (above). By putting out food during the winter months, when other foods are scarce, people can help birds to survive.*

*Gulls follow the plough (right) to eat the invertebrates brought to the surface. The actions of humans can have many unforeseen effects on birds.*

*Mute Swans swim in waters near the giant cooling towers of a power station (above). Heat and chemicals from industrial complexes can enter rivers and lakes, affecting the habitats of water birds. Toxic chemicals may poison the birds or their food source, sometimes with disastrous consequences, or encourage massive growths of algae, which strangle other plantlife.*

*A Whooper Swan (right) is held securely by a conservation worker while it is fitted with a tiny radio transmitter. These lightweight devices allow scientists to track migrating birds, gathering vital information without interfering with the bird's movements.*

Feral Pigeons congretate in St Mark's Square, Venice (left). Pigeons are scavengers and will come quite close to people if they think they have food to offer.

Falconry, the art of training birds of prey to hunt game, has been practised by people for centuries. A falconer (right) wears a heavy glove to protect his hand against the bird's claws.

Binoculars, a telescope, a note book and comfortable clothing are essentials for birding (below). Birdwatching has replaced hunting and egg collecting in the 20th century as conservation has become increasingly important.

The cutting of reeds (left) and other natural cover can devastate breeding birds, but delaying such cuts by as little as two or three weeks can be enough to give time for nestlings to fledge.

A Puffin is released after being ringed (right). When birds are ringed, they are weighed, measured and inspected for age, sex, health and other features. This builds up a picture of the bird population and, if the bird is recaptured, shows where the bird has moved to.

# BIRD GARDENING

The House Sparrow, a popular visitor

**N**o one knows exactly when the practice of putting out food for wild birds began, but bird gardening today is a thriving industry.

Peanut dispensers, seed hoppers, bird tables, bird baths and drinking pools are now standard in many European gardens – and the birds have responded gratefully. In Britain, House Sparrows, Blue and Great Tits, Starlings and Greenfinches dominate, but Robins, Hedge Accentors, Blackbirds and Song Thrushes can all be seen. Even specialist feeders, such as the Great Spotted Woodpecker and the Siskin, may become regular visitors.

The provision of food and water is only the most obvious form of bird gardening. There is much more to it than that – such as providing places to breed. Nestboxes, with small holes for tits and Tree Sparrows or left open-fronted for Robins and Spotted Flycatchers, come in a wide variety of designs. Some are large enough to hold a pair of owls or Kestrels. Others are made of concrete to prevent the depredations of Great Spotted Woodpeckers. Yet others can be filled with expanded

*Great Tits (above), which are larger than other species of tit, often dominate at peanut dispensers. Tits in general are inquisitive birds and not particularly shy. This makes them regulars at the bird table.*

*The Starling (above) is a versatile feeder and enjoys insects, berries, fruit and seeds. City*

*Starlings make the most of urban ad hoc bird tables, like this one made from a tree stump.*

polystyrene to enable Willow Tits to excavate their own nest chambers, as they would do naturally in a rotten tree stump.

Another single-species nestbox, the House Martin nest, can be fixed under the eaves of a house. The advantage of this nestbox is that it is not only occupied by the birds, but also encourages other pairs of House Martins to construct real nests alongside – and perhaps create a significant

colony. These summer visitors build their nests of mud pellets that may be gathered from a pond, or even a muddy puddle, up to a kilometre (more than half a mile) distant. Providing mud may encourage House Martins to nest in otherwise totally dry environments. Similarly, providing feathers, cotton and wool for the birds to line their nests can create more opportunities for close observation of birds in the garden environment.

**Larger Bird Gardens**

For those fortunate enough to have a large garden, the thoughtful planting of berry-bearing shrubs provides food in a more natural manner. It is not only shrubs offering food that attract birds but also those that have foliage year-round. Greenfinches, Blackbirds and other garden species like coniferous shrubs because they provide safe roosting sites. Fruit trees, too, attract birds, offering autumn and winter food, particularly where fallen apples are allowed to stay on the ground. Redwings, Fieldfares and other

74

## HOW TO BUILD A NESTBOX

First of all, decide which birds you want to attract. To entice Spotted Flycatchers and Robins, you will need to provide a half-front to the box; but for tits, you must drill a hole 3cm (1¼in) in diameter in the front.
1. To make the box, cut six pieces of plywood to the required sizes.
2. Fit the pieces together with wood glue.
3. Secure the sides with short brass screws or copper tacks.
3. To attach the lid, you can use hinges – but a simple piece of roofing felt or a piece of tyre inner tube is just as effective.
4. If you wish, add a peg perch to improve the overall appearance of the nestbox.
5. Fix the box to a tree or a wall that faces away from the sun and prevailing wind. Over most of Europe this means facing northeast.
Remember to clear the box of all nesting materials at the end of each breeding season.

*A Eurasian Jay in a nestbox (above) awaits the return of its parent with food. The parents have filled the box with dry twigs in the way they would have lined a nest in the wild.*

*Water is an important feature in bird gardening, as this Robin, shown bathing in a puddle (right), demonstrates.*

*A Robin and a group of Blue Tits have a midwinter feast at a custom-built bird table (above). On the floor of the bird table there are nuts, seeds and kitchen scraps bound together with meat fat – a high-protein and fat combination that is important in the winter. There are also two hanging bags of unsalted peanuts, which offer food to the more agile tits. It is most essential to feed birds in winter when many of them die of starvation, but feeding can be continued throughout the year.*

thrushes may gather in large numbers around such fruit trees, particularly in cold weather.

Birds respond to a huge variety of opportunities, so it is not necessary to spend a fortune on either gourmet meals or purpose-built homes. For example, an old kettle fixed against a wall, may form the perfect home for a Spotted Flycatcher. Arranging a garden hose to drip slowly into a pond or upturned dustbin lid creates moving water, which warblers find irresistible. A ledge inside a garden shed may encourage Swallows to breed – but remember to keep a door or window open throughout the breeding season. Above all, remember the birds when performing any garden management, such as removing trees or shrubs that may contain nests.

**I**t is said that all you need to start watching birds is a pair of eyes. This is true, but since many birds are small, shy creatures that fly away when you approach, some sort of optical aid, such as binoculars or a telescope, is also useful.

The field notebook, a birdwatching essential

Today, even casual birdwatchers usually own a pair of binoculars. As a guide, the ideal binocular is a compromise between magnification, field of view (i.e. the area that can be seen), depth of field (i.e. the focusing power) and weight.

When it comes to choosing a pair of binoculars, bigger is not always better. Big binoculars with large lenses provide great field of view and depth of field – you can see over a large area and focus very accurately. However, the weight is a hindrance during a whole day's birdwatching.

All binoculars are marked with two numbers: the power of *magnification* (e.g. x7, x8) and the *diameter* of the large piece of glass at the front of the binoculars, called the object lens (e.g. 40mm, 50mm). A binocular with 7 x 50 specification provides a magnification of 7 with a 50mm object lens. The higher the magnification, the narrower the field of view and the less the depth of field.

## PRISM BINOCULARS

Ordinary, or porro, prisms are distinctly wider at the front than the rear and have big, angled 'shoulders'. Both ordinary and roof prisms have a central-focusing adjustable eyepiece to compensate for differences between an individual's eyes, and can be 'broken' to allow for personal 'eye apart' measurements.

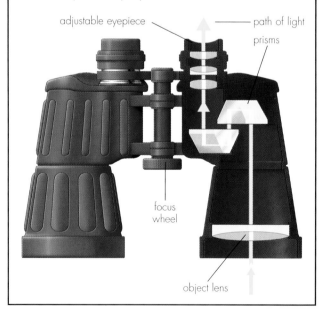

adjustable eyepiece — path of light

prisms

focus wheel

object lens

*When birdwatching in a wide, open landscape (above), it is more effective to keep your eye on a specific area and bring your binoculars up to your line of vision.*

*In poor light conditions, such as those prevalent at dusk (above) or dawn, a light-gathering power of 5mm is suitable. A lower magnification than x10 provides a slightly higher light-gathering power.*

Field and depth factors can be increased to a given magnification by using a larger object lens. The ideal diameter for the object lens is between 30mm and 50mm, while the magnification range recommended by experienced birders is between x7 and x10. A good compromise is a lens with a x8 magnification, which has a wider field of view and depth of field than a lens with, say, a x10 magnification.

One further practical consideration is the light-gathering power of binoculars. In the poorest light conditions, the

## CHOOSING A TELESCOPE

If you plan to do a lot of long-range viewing, you should probaly invest in a telescope. There are two types: draw telescopes and prismatic telescopes. Draw telescopes are out of date, so most birdwatchers use prisms, but the choice boils down to a compromise between weight, magnification and depth and view features. Good modern telescopes have object lenses between 50mm and 80mm. Their weight increases with the size of the lens.

Magnifications vary from x20 to x50, but anything larger than x30 can be difficult to fine-focus.

Unlike zoom-lens binoculars, telescopes with zoom lenses can be useful, although loss of field is inevitable. Wide-angled eyepieces are increasingly available, enlarging the field of view. A typical specification is 20 x 50mm. Prismatic telescopes also come either 'straight-through' or 'angled' at 45 degrees (see below). Angled eyepieces make it easier to pick up flying birds, and can be used with lower and lighter tripods. Leaders in

the field include Swarovski, Kowa, Nikon and Optolyth, with Bushnell at a lower price – a good choice for those who are not sure how much they are likely to use a telescope.

Finally, astronomical mirror telescopes have now been adopted by the most serious modern birders, where a feather-by-feather examination may be required to clinch an identification. The American-made Questar is very expensive and, because of its mirror image, can be confusing to use initially, but it is undoubtedly the leader in this field.

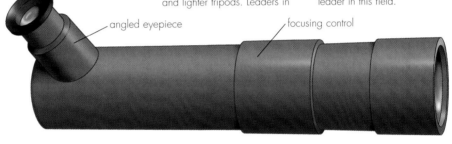

angled eyepiece       focusing control

---

human eye is physically unable to open much more than 6mm (¼in), so a pair of binoculars with a light-gathering power of 5mm is probably suitable. Light-gathering power can be calculated by dividing the object lens size by the magnification specification. So if you have a pair of 10 x 50 binoculars, divide 50 by 10, and you come up with a light-gathering power of 5mm. If you wish to choose binoculars with a higher light-gathering power, buy a lower magnification than x10.

Modern prismatic binoculars can be divided into two basic types: those that contain ordinary prisms (see box opposite) and those that contain roof prisms. Roof prisms, more modern and more expensive than ordinary prisms, were developed in the 1960s. Their parallel tubes fit into a very compact design resembling opera glasses.

Some binoculars, but not all, are fully waterproof but these are usually more complex and more expensive. Leica, Zeiss, Swarovski, and Bausch & Lomb are all top-of-the-range European makes. Japanese optical companies all make binoculars, but although their camera lenses are the best in the world, they have yet to take binoculars seriously enough to produce one to beat the European brand leaders.

*Telescopes become even more useful when combined with tripods, especially in open areas, (above). Tripods should be easily adjustable and lightweight yet sturdy – particularly when there is competition for space (left).*

# BIRD IDENTIFICATION

**E**veryone can place an unknown bird, be it duck, thrush, hawk, crow, finch or wader, in some sort of broad category.

For example, on spotting an unknown bird, a non-birder might observe that 'It was about the same size as a thrush.' In stating this, they are actually comparing a bird they don't know with one they do know – which is exactly what birdwatchers do. In addition, the same non-birder is unlikely to say that the mystery bird was the size of a thrush if it was seen on, say, a pond. Why? Because even non-birders know that thrushes do not swim. People are more likely to compare a bird seen on a pond with another known *swimming* bird. In this way, the non-birder has hit upon the most crucial question of bird identification: What type of bird have I seen? To help answer this question, he or she must analyse the bird's physical appearance, where and when it was seen, and what it was doing when seen.

*Pied Flycatcher, identified with care by the head and wing marks*

## The How, Where and When of Bird Identification

How a bird behaves is almost as crucial as its type, and is the second stage of identification. A bird feeding on the shoreline may be a duck, a heron or a bunting. However, if it has a relatively long bill and long legs then it is likely it could be a wader, and the search for a name is narrowed.

Behaviour is closely linked to the third factor – habitat, or where a bird is usually to be found. Birds are highly mobile and can turn up anywhere, especially after an exhausting migratory flight. For example, under duress, seabirds may appear miles inland on lakes and other freshwaters. But birds do have definite preferences; they are generally creatures of both habit and habitat.

The appearance of a bird in a certain habitat is very regular, so the 'when' factor is another crucial part of identification. For instance, Common Cuckoos do not sing in January, flycatchers do not appear in February

*A Common Buzzard can be identified as a bird of prey at a distance by its hooked bill and the shape of its body.*

and Common Swifts do not arrive before the end of April. Timing varies within Europe, but a sound knowledge of the birds' arrival and departure dates for your local area is more important than other details, such as a bird's size.

## Getting to Know Jizz and Field Marks

Combining the way that a bird behaves with its structure creates a picture of its character, and this, in birders' language, is known as its 'jizz'. Jizz may be a combination of the way a bird perches, its feeding behaviour, its habitat, its size, its length of leg and bill, the shape of its wings, the way it flies and the length of its tail. A duck with white in

*The combination of aquatic habitat, size, shape, and the length of its bill identifies this bird as a wader. Other features, including the pale supercilium, mark it as a Wood Sandpiper.*

the wing that lands on a meadow to graze is a Wigeon; one that lands on a marsh and 'up-ends' is a Gadwall.

The final factor in identification is field marks – bold patches of plumage that are specific to a particular bird, or group of birds. The great American Roger Tory Peterson's field guides described field marks so well that a generation of birders was able to improve their identification skills.

# FIELD MARKS

Field marks are striking markings that are specific to a particular bird, or at least to a group of birds. The presence or absence of features such as wingbars, white or coloured outer tail feathers, white patches on the rump, extended tail feathers, particular head markings, or the colour of legs and bill, enable us to distinguish birds that have a similar structure from one another.

## WINGBARS

### Brambling
White rump and short, forked black tail. Breeding male has a black head and mantle, bold orange shoulder patch and breast.

### Siskin
Male is greenish with a yellow rump and a distinctive black crown.

## HEAD MARKINGS

### Sedge Warbler
The dark brown crown has distinct streaks and there is a cream stripe above the eye.

### Little Ringed Plover
Bold head markings. This bird has a narrow white line above a black crown bar and a yellow ring around the eye.

### Whinchat
White stripes outline dark cheeks on the male with a blackish brown crown, broad white supercilium and a white moustache stripe.

### Cirl Bunting
The male has a black throat and chin below a striking olive green and yellow-streaked face.

## TAILS

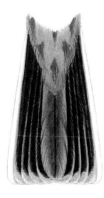

### Chaffinch
White sides to long tail feathers distinguish the Chaffinch from a variety of other finches.

### Wheatear
This tail is dark in the centre with white and black on the edges. It forms an inverted 'T'-shape when fanned.

### Bar-tailed Godwit
As its name suggests, this wader has a barred greyish tail pattern on top of a white rump.

### Fan-tailed Warbler
The tail of the Fan-tailed Warbler is tipped black and white on the outer feathers.

### Wood Lark
This species is easy to distinguish from other birds in flight by its whitish outer tail tips.

**B**irds tend to restrict themselves to specific habitats, such as mountains, forests, salt marshes, reedbeds or freshwater lakes.

The Crested Tit, found only in woodland

Birders need to teach themselves the appropriate field tactics – or behaviour – in each of these habitats to make the most of their birdwatching.

The Pyrenees, which separate Spain from France, are high mountains crossed by road passes that are free from snow only during high summer. Their mountain fastnesses are the major European stronghold of that huge vulture, the Lammergeier, as well as other high-altitude species. In the Pyrenees, the birders main tactic has to be to get as far away as possible from the tourists who congregate at major passes. He or she must find a good vantage point that is relatively quiet and settle down to observe patiently.

The forest region of Bialowieska in Poland – the home of the rare European Bison – contains a splendid collection of breeding birds, including the elusive Hazel Grouse. The region also boasts an impressive variety of woodpeckers and several other rare birds, such as the Greenish Warbler and Red-breasted Flycatcher. As with all woodland, a quiet and unobtrusive approach is necessary – and in Bialowieska particularly, it is essential to have waterproof boots.

The Camargue in France is the delta area of the mighty River Rhône, a maze of channels and shallow lagoons set on the tideless Mediterranean. There is a huge array of birds breeding here, including a splendid colony of Greater Flamingos – one of only three colonies in Europe – which find their northern outpost among the marshes. Most of the Camargue's birdwatching takes place from the public roads, so you need to be mobile and use the 'stop-and-look' tactic.

The low-lying island of Texel, in the Netherlands, is set among the vast mudflats of the Waddenzee. In this region, Avocet, Ruff, Black-tailed Godwit and Black Tern are the stars, but an abundance of other waders and terns can also be seen. The region has a large number of reserves through which to walk – visit as many as possible and make full use of the well-sited hides available.

Varanger Fjord, Norway, is as near as one can get to tundra in Europe. Facing eastwards on to the Arctic Ocean close to Russia, this fjord boasts exciting breeding species, such as Steller's Eider, Brünnich's Guillemot and Bar-tailed Godwit. This vast area needs to be explored by car and on foot. High-latitude weather is always unpredictable, so be prepared to get hot, cold, wet and dry all on the same day.

*The Pyrenees at Riglos (above) are home to a wealth of high-altitude specialities, including the Lammergeier and the Wallcreeper.*

*Bialowieska, Poland (below), is the last large remnant of the native deciduous forest that once covered much of Europe.*

## WHERE TO GO

One can go birdwatching almost anywhere in the world, but some places are so good, by virtue of their geographical position or variety of habitats, that they have become 'bird resorts' – or at least resorts for birdwatchers. Over the years, guidebooks about birdwatching have proliferated and there are now guides to countries, regions and even single cities. Below is a selection of the best bird locations in Europe.

*The spectaclar Varanger Fjord, Norway (above), is home to a wide variety of tundra breeding species.*

| | | | |
|---|---|---|---|
| **Austria** | Neusiedl | **Holland** | Texel |
| **Britain** | Isles of Scilly | **Hungary** | Hortobágy |
| | North Norfolk | **Iceland** | Myvatn |
| | Shetland | **Ireland** | Wexford |
| **Cyprus** | | **Italy** | Sardinia |
| **Czech** | Lednice | **Norway** | Dovrefjell |
| **Denmark** | Limfjørden | | Varanger Fjord |
| | Ringkøbing | **Poland** | Bialowieska |
| **Finland** | Lapland | | Biebrza |
| | Parikkala | **Portugal** | Alentejo |
| **France** | Baie d'Aiguillon | **Romania** | Danube Delta |
| | Camargue | **Spain** | Coto Doñana |
| | Gavarnie | | Monfragüe |
| **Germany** | Munich | | Pyrenees |
| | Muritz Lakes | **Sweden** | Hornborgasjön |
| **Gibraltar** | | | Lapland |
| **Greece** | Evros | | Öland |
| | Kerkini Lake | **Turkey** | Bosphorus |
| | Prespa | **Yugoslavia** | Kopački Rit |
| **Holland** | Flevoland | | Obedska Bara |

*Flamingos in the Camargue, France (above), live on tiny invertebrates that flourish in extremely salty conditions.*

*The Dutch island of Texel (right), one of the best marsh breeding sites in northern Europe, provides bird interest throughout the year.*

The Osprey, confined to mountains

**M**any of Europe's – and the world's – bird populations are at risk. The reasons for this include hunting, disappearing habitats and pollution.

Birds have been hunted for food since prehistory and, in many areas, birds such as Crane and Great Bustard, Black-tailed Godwit and Ruff were eaten and eliminated long before their habitat disappeared. Today, despite government legislation, bird hunting for both food and sport still takes place. For example, in defiance of Italian laws protecting migrating Honey Buzzards, Sicilians shoot many each year; the French government bans bird hunting, yet pâté made from larks' tongue or Blackbirds is sold openly. The Dutch actually subsidize their farmers for damage caused by vast flocks of wintering geese.

In spite of such direct persecution, the birds of Europe would survive and even prosper were it not for the changes humankind inflicts on the landscape. The advent of power, first in the form of wind power and later in the form of the

internal combustion engine, has made the wholesale clearance of forest and marshland possible. In addition, in an effort to increase crop yields all over the world, farmers now use chemicals to protect seeds from destruction by pests. Many of these chemicals and pesticides take a long time to decay naturally and build up through the food chain to produce disastrous effects. Despite early promise, organic farming methods have not proved a successful alternative, since the food produced is so much more expensive.

Crane, Great Bustard and Mute Swan were served at medieval banquets in England, but it was only the royal status of the Mute Swan (above) that prevented it from following the Crane and Bustard into local oblivion.

In parts of Cyprus, the practice of bird liming still takes place (right). Migrant warblers and chats, including Nightingales, as shown in this photograph, are caught on lime sticks and pickled to be eaten as delicacies.

The shooting of pigeons and doves (left) is still part of everday life in Malta and in the Pays-Basque region of France.

In the world of dying birds, as described in Rachel Carson's book Silent Spring (1962), raptors, such as Peregrines, ate their own abnormally thin-shelled eggs (right), as did Golden Eagles.

# ENDANGERED SPECIES

Europe has its rare birds, but most of these can be found elsewhere in the world and will survive as species even if they are extirpated in Europe. There are several species, however, that are highly endangered both in Europe and worldwide. A few pairs of the Slender-billed Curlew winter in Morocco and have been seen more recently in Italy – otherwise we have no knowledge of where the bird is to be found. The Lesser Kestrel has suffered a catastrophic population crash, with their numbers in Spain falling from 100,000 to barely 5000–6000 pairs in the last 30 years. The population of the Lammergeier was probably never great, but with fewer than 50 or 60 pairs in the whole of Europe, it must now be regarded as endangered. In some instances, human intervention, such as active conservation measures, can help to redress the balance, but there is a limit to what can be achieved. The following are some of Europe's most endangered birds.

## Golden Eagle

The absorption of pesticides in the 1960s damaged eggs so that they became abnormally thin-shelled. They cracked in the nest and were eaten by their parents, causing the raptor population to fall. The Golden Eagle (below) has continued to decline in Europe. Confined to remote mountains, they are still shot and poisoned by gamekeepers and their nests raided by egg collectors, who ignore conservation laws.

saved the Peregrine (above) just in time, but it was virtually wiped out in Europe and North America. However, by 1980, Peregrines had made a comeback in North America.

## Great Bustard

Just how such a large, ground-dwelling bird as the Great Bustard (below) survives in Europe is something of a mystery. These birds lay their eggs in grassland but also in fields of cereal, where the chances of the young surviving are slim. It is possible that we have an aging population of these great birds.

## Peregrine

Generations of Peregrines have faced crisis after crisis. During World War II, they were destroyed on government orders so that messenger pigeons could get through from the front. In the 1960s, they were poisoned by agricultural chemicals. Young Peregrines have recently been in high demand among falconers. In Britain, work by a handful of conservation bodies

Red Kite, a very graceful flier

**I**n Europe, changes wrought on the landscape, particularly in the nineteenth and twentieth centuries, forced a wide audience into taking notice of the issue of conservation, which was previously considered the territory of cranks.

Bird protection, as it was called at first, started in England with protestors complaining about the use of feathers and bird plumes as fashion items for decorating hats and clothes. For example, aigrette feathers, the nuptial plumage of egrets, were in great demand and these birds were ruthlessly slaughtered in order to get their breeding finery.

*The ringing of birds is an essential part of controlling and protecting their populations. Above, a dedicated conservationist is shown ringing Shags on the rocky, coastal cliffs in a bird reserve along the coast of Britain.*

### The Birth of the RSPB
From this small start, the Royal Society for the Protection of Birds (RSPB) was born. It is now the largest private sector wildlife conservation organization in Europe and has more than a million members. At first, the fledgling society spent its money mainly on 'watchers' to help keep an eye on Britain's marshes and moorlands, where rare birds could be found breeding. Then the RSPB became involved in more specialized areas of conservation – such as the purchase of large tracts of coastal land to protect the breeding Avocet

population. Since then, all over the world, the enormous popularity of televised nature programmes has meant that millions of people have become aware of wild birds as well as the great mammal populations of Africa, and the wildlife of North and South America, Asia, Australia and Antarctica.

Conservation has now moved from the small-scale protection of a few individual animals and birds to a mass

*A sound technician uses a parabolic reflector (above) to make high-quality recordings of birdsong. Dawn, when singing birds are in full flow, is the best time to make such recordings.*

movement with huge support. Instead of targeting particular endangered species, conservation societies now tend to use a combined approach that involves preserving the habitats of birds, banning hunting for sport and preventing pollution.

Today, more people are 'green' than ever before. This greater awareness of the natural environment has also led to the growth of outdoor activities, such as birdwatching, bird recording and bird photography.

# BIRDWATCHING BY EAR

A knowledge of birdsong and calls is crucial in locating many of Europe's less obvious birds, as well as in identifying disappearing species and birds in flight. Such knowledge can save valuable time when trying to track down an unknown call – time that can be spent searching for other birds. If you have a reasonably good ear, walk through the

countryside with an expert and note what you can hear. You can learn to identify bird after bird without actually seeing it. How do you learn these calls and songs? By playing recordings, available on both tape and CD. Play them daily until they are built into the computer of your mind. Start with common birds that live alongside you, such as Song Thrush, Chaffinch, Blackbird and Robin.

## Song Thrush

The voice of the Song Thrush is loud and musical. Its song consists of brief but varied phrases, repeated two to four times, and punctuated by short pauses. The notes are soft and flutelike. The singing of the Song Thrush peaks during courtship but there is a second peak between the first and second broods. It can also be heard during the winter months. The Song Thrush prefers to live in woodlands and to sing high off the ground, while perched on a tall tree.

## Chaffinch

The Chaffinch's song is a descending phrase of about 12 notes that ends with a flourish. The bird is found in woodlands, parks and gardens and starts singing in February, when the male claims its territory. Although the basis of a Chaffinch's song is instinctive, the flourish at the end is learned from an adult. This means that the Chaffinch's song develops regional dialects.

## Blackbird

The song of the Blackbird is a rich, mellow warble that makes up a major part of the dawn and dusk choruses. The song is loud, with phrases strung together without repetition. It sings mainly in gardens and parks and, like the Song Thrush, prefers to sing high off the ground, perched on a TV aerial or tree. The Blackbird's song is heard between February and late July and reaches its peak when birds are setting up their territories at the beginning of the breeding season.

*Thanks to modern environmental awareness, many wetland areas are now bird reserves. The worker at a Wildfowl and Wetlands Trust reserve (left) is checking the purity of the water from a reed filtration system.*

*This sign (above) at Akureyri, Iceland, says 'Attention'. It is alerting road users to the fact that young broods of Eider duck, which prefer to breed along coasts, may be crossing the road to reach the sea.*

# BIRD SPECIES

Masked
Shrike

**M**uch of the fascination in birding comes from identifying birds, and that means recognizing their species. Some species look the same all the time, but others have plumages that vary according to age, sex or time of year. Knowing the different appearances of a species is the mark of an experienced birder.

The following pages give details of all European bird species, to allow the birdwatcher to make a clear identification. Maps and habitat details provide the birder with information about where a bird is likely to be seen and the frequency of its occurrence on a monthly basis. Each species has an entry to itself, with the various species arranged so that closely related birds appear next to each other. The species order follows a generally agreed scientific format, with the more primitive birds such as divers first, and the more recently evolved perching birds, such as warblers, last.

Puffins (above) belong to the auk family. Auks are black and white seabirds that dive from the water surface to catch fish. They have short legs and stand upright.

The Great Crested Grebe (right) is the largest of the grebes, a family of freshwater diving birds that build floating nests and have bright summer plumage.

The Waxwing (above) is the only member of the family Bombycillidae that is resident in Europe. However, the Cedar Waxwing from North America has once strayed across the Atlantic, to be seen as a rare vagrant in England.

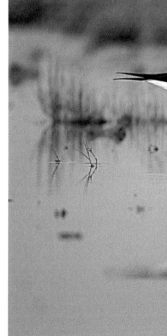

The Merlin (right) is a typical falcon, with its streaked underparts and long, pointed wings. The falcons are small to medium-sized birds, which are able to use their powerful wingbeats to chase after prey. Like other birds of prey, or raptors, they have strongly hooked beaks and long, sharp talons to help them seize and then dismember their catch.

The European Roller (left) is the only species of roller native to Europe. The family takes its name from the courtship display flight of the male, which involves tumbling and rolling in the air.

The Red Grouse (right) is a typically plump and well-camouflaged gamebird of the grouse family. Five species of this family live in Europe, all related to other gamebirds such as partridges, quails and pheasants.

The Red-breasted Goose (below) is one of nine species of goose found in Europe. Of these, four, including the red-breasted, are classed as black geese in the genus Branta, and the others as grey geese in the genus Anser.

There are more than 40 species of wader in Europe, but the Black-winged Stilt (left) is the one with the longest legs. Apart from flamingos, the Black-winged Stilt has longer legs in proportion to its body than any other bird in the world.

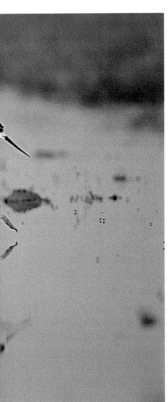

Only one species of flamingo is present in Europe – the Greater Flamingo (right). Other species are found in Africa, Asia and South America, but none lives as far north as this species. In Europe, the bird inhabits shallow lakes and lagoons in southern France and Spain.

**T**he 423 species that are most likely to be found in Europe appear as individual entries in this section. The introductory text gives a brief outline of the bird before describing its appearance to aid identification. A data panel gives details about the bird's size, call, habitat and other facts.

There is some argument about the geographical limits of Europe, but for the purposes of this book, we have taken the view that Europe is the western peninsula of the great Eurasian landmass. The eastern limit runs from the shores of the Arctic Ocean near the island of Novaya Zemlya, south along the Ural Mountains before turning west to follow the Volga River to the Sea of Azov. The southern limit runs from the Sea of Azov through the Black Sea and the Bosphorus, before looping around the Greek islands and southern Italy to pass out through the Strait of Gibraltar into the Atlantic. Iceland is included in Europe for historic and cultural reasons.

**Species name:** Common name

**Species name:** *Latin name*

**Abundance charts:** For abundance charts see species maps box below.

**Size:** This is the length of the bird from the tip of the bill to the tip of the tail, measured as if the bird were stretched out straight. In the field, most birds appear shorter as they hold their necks upright.

**Wing:** This is the measurement from the carpal joint (the bend of the wing) to the tip of the longest primary feather held flat and straight.

**Bill:** This is the length of the bill from its tip to where it meets the head.

**Weight:** The weight of a bird can vary not only according to its age or size, but also to the season of the year as individuals fatten up prior to migration.

**Voice:** A bird's song or call may be described, or an approximation of the sound it makes may be given in *italic*.

**Habitat:** The type of vegetation or landscape preferred by the bird is described here.

**Food:** The food preferred by the adult bird is described here; the chicks of many species are fed on insects, whatever the adults eat.

**Range:** The geographical spread of the bird species is described both in and outside Europe. If the breeding and wintering grounds are different, these are given.

**Movements:** Any large-scale movements made by the bird species, be they migrations or more localized movements, are described.

**Breeding:** The number and appearance of eggs, type of nest and incubation or fledging periods are outlined here.

**Similar Species:** Any easily confused species is mentioned here. If there are no similar species of bird, the entry is omitted.

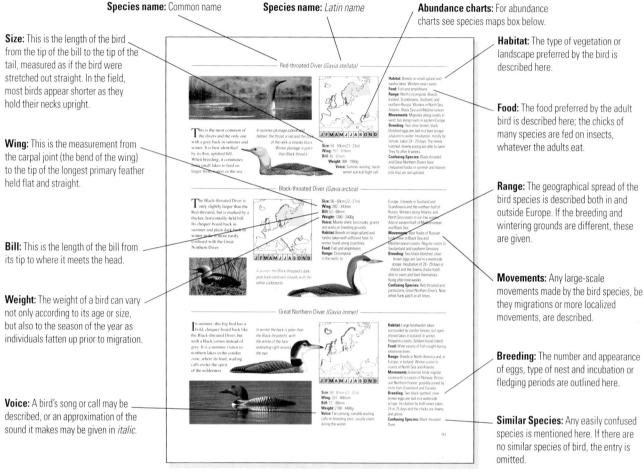

# SPECIES MAPS

The maps show the range and distribution of each species. Areas coloured yellow are the breeding grounds where the birds spend the summer. The areas shaded blue are the wintering grounds of the species. Those areas shaded green, where yellow and blue overlap, are the areas where the bird species can be found throughout the year, although individual birds may move within this area. The birds are not found everywhere within the area shaded, but only in suitable habitats within that region. A few bird species are seen only on migration as they pass to and from breeding grounds, and this is shown in grey.

## Key to Species ranges

☐ Summer visitor

☐ Winter visitor

☐ Present all year round

☐ Occurs on migration

## Reading abundance charts

The abundance chart below each map shows how likely the bird is to be seen within its range for each month of the year. It is assumed that observation is by a person in the correct habitat, who is reasonably skillful and is keeping a careful watch for the particular species.

☐ Rarely seen

☐ Seen if searched for

☐ Seen most days

☐ Seen every day

☐ Impossible to miss

## Red-throated Diver *(Gavia stellata)*

This is the most common of the divers and the only one with a grey back in summer and winter. It is best identified by its thin, uptilted bill. When breeding, it commutes from small lakes to feed on larger fresh waters or the sea.

*In summer plumage (above and below), the throat is red and the back of the neck is streaky black. Winter plumage is paler than Black-throat's.*

**J F M A M J J A S O N D**

**Size:** 53–59cm (21–23in).
**Wing:** 257–310mm.
**Bill:** 46–61mm.
   **Weight:** 988–1900g.
      **Voice:** Summer wailing; harsh winter *kuk-kuk* flight call.

**Habitat:** Breeds on small upland and tundra lakes. Winters near coasts.
**Food:** Fish and amphibians.
**Range:** North circumpolar. Breeds Iceland, Scandinavia, Scotland, and northern Russia. Winters in North Sea, Atlantic, Black Sea and Mediterranean.
**Movements:** Migrates along coasts in west, but along rivers in eastern Europe .
**Breeding:** Two olive-brown, black-blotched eggs are laid in a bare scrape adjacent to water. Incubation, mostly by female, takes 24–29 days. The newly hatched, downy young are able to swim. They fly after 6 weeks.
**Confusing Species:** Black-throated and Great Northern Divers have chequered backs in summer and heavier bills that are not uptilted.

## Black-throated Diver *(Gavia arctica)*

The Black-throated Diver is only slightly larger than the Red-throated, but is marked by a thicker, horizontally-held bill. Its chequer-board back in summer and plain dark back in winter make it more easily confused with the Great Northern Diver.

**J F M A M J J A S O N D**

*In winter, the Black-throated's dark grey back contrasts sharply with the white underparts.*

**Size:** 56–69cm (22–27in).
**Wing:** 282–343mm.
**Bill:** 52–68mm.
**Weight:** 1300–3400g.
**Voice:** Mainly silent, but croaks, grunts and wails on breeding grounds.
**Habitat:** Breeds on large upland and tundra lakes with sufficient food. In winter found along coastlines.
**Food:** Fish and amphibians.
**Range:** Circumpolar in the north. In

Europe, it breeds in Scotland and Scandinavia and the northern half of Russia. Winters along Atlantic and North Sea coasts in ice-free waters. Also in eastern half of Mediterranean and Black Sea.
**Movements:** Vast flocks of Russian birds move to Black Sea and Mediterranean coasts. Regular visitor to Switzerland and southern Germany.
**Breeding:** Two black-blotched, olive-brown eggs are laid in a waterside scrape. Incubation of 28–29 days is shared and the downy chicks hatch able to swim and feed themselves, flying after nine weeks.
**Confusing Species:** Red-throated and, particularly, Great Northern Divers. Note white flank patch at all times.

## Great Northern Diver *(Gavia immer)*

In summer, this big bird has a bold, chequer-board back like the Black-throated Diver, but with a black crown instead of grey. It is a summer visitor to northern lakes in the conifer zone, where its loud, wailing calls evoke the spirit of the wilderness.

*In winter the back is paler than the Black-throated's, with the white of the face extending right around the eye.*

**J F M A M J J A S O N D**

**Size:** 69–81cm (27–32in).
**Wing:** 331–400mm.
**Bill:** 72–89mm.
**Weight:** 2780–4480g.
**Voice:** Far-carrying, variable wailing calls on breeding sites; usually silent during the winter.

**Habitat:** Large freshwater lakes surrounded by conifer forests, but open-shored lakes in Iceland. In winter, frequents coasts. Seldom found inland.
**Food:** Wide variety of fish caught during extensive dives.
**Range:** Breeds in North America and, in Europe, in Iceland. Winter visitor to coasts of North Sea and Atlantic.
**Movements:** Icelandic birds migrate eastwards to coasts of Norway, Britain and Northern France; possibly joined by birds from Greenland and Canada.
**Breeding:** Two black-spotted, olive-brown eggs are laid in a waterside scrape. Incubation by both sexes takes 24 or 25 days and the chicks are downy and active.
**Confusing Species:** Black-throated Diver.

## Little Grebe *(Tachybaptus ruficollis)*

The Little Grebe is the smallest of the grebes. It is box-shaped, with a short neck, stubby bill, and a 'sawn-off' rear end. Summer features include the rich rufous sides of the head and neck, and a bare yellow patch at the base of the bill. In winter, a combination of shape and stubby bill are the best means of distinguishing it from other small grebes. It swims with ease, diving to hide among vegetation when disturbed. It favours waters with emergent vegetation.

JFMAMJJASOND

*In winter (right), the Little Grebe lacks the attractive rufous colouring of its summer plumage (above), and is generally paler all over, with a whitish throat and cheeks and a dull, brownish cap.*

**Size:** 25–28cm (10–11in).
**Wing:** 90–106mm.
**Bill:** 15–21mm.
**Weight:** 117–236g.
**Voice:** Loud whinnying call; made less frequently in winter.
**Habitat:** Freshwater lakes, ponds and slow-moving rivers; reservoirs and gravel pits.
**Food:** Small fish, crustaceans, molluscs and insects, caught during brief dives.
**Range:** Breeds across Europe and Asia to Japan and the Far East, and throughout sub-Saharan Africa. Absent from most of Scandinavia and northern Russia. Winters from Poland southwards and westwards.
**Movements:** Eastern European birds move west and south to Turkey.
**Breeding:** Four to six white eggs are laid on a platform of floating vegetation attached to waterweeds. Parents share the incubation period of 19–25 days. The downy, self-feeding young can fly after 44–48 days.
**Confusing Species:** Black-necked and Slavonian Grebes are of similar size, but are always distinct in shape and plumage.

## Great Crested Grebe *(Podiceps cristatus)*

The Great Crested Grebe raises its summer head plumes in courtship. In winter, when the plumes are lost, it can be identified by its long neck and pink, spear-like bill; a white foreneck and face above the eyes distinguish it from the Red-necked Grebe. It inhabits freshwater habitats in summer. The young chicks hitch a ride on their parents' backs.

JFMAMJJASOND

*In the intricate courtship display, a pair of Great Crested Grebe dive, then emerge, clutching waterweed in their bills, and shake their heads as they rise up breast to breast.*

**Size:** 46–51cm (18–20in).
**Wing:** 168–209mm.
**Bill:** 38–55mm.
**Weight:** 568–1490g.
**Voice:** Barking, croaking calls.
**Habitat:** Freshwater lakes and ponds – including park lakes – with emergent vegetation or overhanging trees or shrubs; also bare-banked reservoirs and sheltered coasts in winter.

**Food:** Fish, crustaceans and molluscs.
**Range:** Breeds across Eurasia from Atlantic to Pacific. Patchily distributed in Europe; absent from northern Scandinavia and northern Russia. Winters westwards from Denmark and Italy and across the Mediterranean.
**Movements:** Birds breeding eastwards of Berlin and Vienna move south and west, mainly to the Mediterranean area and Turkey.
**Breeding:** Four white eggs laid on floating vegetation anchored to overhanging or emergent plants are incubated by both sexes for 25–29 days. Downy chicks fly after 71–79 days.
**Confusing Species:** Red-necked Grebe has short, heavy bill and a dark foreneck.

# Red-necked Grebe *(Podiceps grisegena)*

The Red-necked Grebe's foreneck is a bright rust-red in summer and a dusky grey in winter, while the Great Crested shows a white foreneck in all plumages. The cap is black and extends to below the eyes. In summer, it has an obvious silvery cheek patch. A mainly eastern European grebe, it is a passage migrant in other areas. This grebe usually occupies smaller waters than the slightly larger Great Crested Grebe and nests deep inside reedbeds, often alongside Black-headed Gulls.

*The rust-red neck (above) becomes a dull grey colour in winter (right).*

**Size:** 40–46cm (16–18in).
**Wing:** 153–193mm.
**Bill:** 33–44mm.
**Weight:** 476–1270g.
**Voice:** Loud wailing or hooting; more vocal than other grebes. Silent in winter.
**Habitat:** Lowland waters with emergent vegetation, usually reeds. In winter, on larger and more open waters, often along coasts and estuaries.
**Food:** Fish, molluscs, crustaceans and insects.
**Range:** Circumpolar in north. In Europe, breeds from Denmark and Yugoslavia eastwards across temperate Russia. Winters westwards to Italy and Britain.
**Movements:** Westward migration, outside its breeding range.

**Breeding:** Four to five white eggs on a floating heap hidden in reeds; shared incubation lasts 20–23 days. Fledging period of self-feeding chicks unknown.
**Confusing Species:** Great Crested Grebe.

J F M A M J J A S O N D

# Slavonian Grebe *(Podiceps auritus)*

In summer, the Slavonian Grebe sports golden 'horns', while its neck and body are rust-red. The horns are usually quite distinct, but, after diving, these feathers may spread over the head, like those of the Black-necked. It is black above and white below in winter, with a black cap and white foreneck.

J F M A M J J A S O N D

**Size:** 28–33cm (11–13in).
**Wing:** 131–158mm.
**Bill:** 20–25mm.
**Weight:** 300–720g.
**Voice:** Variety of trilling calls.
**Habitat:** Breeds on shallow lakes in conifer zone with surrounding vegetation. Winters on estuaries and along sheltered shorelines.
**Food:** Molluscs, crustaceans and insects, as well as small fish.
**Range:** Northern circumpolar. In Europe, breeding in Iceland, Scotland, Scandinavia and northern, non-Arctic Russia. Winters on western coasts and around the Mediterranean.
**Movements:** Abandons summer range, with large movements through Baltic.

*The Slavonian's orange plumes are more horn-like compared with the brush-like plumes of the Black-necked Grebe.*

**Breeding:** Four to five white eggs are laid on a floating platform. Downy, self-feeding chicks hatch after 22–25 days of shared incubation. Fledging period is 55–60 days.
**Confusing Species:** Black-necked Grebe; Slavonian has distinguishing red summer neck and white winter neck.

# Black-necked Grebe *(Podiceps nigricollis)*

The Black-necked Grebe replaces the similar-looking Slavonian in the south of the conifer forest zone. Summer head and neck are black, with a golden fan on the ear coverts. Winter face and neck are a scruffy grey, in contrast with the Slavonian's clean-cut winter plumage. It is highly colonial during breeding, with perhaps 250 or more pairs on one lake.

*In all plumages, the Black-necked Grebe's slender, uptilted bill helps to distinguish it from the Slavonian Grebe.*

**Size:** 28–33cm (11–13in).
**Wing:** 124–139mm.
**Bill:** 20–26mm.
**Weight:** 213–402g.
**Voice:** Wails and hoots; quieter and less harsh than Slavonian.
**Habitat:** Breeds on small waters with masses of emergent vegetation. Winters on fresh waters more than other migratory grebes, but also on sea.
**Food:** Insects and molluscs.
**Range:** Breeds North America, Europe, China and locally in Africa. In Europe, it is confined to the temperate zone eastwards to Ukraine and southern Russia. Winters in western Europe, the Mediterranean and Turkey.
**Movements:** Summer visitor in the east. Huge numbers winter in Iran, with large migratory flocks.

**Breeding:** Three to four white eggs are laid on a floating nest and incubated by both parents for 20–21 days. The downy chicks are self-feeding. The fledging period is not known.
**Confusing Species:** Slavonian Grebe has red summer neck and white winter.

J F M A M J J A S O N D

## Fulmar *(Fulmarus glacialis)*

The Fulmar is an abundant, stocky, gull-like petrel that flies on stiff wings over the waves – a technique known as 'shearwatering'. It is grey above and white below, with a thick neck and a small, yellow, 'plated' bill. A close-up view shows a tube-like nose on top of its bill. It spends most of its life at sea, often well out of sight of land, coming ashore only to breed. Fulmars defend their nesting sites by 'spitting' a foul-smelling liquid, regurgitated from the stomach, at intruders.

**Size:** 43–51cm (17–20in).
**Wing:** 312–353mm.
**Bill:** 33–40mm.
**Weight:** 535–1000g.
**Voice:** Harsh cackles at breeding sites; silent at sea.
**Habitat:** Breeds on wide, cliff-top ledges, as well as among broken walls and buildings that can be a kilometre or more from the sea; otherwise roams the oceans.
**Food:** Squid, fish and offal, taken near the surface.
**Range:** Northern circumpolar. After a huge population increase in the 20th century, it is far more widespread than 100 years ago. In Europe, it breeds on the coasts of Iceland, Norway, Britain and northern France. Winters in the North Atlantic and Arctic Oceans.
**Movements:** Dispersal, with the birds roaming over adjacent seas, rather than true migration.
**Breeding:** A single white egg is laid on a grassy ledge on a cliff or on buildings near the coast, and is incubated by both members of the pair for 49–53 days. The down-covered chick is helpless, and fledges in about 46–51 days. Fulmars do not breed until they are seven to nine years old.

*All petrels have a complex beak structure (left and above), made up of a number of horny plates with clearly visible joints. The ridge of the beak is topped with a horny tube, containing the nostrils, which is why the petrel group are often referred to as 'tube-noses'.*

## Cory's Shearwater *(Calonectris diomedea)*

Cory's Shearwater is the largest breeding European shearwater, confined to the Mediterranean during summer but ranging into the North and South Atlantic Oceans in winter. It is a typical long-winged shearwater, with a stiff-winged, flap-and-glide flight low over the waves. Its brown upperparts merge with white underparts. Its underwing is white with narrow, darker margins. Birds of the Atlantic islands are now regarded as a separate species, the Cape Verde Shearwater.

*The head of Cory's Shearwater is uniformly grey, with a dark area around the eyes to the base of the bill. The large, pale yellow bill shows a darker area towards the tip when viewed at close range.*

**Size:** 43–48cm (17–19in).
**Wing:** 347–367mm.
**Bill:** 49–59mm.
**Weight:** 560–1014g.
**Voice:** Harsh wails and screams on breeding grounds; silent when at sea.
**Habitat:** Uninhabited rocky islands; otherwise at sea.
**Food:** Fish, crustaceans and squid taken in shallow dives.
**Range:** Mediterranean. In winter, it ranges northwards into the North Atlantic Ocean as far as eastern North America and southern Ireland.
**Movements:** Outside the breeding season, many birds move across the Atlantic Ocean and southwards as far as Cape Town.
**Breeding:** A single white egg is laid in a burrow or rock crevice and incubated by both parents for about 60 days. The downy chick is cared for by the adults for about 97 days before flying.
**Confusing species:** The Great Shearwater of the South Atlantic is an autumn visitor to the North Atlantic. It is similar in shape and size, but has a clear-cut dark cap, with a white collar and rump.

## Manx Shearwater *(Puffinus puffinus)*

Abundant in the North Atlantic, the Manx breeds in huge colonies, often on uninhabited islands. Its white underwing is margined in black.

**Size:** 30–38cm (12–15in).
**Wing:** 226–243mm.
**Bill:** 31–38mm.
**Weight:** 375–459g.
**Voice:** Wild wailing calls at colonies.
**Habitat:** Breeds on remote, rocky islands, sometimes high on mountain-top screes; otherwise at sea.

**Food:** Fish, squid and crustaceans.
**Range:** North Atlantic. In Europe, it breeds in Iceland, Britain, Ireland and northern France. Ranges over the oceans outside of the breeding season.
**Movements:** Some Manx Shearwaters cross the Equator to winter off the coasts of southern South America.

*The Manx Shearwater alternately shows its clearly demarcated black upperparts and white underparts when flying, often well out of sight of land.*

**Breeding:** One white egg, laid in a burrow or crevice, is incubated by both sexes for 52–54 days. The downy, helpless chick takes 59–62 days to fly.
**Confusing species:** Levantine Shearwater is less clearly marked.

| J | F | M | A | M | J | J | A | S | O | N | D |

---

## Balearic Shearwater *(Puffinus mauretanicus)*

The Balearic Shearwater is similar in size and behaviour to the Manx. However, it is much browner above and more buff below, with its upperparts and underparts merging, rather than being clear-cut as they are on the Manx. The Balearic regularly wanders into the eastern Atlantic.

*In flight, the Balearic's axillary feathers (those in its 'armpits') display buff coloration and contrast with the rest of the creamy underwing.*

**Size:** 30–38cm (12–15in).
**Wing:** 235–256mm.
**Bill:** 36–42mm.
**Weight:** 472–565g.
**Voice:** Wailing, eerie cries at breeding colonies; silent at sea.
**Habitat:** Wild, offshore rocky islets and headlands in breeding season; at sea.
**Food:** Fish, crustaceans and squid taken near the surface.
**Range:** Mediterranean, from the Balearics to the Adriatic. Some birds move into the eastern Atlantic in winter.
**Movements:** These birds regularly range northwards, moving along the coasts of France to Ireland and the English Channel.
**Breeding:** A single white egg is laid in a burrow or rock crevice; incubated by both sexes for more than 50 days. The downy chick is cared for by both parents for about 60 days before flying.
**Confusing species:** Manx, Levantine or the larger Cory's Shearwater.

| J | F | M | A | M | J | J | A | S | O | N | D |

---

## Levantine Shearwater *(Puffinus yelkouan)*

When viewed from afar, the Levantine Shearwater looks far blacker than the Manx. It overlaps with the Balearic in the central Mediterranean but looks much more black and white. There is little evidence of it moving from the eastern Mediterranean into the Manx's normal range.

*The Levantine closely resembles the Manx.*

**Size:** 28–35cm (11–14in).
**Wing:** 224–244mm.
**Bill:** 32–38mm.
**Weight:** 349–416g.
**Voice:** Loud wailing at breeding colonies; otherwise silent.
**Habitat:** Uninhabited islands and remote headlands during the breeding season; otherwise at sea.
**Food:** Fish, crustaceans and squid taken in shallow dives near the surface.
**Range:** Virtually confined to the Greek Aegean as a breeding bird, but perhaps also at unknown sites in the Black Sea. Winters in the eastern Mediterranean.
**Movements:** Many migrate into and out of the Black Sea via the Bosphorus.
**Breeding:** A single white egg is laid, usually in a rock crevice, and incubated for about 50 days by both sexes. The

| J | F | M | A | M | J | J | A | S | O | N | D |

downy chick fledges after some 50–54 days.
**Confusing species:** Very similar to the Manx Shearwater except for gradations in colouring; also similar to the Balearic Shearwater, which is browner.

95

The European Storm-petrel is a tiny, black-and-white seabird that flits, swallow-like, over the waves and survives the roughest of seas. It has a rounded head with a tiny bill. It has a square white rump and the tail is square, rather than forked like that of Leach's Storm-petrel; it also lacks the pale line across the upperwing coverts. It can be seen pattering over the surface of the sea, picking up small food items as it goes, and often follows ships in search of scraps.

*In flight, the European Storm-petrel's square-cut white rump (extending to the sides of its undertail) and a white line along its underwing coverts, break the almost entirely soot-black plumage.*

| J | F | M | A | M | J | J | A | S | O | N | D |

**Size:** 14–16cm (5–6in).
**Wing:** 116–127mm.
**Bill:** 10–12mm.
**Weight:** 18–38g.
**Voice:** High-pitched squeaks and low purring during the breeding season. Silent at sea.
**Habitat:** Uninhabited islands; or at sea.
**Food:** Plankton, small fish and the debris of meals of larger birds and seals.
**Range:** Confined to eastern North Atlantic, Britain, Ireland, France and western Mediterranean. Outside the breeding season it ranges the eastern North and South Atlantic Oceans.
**Movements:** Some birds range as far north as Iceland and as far south as Cape Town, being a regular migrant off African coasts.
**Breeding:** A single white egg laid in a rock crevice is incubated by both sexes for 38–40 days. The downy, helpless chick is fed for 56–64 days before flying.
**Confusing species:** Leach's Storm Petrel has smaller, divided white rump, pale upperwing coverts and a forked tail.

Similar to the European Storm-petrel in coloration and behaviour, Leach's Storm-petrel is larger, with a divided white rump and a pale bar across the upperwing coverts. Unlike the direct, rapid-wingbeat flight of the European Storm-petrel, The Leach's flight is jerkier, with much deeper wingbeats and shearwater-like glides. It breeds on only a handful of remote islands. Unlike the European Storm-petrel, it does not follow ships in search of food.

| J | F | M | A | M | J | J | A | S | O | N | D |

**Size:** 19–22cm (7½–9in).
**Wing:** 148–166mm.
**Bill:** 14–17mm.
**Weight:** 40–50g.
**Voice:** Repeated screeches and cooing notes during summer. Silent at sea.
**Habitats:** Remote, uninhabited islands during the breeding season, but otherwise oceanic.
**Food:** Fish and plankton.
**Range:** Isolated islands of Norway, Scotland, Ireland and Iceland, and off both Pacific and Atlantic coasts of North America. Winters at sea.
**Movements:** Moves southwards off the coasts of Africa as far as Cape Town in winter, but may be found right across the tropical Atlantic Ocean.
**Breeding:** A single white egg is laid in a burrow or rock crevice and is incubated by both members of the pair for 41 or 42 days. The helpless, down-covered chick is able to fly after 63–70 days.
**Confusing species:** European Storm-petrel has a square tail.

*Although similar to its European relative, Leach's Storm-petrel is identified in flight (right) by its forked tail, bisected white rump, pale band on the upperwing coverts and longer, more pointed wings.*

## Gannet *(Morus bassanus)*

*In flight, on its long, angular wings, the Gannet's body has a cigar-like shape. With wings folded back, it dives spectacularly into the sea from heights of up to 30m (90ft).*

This large, goose-like, black and white seabird ranges over the open oceans and nests in dramatic, densely packed colonies, where the birds are crowded together approximately one per 1m sq (9sq ft). Storm-driven gannets sometimes visit inland lakes and rivers. The adult is white, with black wing tips and, in the breeding season, a yellow wash over its head. The bill is long and sharp. Over five years, immature birds pass from an all-dark plumage to the mainly white adult one.

**Size:** 86–94cm (34–37in).
**Wing:** 460–520mm.
**Bill:** 92–101mm.
**Weight:** 2300–3610g.
**Voice:** Mooing, cackling and grunting at breeding colonies. Silent at sea.
**Habitat:** Rocky stacks and sheer cliffs. Outside the breeding season, they range over the seas but they are usually more coastal than shearwaters.
**Food:** Fish.
**Range:** Confined to both sides of the North Atlantic. In Europe, colonies occur in Iceland, Norway, Britain, Ireland and France. Winters at sea.
**Movements:** Breeding birds regularly range to Biscay to find fish. In winter, birds are found as far south as the bulge of Africa.
**Breeding:** Colonies mainly on flat-topped stacks, but also on sheer mainland cliffs. A single white egg is laid on a pile of seaweed and incubated for 43–45 days by both members of the pair. The helpless, down-covered chick fledges after approximately 100 days.

## Cormorant *(Phalacrocorax carbo)*

This large, dark waterbird is equally at home at sea or on fresh water. The adult's plumage is black, but has a bronzy sheen that can be seen at close range. There are white patches on its thighs and face in summer, but in winter the thigh patches are lost and the face patch becomes smaller. The bill is yellow. Immature birds are brown above and buff below. Cormorants can swim and dive well, grabbing fish underwater in their strong, hooked bills. Out of water, they often have a strangely snake-like, or serpentine, appearance. Cormorants breed in colonies on exposed sites.

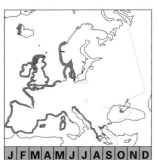

*Cormorants, like Pygmy Cormorants and Shags, have feathers that are less water-repellent than those of most other waterbirds. After each session in the water, Cormorants find an open spot where they can spread out their saturated wings to dry in the breeze.*

**Size:** 84–91cm (33–36in).
**Wing:** 318–363mm.
**Bill:** 59–73mm.
**Weight:** 1673–2555g.
**Voice:** Harsh croaking and grunting while breeding.
**Habitat:** Nests at foot of sea cliffs or inland in trees. In winter frequents large fresh waters, coasts and estuaries.
**Food:** Fish of a variety of species, caught underwater.
**Range:** Widespread throughout the Old World and in northeastern North America. Winters at sea, mainly along coasts and in estuarine waters. Patchily distributed in Europe.

**Movements:** Inland breeders move to nearby coasts.
**Breeding:** Three or four pale blue eggs are laid on a large mound of rotting seaweed and incubated by both members of the pair for 28 or 29 days. The naked, helpless chicks fledge after 50–60 days.
**Confusing species:** The Shag is smaller, all black, and has thinner neck.

This small, totally marine version of the Cormorant is black with a metallic-green sheen. It has a small forward-curving crest in summer. The neck is long and thin, and the thin bill has a yellow base. Immatures are brown above, buff below.

*Shags swim low in the water and, propelled by their feet, actively pursue fish below the surface.*

**Size:** 72–79cm (28–31in).
**Wing:** 251–278mm.
**Bill:** 51–59mm.
**Weight:** 1760–2154g.
**Voice:** Aggressive hisses and grunts.
**Habitat:** Exclusively sea coasts, usually with rocky shores.
**Food:** Fish, caught under water.
**Range:** Breeds around the rocky coasts of Europe, including Iceland, Norway, Britain, Ireland, France, Iberia and in the Mediterranean. Endemic to the Western Palearctic region. Winters locally.
**Movements:** Only the birds of northern Norway actually migrate southwards.

**Breeding:** Breeds in colonies, usually among debris at foot of coastal screes and on offshore stacks and islets. Three pale blue eggs are laid on a heap of seaweed and incubated by both sexes for 30 days. The naked, helpless young fledge in 55 days.
**Confusing species:** Cormorant's neck is thicker, its head larger and less round and its bill longer and thicker.

J F M A M J J A S O N D

---

**Size:** 48–49cm (19in).
**Wing:** 193–217mm.
**Bill:** 27–33mm.
**Weight:** 565–870g.
**Voice:** Harsh barks, croaks and grunts during the breeding season.
**Habitat:** Extensive marshlands, reedbeds and deltas.
**Food:** Fish caught under water.
**Range:** Breeds from the Balkans eastwards across the Ukraine to west-central Siberia.
**Movements:** Mainly residential, although there is some movement away from the Black Sea colonies.

*The Pygmy Cormorant is a highly gregarious bird, and is often abundant in marshland. It forms nesting colonies in bushes and trees beside reedy lakes and rivers, often together with Cormorants, herons and egrets.*

**Breeding:** Four to six white eggs laid in a substantial cup of twigs and other available material, either among reeds or in a tree. The eggs are incubated for 27–30 days by both sexes, and the naked, helpless chicks take 30 days to learn to fly.
**Confusing species:** Cormorant and Shag, but both are considerably larger and have much longer bills.

Though a typical cormorant, this is a smaller bird than its relatives. At the start of the breeding season, it has white spots on its head and neck, but otherwise has all-dark plumage with a brown head and, in winter, a white-buff throat. Like other cormorants, the Pygmy swims low in the water and stretches its wings out to dry.

J F M A M J J A S O N D

# White Pelican (*Pelecanus onocrotalus*)

About the size of a swan, this huge, white waterbird, has an enormous bill and a massive yellow-orange pouch. The legs and feet are pink, not blackish as in the Dalmatian Pelican. Though it takes great effort and a long run over the water to get into the air, once airborne White Pelicans fly with ease on strong wings, often in a goose-like V formation or gliding low over the water's surface in long lines. The young have brown wings that gradually become white, except for the black flight feathers.

JFMAMJJASOND

*Although clumsy-looking on the ground, the White Pelican is a surprisingly graceful flyer. In the air, with its neck folded back, the White Pelican's black flight feathers contrast sharply with the white coverts above and below.*

**Size:** 140–180cm (55–70in).
**Wing:** 710–730mm.
**Bill:** 420–450mm.
**Weight:** 9100–12,000g.
**Voice:** Various grunts, growls and cooing notes.
**Habitat:** Extensive freshwater marshes and deltas with large stand of plentiful emergent vegetation.

**Food:** Fish, often caught cooperatively by flocks.
**Range:** Breeds from eastern Europe to south-central Siberia and in India and Africa. In Europe, it is confined to a few major sites in the Balkans.
**Movements:** Most European birds move through Turkey to winter in the Nile valley and Euphrates delta.
**Breeding:** Highly colonial, with two white eggs laid on a large platform of aquatic vegetation hidden among reeds adjacent to open water. Incubation of 29 or 30 days is shared. The naked, helpless chicks are cared for and fed for 70 days before they fly.
**Confusing species:** Dalmatian Pelican has greyish flight feathers, not black.

# Dalmatian Pelican (*Pelecanus crispus*)

The Dalmatian Pelican is similar in appearance, behaviour and habits to the White, but is more widespread, being less restricted to large colonies. Male and female plumage is white with a steel-grey tinge. This, combined with the ragged head crest, makes it look like a dingy White Pelican. Legs are blackish grey.

JFMAMJJASOND

*The Dalmatian Pelican's flight feathers are dark (not black), and merge into grey-white coverts, so the contrast is not as great as those of the White Pelican. The Dalmatian's flight is direct, with a few slow wingbeats followed by gliding.*

**Size:** 160–180cm (63–70in).
**Wing:** 570–620mm.
**Bill:** 292–378mm.
**Weight:** 5200g.
**Voice:** Harsh, barking notes.
**Habitat:** Shallow marshes with strong growth of reeds.
**Food:** Fish, caught by foraging in groups in coastal inlets or on the open sea.
**Range:** From Europe across Russia to central Asia. In Europe, it breeds at several locations in the Balkans, but it is never numerous.
**Movements:** European birds are mostly resident or local wanderers. Asian birds move to the Middle East and the Indian subcontinent.
**Breeding:** Two to four white eggs are laid on a platform of reeds or rushes. Incubation, lasting 30–32 days, is undertaken mainly by the female. The chicks are naked and helpless when they hatch, and it is 70–80 days before they are able to fly. The Dalmatian Pelican is colonial, but breeding colonies are smaller than those of the White Pelican.
**Confusing species:** White Pelican.

# Bittern *(Botaurus stellaris)*

**Size:** 69–79cm (27–31in).
**Wing:** 238–291mm.
**Bill:** 63–80mm.
**Weight:** 372–571g.
**Voice:** Deep booming, usually uttered in early morning and late evening in

spring and early summer. Also makes a grating *oork* when disturbed.
**Habitat:** Extensive reedbeds.
**Food:** Fish and amphibians.
**Range:** Breeds right across Europe and Asia to northern Japan. In Europe, it has a disrupted distribution due to a lack of suitable habitats. Winters west of a line drawn from Denmark to Romania.
**Movements:** North- and east-European birds move westwards, though those from Russia move south to the Balkans, Turkey and Iraq. Asian birds head south to India and China.
**Breeding:** Three or four greenish blue eggs are laid on a platform of reeds and are incubated by both sexes for approximately 21 days. The downy, helpless young fly after about 42 days. Occasionally has two broods.
**Confusing species:** Juvenile Night Heron has white spots on wing coverts.

This highly secretive and well-camouflaged heron spends most of its time in dense reedbeds, where its presence is betrayed only by the occasional booming call in early summer. In flight, its rounded wings, trailing feet and tucked-back neck make it resemble a juvenile Night Heron – or even an old flying sack.

*The bittern is heavily barred and streaked in buffs, browns and blacks to help to conceal it in reedbeds. To avoid detection, it also points its bill skywards, as shown on the left, and sways in time with wind-blown reeds.*

# Little Bittern *(Ixobrychus minutus)*

*The female Little Bittern has less pronounced markings than the male (above), with 'dirtier' buff wing patches and a more streaked breast.*

**Size:** 33–38cm (13–15in).
**Wing:** 142–157mm.
**Bill:** 44–53mm.
**Weight:** 140–150g.
**Voice:** A croaking call that is repeated at regular intervals.
**Habitat:** Marshes, lakes and slow-flowing rivers with a strong growth of reeds.
**Food:** Amphibians and fish.
**Range:** Breeds right across Europe to central Asia and northern India, as well as across most of sub-Saharan Africa. In Europe, breeds over most of the continent except Scandinavia and also Britain, where it has been proven to have bred only once.
**Movements:** European birds migrate to sub-Saharan Africa, many making a non-stop flight across the Mediterranean and Sahara in autumn.

**Breeding:** Five or six white eggs are laid in a neat cup of vegetation constructed among reeds or in a waterside thicket. The down-covered, helpless young hatch after 16–19 days of incubation by both members of the pair. It is 25–30 days before the young are able to fly.

The Little Bittern is a tiny heron that breeds in the reedbeds and marshes of temperate and Mediterranean Europe during the summer months. The male is black above, warm buff below, and marked by bold pinkish white wing patches that are most obvious in flight. The female is similar, but less clearly marked. Little Bitterns are usually seen flying low over the reedbeds, with quick wingbeats and long glides. Occasionally, they perch openly on top of a reed stem.

## Night Heron *(Nycticorax nycticorax)*

This heron spends the day among trees and flies out at dusk and dawn to feed in the surrounding marshes. Adults have a black back, grey wings and pale, grey-white underparts. The black cap, white cheeks and heavy black bill are conspicuous features. A stocky build, large rounded wings and a short head and tail produce an easily identifiable silhouette when the bird is in flight. Nesting is often in tall bushes among egret colonies.

J F M A M J J A S O N D

*The juvenile Night Heron (below left) is brown above and whitish below, with heavy brownish grey streaks. White spots on its wing coverts distinguish it from the Bittern. By the second summer, juveniles resemble adults.*

**Size:** 59–64cm (23–25in).
**Wings:** 278–308mm.
**Bill:** 64–78mm.
**Weight:** 525–800g.
**Voice:** Loud, croaking calls.
**Habitat:** Marshes, lakes, backwaters and other fresh waters with trees and a dense growth of marginal vegetation.
**Food:** Fish and amphibians.

**Range:** Cosmopolitan in the Americas, Africa, Asia and Europe. In Europe, it is a summer visitor to the Mediterranean and temperate zones, but with a patchy distribution owing to its habitat requirements.
**Movements:** European birds are trans-Saharan migrants, wintering across central Africa's Sahel region.

**Breeding:** Three or four pale blue eggs are laid on a platform of twigs placed in a tree or thicket. Incubation is undertaken by both members of the pair and usually takes about 21 days. The downy, helpless chicks are able to fly after about 40 days. Night Herons occasionally have two broods.
**Confusing species:** Bittern.

## Squacco Heron *(Ardeola ralloides)*

This small, secretive heron is difficult to locate unless it flies, when its flashing white wings betray its presence. In summer, the adult is a rich buff-orange colour, with black and white head plumes, a grey, dagger-like bill and pink legs and feet. The immature plumage is streaky brown. The Squacco is generally a solitary bird that inhabits waterside margins. It stands and waits for prey, usually among vegetation, but also in open fields and wet meadows in the early morning.

J F M A M J J A S O N D

*Like the juvenile (above), the winter adult Squacco Heron is drably streaked with brown, both above and below. It loses the long head plumes of the summer plumage (right), while its grey bill takes on a yellowish hue.*

**Size:** 43–48cm (17–19in).
**Wing:** 208–234mm.
**Bill:** 58–70mm.
**Weight:** 230–370g.
**Voice:** Variety of harsh, croaking calls, though usually silent.
**Habitat:** Margins of marshes, lakes, canals and other fresh waters.
**Food:** Fish, insects and amphibians.
**Range:** Breeds right across southern Europe, but is more widespread in Balkan river systems to the east than in the west. Also occurs in sub-Saharan Africa.
**Movements:** European birds migrate across the Sahara to winter in, and south of, Africa's Sahel region.
**Breeding:** Three to five greenish blue eggs are laid on a platform of twigs, hidden in the branches of a tree or bush over water. Duties during the 24-day incubation period are shared between the male and the female, and the helpless, downy young make their first flight after about 45 days.

101

## Cattle Egret *(Bubulcus ibis)*

This stocky bird has a hunched posture and jowled look. Its stubby bill is yellowy orange, while its legs are green in summer and dark in winter. Winter plumage is all-white, but the head, breast and back turn a rich buff in summer.

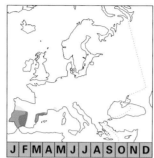

J F M A M J J A S O N D

*This bird takes its name from its habit of feeding beside grazing cattle, which disturb the insects and small animals on which it feeds.*

**Size:** 48–53cm (19–21in).
**Wing:** 240–266mm.
**Bill:** 52–60mm.
**Weight:** 304–387g.
**Voice:** Mostly silent.
**Habitat:** Breeds among marshy thickets and waterside trees, and on islands in lakes. Forages on marsh and farmland.

**Food:** Insects and amphibians.
**Range:** Widespread through Asia to Australia. In the 20th century, it colonized North and South America. In Europe, confined to Iberia and France.
**Movements:** French birds move southwest into Iberia.
**Breeding:** Four or five bluish-white eggs are laid in a shallow cup of twigs in a marshy thicket. Both sexes incubate the eggs for 21–25 days; downy, helpless chicks take 30 days to fledge.
**Confusing species:** Squacco Heron.

## Little Egret *(Egretta garzetta)*

The Little Egret is the most widespread of all the white herons in Europe. It has long, white plumes in summer. The bill and legs are black, and the feet a distinctive yellow. Its thin black bill distinguishes it from other egrets. It nests colonially with other herons.

J F M A M J J A S O N D

*During the breeding season, the birds grow showy white plumes on their heads, chests and backs.*

**Size:** 53–59cm (21–23in).
**Wing:** 251–303mm.
**Bill:** 67–93mm.
**Weight:** 305–614g.
**Voice:** Silent.
**Habitat:** Marshes, deltas, estuaries, salt pans and shorelines. More marine than other European herons.
**Food:** Small fish.
**Range:** Summer visitor to southern Europe, extending north to France and England, and along the Danube river. Resident in southern Spain.
**Movements:** Trans-Saharan migrants.
**Breeding:** Four blue-green eggs, laid on a platform of twigs in a tree; incubation by both sexes for 21–25 days. The helpless, downy chicks fly after 40 days.
**Confusing species:** Great White Egret.

## Great White Egret *(Egretta alba)*

Almost as large as the Grey Heron, the Great White Egret is now scarce in Europe, being confined largely to the Balkans. It has an all-white plumage, with a yellow bill that becomes black-tipped in summer, and dark legs that are yellow above the 'knee' joint. In flight, its size distinguishes it from the Little Egret.

J F M A M J J A S O N D

**Size:** 86–100cm (34–39in).
**Wing:** 400–485mm.
**Bill:** 110–135mm.
**Weight:** 960–1680g.
**Voice:** Silent.
**Habitat:** Extensive reedbeds.
**Food:** Fish, amphibians and insects.
**Range:** Cosmopolitan, found on all the world's large landmasses. In Europe, it breeds in several areas of the Balkans eastwards across the Ukraine to the Caspian Sea.
**Movements:** European birds winter in the former Yugoslavia and Greece, and in the Nile delta.
**Breeding:** Three or four pale blue eggs are laid on a platform among dense stands of reeds. The eggs are incubated by both members of the pair for 25–26 days and the downy, helpless chicks fledge after 42 days.
**Confusing species:** Little Egret.

*Like other herons, the Great White Egret hunts by standing motionless and suddenly lunging at passing prey, or by advancing slowly and deliberately on its victims.*

# Grey Heron (*Ardea cinerea*)

The Grey Heron is the largest European heron and the most widespread member of the family. Its all-grey plumage is marked by a black crest and black streaking on its foreneck and breast. The juvenile has a dark cap rather than a crest. The dagger-like bill is yellow, as are the legs of the adult. In the air, its black flight feathers contrast with the otherwise grey wings, and the head and neck are tucked back in the typical heron fashion.

J F M A M J J A S O N D

*The Grey Heron's bow-winged flight, with slow, heavy beats (far left), is distinctive. A flying Grey can be confused with a Purple Heron, but the Purple (left) is a warmer colour on the back and the neck bulge.*

**Size:** 89–100cm (35–39in).
**Wing:** 428–485mm.
**Bill:** 101–131mm.
**Weight:** 1071–2073g.
**Voice:** Loud, harsh *snark*.
**Habitat:** Various freshwater habitats, from rivers and streams to ponds, reservoirs and marshes. Also estuaries and shorelines. Its success is due to its catholic choice of habitat.
**Food:** Fish and amphibians.

**Range:** Throughout the Old World. In Europe, it is found mainly in the temperate zone northwards through Scandinavia and Russia. Eastern birds are summer visitors.
**Movements:** Grey Herons from eastern and central Europe move south and west to winter, some as far as West Africa.
**Breeding:** Three to five greenish blue eggs are laid on a platform of twigs placed high in a tree often, but not necessarily, near water. Incubation, by both sexes, takes 23–28 days. The helpless, down-covered chicks take 50–55 days to fly. Forms colonies, often with other species.
**Confusing species:** Purple Heron is smaller and browner.

# Purple heron (*Ardea purpurea*)

This large, dark heron is a summer visitor, mostly to southern Europe. Both male and female adults have a similar plumage, with grey wings with black flight feathers, and a grey back with buff-tipped scapular feathers. The neck is orange-buff, liberally streaked with black; the streaking extends to the chest. A black cap, yellow eye and sharply pointed yellow bill combine to create a rather fierce appearance.

*The Purple Heron could be confused with the even larger Grey Heron, but it always has brown elements in its plumage, giving it a much warmer appearance. The neck is also more slender and snake-like.*

J F M A M J J A S O N D

**Size:** 75–84cm (29–33in).
**Wing:** 337–383mm.
**Bill:** 109–131mm.
**Weight:** 525–1215g.
**Voice:** Harsh call like that of the Grey Heron, but higher pitched.
**Habitat:** Extensive marshes and rivers, especially among reedbeds.
**Food:** Fish, insects and amphibians.
**Range:** Widespread. It is a summer visitor to much of southern Europe and ventures northwards to Holland. It is absent from Britain, Scandinavia and Russia, except as a rare vagrant.
**Movements:** European birds are trans-Saharan migrants and winter in African savannas. Though the results of ringing suggest that some European birds may be among birds in the east, they are largely confined to West Africa.
**Breeding:** Four or five greenish blue eggs are laid on a platform of reeds hidden deep in a reedbed. Both members of the pair share the incubation, which lasts 24–28 days. The downy, helpless young are able to fly after 45–50 days.
**Confusing species:** Larger Grey Heron lacks the warm brown tones. Beware confusing the Purple Heron with the juvenile Bittern.

## Glossy Ibis *(Plegadis falcinellus)*

From a distance, this Curlew-like bird, with its long, curved bill, appears entirely brownish-black. A closer approach reveals its glossy purple and metallic-green plumage, particularly on the back and wings. The legs are yellow-green. Its flight, with neck extended and quick wingbeats interspersed with short glides, is similar to the Spoonbill's. Glossy Ibis flocks form long lines that undulate neatly as the birds lose height in the gliding phase.

*The Glossy Ibis nests colonially in reedbeds, bushes or trees, sometimes with herons, egrets, storks and Pygmy Cormorants.*

**Size:** 51–64cm (20–25in).
**Wing:** 267–306mm.
**Bill:** 106–141mm.
**Weight:** 530–768g.
**Voice:** Various croaking calls.
**Habitat:** Marshes, lakeside margins, and reedbeds with thickets.
**Food:** Insects and molluscs.
**Range:** Virtually cosmopolitan, but only a recent colonist of southeastern North America. In Europe, it is confined to the Balkans, with the largest numbers to be found in the Danube delta and river system, though vagrant birds have been seen as far north as Denmark and the British Isles.
**Movements:** Summer visitor to Europe that is a trans-Saharan migrant, wintering in Africa's Sahel region.
**Breeding:** Three or four blue eggs are laid in a well-constructed cup among reeds, or in an emergent thicket. They are incubated mainly by the female for 21 days. The downy chicks, which are semi-helpless when they hatch, take 40 days to fledge. The Glossy Ibis is a highly colonial bird and is gregarious at all times.

## Spoonbill *(Platalea leucorodia)*

The Spoonbill is a large white waterbird marked by a long, spatulate black bill and black legs. It can be identified from afar by the rhythmic side-to-side sweeps of its broad, long bill as it sifts small animals, such as fish and insects, from the water. In summer, the adult has a yellow wash on its chin, breast and bill-tip.

**Size:** 69–79cm (27–31in).
**Wing:** 360–412mm.
**Bill:** 168–231mm.
**Weight:** 1130–1463g.
**Voice:** Usually silent, with rare grunts.
**Habitat:** Extensive shallow marshes, lakes, deltas, lagoons and estuaries.
**Food:** Invertebrates, small molluscs and crustaceans.
**Range:** Breeds right across Eurasia. In Europe, it has a highly disjointed distribution, with isolated colonies in Spain, Holland and Hungary, and from the Balkans to the Caspian.
**Movements:** The Spoonbill is a summer visitor to Europe and spends the winter in the Nile Valley and the Middle East.
**Breeding:** Four red-spotted eggs are laid on a platform of twigs and reeds among reedbeds or in trees; incubated by both parents. Helpless, downy young hatch after 21 days and fledge after a further 55 or 56 days. Generally a sociable bird, the Spoonbill is often seen in small, close-knit groups.

*Spoonbills fly with faster wingbeats than storks, and form a line abreast (above left) when flying together. The summer plumage has a yellow wash on the breast (left).*

## White Stork *(Ciconia ciconia)*

**Size:** 95–105cm (37–41in).
**Wing:** 542–580mm.
**Bill:** 158–191mm.
**Weight:** 2610–4400g.
**Voice:** Silent, but claps bill loudly in greeting ceremony.
**Habitat:** Towns and villages, and among trees bordering rich marshes and river systems.
**Food:** Amphibians, insects, small mammals and edible rubbish.
**Range:** Breeds in Europe, North Africa, Middle

East and in China. Some Iberian birds are resident. Birds of central and eastern Europe and Russia are summer visitors.
**Movements:** Eastern European population concentrates over the Bosphorus in August in great swirling flocks, then moves south to winter on African savannas.
**Breeding:** Three to five white eggs are laid in a bulky nest of twigs and rubbish on a chimney pot, roof, tree-top or specially erected platform. Incubation of 29 or 30 days is by both sexes. The downy, helpless young fly after about 53–55 days.
**Confusing species:** Black Stork is black, with white confined to lower breast and belly.

The White Stork, once widespread over most of continental Europe, has now disappeared from much of France and Germany. This tall, white bird has black flight feathers and a long, red bill and legs. It soars easily, but is most often seen nesting on rooftops or walking in fields, marshes and rubbish dumps close to its nest. It is easy to approach.

*The White Stork will return to the same nesting site year after year to raise its young. The pairs, which form for life, engage in elaborate greeting displays in which they bend their heads over their backs and clap their bills.*

J F M A M J J A S O N D

## Black Stork *(Ciconia nigra)*

This large, black-and-white bird is similar in structure to the White Stork, but is less numerous and more secretive in its behaviour, making it more difficult to observe. It is seen in large numbers only on migration. The whole plumage is black, except for the lower breast, belly and axillary feathers. The bill and legs are red. Juvenile birds have pale green bills and legs. The Black Stork is less demonstrative in bill-clapping when greeting its mate than its white relative.

J F M A M J J A S O N D

*In flight, when soaring easily on rising air currents (right), the Black Stork displays the bold black-and-white pattern on its breast and belly, making it easy to distinguish from the White Stork.*

**Size:** 89–100cm (35–39in).
**Wing:** 520–600mm.
**Bill:** 160–180mm.
**Weight:** 2400–3000g.
**Voice:** Silent, but claps bill in greeting ceremony.
**Habitat:** Dense forests, mountain ranges and undisturbed marshes.
**Food:** Fish, amphibians and insects.
**Range:** Breeds right across Eurasia, from Iberia to Japan, and in South Africa. In Europe, it is resident in central Iberia. From eastern Europe across Russia and Asia, it is a summer visitor.

**Movements:** East European birds cross the Bosphorus and head down the Nile valley to winter in East Africa.
**Breeding:** Three to five white eggs are laid in a large stick nest in a cave, on a cliff ledge, or in a tree. The same nest may be used year after year and grows to a huge size. Incubation of 30–35 days is by both sexes, and the helpless, downy chicks fly after 63–70 days.
**Confusing species:** White Stork, but only its flight feathers are black.

105

## Greater Flamingo *(Phoenicopterus ruber)*

Greater Flamingoes are tall, slender pink and white birds with exceptionally long pink legs and equally long necks. The large, blunt, angled bill is pink and black, and contains a comb-like filter made out of fine plates. The bird feeds in saline water by holding its bill upside down and sucking water through the filter to sieve out microscopic plants and animals. The Greater Flamingo is highly gregarious and is often seen feeding in large flocks. It is confined to three large breeding sites in Europe.

*With its large size, long legs, serpentine neck and pink colouring, the Greater Flamingo is unmistakable among European birds.*

**Size:** 125–145cm (49–57in).
**Wing:** 360–460mm.
**Bill:** 112–125mm.
**Weight:** 2100–4100g.
**Voice:** Goose-like honking call.
**Habitat:** Saline lakes, deltas, estuaries and shorelines.
**Food:** Crustaceans and algae.
**Range:** Found on all major landmasses.

In Europe, it is confined to the Camargue in France and to Doñana and Laguna Fuente Piedra in Spain.
**Movements:** While most European birds remain on the breeding grounds, some move around Iberia and some birds reach Morocco.
**Breeding:** One or two pale green eggs are laid on a large mound of clay and salt and incubated by both sexes for 28–32 days. The active, downy chicks are able to fly after about 75 days, but often form crèches within the huge, tightly packed colonies. Flamingos do not breed successfully every year and may abandon the breeding site in the middle of an attempt, leaving their dead and dying chicks behind.

## Bewick's Swan *(Cygnus columbianus)*

Bewick's Swan is slightly smaller than Europe's other two swans. The adult is white, with a black bill based with yellow that ends squarely, while the Whooper Swan has a yellow area on its beak that extends to a point. Bewick's has a shorter neck than the Whooper. The juvenile is grey and its bill has a concave profile, like the adult's.

*The shape of the yellow at the base of the bill varies, enabling individuals to be recognized among a flock of otherwise identical birds.*

**Size:** 116–125cm (46–49in).
**Wing:** 469–548mm.
**Bill:** 82–102mm.
**Weight:** 3300–7800g.
**Voice:** Goose-like honking notes, mostly in flight.
**Habitat:** Breeds on tundra lakes and marshes. Winters on temperate extensive coastal floodlands.
**Food:** Grass, grain and roots.
**Range:** Breeds from Novaya Zemlya eastwards across northern Siberia. Winters around the low-lying shores of the North Sea.
**Movements:** It is a winter visitor from the extreme northeast of European Russia and eastwards into Siberia. Several thousand birds migrate through the Baltic to winter in Denmark, Germany, Holland and Britain.
**Breeding:** Four creamy white eggs are laid on a mound of vegetation. They are incubated by the female for 29 or 30 days. The down-covered chicks are active as soon as they hatch and fledge after 40–45 days. They are proficient enough flyers to accompany their parents on their first migration flights.
**Confusing species:** The Whooper Swan is larger, with a longer neck and a pointed yellow area on its bill.

## Whooper Swan *(Cygnus cygnus)*

This large, all-white swan is mainly a winter visitor to Europe. Its black bill has a straight profile, not concave like that of Bewick's Swan, and a yellow base that terminates in a distinct point. The neck is longer and usually straighter than Bewick's or the Mute Swan's. Its flight is powerful and direct, accompanied by loud trumpeting calls, rather than the wing-beating produced by the Mute Swan. Flocks of Whooper Swans fly in a V-shaped formation or an oblique line.

J F M A M J J A S O N D

*The juvenile Whooper Swan has a pink and grey bill. It is more uniformly grey than the juvenile Mute Swan, and has a paler bill base that contrasts with its darker face.*

**Size:** 145–160cm (57–63in).
**Wing:** 562–635mm.
**Bill:** 92–116mm.
**Weight:** 7400–10,300g.
**Voice:** Loud, trumpeting calls.
**Habitat:** Breeds in upland and tundra lakes. Winters in lowland lakes and marshes.
**Food:** Grass, grain and roots.
**Range:** Breeds across Eurasia from Iceland to the Bering Strait. Winters in Japan, China, Caspian and Black Seas, the Balkans and shores of the North Sea.

**Movements:** Large migration through the Baltic to winter in northwest Europe.
**Breeding:** Five or six creamy eggs are laid on a huge mound of vegetation beside water, often on an island in a lake. They are incubated for 35–42 days by the female and the active, downy young fledge after 2–3 months. Like Bewick's, the youngsters fly with their parents to the wintering grounds.
**Confusing species:** Bewick's Swan is smaller, shorter-necked and has a truncated yellow base to its bill.

## Mute Swan *(Cygnus olor)*

The Mute Swan is one of the world's heaviest flying birds. Its legs are short and strong to support its great weight. Unlike that of other European swans, the long neck, which enables it to reach underwater for aquatic plants and roots, is usually held in a distinctive 'S' curve. In flight, however, its long neck is outstretched as in other swans. It is sociable, except when breeding, when nesting pairs fiercely defend their territories against intruders.

J F M A M J J A S O N D

*The distinguishing feature of the Mute Swan is its orange bill (grey in the juvenile) backed by a bare black knob, which is larger in the male than the female.*

**Size:** 145–160cm (57–63in).
**Wing:** 533–623mm.
**Bill:** 69–88mm.
**Weight:** 5500–13,500g.
**Voice:** Silent. In flight, wings make a throbbing sound.
**Habitat:** A wide variety of fresh waters, and sheltered estuaries and shorelines.
**Food:** Aquatic vegetation.
**Range:** Natural range confused by domestications and introductions, but probably across Europe to central Siberia. In Europe, it now breeds from France across temperate and northern areas to western Russia and the land around the Black Sea.
**Movements:** Scandinavian and east European birds move westwards in winter, with large numbers off Denmark.
**Breeding:** Five to seven white eggs are laid on a huge mound of vegetation among reeds or alongside water. They are incubated mainly by the female for the 34–38 days the active, downy chicks take to hatch. They take up to 150 days to fledge.
**Confusing species:** Both other European Swans have clear yellow bases to their bills.

# Greylag Goose *(Anser anser)*

The largest of the grey geese, the Greylag has a large, orange bill, pink legs and prominent grey forewing (or 'lag') in flight. It has brown, narrow-barred black and buff upperparts; its underparts are creamy buff and its undertail white. The Greylag is the ancestor of the 'farmyard' goose that has been domesticated throughout Europe.

| J | F | M | A | M | J | J | A | S | O | N | D |

*The large head and bill are major distinguishing marks.*

**Size:** 77–89cm (30–35in).
**Wing:** 412–480mm.
**Bill:** 58–74mm.
**Weight:** 2160–4560g.
**Voice:** Familiar nasal honking.
**Habitat:** Marshes, lakes, floods and, in winter, estuaries and dry fields.
**Food:** Grass, grain, roots.
**Range:** Breeds from Iceland to the Sea of Japan. Winters in China, India, Middle East and western Europe.
**Movements:** In Europe, winters on the shores of North Sea; a few reach Iberia.
**Breeding:** Four to six white eggs are incubated by the female for 27 or 28 days. The active, downy chicks fly after about 56 days.
**Confusing Species:** Other grey geese are generally smaller.

# Bean Goose *(Anser fabalis)*

This large, grey goose is marked by a dark head and neck, orange and black bill, and orange legs. In flight its upperwing is uniformly brown. Some researchers think that the two types of Bean Goose may be two species, Tundra Bean Goose and Taiga Bean Goose, which are separated by neck length and the extent of black on the bill. However, others maintain that the birds are merely subspecies, the former being classified as *Anser fabalis rossicus* and the latter as *A. f. fabalis.*

| J | F | M | A | M | J | J | A | S | O | N | D |

*The black bill with an orange ring near the tip distinguishes the Bean Goose from other geese, and the amount of black separates the two types of Bean Goose.*

**Size:** 72–89cm (28–35in).
**Wing:** 434–520mm.
**Bill:** 55–70mm.
**Weight:** 2220–4060g.
**Voice:** Low-pitched *ung-unk.*
**Habitat:** Tundra lakes and marshes; freshwater marshes in winter.
**Food:** Grass, grain.
**Range:** Breeds tundra and taiga from Scandinavia to Bering Straits. Winters Japan, China and western Europe.
**Movements:** Migrates through Baltic to winter along shores of North Sea.
**Breeding:** Four to six white eggs are laid in a scrape near water, incubated by the female for 27–29 days; downy, active chicks fly after 56 days.
**Confusing Species:** Smaller dark Pink-footed Goose shows grey forewing.

# Pink-footed Goose *(Anser brachyrhynchus)*

This small, grey goose has a short dark neck, dark head, pink and black bill and pink legs. It shows a grey forewing in flight. The world population is found in Europe in winter. The geese feed on arable fields and fly in dramatic formations across the evening sky to roost on offshore shoals.

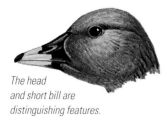

*The head and short bill are distinguishing features.*

| J | F | M | A | M | J | J | A | S | O | N | D |

**Size:** 61–77cm (24–30in).
**Wing:** 405–460mm.
**Bill:** 40–52mm.
**Weight:** 1810–3350g.
**Voice:** Barking yelps, highly vocal.
**Habitat:** Summer on tundra deltas and marshes. They winter in coastal fields,

along shorelines, estuaries and on offshore banks.
**Food:** Grass, grain, potatoes.
**Range:** Breeds in eastern Greenland, Iceland and Spitzbergen. Winters along North Sea shorelines.
**Movements:** Greenland and Iceland birds winter in Scotland. Spitzbergen birds winter in Germany and Holland, a few of them reaching southern England.
**Breeding:** Four or five white eggs are laid in a scrape near water or on a cliff ledge. They are incubated by the female alone and take about 25–28 days to hatch. The active, down-covered chicks are ready to fly after about 55 days. They are highly gregarious and form vast, noisy flocks.
**Confusing Species:** Bean Goose lacks grey forewing in flight.

# White-fronted Goose (Anser albifrons)

The White-fronted Goose is a dainty, well-proportioned grey bird, marked by dark, smudged barring on the belly and white around the bill. In flight, it shows greyish outer wings. Two distinct subspecies are regular in Europe: *Anser albifrons flavirostris* from Greenland has darker plumage and an orange bill; *A. a. albifrons* from Russia has a pink bill. Both have orange legs and feet. The birds often gather in large flocks of up to 10,000 during the winter.

The characteristic white face of the White-fronted Goose appears only in adulthood – the juveniles have an overall brown colouring, lacking the breast bars as well as the white face markings.

**Size:** 66–77cm (26–30in).
**Wing:** 389–463mm.
**Bill:** 44–60mm.
**Weight:** 1430–3340g.
**Voice:** A musical *kow-yow* and other high-pitched notes.
**Habitat:** High-Arctic tundra lakes, deltas and marshes and, in winter, grasslands and saltings.
**Food:** Grass, cereals.
**Range:** High northern circumpolar. In Europe breeds only in Arctic Russia east of the Urals. Winters in a broad swathe across Europe from northwest to southeast, but becoming rarer.
**Movements:** Greenland birds migrate through Iceland to winter in Ireland, Scotland and Wales. Russian and Siberian birds move through the Baltic to winter along the southern shores of the North Sea on the Hungarian plain and along the Black Sea.
**Breeding:** Five or six white eggs are laid in a scrape beside a bog or hidden in a thicket and are incubated by the female alone for 27 or 28 days. The chicks are active and downy.
**Confusing Species:** Lesser White-fronted Goose has a less barred belly, more white on the head and a bold yellow eye-ring.

# Lesser White-fronted Goose (Anser erythropus)

A scarce, high-Arctic relative of the White-fronted Goose whose numbers are declining. Similar to White-fronted, but with a shorter, thicker neck and more rounded head. The white around the bill extends on to the forehead, the eye has a prominent yellow ring in the adult, and the bill is pink. The belly bars are reduced to three or four smudges and there is no grey in the wing in flight. At rest, the wing tips extend back beyond the tail. Juveniles lack most of these features and should be distinguished from juvenile Russian White-fronteds with great care.

*The Lesser White-fronted Goose has a distinctive yellow eye-ring which can be seen at a surprising distance. Care should be taken at close quarters, however, as some White-fronted Geese have a faint yellow eye-ring.*

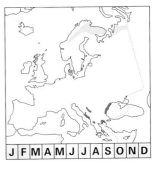

**Size:** 66–77cm (26–30in).
**Wing:** 389–463mm.
**Bill:** 44–60mm.
**Weight:** 1430–3340g.
**Voice:** A higher pitched *kow-yow* than the White-fronted.
**Habitat:** Tundra lakes and marshes and, in winter, grasslands and saltings.
**Food:** Grass, cereals.

**Range:** Breeds right across Eurasia in the northernmost tundra. Winters China, Middle East and Balkans. In Europe breeds northern Scandinavia and Russia.
**Movements:** Birds winter in Ireland, Scotland and Wales, in Hungary and on shores of North and Black Seas. Some passage through central Europe on way to Danube delta area and river system.
**Breeding:** Five or six white eggs are laid in a scrape beside a bog or in a thicket, often at altitude. They are incubated by the female alone for 25–28 days. The chicks are active and downy and fly after 35 days.
**Confusing Species:** White-fronted Goose has a barred belly, less white on head and a faint yellow eye-ring.

## Canada Goose *(Branta canadensis)*

This large 'black' goose has been introduced to several parts of Europe from its native North America and has prospered and multiplied. The large brown body is darker above and paler below, with a black neck and head broken by a broad white chin strap. Size can vary enormously, and the appearance of smaller Canada Geese with flocks of wild Barnacle and White-fronted Geese in Scotland indicates immigration of wild Canada geese from across the Atlantic.

J F M A M J J A S O N D

*Like most geese, the Canada Goose can be aggressive. If the lowered head and hissing of the threat display (right) does not deter the intruder, powerful blows from the wings may follow.*

**Size:** 91–102cm (36–40in).
**Wing:** 325–550mm.
**Bill:** 25–65mm.
**Weight:** 2900–5410g.
**Voice:** Loud, repeated *wagh-onk*.
**Habitat:** Naturally breeds in a wide variety of wetlands from tundra to temperate lakes. In Europe, mainly in and around parks and ornamental waters.
**Food:** Grass, aquatic plants, cereals.
**Range:** Breeds over most of Canada and the central United States. Winters southwards as far as Mexico. In Europe, it is resident in the British Isles, Germany, Netherlands, Belgium and at a few places in Norway. It is a summer visitor to southern Sweden and Finland.
**Movements:** British and Irish birds largely resident, though gather at large local waters to moult. Scandinavian birds move to southern Baltic in winter.
**Breeding:** Five or six white eggs are laid in a scrape beside water and incubated by the female for 28–30 days. The active and downy chicks take about 63 days to fledge.
**Confusing Species:** Barnacle Goose is grey not brown, the face is white, and the black of head and neck extends to the breast.

## Barnacle Goose *(Branta leucopsis)*

This dainty, well-marked 'black' goose has neatly barred grey and black upperparts, white underparts and black on the head and neck that extends to the breast to form a band. The whole face is white. In flight, it shows heavily barred grey wings. It is highly gregarious, forming huge winter flocks at a few traditional sites.

J F M A M J J A S O N D

*The contrast between the white belly and black neck is a sure means of distinguishing this from other geese.*

**Size:** 59–69cm (23–27in).
**Wing:** 376–429mm.
**Bill:** 27–33mm.
**Weight:** 1290–2400g.
**Voice:** High-pitched barking notes, creating considerable noise when large flocks take off.
**Habitat:** Tundra cliffs and marshes; winters on grassland and estuaries near the sea.
**Food:** Grass.
**Range:** Breeding confined largely to Greenland, Sptizbergen and Novaya Zemlya. Winters in Netherlands, Germany and Britain.
**Movements:** Three breeding areas and three equally distinct wintering zones. Greenland birds cross the North Atlantic to winter in Ireland and Scotland. Spitzbergen birds winter exclusively on the Scottish Solway. Siberian birds in the Netherlands and Germany.
**Breeding:** Three to five white eggs are laid in a downy cup on a cliff ledge and incubated by the female for 24 or 25 days. The active, downy chicks throw themselves to the ground and take about 50 days to fledge.
**Confusing Species:** Canada Goose is much larger and brown rather than grey.

Brent Geese are dark grey, almost black above, with a black head, neck and breast broken only by a white neck slash. Dark-bellied birds show virtually no breast band, whereas pale-bellied birds have a distinct and contrasting breast band. Two subspecies are regular in Europe and another, from North America, is a rare visitor.

*The size of the white neck slash varies according to subspecies and age.*

**Size:** 56–61cm (22–24in).
**Wing:** 317–353mm.
**Bill:** 29–38mm.
**Weight:** 1385–1585g.
**Voice:** Murmuring, grumbled *knook*.
**Habitat:** Breeds on high-Arctic tundra river systems and bogs. In winter the bird frequents estuaries and open shorelines.
**Food:** Seaweeds and, progressively, more grass.
**Range:** Circumpolar as far north as ice-free land exists. Dark-bellied *B. b. bernicla* breed in mainland Siberia. Pale-bellied *B. b. hrota* breed in Spitzbergen and Franz Joseph Land, as well as in Greenland and the Arctic Canadian islands.
**Movements:** Dark-bellied *B. b. bernicla* move through Baltic to Denmark and on to Germany, Holland and southern England. Pale-bellied *B. b. hrota* from Greenland and Canada winter in Ireland. Pale-bellied *B. b. hrota* from Spitzbergen and Franz Joseph Land winter in Northumberland, England.
**Breeding:** Three to five, yellow-washed white eggs are laid in a scrape near water and incubated by the female for 24–26 days. The young birds are active and downy.

**Size:** 51–59cm (20–23in).
**Wing:** 332–379mm.
**Bill:** 22–27mm.
**Weight:** 1058–1625g.
**Voice:** High-pitched, rather shrill *kee-wa*.
**Habitat:** Breeds on high-Arctic tundra river systems and bogs. Winters on grasslands and floods.
**Food:** Grass.

**Range:** Single breeding area in north central Siberia. Winters on the Caspian and Black Seas.
**Movements:** Performs huge, cross-country migration across Siberia and Russia to Caspian Sea, Bulgaria and Romania. Numbers vary between these zones year by year, but Bulgaria and Romania have been main wintering areas for the past 30 years.
**Breeding:** Three to eight cream-coloured eggs are laid in a neat cup on a cliff, where they are incubated by the female for 24 to 30 days. The down covered chicks throw themselves to the ground and fledge after about a month.

A delightfully marked 'black' goose, this bird is a winter visitor in variable numbers to the Black Sea and a vagrant farther west. The body, above and below, is black separated by a bold white flank slash. The breast and face is rusty red and the head a harlequin pattern of black, red and white. The tiny black bill and thick neck are distinctive.

*The black wings, both above and below, are as distinctive in flight as the red chest and face markings are at rest.*

111

A well-marked, unmistakable goose-like duck, the Common Shelduck is a familiar sight on estuaries and along shorelines. The adult is white with black and white wings and a bold chestnut breast band. The head and neck are green, and the bill red. The female lacks the red knob on the bill and young lack a chestnut breast band.

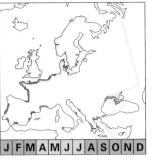

J F M A M J J A S O N D

*The young from different broods may join together in the care of a single adult female (below) as the adults fly off to moult. Far right: Adult male.*

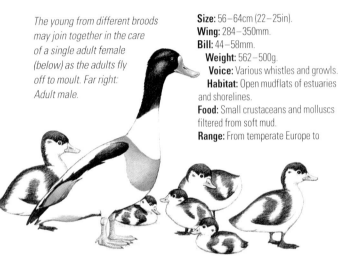

**Size:** 56–64cm (22–25in).
**Wing:** 284–350mm.
**Bill:** 44–58mm.
**Weight:** 562–500g.
**Voice:** Various whistles and growls.
**Habitat:** Open mudflats of estuaries and shorelines.
**Food:** Small crustaceans and molluscs filtered from soft mud.
**Range:** From temperate Europe to south central Siberia. The latter is a highly migratory population that winters in China, northwest India and the Middle East. European birds are mainly resident, though some winter in Iberia.
**Movements:** Large moult migration of European birds to Heligoland Bight, Germany and Bridgwater Bay, England in late summer. During the moult, the birds cannot fly for up to 30 days and find safety in numbers during this dangerous period. At this time, the young are left in crèches cared for by a number of adult female 'aunties'.
**Breeding:** Eight to twelve creamy eggs are laid in a down-lined cup in a burrow or hollow tree and incubated for 28–30 days. Chicks fledge at about 56 days.

This large goose-like duck is similar in shape and size to the more widespread and familiar Common Shelduck, but it is easily identified by the orange-chestnut coloration. In flight, black flight feathers contrast with white wing coverts. It is usually seen as it wades along marsh edges feeding from the surface.

J F M A M J J A S O N D

*The male Ruddy Shelduck has a darker head with a distinctive neck ring, while the female has a white head and no neck ring.*

**Size:** 61–66cm (24–26 in).
**Wing:** 321–383mm.
**Bill:** 35–49mm.
**Weight:** 1200–1600g.
**Voice:** Honking calls and a repeated *gorrr* sound.
**Habitat:** Shallow marshes often, but not always, near the sea or around the fringes of large river systems.
**Food:** Aquatic vegetation, crustaceans.
**Range:** The species breeds right across Eurasia from the Mediterranean almost to the Sea of Japan and southwards to central Asia. In Europe, it is confined to coasts of Greece, Black Sea and major rivers of Ukraine; though escapees are known elsewhere. Asian populations winter in India and across Southeast Asia to China.
**Movements:** East European birds are presumed to join the larger Turkish population in winter.
**Breeding:** Eight to twelve white eggs are laid in a tree hole or rock crevice and incubated by the female for 27–29 days. The active and downy young fly after about 55 days.

## Wigeon *(Anas penelope)*

A surface-feeding duck, the Wigeon spends its time grazing meadows or loafing on the water in large flocks. The male is grey with a black and white rear end and a rusty head topped by a golden crown, and the female a warm buff. Both have rounded heads and silver bills. In flight, male shows white patch on inner wing. A flock that has some ducks with white in the wing and some without is usually Wigeon.

*A small grey bill and rounded head distinguish the female Wigeon (left) from other female ducks. The male (above) is more colourful.*

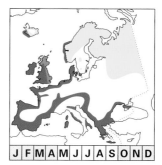

**Size:** 43–48cm (17–19in).
**Wing:** 228–281mm.
**Bill:** 32–40mm.
**Weight:** 400–1090g.
**Voice:** Male gives shrill whistles, female growls.
**Habitat:** Marshes and bogs in summer; wintering on estuaries and shorelines.

**Food:** Grass, eelgrass.
**Range:** Breeds right across tundra and boreal zones of Eurasia. In Europe, breeds from Iceland, northern Britain and Scandinavia to Russia. Winters throughout western Europe.
**Movements:** Vast numbers move south-west to western and southern Europe.

**Breeding:** Seven or eight creamy eggs are laid in a down-filled hollow near water and incubated for 22–25 days by the female. The active, down-covered young fledge after about 40 days.
**Confusing Species:** No other surface-feeding duck has such a neatly rounded head and small bill.

J F M A M J J A S O N D

## Gadwall *(Anas strepera)*

The Gadwall is a somewhat dull-coloured duck that is marked grey in the male, with a black rear end and a white speculum in the wing; the bill is silver-grey. The female resembles a female Mallard, but has orange margins to the bill and a white speculum. Lighter in build than Mallard.

J F M A M J J A S O N D

*The female Gadwall has a white flash on the wing, which marks it out from the females of other species.*

**Size:** 46–53cm (18–21in).
**Wing:** 243–282mm.
**Bill:** 37–46mm.
**Weight:** 470–1300g.
**Voice:** Male whistles, female quacks.
**Habitat:** Freshwater marshes with good growth of emergent vegetation, also on open estuaries.
**Food:** Mostly aquatic vegetation found by up-ending.
**Range:** Circumpolar in north temperate zone. In Europe, the bird is patchily distributed in the west, though more continuously in Russia. Winters from Britain westwards to the Balkans.
**Movements:** The whole population of eastern Europe and Russia migrates westwards and southwards to winter in northern Greece and Turkey. Introductions to many areas have created resident populations.
**Breeding:** Eight to twelve creamy eggs are laid in a down-lined hollow, usually near water. They are incubated by the female for 25–27 days, and the active and down-covered young take about 50 days to fledge.
**Confusing Species:** Male unlike any other male surface-feeding duck, though easily overlooked. Female similar to females of many other duck species.

113

## Common Teal (Anas crecca)

This tiny, well-marked duck forms winter flocks that perform aerial displays similar to those of several species of wader. The male is grey with a yellowish rear patch, white flank slash and a rusty coloured head, marked by a green eye patch edged yellowish.

The head of the female Common Teal is plain, lacking the distinct stripes of female Garganey.

**Size:** 33–38cm (13–15in).
**Wing:** 175–196mm.
**Bill:** 32–40mm.
**Weight:** 200–500g.
**Voice:** Male whistles, female quacks.
**Habitat:** Marshes, lakes, bogs, estuaries and open shorelines.
**Food:** Aquatic vegetation and seeds.
**Range:** Breeds across Eurasia in tundra, boreal and temperate zones. Winters throughout Europe and east to Japan.
**Movements:** Migration south and west from Scandinavia, Russia and Poland.
**Breeding:** Eight to twelve buff eggs laid in a hollow and incubated for 21–28 days by the female. The active and downy chicks fly after about 44 days.
**Similar Species:** Female same size as female Garganey, but has plain face.

JFMAMJJASOND

## Garganey (Anas querquedula)

The Garganey is the only duck that abandons Europe completely for the winter. The male is warm grey, with a rufous head marked by a prominent white supercilium; extended black and white scapulars cascade over the back. Both sexes show a blue-grey inner wing and dark leading edge to the underwing in flight.

The distinctly striped face pattern of the female separates it from the female Teal.

**Size:** 35–40cm (14–16in).
**Wing:** 182–211mm.
**Bill:** 36–43mm.
**Weight:** 250–600g.
**Voice:** Male rattling call; female quack.
**Habitat:** Freshwater pools and marshes.
**Food:** Aquatic plants and invertebrates.
**Range:** In Europe, breeds from Britain to Balkans, Russia and Ukraine.
**Movements:** European population crosses the Sahara to winter in Africa.
**Breeding:** Eight to eleven buff-coloured

JFMAMJJASOND

eggs are laid in a hollow near water, where they are incubated for 21–23 days by the female. The active, downy chicks fledge after 35–42 days.
**Similar Species:** Female Teal lacks striped face pattern of female Garganey.

## Marbled Duck (Marmaronetta angustirostris)

This is a bland-coloured little duck, in which the sexes are similar, and which has only a remnant distribution through the Mediterranean. Both sexes are buffy brown, heavily spotted whitish. There is a dark area around the eye and the hint of a crest, which may be raised in display.

The common name of this duck comes from its mottled flanks, which resemble the patterns found in marble.

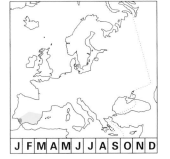

JFMAMJJASOND

**Size:** 38–40cm (15–16in).
**Wing:** 186–215mm.
**Bill:** 39–47mm.
**Weight:** 400–590g.
**Voice:** Silent.
**Habitat:** Shallow, well-vegetated fresh waters.

**Food:** Aquatic vegetation obtained from the surface and by up-ending.
**Range:** Highly localized and in Europe breeds at only a handful of places in Spain. It is found in greater numbers in North Africa, Turkey, the Middle East and in the Caspian and Aral Sea areas.
**Movements:** Perhaps more dispersive than truly migratory in Spain, but some birds probably cross into nearby Morocco. In the east, the largest concentrations in the world winter in Iran. The European population is now thought to have fallen dramatically, probably to below 100 pairs.
**Breeding:** Nine to thirteen creamy eggs are laid in a hollow near water and incubated by the female for 25–27 days. When the youngsters hatch they are active and down-covered.

## Mallard *(Anas platyrhynchos)*

Most widespread, common and familiar of European ducks, the Mallard is as at home on a pond in a city park as on a wild coastal estuary. It is also the original species from which most domestic ducks have been bred. The male is grey, with a black rear and a brown breast separated from a green head by a narrow white collar. The female is brown and buff with an orange bill. Both sexes show white and blue speculums.

J F M A M J J A S O N D

**Size:** 56–61cm (22–24in).
**Wing:** 252–298mm.
**Bill:** 47–59mm.
**Weight:** 750–1572g.
**Voice:** Male whistles and grunts; female quacks.
**Habitat:** Virtually any fresh water as well as estuaries and sheltered shorelines.
**Food:** Seeds, plants, aquatic vegetation, invertebrates, bread.
**Range:** Northern circumpolar, mostly in temperate zone. Breeds throughout Europe. Winters over most of Europe, except Scandinavia and Russia, as well as in India, China and Japan.
**Movements:** Large numbers of northern Russian birds move westwards to Britain and the North Sea. Southern Russian and Ukrainian birds move to Balkans, particularly Greece. As many as nine million birds winter in Europe.
**Breeding:** Ten to twelve creamy eggs are laid in a hollow and incubated by the female for 28 or 29 days. The downy chicks are active and fledge after 50-56 days. Females may raise more than one brood each season and the males are promiscuous.
**Confusing Species:** Female similar to other female ducks, but with blue and white speculum.

*The female Mallard has a dull brown plumage which camouflages the bird while it sits on the nest incubating the eggs. The male (left) is more showy.*

## Pintail *(Anas acuta)*

Most elegant and finely marked of all surface feeding ducks, the Pintail may spend lengthy periods feeding in a tiny area. The male is grey, with a yellowish cream and black rear end marked by the extended 'pin tail'. The white of the breast extends up the back of the brown head. The female is like other female ducks, but slimmer, and has a 'low in water' base to neck.

**Size:** 53–69cm (21–27in).
**Wing:** 254–282mm.
**Bill:** 44–56mm.
**Weight:** 400–1300g.
**Voice:** Male whistles and growls; female quacks.
**Habitat:** Marshes, floods and estuaries, though will avoid some apparently suitable areas.
**Food:** Aquatic vegetation and invertebrates.
**Range:** Northern circumpolar in tundra and boreal zones. In Europe, breeds from Iceland to Russia. More sporadically in Britain, Denmark, Germany and Poland. Winters from Britain to the Balkans westwards.
**Movements:** Large migration through the Baltic to wintering grounds in south and west.
**Breeding:** Seven to nine yellow-washed eggs are laid in a down-lined hollow and incubated by the female for 21–23 days. The active, down-covered chicks fly after about 50 days.
**Confusing Species:** Female resembles other female ducks, but is slimmer, more elegant and has a long, pointed tail.

*The female Pintail's long neck is a major distinguishing feature (left). Below: the male.*

J F M A M J J A S O N D

## Shoveler *(Anas clypeata)*

J F M A M J J A S O N D

The Shoveler is a robust, well-marked duck, with a large spatulate sieve of a bill. The male is white with rich chestnut flanks and belly and green head. In flight it shows pale blue inner wings. The female is similar to other female surface-feeding ducks. At a distance the male's white breast acts as a fine field mark.

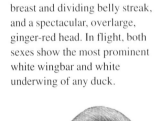

*The size of the bill marks out the female (below and above right) from other female ducks.*

**Size:** 46–53cm (18–21in).
**Wing:** 222–249mm.
**Bill:** 56–72mm.
**Weight:** 300–1000g.
**Voice:** Male utters harsh double note: female quacks.
**Habitat:** Shallow marshes, floods, estuaries.
**Food:** Small crustaceans, molluscs, insects, aquatic seeds and plants.
**Range:** Circumpolar in the northern boreal and temperate zones. In Europe, breeds from Iceland and Britain across

Baltic Scandinavia and Russia, southwards to France and the Ukraine. Winters in south and west, though some eastern birds cross the Sahara.
**Movements:** Russian birds migrate southwards as far as East Africa. Some European birds may move as far as West Africa, where they can be found from Senegal to the Niger Inundation Zone.
**Breeding:** Eight to twelve buff eggs are laid in a down-lined hollow located near water where they are incubated by the female for 22 or 23 days. The down-covered young are active and fly after 42–49 days.
**Confusing Species:** Female is like other female surface-feeding ducks, but with a very large bill.

## Red-crested Pochard *(Netta rufina)*

A boldly marked diving duck that tends to concentrate in large numbers at favoured locations, the Red-crested Pochard is otherwise scarce. The male is brown above, white below with black rear end, breast and dividing belly streak, and a spectacular, overlarge, ginger-red head. In flight, both sexes show the most prominent white wingbar and white underwing of any duck.

*The white cheeks and throat of the female Red-crested Pochard (right) make it more noticeable than most female ducks.*

J F M A M J J A S O N D

**Size:** 53–59cm (21–23in).
**Wing:** 251–273mm.
**Bill:** 42–52mm.
**Weight:** 830–1420g.
**Voice:** Mostly silent.
**Habitat:** Freshwater lakes with floating islands and/or plentiful emergent vegetation, and sometimes along sheltered seashores.
**Food:** Aquatic vegetation, obtained chiefly by diving.
**Range:** Breeds from Europe through

Turkey to south and central Siberia. Winters India, Middle East and Balkans.
**Movements:** Resident Iberian population augmented by French, German, Dutch and Central European breeders. Ukrainian birds migrate southwest to the Balkans in winter.
**Breeding:** Six to twelve creamy eggs

are laid in a hollow among dense vegetation. They are incubated by the female for 26–28 days and the active and down-covered chicks take 40–50 days to fledge.
**Similar Species:** The female resembles the female Common Scoter, but has a larger, rounded head.

## Common Pochard *(Aythya ferina)*

Anumerous and widespread diving duck, the Common Pochard often gathers in huge rafts at suitable waters. The male is grey with black fore and aft, a rust, triangular-shaped head and a concave bill profile. The female is brown with a similar profile. In flight, the wings are grey, with a paler grey wing bar. The bird dives easily in search of food.

J F M A M J J A S O N D

*The distinctive pale band around the bill and the black bill tip (left) are features shared by both the male (above) and female Pochard.*

**Size:** 43–48cm (17–19in).
**Wing:** 200–223mm.
**Bill:** 42–52mm.
**Weight:** 467–1240g.
**Voice:** Female growls in flight, otherwise silent.
**Habitat:** Large fresh waters, reservoirs, estuaries, sheltered shorelines.
**Food:** Aquatic vegetation obtained by diving, also invertebrates.
**Range:** Breeds from Ireland across temperate and boreal Europe to Russia and the Ukraine, eastwards to eastern Siberia. Winters Japan, China, India, Middle East and western Europe.
**Movements:** Vast movements westwards from Russia, with some birds crossing the Sahara. About a quarter of a million Pochard winter in Europe.

**Breeding:** Six to eleven green-washed eggs are laid on a mound of vegetation, usually close to water. They are incubated for 24–26 days by the female and the active, downy chicks fly after 50–56 days.

## Tufted Duck *(Aythya fuligula)*

Common, widespread and easily recognized, the Tufted Duck is a diving duck that is often seen on city ponds and lakes. The male is black with white flanks and a neatly rounded purple-glossed head, marked by a drooping crest. The female is brown all over, slightly paler on the flanks. The bird dives easily and gathers in large rafts on suitable waters, often with Common Pochard.

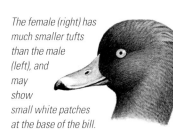

*The female (right) has much smaller tufts than the male (left), and may show small white patches at the base of the bill.*

**Size:** 40–43cm (16–17in).
**Wing:** 193–215mm.
**Bill:** 36–44mm.
**Weight:** 335–1028g.
**Voice:** Generally silent, although the female may growl.
**Habitat:** Fresh waters, from marshes to open reservoirs, as well as estuaries.
**Food:** Aquatic invertebrates, insects.
**Range:** Breeds from Iceland across boreal Eurasia to Japan. It winters in the Nile marshes, in many parts of the Mediterranean, Middle East, India, China and Japan.
**Movements:** Scandinavian birds migrate to shores of North Sea, the Siberian birds to Sudan and Ethiopia.
**Breeding:** Five to twelve green-washed eggs are laid in a hollow near

water and incubated for 23–25 days by the female. The down-covered chicks are active and take 40–42 days to fledge.
**Confusing Species:** Male Scaup has grey back; female Scaup has more white at base of bill, and different head shape.

J F M A M J J A S O N D

## Ferruginous Duck *(Aythya nyroca)*

Agenerally scarce, mainly eastern, diving duck, the Ferruginous Duck has a highly disjointed breeding distribution. Both sexes are a rich dark chestnut, with a darker back and white rear end and wingbar.

*Although the sexes are broadly similar, at close quarters the two are distinct, since the male (below) has a white eye, while that of the female (left) is dark.*

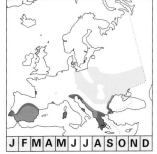

J F M A M J J A S O N D

**Size:** 38–43cm (15–17in).
**Wing:** 171–196mm.
**Bill:** 36–43mm.
**Weight:** 410–730g.
**Voice:** A quiet *tuk-tuk*.
**Habitat:** Marshes and lakes with dense vegetation to hide in when disturbed.
**Food:** Aquatic vegetation and invertebrates.
**Range:** Breeds from Spain to Caspian Sea and to Siberia in the temperate zone. Winters in the Balkans, Turkey, the Nile Valley and in northern India.
**Movements:** European birds migrate to the Balkans, but some cross the Sahara.
**Breeding:** Seven to eleven creamy eggs are laid in a hollow, among waterside vegetation. They are incubated for 25–27 days by the female. The active, downy chicks fly after 56–60 days.

117

## Scaup *(Aythya marila)*

This is the marine equivalent of the Tufted Duck, and the female especially could be confused with that bird. Scaup form large flocks on the sea over feeding grounds. The male has white flanks with a pale grey back and black front and rear ends. A close view shows that the head has a metallic green sheen. The head shape of Scaup, with a distinctly sloping rear crown, is different to that of the Tufted Duck. Both males and females show a bold white wingbar in flight.

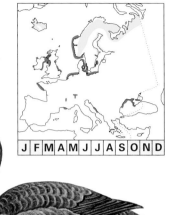

*The female is brown like the female Tufted Duck, which may have a white base to its bill. This is always more extensive and clear cut in the Scaup.*

**Size:** 46–51cm (18–20in).
**Wing:** 211–237mm.
**Bill:** 40–47mm.
**Weight:** 690–1372g.
**Voice:** Females growl.
**Habitat:** Mountain lakes and marshes; sheltered bays.
**Food:** Molluscs, vegetation.
**Range:** Circumpolar in tundra. Breeds in Iceland, Scandinavia and Russia. Winters on coasts.
**Movements:** From Russia to the Baltic; to Britain; Icelandic birds to Ireland and Scotland.
**Breeding:** Six to fifteen greenish eggs in an open hollow near water; incubated by female for 24–28 days. The young fledge at 35–42 days.
**Confusing Species:** Tufted Duck.

## Common Eider *(Somateria mollissima)*

Robust, chunky seaducks Eiders form large breeding colonies at many northern sites. The male is white above, black below and is marked by a triangular-shaped head with a black cap and pale green nape. The female is a mottled dark brown, but with a similar build and triangular head. A flat forehead and bill are characteristic. Dives well and seemingly ignores heavy seas.

*Sub-adult males (right) show a variety of patchy plumages. Initially, they resemble the female with warm brown and black-barred plumage.*

**Size:** 53–61cm (21–24in).
**Wing:** 286–315mm.
**Bill:** 51–61mm.
**Weight:** 1192–2800g.
**Voice:** Gentle, cooing calls.
**Habitat:** Rocky sea coasts.
**Food:** Marine molluscs and crustaceans.
**Range:** Circumpolar on ice-free land. In Europe, northern coasts of Britain, Scandinavia and Iceland.
**Movements:** Westward.
**Breeding:** Four to six greenish eggs in a hollow lined with down; incubated by the female for 27 or 28 days; down-covered chicks spend 60–75 days by the sea prior to fledging.
**Confusing Species:** Other female eider species.

## King Eider *(Somateria spectabilis)*

A scarce, winter wanderer southwards to northern Europe, the King Eider winters along Norway's coasts. The male is black with a white patch on the rear flank. The head is a motley of colours, and the breast is a rich peach. The male has a white patch on the inner forewing.

*The female King Eider resembles a female Common Eider, but has a distinct bump on an otherwise flat forehead/bill profile.*

**Size:** 46–64cm (18–25in).
**Wing:** 256–293mm.
**Bill:** 27–35mm.
**Weight:** 1213–2013g.
**Voice:** Resounding, hollow calls, grunts, hisses and cooing.
**Habitat:** Rocky coastlines.
**Food:** Marine molluscs and crustaceans.
**Range:** Circumpolar in northern latitudes. Breeds Spitzbergen and Russian Arctic; winters coastal Norway, Iceland.
**Movements:** East or west to open water as far as Norway.
**Breeding:** Four or five greenish eggs in a hollow lined with down, near water; incubated by the female for 22–24 days. The chicks are active and downy.
**Confusing Species:** Female Common Eider.

## Long-tailed Duck (Clangula hyemalis)

This attractive seaduck boasts distinctive plumages year-round, and has a unique structure. In summer, the male has a chocolate-brown head and a large white eye-patch; the female is similar, but with a brown smudge below the eye.

*In winter the male has a white head with a brown ear covert patch. The tail in all plumages is exceptionally long.*

| J | F | M | A | M | J | J | A | S | O | N | D |

**Size:** 40–43cm (16–17in). Tail of male an extra 12–15cm (5–6in).
**Wing:** 204–241mm.
**Bill:** 24–30mm.
**Weight:** 510–910g.

**Voice:** Male yodels; female quacks.
**Habitat:** Mountain and tundra marshes, lakes and coasts.
**Food:** Molluscs and crustaceans.
**Range:** Circumpolar in northern tundra. Breeds in Scandinavia, Iceland and Russia. Winters Baltic and North Seas.

**Movements:** Through Murmansk, St Petersburg, Baltic and Norwegian coast.
**Breeding:** Five to nine yellowish eggs are laid in a hidden hollow; incubated by the female for 23–25 days. The downy chicks fly at about 35 days.

## Goldeneye (Bucephala clangula)

The Goldeneye, a compact, well-marked diving duck, is a widespread winter visitor to western Europe. The male is black and white, with a triangular, metallic green head marked by a round white spot between the bill and the bright yellow eye. It swims low in the water and dives easily.

*The female's head (right) is of a similar shape to that of the male, but it is brown.*

| J | F | M | A | M | J | J | A | S | O | N | D |

**Size:** 40–48cm (16–19in).
**Wing:** 186–231mm.
**Bill:** 28–36mm.
**Weight:** 500–1245g.
**Voice:** Rolling calls in courtship.
**Habitat:** Boreal lakes in the breeding season. In winter, on large fresh waters, estuaries and the sea.
**Food:** Molluscs and crustaceans.
**Range:** Circumpolar in boreal zone. In Europe, breeds in Scandinavia and northern Russia. Winters from Germany westwards across central Europe to the Balkans. Absent from Iberia.
**Movements:** Most migrate through the Baltic to winter around Jutland. Fewer fly south and west.
**Breeding:** Six to eleven greenish-blue eggs in a tree hole; incubated by the female for 27–32 days. Downy chicks leap to the ground and fledge in 51–60 days. Nestboxes have created a population boom in some areas.
**Confusing Species:** Barrow's Goldeneye is confined to Iceland.

## Barrow's Goldeneye (Bucephala islandica)

black above and white below. The purple-glossed head is large with a steep forehead and distinctly sloped rear to the crown. The female resembles the female Goldeneye, but has a steep forehead and a sloped rear crown, similar to the male. This bird dives easily.

Very similar to the Goldeneye, but Barrow's Goldeneye breeds only in Iceland and is a rare vagrant south and east. The male is

| J | F | M | A | M | J | J | A | S | O | N | D |

*The male (above left) is black above and white below, with a series of white spots on the sides of the folded wing. There is also an oval white spot between bill and eye.*

**Size:** 40–53cm (16–21in).
**Wing:** 211–248mm.
**Bill:** 29–34mm.
**Weight:** 737–1304g.
**Voice:** Various grunts and growls.
**Habitat:** Freshwater lakes, as well as clear, fast-flowing rivers and streams.
**Food:** Insects, molluscs and crustaceans.
**Range:** Breeds Alaska southwards through western North America, eastern Canada, Greenland and Iceland.
**Movements:** Moves only as far as necessary to find ice-free waters and may then frequent sheltered sea bays.
**Breeding:** Eight to fourteen pale green eggs in a hole among rocks; incubated by the female for 28–30 days. Young are active and down-covered.
**Confusing Species:** Goldeneye.

## Common Scoter *(Melanitta nigra)*

Usually seen either in lines or bunched together in groups, the Common Scoter flies low over the waves offshore and disappears as it lands among the sea swells. The male is the only entirely black duck and is marked by a difficult-to-see yellow bill topped by a black knob. The female appears dark, but is actually brown with a whitish belly and pale brown cheeks, which can be picked out at a great distance.

*In mixed flocks with Velvet Scoter, the large pale cheeks of the female Common Scoter (above right) contrast with the two smaller pale cheek spots of the female Velvet Scoter. The male (right) is usually all black.*

**Size:** 46–51cm (18–20in).
**Wing:** 206–247mm.
**Bill:** 41–51mm.
**Weight:** 600–1450g.
**Voice:** Utters occasional whistles.
**Habitat:** Breeds on mountain and tundra lakes and winters at sea.
**Food:** Molluscs and crustaceans.

**Range:** Breeds mainly in tundra zone across Eurasia, from Iceland, Scotland and Ireland to Scandinavia, and northern Russia across Siberia to Alaska. Also at several isolated breeding sites in northern Canada. Winters Atlantic and North Sea coasts.
**Movements:** Russian birds migrate through the Baltic to winter southwards as far as Iberia and Morocco.

**Breeding:** Six to nine creamy eggs are laid in a lined hollow near water; incubated by the female for 27–31 days. The active, down-covered chicks fly after 42–50 days.
**Confusing Species:** Velvet Scoter has white in wing when flapping or flying, and the female has two pale spots on face, not large pale cheeks like the Common Scoter.

## Velvet Scoter *(Melanitta fusca)*

The Velvet Scoter is very similar to the Common Scoter in both plumage and behaviour. The male has all-black plumage broken by a white speculum, which is obvious in flight. The female is dark brown with a white speculum and two pale spots on the cheek, which helps identify flocks at sea from a distance.

*Female head marks (right) are useful in identifying non-flying flocks. The male (above) is black with a white speculum.*

**Size:** 51–59cm (20–23in).
**Wing:** 232–286mm.
**Bill:** 37–51mm.
**Weight:** 1140–2014g.
**Voice:** Silent, apart from a few croaks.
**Habitat:** Breeds southwards of tundra and of range of Common Scoter among taiga and boreal lakes. Winters at sea.
**Food:** Molluscs and crustaceans.
**Range:** Circumpolar in the north, though absent from eastern Canada, Greenland and Iceland. In Europe, breeds from Scandinavia to northern Russia. Winters mainly North Sea, north to Norwegian coast and east to Baltic.
**Movements:** Large migration through the Baltic to Jutland.
**Breeding:** Seven to ten cream-coloured eggs are laid in a hollow near water. Incubation, by the female alone, lasts 27 or 28 days and the active and downy chicks fly after 42–50 days.
**Confusing Species:** Common Scoter lacks the white in wings and the female lacks the two pale spots on the cheeks.

## White-headed Duck *(Oxyura leucocephala)*

Highly localized and scarce, this duck has only a few European toeholds. The male is buff-brown with a white head, a small black cap, and a pale blue bill. The female is similar, but the cap extends to below the eye and there is a black bar across the face.

*The White-headed Duck is Europe's only native stiff-tailed duck. It is a peculiar shape, with a round body, deep head, short wings and swollen-looking bill. The stiff tail is often erect.*

**Size:** 43–48cm (17–19in)
**Wing:** 148–172mm.
**Bill:** 43–48mm.
**Weight:** 553–900g.
**Voice:** Female produces a sharp *gek*.
**Habitat:** Marshy edges of fresh waters.
**Food:** Aquatic vegetation, invertebrates
**Range:** Resident southern Spain, Tunisia, Danube Delta, and locally through Turkey to beyond the Caspian Sea. Winters locally in Europe.
**Movements:** Local dispersal in Spain and Romania. Elsewhere large movement westwards to Turkey.
**Breeding:** Five to twelve white eggs laid in a nest of vegetation; incubated by the female for 25–27 days. The downy young fly after 35 days.
**Confusing Species:** Ruddy Duck.

## Ruddy Duck *(Oxyura jamaicensis)*

The male of this stiff-tail duck is chestnut with white undertail coverts, a black cap, white face and a bold, cobalt-blue bill. The female is brown, with a black cap and a single, narrow dark line across the face.

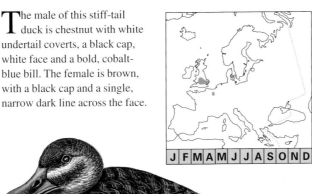

*The Ruddy Duck was introduced to Britain and has since prospered and spread to continental Europe. It has reached Spain, where it interbreeds with the local White-headed Duck, threatening its survival.*

**Size:** 36–43cm (14–17in).
**Wing:** 135–154mm.
**Bill:** 37–41mm.
**Weight:** 310–795g.
**Voice:** Grunts and hisses in courtship.
**Habitat:** Lakes, marshes, reservoirs.
**Food:** Seeds and aquatic larvae.
**Range:** In Europe, progressively more widespread in England extending to France, Belgium and Spain.
**Movements:** Dispersal mainly south and east leading to colonizations.
**Breeding:** Six to ten white eggs on a floating mound of vegetation hidden in waterside growth; incubated by the female for 20 or 21 days. The young are active and downy.
**Confusing Species:** Female White-headed Duck has broader facial band.

## Harlequin Duck *(Histrionicus histrionicus)*

The Harlequin is a robust white-water specialist. The male shows a complex pattern of blue, white and maroon, with a white face. The bill is short. The female has brown plumage and white patches on the face.

*The male (above right and below) is more colourful than the female (above left). This duck likes torrents and waterfalls. It winters along the coasts of Greenland and Iceland.*

**Size:** 40–46cm (16–18in).
**Wing:** 194–214mm.
**Bill:** 24–28mm.
**Weight:** 500–736g.
**Voice:** Female utters a harsh quack.
**Habitat:** Fast-flowing rivers and sea.
**Food:** Molluscs and crustaceans.
**Range:** Breeds Iceland, eastern Siberia south to Japan, and North America and Greenland.
**Movements:** Icelandic breeders move only to adjacent coasts. Vagrant exceptionally to Scotland and Norway.
**Breeding:** Six to eight creamy eggs in a down-lined thicket hidden in dense cover near water. They are incubated for 27–33 days by the female and the active, downy young fly after 40 days.
**Confusing Species:** Female Velvet Scoter also shows pale face patches.

121

# Smew *(Mergus albellus)*

A delightful, well-marked, little diving duck, the Smew is mostly a winter visitor. The male is white, marked by a network of vein-like black lines and a black mask and nape patch. The large head creates a unique appearance. In flight, it shows black wings with a white inner patch. It dives easily.

*Females (left) and immatures, known as 'Redheads', are grey with a white face and maroon cap. The male (above) is white with black markings.*

**Size:** 35–43cm (14–17in).
**Wing:** 171–208mm.
**Bill:** 25–32mm.
**Weight:** 500–935g.
**Voice:** Mostly silent.

J F M A M J J A S O N D

**Habitat:** Fresh waters and marshes near coast; breeds on large rivers with trees.
**Food:** Fish.
**Range:** Breeds across Eurasia in northern Sweden, Finland and Russia. Winters in Japan, China, Pakistan, southern Siberia and on the Black and North Sea coasts.
**Movements:** Through Baltic to Denmark, northern Germany and Holland. Smaller numbers westward to Britain.
**Breeding:** Six to nine creamy eggs laid in a tree hole; incubated by the female for 26–28 days; downy chicks jump to the ground and fly at about 70 days.
**Confusing Species:** Winter Slavonian Grebe from afar because the maroon cap of females and immatures appears dark.

# Red-breasted Merganser *(Mergus serrator)*

Typical 'sawbill' duck, with a sloping rear end, that sits low in the water. The male is black, white and grey with a distinctive brown-speckled breast band. The head is dark green and has a horizontal ragged crest. The long, thin bill is red and serrated. The Merganser swims and dives expertly in pursuit of fish.

J F M A M J J A S O N D

*Where the male (left) has a bottle-green head and speckled brown chest, the female is grey with a rufous-brown head. Both sexes have a ragged crest.*

**Size:** 51–61cm (20–24in).
**Wing:** 208–255mm.
**Bill:** 48–64mm.
**Weight:** 780–1350g.
**Voice:** Purring and croaking in display.
**Habitat:** Boreal/mountain rivers and tundra; winters at sea.
**Food:** Fish.
**Range:** Northern circumpolar. Iceland, Britain, Scandinavia and north Russia. Winters Atlantic and North Sea coasts, east Mediterranean and Black Seas.
**Movements:** Through Baltic to Jutland, Holland and Britain.
**Breeding:** Seven to fourteen creamy eggs on a bed of down in a tree hole or rock crevice; female incubates for 32 to 35 days; downy chicks fly in 35 days.
**Confusing Species:** Goosander.

# Goosander *(Mergus merganser)*

J F M A M J J A S O N D

**Size:** 56–69cm (22–27in).
**Wing:** 242–295mm.
**Bill:** 44–60mm.
**Weight:** 989–1390g.
**Voice:** Female cackles during courtship.
**Habitat:** Rivers/lakes in boreal zone; winters at coasts.
**Food:** Fish.
**Range:** Circumpolar in the northern boreal zone. From Iceland, Britain and Scandinavia to Russia. Winters Japan, China, northern India, south-central

Siberian lakes and rivers, the Caspian and Black Seas, and temperate areas of western Europe.
**Movements:** Westwards along the coasts of Norway.
**Breeding:** Seven to fourteen creamy eggs in a tree hole or rock crevice; incubated by the female for 32–35 days. The down-covered and active young fledge at 60–70 days.
**Confusing Species:** Female Red-breasted Merganser.

Europe's largest duck, the Goosander is about the same size as a Shelduck, and is closely related to the other 'sawbills' – the Red-breasted Merganser and Smew. The male

is creamy white with a pinkish flush on the breast, visible at surprising distances. The head is bottle green with a smooth rounded crest. The eye and narrow bill are red.

*The female (left) is like the female Red-breasted Merganser, but with a smoothly rounded, drooping crest on the rust-red head.*

## Honey Buzzard *(Pernis apivorus)*

**Size:** 51–59cm (20–23in).
**Wing:** 386–439mm.
**Bill:** 19–23mm.
**Weight:** 450–1050g.
**Voice:** A high-pitched *kee-aa.*
**Habitat:** Deciduous and coniferous forests and woods.
**Food:** Bees, wasps, amphibians and birds.
**Range:** Western Palearctic eastwards to western Siberia. Winters in the Sahel and in southwest Africa.
**Movements:** Population reaches Africa via Gibraltar, Sicily or the Black Sea.
**Breeding:** One to three reddish brown-speckled, white eggs in a nest of twigs; incubated by female for 30–35 days; downy chicks fledge at 40–44 days.
**Confusing Species:** Common Buzzard.

*The Honey Buzzard's wings droop when soaring, in contrast with the Common Buzzard, which soars on upraised wings. It has a long neck and tail, and a small, rounded head.*

Widespread, but localized, summer visitor to most of temperate Europe, which feeds mostly on the grubs of wasps and bees. The Honey Buzzard is similar to the Common Buzzard, but has a smaller head and bill on a longer neck, decidedly 'waisted' wings, heavily barred underwings and a longer tail. The species may vary in colour, with some darker than others, but birds always show three distinct tail bands.

## Black-shouldered Kite *(Elanus caeruleus)*

Once considered only a 'possible' European breeder, this distinctive and attractive raptor now breeds widely in Iberia, though its numbers remain small. The Black-shouldered Kite is grey above and white below, with an overlarge head that gives it an owl-like appearance. It has black 'shoulders' and pointed black wing tips.

*The Black-shouldered Kite perches openly, often on power poles and pylons. When it hovers in search of prey, the black 'shoulders' that give the bird its name and its pointed black wing tips are particularly obvious.*

**Size:** 30–35cm (12–14in).
**Wing:** 262–292mm.
**Bill:** 16–18mm.
**Weight:** 230–235g.
**Voice:** Mainly silent.
**Habitat:** Copses in grasslands.
**Food:** Mammals, birds, reptiles.
**Range:** Large areas of Africa; winters south of the Sahara. Resident India and Southeast Asia; Spain and Portugal.
**Movements:** Local wandering outside the breeding season.
**Breeding:** A single brood of three or four brown-blotched, creamy eggs are laid in a nest of twigs in a bush or a small tree, and incubated by the female for 25–28 days. The helpless, downy young fledge after 35 days.

123

The Black Kite is an abundant summer visitor to continental Europe. It performs dramatic migrations at the narrow sea crossings at either end of the Mediterranean Sea. The bird is dark grey-brown with paler upperwing coverts. Its head and bill are small, and the wings long and angular in shape. The Black Kite's tail, which acts as a rudder during flight, is long and distinctly notched rather than forked.

J F M A M J J A S O N D

**Size:** 53–59cm (21–23in).
**Wing:** 426–482mm.
**Bill:** 23–28mm.
**Weight:** 630–941g.
**Voice:** Squeals and chattering.
**Habitat:** River banks, woods, marshes, towns, rubbish tips.
**Food:** Carrion, insects.
**Range:** Breeds across Eurasia to Australia and Japan. Absent from Scandinavia, Britain and Holland. Winters south of the Sahara.
**Movements:** Migrates via Gibraltar in particular, but also via the Bosphorus and eastern end of Black Sea. About 40,000 cross via Gibraltar in autumn.
**Breeding:** Two or three creamy, brown-blotched eggs laid in an untidy cup

*Although flight appears rather laboured, the Black Kite glides and soars well on bowed wings.*

placed high in a tree. Incubation, by the female, lasts 25–28 days, and the down-covered, helpless chicks fledge after about 42 days.
**Confusing Species:** Female Marsh Harrier and Red Kite.

The Red Kite is a slim, long-winged, angular bird of prey that hangs in the air – the children's toy takes its name from this characteristic. Decidedly rufous above and below, it shows black on the wings above and distinctive white patches below. The head and bill are small, the wings long and narrow, the tail long, deeply forked and translucent pinkish in good light. The Red Kite soars on rising air along hillsides and twists its tail to steer in flight on bowed wings.

J F M A M J J A S O N D

*Long angular wings and a long forked tail are the key identification points.*

**Size:** 56–64cm (22–25in).
**Wing:** 448–535mm.
**Bill:** 26–29mm.
**Weight:** 960–1389g.
**Voice:** Repeated *ha–hee–haa.*
**Habitat:** Mainly deciduous woodland with adjacent open country.
**Food:** Mammals, birds and carrion.
**Range:** Endemic to Western Palearctic and resident in south and west. Birds from northern France eastwards are only summer visitors. Reintroduction

schemes in England and Scotland. Most abundant in Spain.
**Movements:** Most migrants move southwest, through the passes of the Pyrenees, to winter in Iberia.
**Breeding:** Two or three cream coloured eggs, blotched brown, are laid in a nest of twigs placed in a large tree. They are incubated by the female for 28–30 days, and the downy, helpless chicks take 45–50 days to fly.
**Confusing Species:** Black Kite.

## White-tailed Eagle *(Haliaeetus albicilla)*

This huge, broad-winged eagle catches fish but is also an inveterate scavenger. Buffy brown above, with a pale head and white tail.

**Size:** 69–91cm (27–36in).
**Wing:** 552–715mm.
**Bill:** 47–63mm.
**Weight:** 3200–7500g.
**Voice:** Loud, far-carrying, laughing during courtship.
**Habitat:** Sea coasts, lakes, marshes, ponds, river systems.
**Food:** Fish and carrion.
**Range:** Breeds from Greenland and Iceland across Europe to Bering Strait. Highly localized in Europe with largest populations in Norway and the Danube river system. Reintroduced Scotland.
**Movements:** Russian birds migrate westwards as far as Holland and northern France.
**Breeding:** Two white eggs in a nest of twigs placed in a tree or on a cliff. Eggs

*Huge yellow bill and white tail are obvious, even when plunge diving.*

are incubated for 35–45 days by both members of the pair. The helpless, downy young fledge after about 70 days.
**Confusing Species:** The immature is similar to that of all dark eagles.

## Lammergeier *(Gypaetus barbatus)*

Huge and long-winged, this vulture frequents remote mountains, but numbers are declining. It has a gold body,

black wings and tail, and a prominent bill with black beard-like bristles on either side, which give it its other name of Bearded Vulture.

*This bird drops bones on to rocks to break them, so it can extract the marrow.*

**Size:** 100–114cm (39–45in).
**Wing:** 715–910mm.
**Bill:** 47–52mm.
**Weight:** 4500–7000g.
**Voice:** Squealing notes while breeding.
**Habitat:** High mountain plateaux, gorges, screes, cliff faces, descending to lower levels in winter.
**Food:** Carrion, especially large bones. The decline in use of mules and donkeys has reduced the available food supply.
**Range:** Breeds from Europe, through Turkey to the Middle East and mountains of Asia. Also in Ethiopia and South Africa. In Europe, confined to the Pyrenees, Corsica, Crete and, lingeringly, Greece. Total 75–90 pairs.

**Movements:** None.
**Breeding:** Lays one or two brown-blotched white eggs on a platform of twigs in a cliff cave. They are incubated for 55–60 days by the female and the young fly after 107–111 days.

## Egyptian Vulture *(Neophron percnopterus)*

The smallest European vulture, with bold black and white plumage and peculiar, cigar-like body shape. Immatures are brown. Adult has a short wedge-shaped tail, a small head and bill, and a bare yellow face.

*Black flight feathers and white coverts are the key to in flight identification.*

**Size:** 61–69cm (24–27in).
**Wing:** 480–516mm.
**Bill:** 29–34mm.
**Weight:** 1584–2180g.
**Voice:** Occasional grunts.
**Habitat:** Progressively confined to mountains, though once more widespread over all open country that produced carrion.
**Food:** Carrion and rubbish, scours refuse tips in some areas.
**Range:** Breeds across Iberia and locally across southern Europe to Greece, Turkey and central southern Siberia to India. Winters across the African Sahel. Generally declining as Europe cleans and tidies up its countryside.
**Movements:** European birds cross into Africa at Gibraltar (the major site) and the Bosphorus before moving on

to the Sahel zone to winter.
**Breeding:** Two, brown-blotched white eggs are laid in an untidy nest of twigs and rubbish set in a small cliff cave. Incubation, which is shared, lasts 42 days and the downy, helpless chicks fledge after about 80 days.

125

*Usually seen soaring overhead, often in small groups, the Griffon Vulture has a distinctive buff body and wings, contrasting with black flight feathers.*

This huge vulture has broad wings that span more than 2.5m (8ft). In flight, the small head is surrounded by a whitish ruff and the tail is short and square. The dark flight feathers contrast with buffy wing linings and body. At rest a long neck is apparent, particularly when squabbling over food. It is gregarious at all times.

**J F M A M J J A S O N D**

**Size:** 94–104cm (37–41in).
**Wing:** 685–775mm.
**Bill:** 48–56mm.
**Weight:** 4250–10,500g.
**Voice:** Harsh grunts and hisses.
**Habitat:** Wilderness areas, particularly mountains with gorges and cliffs.
**Food:** Carrion, of which an ever-tidier Europe provides less and less.
**Range:** Across southern Europe through Middle East to India and mountains of south-central Asia. Mostly resident.

Largest European population is in Spain.
**Movements:** Turkish birds leave central Anatolia.
**Breeding:** A single white egg is laid in a nest of sticks placed in a cliff cave or ledge. Incubation lasts 48–54 days and is performed by both sexes. The chicks hatch helpless and downy and fly after 110-115 days.
**Confusing Species:** Black Vulture is darker, with a short, wedge-shaped tail.

Only fractionally larger than the Griffon Vulture, the Black Vulture has equally huge broad wings, and a similar flight silhouette of small head and tail. The tail is distinctly wedge-shaped, and the head is a contrasting white.
Confined to wooded hills and mountains, it soars easily, often with Griffons.

*Most often seen alone, the Black Vulture patrols the skies above the remote groves and grasslands where it lives. Although actually sooty brown, it appears black from a distance.*

**J F M A M J J A S O N D**

**Size:** 100–109cm (39–43in).
**Wing:** 720–845mm.
**Bill:** 58–64mm.
**Weight:** 7000–12,500g.
**Voice:** Silent.
**Habitat:** Mountains and hills with seldom-disturbed woods or forests. Also forages over open ground.
**Food:** Carrion.
**Range:** Localized resident in southern Europe eastwards through Turkey and the Middle East to south-central Asia

and northern China. In Europe, confined to Portugal and Spain, the Balearics, Greece and the adjacent areas of the former Yugoslavia.
**Breeding:** One brown-spotted, white egg is laid in a stick-built nest at the top of a tree and incubated by both members of the pair for 52–55 days. The downy, helpless young fly after about 100 days.
**Confusing Species:** Griffon Vulture always shows buffy wing coverts and body and is far more numerous.

126

## Marsh Harrier *(Circus aeruginosus)*

L argest of the harriers, the Marsh Harrier has the typical harrier flap-flap-glide flight on V-shaped wings, low over the ground. The long, narrow wings and long tail distinguish it from other raptors, except other harriers and the kites. The male has black wing tips, grey tail and inner flight feathers and dark brown wing coverts and body. The female is brown with a creamy crown and leading edge to the wings. Immatures are also brown, but are cream only on the crown.

*Sweeping low over dense reedbeds in marsh or fenland, the Marsh Harrier will suddenly plummet down to pounce on prey. The female (below) has grey flight feathers, while those of the male (left) are dark brown.*

**Size:** 48–56cm (19–22in).
**Wing:** 372–426mm.
**Bill:** 20–37mm.
**Weight:** 405–800g.
**Voice:** A *kee-a* in courtship, otherwise silent.
**Habitat:** Marshes with reedbeds, also cereal fields near wetlands.
**Food:** Birds, small mammals, carrion.
**Range:** Breeds right across temperate Eurasia from Britain to Japan. In Europe, breeds Spain to southern Scandinavia, Ukraine and Russia. Winters in China, Southeast Asia and India, and in sub-Saharan Africa.
**Movements:** Populations breeding west of a line from Britain to Greece are

resident. Eastern birds migrate via Gibraltar and Sicily, but probably also on a broad front across the Mediterranean Sea and Sahara.
**Breeding:** Four or five bluish eggs are laid on a platform of stems in a reedbed or cereal field and incubated by the female for 33–38 days. The helpless, downy chicks fly after 35–40 days.
**Confusing Species:** Females of other harriers all have white rump. Black Kite has similar shape, but flies differently.

## Hen Harrier *(Circus cyaneus)*

A typically angular, long-winged, long-tailed harrier, the Hen Harrier has a flap-and-glide flight low over the ground. Both sexes are more heavily built than other harriers with similar plumage. The male is

grey above and white below with black wing tips and white rump. The female is brown with white rump and pale facial collar. The latter separates it from female Montagu's and Pallid Harriers.

*The elegant, pale grey and black male Hen Harrier (left) is distinguished from the smaller male Montagu's and Pallid Harriers by its white rump. Far left: the female.*

**Size:** 43–51cm (17–20in).
**Wing:** 323–392mm.
**Bill:** 15–20mm.
**Weight:** 300–708g.
**Voice:** Squabbling and cackling confined to the breeding season.
**Habitat:** Marshes and moorland in tundra, boreal and temperate zones.
**Food:** Birds and small mammals. Its depredations on grouse chicks brings it into conflict with shooting interests.
**Range:** South America, and circumpolar in the north. In Europe, breeds from Britain and Spain to Scandinavia, Russia and the Ukraine. Winters throughout western Europe.
**Movements:** Swedish and Russian birds move south and west to Europe and Turkey.
**Breeding:** Four to six pale blue eggs are laid on a shallow cup of twigs and stems, well hidden among ground vegetation. They are incubated for 29–39 days by the female, and the downy and helpless chicks fly after about 37 days.
**Confusing Species:** The male is like Montagu's and Pallid Harriers but with a white rump. The female can easily be confused with females of those species, but has a clear pale collar around an otherwise plainish face.

# Pallid Harrier *(Circus macrourus)*

J F M A M J J A S O N D

A mainly eastern harrier, the Pallid Harrier is similar to both Hen and Montagu's Harriers, especially the latter. The male is very pale grey, with diamond-shaped black wing tips. The female is brown, with a narrow white rump and distinctive brown and buff face pattern and pale collar. This is not easy to see, but is diagnostic after a little experience.

*The female Pallid Harrier is very similar to the equally lightweight female Montagu's, but has more pronounced facial barring, visible at close range.*

**Size:** 40–48cm (16–19in).
**Wing:** 327–393mm.
**Bill:** 15–20mm.
**Weight:** 318–379g.
**Voice:** A high-pitched *pree-pre-pre*.
**Habitat:** Marshes, extensive grasslands, heathlands.

**Food:** Small birds and voles.
**Range:** Confined to steppes of Ukraine and Russia from Black Sea to south central Siberia. Winters in India, sub-Saharan Africa, and locally in Greece.
**Movements:** Migrates through the eastern Mediterranean in autumn, before crossing the Sahara on a diagonal route. Follows a more westerly route in spring, when birds are more likely to appear in Europe.
**Breeding:** Four or five pale blue eggs are laid in a lined hollow and incubated by the female for 28–30 days. The downy, helpless chicks fledge after 35–40 days.
**Confusing Species:** Montagu's and Hen Harriers.

# Montagu's Harrier *(Circus pygargus)*

More lightly built than the similar Hen Harrier, the Montagu's Harrier has the same flap-and-glide flight on V-shaped wings low over the ground. The male is grey with black wing tips and a black line along the upper wing. The breast is streaked chestnut, unlike that of any other male harrier. The female is brown with a white rump and stronger face pattern than the female Hen Harrier, but is less marked than the female Pallid.

*The handsome male Montagu's Harrier is characterized by grey plumage with bold black wing tips and clear black bars on the underside of the wings, as well as above.*

J F M A M J J A S O N D

**Size:** 38–46cm (15–18in).
**Wing:** 346–393mm.
**Bill:** 13–17mm.
**Weight:** 227–445g.
**Voice:** A high pitched *kee-kee-kee* during courtship.
**Habitat:** Heaths, cereal fields, marshes.

**Food:** Small mammals and birds.
**Range:** Summer visitor, across Europe to south-central Siberia. Winters in India and sub-Saharan Africa. In Europe, its range extends from England and Denmark to Russia and the Ukraine.
**Movements:** Southwesterly orientation in autumn, probably across the Mediterranean and Sahara on a broad front. Gibraltar is a primary watchpoint.
**Breeding:** Four or five bluish eggs are laid on a platform of twigs on the ground and incubated by the female for 27–30 days. The down-covered, helpless chicks fly after 35–40 days.
**Confusing Species:** Female separated from the larger Hen Harrier and similar-sized Pallid Harrier by face pattern.

## Goshawk *(Accipiter gentilis)*

**Size:** 48–59cm (19–23in).
**Wing:** 306–366mm.
**Bill:** 20–26mm.
**Weight:** 300–365g.
**Voice:** A chattering note.
**Habitat:** Extensive forests of a wide variety of types.
**Food:** Birds and mammals.
**Range:** Circumpolar, breeds throughout Europe, though seldom common.
**Movements:** Some winter wandering to areas where it does not breed.
**Breeding:** Two or three bluish eggs are laid in a nest of twigs placed next to the trunk in a tall tree. The female incubates them for 36–41 days, and the downy, helpless young fledge in up to 45 days.
**Confusing Species:** Large female Sparrowhawk.

Although the larger female Goshawk is almost the size of a Common Buzzard, the male is only the size of a large female Sparrowhawk, so they are easily confused. The female is grey-brown above and heavily barred black and white below. In flight, both sexes show bulging secondaries.

*When soaring, the Goshawk often fans the white undertail coverts into a 'powder-puff', especially in display.*

## European Sparrowhawk *(Accipiter nisus)*

This widespread bird of prey frequents woodland and adjacent open land. The male is blue-grey above, closely barred rufous on white below. The female is larger and grey above, showing a bold supercilium.

*The male (right) has red barring unlike the female (left).*

**Size:** 28–38cm (11–15in).
**Wing:** 207–250mm.
**Bill:** 10–15mm.
**Weight:** 110–342g.
**Voice:** Ringing *kek-kek-kek.*
**Habitat:** All manner of woodlands.
**Food:** Small birds.
**Range:** Circumpolar in boreal and temperate zones. In Europe, breeds virtually everywhere except central European plains. Resident save in Scandinavia and northern Russia. Siberian birds winter in the Middle East, India and China.
**Movements:** North European birds move south and west in winter. Some migration over Gibraltar and the Bosphorus.

**Breeding:** Four or five brown eggs are laid in a cup of twigs in a tree and incubated by the female for 42 days. The downy, helpless chicks fly after 32 days.
**Confusing Species:** Male Goshawk shows bulging secondaries in flight.

## Levant Sparrowhawk *(Accipiter brevipes)*

This bird is blue-grey above and lightly barred rufous on white below. In flight, the whitish wings with black tips are by far the best means of identification.

**Size:** 33–38cm (13–15in).
**Wing:** 210–244mm.
**Bill:** 11–15mm.
**Weight:** 150–275g.
**Voice:** High pitched *kee-wick.*
**Habitats:** Woodlands, especially riverine forests.
**Food:** Insects and reptiles.
**Range:** Virtually endemic to the Western Palearctic. Breeds Balkans and western Ukraine. Presumed to winter in savanna Africa.
**Movements:** Vast numbers cross the Bosphorus and move around the eastern shores of the Black Sea. Passage continues through the eastern Mediterranean, but then disappears.
**Breeding:** Four or five bluish eggs, lightly spotted brown, are laid in a platform in a tree. They are incubated by the female for 30–35 days and the chicks fledge after 40–45 days.
**Confusing Species:** Only the Lesser Kestrel is as pale below, but black margins to the underwing are a fine field mark for the Levant Kestrel.

*The female (left) has a more extensive rosy flush across the chest and underwing coverts than does the generally paler male.*

## Common Buzzard *(Buteo buteo)*

There is a huge range of plumages, from virtually white below to dark brown, on this abundant, large bird of prey.

Typical birds have white bodies with a dark breast and lightly barred underwings, with dark carpal patches. In all plumages, broad wings, shortish tail and a compact head are good features.

*When soaring, the broad wings are held in a shallow V-shape.*

**Size:** 51–56cm (20–22in).
**Wing:** 368–419mm.
**Bill:** 19–25mm.
**Weight:** 525–1176g.
**Voice:** A mewing *pee-oo*.
**Habitat:** Woodland, but also moorland and hills, and grassy fields with adjacent copses or shelter belts.
**Food:** Small to medium-sized mammals.
**Range:** Boreal and temperate Eurasia. Breeds through Europe except upland Scandinavia. Winters from India to China and in South and East Africa.
**Movements:** Scandinavian birds cross to mainland Europe at Falsterbo. Russian birds, including huge numbers of red-tailed 'Steppe Buzzards' *B.b.vulpinus*, cross the Bosphorus.
**Breeding:** Three or four red-blotched white eggs in a bulky nest of sticks in a tree or on a rocky ledge; incubated by the female for about 42 days. Downy, helpless chicks fly after 40–45 days.
**Confusing Species:** Long-legged and Rough-legged Buzzards.

J F M A M J J A S O N D

## Long-legged Buzzard *(Buteo rufinus)*

Structurally like Common Buzzard, this bird similarly soars on wings held in a shallow V. It is brown above and below with a pale head. The tail is unbarred and pale rufous. The 'Steppe Buzzard' subspecies shows a similar tail but dissimilar underwings.

*In flight, pale wings contrast with distinct rufous underwing coverts and a rufous tail.*

**Size:** 51–64cm (20–25in).
**Wing:** 425–496mm.
**Bill:** 24–32mm.
**Weight:** 590–1760g.
**Voice:** Mostly silent.
**Habitat:** Semi-desert, barren hills.
**Food:** Small mammals, reptiles and insects.
**Range:** From Morocco through Balkans and Turkey to the Middle East and Ukraine to south-central Siberia. Winters Sahel zone of eastern Africa, Arabia and northern India.
**Movements:** Small Balkan population mostly migrants, but little solid evidence of passage anywhere.

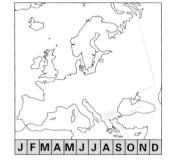

J F M A M J J A S O N D

**Breeding:** Two or three brown-blotched, white eggs in a bulky nest on a crag and incubated by the female for 28 days. The chicks fly after 40–42 days.
**Confusing Species:** Common Buzzard, especially subspecies *B.b.vulpinus*.

## Rough-legged Buzzard *(Buteo lagopus)*

This high-Arctic equivalent of the Common Buzzard is mainly a winter visitor to temperate Europe. It is similar in size and structure to the Common Buzzard, but soars on flat, not V-shaped wings. It hovers more than other European buzzards. It is dark brown above, with a prominent pale head.

*In flight, shows a dark belly (not breast) patch, pale underwing with prominent dark carpal patches, and white tail with a broad black terminal band.*

J F M A M J J A S O N D

**Size:** 50–61cm (20–24in).
**Wing:** 403–454mm.
**Bill:** 20–25mm.
**Weight:** 600–1660g.
**Voice:** Usually silent.
**Habitat:** Tundra with crags and cliffs, also mountain ranges. Winters mostly on marshes and other lowland wilderness areas.
**Food:** Small mammals, mostly lemmings and voles.
**Range:** Circumpolar in the north. In Europe breeds Scandinavian mountain chain and across Lapland and northern Russia. Winters temperate Europe east of a line from Britain to Yugoslavia and across central southern Siberia.
**Movements:** Whole population moves southwards on broad front.
**Breeding:** Two or three brown-blotched white eggs are laid in a nest of sticks placed on a rocky outcrop and are incubated, mainly by the female, for about 28 days. The helpless, down-covered chicks fly after 40–42 days.
**Confusing Species:** Common Buzzards often have a well-marked tail band.

## Imperial Eagle (Aquila heliaca)

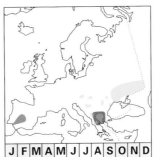

This large eagle is dark brown, with a pale crown and pale 'braces' over the back. The juvenile is sandy brown, with sandy wing coverts and a white rump; black flight feathers are marked by a narrow white wingbar, a white trailing edge and a pale inner primary patch. The Spanish Imperial Eagle, *A. adalberti*, is a distinct species and differs in having a white leading edge to the wing and bigger, whiter 'braces'.

**Size:** 72–84cm (28–33in).
**Wing:** 540–634mm.
**Bill:** 39–47mm.
**Weight:** 2410–4530g.
**Voice:** Deep barking notes.
**Habitat:** Woodlands in mountain and lowland areas.
**Food:** Mammals, birds and carrion.
**Range:** Spanish Imperial Eagle resident Spain and locally Portugal. Imperial Eagle breeds from Czech Republic and Romania eastwards through Ukraine and Turkey to south-central Siberia. Winters Turkey, Middle East, India and China. Central European and Ukrainian breeders are summer visitors.

**Movements:** Small European population moves to Balkans, with some continuing into Asia via the Bosphorus.
**Breeding:** Two brown-spotted white eggs are laid in a huge nest in a tree, used year after year, and are incubated by both sexes for 43 days. The downy, helpless young fly after 60 days.
**Confusing Species:** Steppe, Lesser Spotted and Spotted Eagles are all equally dark, but lack the pale crown and braces of the Imperial Eagle.

*This well-proportioned bird flies majestically on flat wings, which it seldom flaps.*

## Golden Eagle (Aquila chrysaetos)

Typical of the *Aquila* eagles, this is a broad-winged bird, marked by a prominent head and large tail. Most of the plumage is brown. Immature has white flashes at the base of the primaries and inner secondaries, and a white tail with a broad black band.

**Size:** 76–90cm (30–35in).
**Wing:** 565–685mm.
**Bill:** 40–50mm.
**Weight:** 550–720g.
**Voice:** A yelping *kaa*, but mostly silent.
**Habitat:** Mountains and a few lowland wilderness. Also Russian boreal zone.

*Living mainly in hill and mountain areas, this large, majestic eagle soars on 'waisted' wings, held in a V. As its name suggests, it has golden upperwing coverts and a golden crown.*

**Food:** Mammals and birds.
**Range:** Northern circumpolar. Breeds Scotland, Spain, Alps, Italy, Greece, Romania, Yugoslavia, thence east across Siberia to Asia and Japan. Mainly resident, but northern Russian birds move south and west.
**Movements:** Regular wintering in southern Sweden suggests immigration.
**Breeding:** Two brown-blotched white eggs in a mass of sticks in a tree or on a cliff ledge; incubated by the female for 43–45 days and the single surviving chick takes 63–70 days to fledge.
**Confusing Species:** Steppe and Imperial Eagle, when upperparts are not seen.

131

## Lesser Spotted Eagle *(Aquila pomarina)*

A medium-sized, dark eagle, which is a widespread summer visitor to eastern Europe, the Lesser Spotted Eagle migrates across the

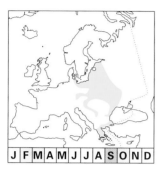

Bosphorus in spectacular numbers. The adult is dark brown at rest. In flight, it shows a white patch at the base of the primaries and a narrow white 'horseshoe' at the base of the tail.

*The most useful identification feature for this eagle is that the wing coverts are paler than the flight feathers when seen from both above and below.*

**Size:** 61–64cm (24–25in).
**Wing:** 446–505mm.
**Bill:** 27–34mm.
**Weight:** 1067–1750g.
**Voice:** High-pitched yelps and barks.
**Habitat:** Woodland, often near rivers.
**Food:** Small mammals.
**Range:** Western subspecies *A. p. pomarina* summer visitor across Poland, Hungary and parts of western Russia.
**Movements:** Vast migration over Bosphorus, over 1000 per day at peak.
**Breeding:** Two, red-spotted white eggs are laid in a twig nest high in a tree near a forest margin. The female incubates for 40–45 days. The downy, helpless chicks fledge after 50–55 days.
**Confusing Species:** The Spotted Eagle is larger and has broader wings.

## Spotted Eagle *(Aquila clanga)*

The adult Spotted Eagle is dark brown with a short tail, less than a third the width of the wing in length. The very broad wings show a prominent

secondary bulge. The underwing pattern shows darker coverts than flight feathers – the reverse pattern of the otherwise very similar Lesser Spotted Eagle.

*The plumage of a Spotted Eagle in its first winter (right) is almost black, with white spots scattered on the coverts and scapulars.*

**Size:** 66–72cm (26–28in).
**Wing:** 477–542mm.
**Bill:** 31–40mm.
**Weight:** 1665–3200g.
**Voice:** High-pitched barking calls.
**Habitat:** Extensive lowland forests and marshes.
**Food:** Birds, small mammals, carrion meat.
**Range:** Summer visitor from Poland across Russia and Siberia to Sea of Japan. Winters in China, India, Turkey and the Middle East. Some winter in Italy, European Turkey and adjacent Greece.
**Movements:** Some passage across Bosphorus, but usually later than normal peak observation period.
**Breeding:** Two greyish eggs, laid in a

large nest of twigs in a forest tree, are incubated by the female for 42–44 days. The downy, helpless chicks fly after 60–65 days.
**Confusing Species:** The Lesser Spotted Eagle.

## Steppe Eagle *(Aquila nipalensis)*

*The adult (below) has plain brown wings with faint black-barred flight feathers. The juvenile (left) has a white wingbar and coverts paler than the flight feathers.*

A brown eagle, that breeds in Russia, the Steppe Eagle wanders westwards only occasionally. At rest, the yellow gape extends to behind the eye. The immature shows a broad white bar separating the brown underwing coverts from the black flight feathers.

**Size:** 66–86cm (26–34in).
**Wing:** 565–645mm.
**Bill:** 34–42mm.
**Weight:** 1950–3900g.
**Voice:** A yapping while breeding, but otherwise silent.
**Habitat:** Steppes, marshes.

**Food:** Small mammals, carrion, piracy.
**Range:** Summer visitor to central Asia, resident India. Winters within range, in Africa south of the Sahara and in the Middle East.
**Movements:** Migrates from Russia on a broad front to Africa, though some concentration around eastern Black Sea. Large concentrations at Eilat occur in spring, but not in autumn.
**Breeding:** Lays one to three, lightly spotted white eggs in a large nest placed on a mound, ruin, haystack or bush. They are incubated by the female only for about 45 days. Once hatched, the down-covered, helpless young take about 60 days to fledge.
**Confusing Species:** All other dark brown eastern eagles are potentially confusing, except when close.

## Booted Eagle (Hieraaetus pennatus)

**Size:** 46–53cm (18–21in).
**Wing:** 342–425mm.
**Bill:** 20–26mm.
**Weight:** 510–1250g.
**Voice:** Whistles and cackles.
**Habitat:** Woodland, especially in hilly regions.
**Food:** Mostly birds.
**Range:** Summer visitor across southern Europe to the Middle East, North Africa and central, southern Asia. Winters in India and savanna Africa.
**Movements:** Regular migrant at Gibraltar, Bosphorus and eastern shores of the Black Sea, but most abundant at Gibraltar with perhaps 20,000 crossing in autumn. Also crosses wider parts of Mediterranean, though in no great numbers.
**Breeding:** Two brown-stained, white eggs are laid in a substantial nest in a tree. They are incubated for 36–38 days by the female and the downy and helpless chicks fly about 50 days after hatching.
**Confusing Species:** Common Buzzard. Short-toed Eagle may be pale below, but has a dark head and a barred tail and lacks the fully black flight feathers.

*White underside with black flight feathers in the pale phase.*

*Almost black with pale tail in the dark phase.*

The Booted Eagle is slightly smaller than a Common Buzzard, but is of typical eagle structure, with its long broad wings, small but prominent head and well-proportioned tail. Pale phase birds are easy to identify, with black flight feathers and white body and wing linings. Dark phase birds are best distinguished from dark Common Buzzard by shape, but pale, unbarred tail is a helpful feature. It soars on flat wings.

## Bonelli's Eagle (Hieraaetus fasciatus)

A large eagle that is resident around the Mediterranean. The adult is grey-brown above and white below, with black streaking on its breast and flanks. The upperparts show a distinct pale patch on middle of upperback. The immature is paler, showing tawny body and wing coverts and pale flight feathers. Soars on flat wings with prominent head and tail.

*At a distance, underwings appear all-dark, but are marked by heavy black bar bordering paler coverts.*

**Size:** 64–72cm (25–28in).
**Wing:** 465–523mm.
**Bill:** 33–36mm.
**Weight:** 1500–2386g.
**Voice:** Dog-like barking and grunts.
**Habitat:** Mountains and hilly country with rocky outcrops and cliffs.
**Food:** Mammals and birds.
**Range:** Resident in southern Europe, North Africa and Middle East to India and China. Also in southern Africa, where known as African Hawk-eagle.
**Movements:** Local wandering, moves to higher mountains in summer.
**Breeding:** Two brown-spotted, white eggs are laid on a large platform of twigs placed on a cliff or in a large tree. They are incubated for 42–44 days by the female and the downy, helpless chicks fledge after 65 days.
**Confusing Species:** The pale phase Booted Eagle has similar markings, but shorter, broader wings.

133

## Short-toed Eagle *(Circaetus gallicus)*

*The Short-toed Eagle is a skilful hunter of snakes and other reptiles, which it captures by pouncing from a hovering, Kestrel-like flight over hillsides.*

A medium-sized eagle, the Short-toed Eagle is a summer visitor to the Mediterranean basin, and eastwards through Russia to central Siberia. It is pale greyish brown above, white below with barred breast and has a dark head. In flight, it often appears very pale below with dark head. It hovers when hunting.

J F M A M J J A S O N D

**Size:** 61–66cm (24–26in).
**Wing:** 506–557mm.
**Bill:** 32–39mm.
**Weight:** 1180–2320g.
**Voice:** Mewing and barking.
**Habitat:** Dry, open, often hilly, country.
**Food:** Snakes and other reptiles.
**Range:** Summer visitor to southern Europe and the east as far north as St Petersburg, eastwards through Turkey and Middle East to southern Siberia. Resident India. Winters in Sahel Africa.

**Movements:** Concentrates especially at Gibraltar, but also at Sicily, Bosphorus and eastern Black Sea coasts. Thence moves southward passing into Africa.
**Breeding:** A single white egg is laid on a twig platform in a tree and incubated by the female for 47 days. The downy helpless chick flies after 70–75 days.
**Confusing Species:** Pale phase Booted Eagle, but it lacks the dark head.

## Osprey *(Pandion haliaetus)*

This medium-sized bird of prey is dark brown above, and white below, with a distinctive small head and bill, dark eye stripe and white crest.

In flight, it is white below with barred flight feathers and tail, contrasting white wing coverts and bold, black carpal patches. It flies on gull-like wings.

**Size:** 51–59cm (20–23in).
**Wing:** 448–518mm.
**Bill:** 30–36mm.
**Weight:** 1208–2050g.
**Voice:** Loud, whistled *tew-tew*.
**Habitat:** Lakes, rivers, reservoirs and sea coasts.
**Food:** Fish taken in spectacular dives after hovering.
**Range:** Cosmopolitan. In Europe, breeds Scotland and Scandinavia, eastwards across Russia and Ukraine, and in the western Mediterranean. Winters Africa south of the Sahara, though most adults concentrate in the north.
**Movements:** Migrates southwards on a broad front; extremely rare in Europe in winter.
**Breeding:** Two or three, red-blotched cream-coloured eggs are laid in a huge nest of sticks placed in a tree, or on an island or cliff top. Incubation, which is shared, takes 35–38 days and the downy, helpless chicks fly after 51–59 days.
**Confusing Species:** No pale European raptors have long, angular gull-like wings and flight.

J F M A M J J A S O N D

*Unique among European birds of prey, the Osprey plunges into lakes to seize fish. These may may weigh up to 1kg (35oz), although most are smaller.*

## Common Kestrel *(Falco tinnunculus)*

**Size:** 33–35cm (13–14in).
**Wing:** 233–272mm.
**Bill:** 13–17mm.
**Weight:** 117–260g.
**Voice:** High pitched *kee-kee-kee*.
**Habitat:** Cities, towns, marshes, heaths, farmland, cliffs and coasts.
**Food:** Small mammals and sometimes small birds.
**Range:** Breeds throughout much of Old World. In Europe, absent only Iceland.
**Movements:** European birds are resident from Denmark to Crimea westwards. Birds that breed to the east migrate south and west to join residents.

As they scan the ground for prey, Kestrels hover (below) over roadside verges or fields, before plummeting down to pounce.

**Breeding:**
Four or five white eggs, heavily speckled brown, are laid in a hole or on a ledge on a cliff or building and are incubated for 27–29 days, mainly by the female. The downy, helpless young fly after 27–39 days.
**Confusing Species:** Lesser Kestrel is smaller.

The most widespread and common European bird of prey, the Kestrel is frequently seen hovering over open land or beside roads. The male has a grey head, marked by a black moustache, a grey tail with a black sub-terminal band and a brown, heavily spotted back. The female is heavily barred black on brown above and streaked black on cream below.

## Lesser Kestrel *(Falco naumanni)*

This dainty, gregarious falcon is a fast declining summer visitor to southern and eastern Europe. The male has an unspotted brown back, grey head, tiny moustache and grey tail. The female has a brown, heavily spotted back and is creamy below with streaking. Both sexes are thinner and smaller than the Kestrel, have a more fluttering flight, hover less frequently and show long central tail feathers.

The male Lesser Kestrel is a beautifully marked bird with a rufous back and inner wings, contrasting with grey wing panels and tail fading to black.

**Size:** 28–33cm (11–13in).
**Wing:** 229–251mm.
**Bill:** 12–14mm.
**Weight:** 90–208g.
**Voice:** High-pitched *kee-kee-kee*.
**Habitat:** Grasslands close to towns and villages.
**Food:** Insects.
**Range:** Summer visitor to the Mediterranean, and from Turkey and Ukraine eastwards to southeastern Siberia and northern China. Winters savanna Africa. The decline in population and disappearance from many previous haunts is due mainly to changing land use and modern farming techniques. The largest population is in Spain.
**Movements:** Some winter southern Spain. Most migrate on a broad front to Africa as far south as the Cape.
**Breeding:** Four or five white eggs, lightly speckled with brown, are laid in a hole in a building or cliff and incubated by the female for 28 days. The down-covered, helpless chicks take 26–28 days to fledge.
**Confusing Species:** Common Kestrel is larger, has a square tail and is more spotted. The male is more rufous on the back of the wings.

## Red-footed Falcon *(Falco vespertinus)*

**Size:** 28–30cm (11–12in).
**Wing:** 237–264mm.
**Bill:** 11–14mm.
**Weight:** 130–197g.
**Voice:** Angry *kee-kee-kee.*
**Habitat:** Open grasslands and savannas, with woods and copses.
**Food:** Insects taken in the air and by shrike-like pounces.
**Range:** Summer visitor from central Europe eastwards to eastern Siberia.
**Movements:** Migrates on a broad front to winter in southern Africa. In spring, isolated birds may often be seen well to the west of the usual breeding range in Europe.
**Breeding:** Three or four speckled, buffy eggs are laid, mostly in nests of Rooks

*Unlike most other birds of prey, the Red-footed Falcon migrates and breeds gregariously.*

Highly gregarious, this little falcon is a summer visitor to eastern Europe. The adult male is slate-grey, marked by a red eye ring, red feet and a rust undertail. The female is barred grey above, with a gingery head and breast. In flight, ginger rufous extends over the underwing coverts. Frequently seen perching on roadside wires and posts, or hovering.

that have fledged. The eggs are incubated by the female alone for 28 days. The downy and helpless chicks fly after 26–28 days.

## Merlin *(Falco columbarius)*

A small falcon that is a summer visitor to northern areas. The male is blue-grey above, with buffy underparts, streaked brown. The female is brown above, with a narrow moustache, and heavily streaked underparts and multiple tail bands. Both sexes are more robust and shorter winged than the similar Hobby.

**Size:** 25–33cm (10–13in).
**Wing:** 191–222mm.
**Bill:** 12–15mm.
**Weight:** 125–300g.
**Voice:** A chattering *kee-kee-kee.*
**Habitat:** Tundra and moorland in boreal and north temperate zones. Winters on marshes, estuaries and coasts.
**Food:** Small birds.
**Range:** Circumpolar in the north. In Europe, breeds Iceland, Britain and Ireland, and from Scandinavia eastwards. Winters over much of temperate Europe.
**Movements:** Migrates on a broad front through Europe, avoiding mountains.

**Breeding:** Five or six, red-spotted buff eggs are laid in a hollow on the ground and incubated for 28–32 days, mainly by the female. The downy, helpless chicks fly after 25–30 days.
**Confusing Species:** The darker Hobby has a bold moustache and is only a summer visitor to Europe.

*This is a long-winged, chunky falcon that regularly preys on flocks of Starlings in winter.*

**Size:** 30–35cm (12–14in).
**Wing:** 237–282mm.
**Bill:** 12–15mm.
**Weight:** 131–340g.
**Voice:** High-pitched *ki-ki-ki.*
**Habitat:** Open country with copses and shelter belts, also marshes and lakes. Winters in savannas.
**Food:** Insects and aerial birds; often hunts at dawn and dusk.
**Range:** Summer visitor across temperate Europe and northern Asia to Japan. In Europe, absent from Iceland, northern Britain and most of Scandinavia. Winters in India and southern Africa.
**Movements:** Migrates on a broad front across the Mediterranean.
**Breeding:** Two or three yellowish eggs, speckled red, are laid in the old nest of another species inside a tree. They are incubated by the female for about 28 days and the downy, helpless young fly after 28–32 days.
**Confusing Species:** Pale phase Eleonora's Falcon is equally angular, but shows dark underwing. The wings of the Merlin and the Kestrel are broader.

*The adult bird has red undertail coverts, which the juvenile lacks.*

J F M A M J J A S O N D

A fast-flying, long-winged falcon, the Hobby is a widespread summer visitor to southern and temperate Europe. Blue-black above, it is marked by a bold black moustache and white spots on the hind neck that create a virtually complete white collar. The white underparts are heavily streaked, and the undertail coverts bright rufous. In flight, it shows heavily barred underwings. The long, sickle-like wings are like those of a large swift. It is often seen hawking for insects.

---

Eleonora's Falcon *(Falco eleonorae)*

A gregarious summer visitor to the Mediterranean, Eleonora's Falcon has a breeding routine geared to the autumn migration of small birds across that sea. There are two distinct colour phases, pale and dark. Pale phase birds resemble the Hobby, but with creamy (not white), heavily streaked underparts and a prominent moustache. Its heavier build and sooty underwing separate it from other species at all times.

*The dark phase bird (right) has a sooty black belly, while the pale phase bird (below right) has a tawny, streaked belly.*

**Size:** 35–40cm (14–16in).
**Wing:** 300–347mm.
**Bill:** 15–19mm.
**Weight:** 340–495g.
**Voice:** A variety of repeated high-pitched calls.
**Habitat:** Rocky islands.
**Food:** Aerial insects and migrating birds caught after dark and often hoarded in 'larders'.
**Range:** Confined to Mediterranean islands and a few islands along the coast of Atlantic Africa, but most concentrated in the Aegean. The birds winter in Madagascar.
**Movements:** Migration obscure.
**Breeding:** Two or three brown-blotched white eggs are laid on a cliff ledge in a colony. They are incubated for 28–33 days by the female and the helpless, downy chicks fly after 28–35 days.

**Confusing Species:** Pale phase birds could be confused with Hobby and Lanner, but all have dark underwings.

J F M A M J J A S O N D

## Lanner Falcon (Falco biarmicus)

This long-winged, angular falcon resembles a pale, thin Peregrine. The upperparts are light grey with a sandy crown and narrow moustache. The underparts are white, lightly streaked black. In flight, white primaries and lightly streaked coverts below create a distinctly pale impression. The tail is neatly barred.

J F M A M J J A S O N D

**Size:** 33–51cm (13–20in).
**Wing:** 310–359mm.
**Bill:** 20–23mm.
**Weight:** 500–900g.
**Voice:** A shrill, repeated *kee-kee-kee.*
**Habitat:** Bare hillsides, steppes and semi-desert.
**Food:** Birds.
**Range:** Resident from Italy eastwards through the Mediterranean to the Middle East and over most of semi-desert and savanna Africa.
**Movements:** Some local wandering.
**Breeding:** Three or four white eggs, spotted with brown, are laid on a cliff ledge or in the old nest of another species in a tree. Incubation, which is shared by the male and the female, lasts 31–38 days, and the downy, helpless chicks take up to 45 days to fledge.
**Confusing Species:** No medium-sized falcon is so pale.

*In flight, the Lanner Falcon shows its pale underside with no contrast between wings and body.*

## Saker Falcon (Falco cherrug)

Large and heavily built, the Saker Falcon is a summer visitor to the steppes of eastern Europe. It is brown above, marked by a contrasting pale head and only the faintest of moustachial streaks. Underparts are white with heavy dark streaking. In flight, the pale flight feathers contrast with heavily barred underwing coverts. The wings are much broader than those of Lanner, especially at their base.

J F M A M J J A S O N D

**Size:** 46–56cm (18–22in).
**Wing:** 347–412mm.
**Bill:** 20–26mm.
**Weight:** 730–1300g.
**Voice:** A repeated *kee-kee-kee.*
**Habitat:** Grassy steppes and hillsides.
**Food:** Mammals, reptiles.
**Range:** Breeds from eastern Europe through Ukraine to southern Siberia and northern China. Winters mainly south of breeding range and in Sahel East Africa. In Europe, breeds Slovakia and in the Danube river system, where it is largely resident.
**Movements:** Though some definite migration occurs, most European birds move no great distance. Some Siberian birds migrate to Sudan and Ethiopia.

**Breeding:** Four, red-spotted cream eggs are laid on a cliff ledge, in an old nest of another species, or on a pylon. They are incubated by both sexes for about 28 days and the downy, helpless young fly after 40–45 days.
**Confusing Species:** Lanner and dark phase Gyr Falcons are pale below, but the Saker's brown upperparts identify it at all times.

*The contrast between the pale head and brown upperparts is a major field mark.*

138

## Gyr Falcon *(Falco rusticolus)*

A huge, pale bird, the Gyr Falcon is an occasional vagrant south of its high-Arctic breeding grounds. The pale phase is white above and below, flecked across the wings with black arrowheads and over the tail with incomplete bars. The dark phase is grey above with white feather margins, creating a scaly effect. The breast is heavily spotted and streaked. In flight, pale birds are all-but white below. Dark birds have pale flight feathers with dark underwing coverts and body.

J F M A M J J A S O N D

*In the medieval sport of falconry, the majestic Gyr Falcon was reserved for use only by royalty.*

**Size:** 50–62cm (20–24in).
**Wing:** 352–415mm.
**Bill:** 22–30mm.
**Weight:** 800–2100g.
**Voice:** Repeated *kee-kee-kee*.
**Habitat:** Tundra, mountains in south.

**Food:** Birds.
**Range:** Northern circumpolar. In Europe breeds Iceland, Scandinavian mountain chain and northernmost Russia. In winter some birds move southwards. Vagrant to rest of northern Europe.

**Movements:** Short distances.
**Breeding:** Up to four red-spotted buff eggs, laid on a ledge, are incubated for 34–36 days by the female. The downy, helpless young fledge at 46–49 days.
**Confusing Species:** A small, dark phase male may be confused with a Peregrine or, when flying, with a Saker.

## Peregrine Falcon *(Falco peregrinus)*

A large, robust and powerful falcon that flies on long pointed wings, the Peregrine Falcon is one of the most effective aerial killers. The upperparts are dark blue-grey; the white cheek, marked by a prominent black moustache, is visible at considerable range. The white underparts are heavily barred black. The juvenile is brown above and streaked brown below. The long, angular, broad-based wings, short tail and deep chest are decisive physical features.

J F M A M J J A S O N D

*In flight, the wing coverts are heavily barred, while the flight feathers are significantly paler.*

**Size:** 38–48cm (15–19in).
**Wing:** 291–367mm.
**Bill:** 18–26mm.
**Weight:** 582–1300g.
**Voice:** Shrill *ke-ke-ke*.
**Habitat:** Mountains, sea cliffs, tundra, boreal forests. Winters in marshes and on estuaries.
**Food:** Birds, particularly Rock Doves and Feral Pigeons.
**Range:** Cosmopolitan. In Europe, widespread but local resident. Scandinavian and eastern birds, from Latvia to the Caspian Sea, are summer visitors which winter southwards throughout Europe.
**Movements:** Migrates on a broad front, but birds living in the north, eastwards of Finland, may cross the Sahara to winter in Africa.
**Breeding:** Three or four reddish-speckled creamy eggs are laid on a rocky ledge and incubated for 28 or 29 days by the female. The helpless, downy chicks fly after 35–42 days.
**Confusing Species:** Saker, Gyr and Lanner Falcons do not show blue-grey upperparts or such a prominent moustache as Peregrine.

## Hazel Grouse *(Bonasa bonasia)*

Grey, spotted upperparts barred with black, brown and white camouflage this secretive grouse. Both sexes have a black band on a large tail.

*Male Hazel Grouse (below) has a small crest, red comb above eye and prominent white-bordered black bib.*

**Size:** 35–38cm (14–15in).
**Wing:** 159–176mm.
**Bill:** 10–11mm.
**Weight:** 305–490g.
**Voice:** Shrill, repeated, whistled call.
**Habitat:** Boreal and mixed forests.

**Food:** Buds, shoots and seeds.
**Range:** Western European mountains across Eurasia in boreal and temperate zones. Breeds from the Alps east to the former Yugoslavia, north to Belgium, and from Scandinavia to Russia.

**Movements:** None.
**Breeding:** Six to ten brown-speckled buffy eggs in a hollow, well-hidden among bushes and incubated by the female for 23–27 days. The active and downy young fly after 20–30 days.

---

## Willow Grouse/Red Grouse *(Lagopus lagopus)*

Male Willow Grouse has white wings and belly in summer. British and Irish subspecies, Red Grouse, lacks white in plumage at all times.

**Size:** 33–38cm (13–15in).
**Wing:** 187–218mm.
**Bill:** 10–12mm.
**Weight:** 405–750g.
**Voice:** Echoing *go-bak go-bak.*
**Habitat:** Tundra, taiga, boreal heaths and moorland.
**Food:** Shoots and buds, mostly of heather.
**Range:** Northern circumpolar. In Europe, breeds in Britain and from Scandinavia across northern Russia.
**Movements:** None, except that extreme northern birds move southwards in winter.
**Breeding:** Six to eleven brown-blotched creamy buff eggs are laid in a hollow and incubated for 20–26 days by the female. The active, down-covered

*In summer, the male Willow Grouse is reddish with a red comb (far left). In winter, both sexes turn white (left), and look similar to Ptarmigan.*

chicks fly after 12–13 days.
**Confusing Species:** Ptarmigan is grey, but white in winter. It is distinguished from the Willow Grouse by black lores.

---

## Ptarmigan *(Lagopus mutus)*

The Ptarmigan is the high-altitude, high-latitude equivalent of the Willow Grouse. The male has a red comb above the eye. In summer, the whole plumage is barred greys and blacks, broken by a white belly and wings. In winter, it turns white, apart from the dark lores.

*The Ptarmigan's summer plumage (left) is effective camouflage among the bare, rocky areas it prefers. In winter, the plumage is white with dark lores (above).*

**Size:** 33–38cm (13–14in).
**Wing:** 187–215mm.
**Bill:** 9–10mm.
**Weight:** 243–586g.
**Voice:** A cackling *ar-ar-ar-ka-ka-ka*
**Habitat:** Rocky plateaux and tundra.
**Food:** Shoots and berries.
**Range:** North circumpolar. Resident as far north as there is open land or rock in summer. In Europe, breeds Iceland, Scotland, Scandinavia and northeastern Russia, as well as in the Pyrenees and Alps, where it has retained a foothold since the last ice age.
**Movements:** None, except that some birds descend to lower levels in severe weather.
**Breeding:** Five to ten brown-blotched white eggs are laid on the ground and

incubated by the female for 24–26 days. The active, downy chicks are able to feed themselves and can fly after only 10 days.
**Confusing Species:** Only Willow Grouse in white winter plumage, but it has white lores instead of black ones.

## Black Grouse *(Tetrao tetrix)*

**Size:** 38–56cm (15–22in).
**Wing:** 217–266mm.
**Bill:** 12–16mm.
**Weight:** 750–1750g.
**Voice:** A repeated *roo-koo* at leks.
**Habitat:** Conifer forests with grassy and moorland margins.
**Food:** Shoots and berries.
**Range:** Breeds right across Eurasia, from Europe to the Sea of Japan. In Europe, breeds Britain, Germany and Scandinavia and across most of Russia, as well as in the Alps and mountains of the Balkans.
**Movements:** Resident.
**Breeding:** Males gather at traditional leks, usually on open ground, where females come to mate. Six to ten brown-spotted buffy eggs are laid in a depression, well-hidden on the ground. Incubated by the female for 23–26 days, and the active, downy chicks fly after 28 days.
**Confusing Species:** Female with female Red/Willow Grouse, but darker, with a notched tail.

The Black Grouse is an almost all-black gamebird of forest edges. The male is black, with a blue metallic gloss, marked by white undertail coverts, a red comb, lyre-shaped tail, and white on the wings in flight. Female is smaller, with brown barring and a notched tail.

*Male Black Grouse (left) congregate at communal grounds, known as leks, to display.*

## Capercaillie *(Tetrao urogallus)*

A huge, Turkey-like gamebird, the Capercaillie inhabits the conifer forests of the boreal zone, as well as the mountains to the south. The male is a stout, all-black bird, with strong head marked by a red eye-ring and a substantial white bill. The female is much smaller, barred brown, buff and black, with a dull-orange breast.

*The male Capercaillie raises its fanned tail in display (left) to attract a female and to warn off other males. The female (right) is a brownish orange colour, and is well camouflaged.*

**Size:** 56–91cm (22–36in).
**Wing:** 286–400mm.
**Bill:** 19–35mm.
**Weight:** 1500–6500g.
**Voice:** Loud, hollow *kok-kok-kok* and a series of clicks ending in a *pop*.
**Habitat:** Conifer forests.
**Food:** Shoots, berries, leaves.

**Range:** Breeds across northern Eurasia. In Europe, in Scotland, Scandinavia and across the northern half of Russia, and also in the Pyrenees and mountains of northern Spain, the Alps, and mountains of the former Yugoslavia, the Carpathians and elsewhere as far north as central Germany.

**Movements:** Mostly resident.
**Breeding:** Five to eight reddish-blotched buffy eggs are laid in a lined hollow and incubated for 26–29 days by the female. The active and downy chicks fly after 14–21 days.
**Confusing Species:** None, but be aware of Black Grouse.

## Chukar Partridge *(Alectoris chukar)*

This is a typical 'red-legged' partridge, with a black line enclosing a white facial bib and chestnut and black flank bars. The upperparts are grey, and the underparts warm buff. The black mask does not touch the bill, as in Rock Partridge.

*The red-legged partridges have distinctive faces. The Chukar Partridge (right) shows white between bill and eye.*

**Size:** 33–35cm (13–14in).
**Wing:** 48–172mm.
**Bill:** 13–16mm.
**Weight:** 460–595g.
**Voice:** A clear *chook-arr chook-arr*

**Habitat:** Dry, rocky hillsides with scanty vegetation.
**Food:** Mainly seeds; also leaves, shoots and some insects.
**Range:** From a toehold in Greece and Bulgaria across Turkey to the Middle East, central Asia to northern China. Introduced western North America and western Europe.
**Movements:** Resident.
**Breeding:** Eight to fourteen buff-coloured eggs with reddish spots are laid in an almost bare ground hollow. Incubation, by the female alone, lasts 24–26 days and the active, downy chicks fly after 15 or 16 days, although they stay with the adults for much longer.
**Confusing Species:** Rock Partridge has narrower and more numerous flank bars.

J F M A M J J A S O N D

## Rock Partridge *(Alectoris graeca)*

The 'red-legged' partridge of southeastern Europe is typical of all members of this group. It has grey upperparts, red bill, black line enclosing a white bib, and chestnut and black flank bars, which are narrower than on other species.

J F M A M J J A S O N D

*The black facial markings of the Rock Partridge (right) links the eyes and bill quite clearly.*

**Size:** 33–35cm (13–14in).
**Wing:** 157–174mm.
**Bill:** 12–16mm.
**Weight:** 450–800g.
**Voice:** A *chuck-chuck-chuck...ar...chuck...ar...chuck.*

**Habitat:** Rocky slopes with low vegetation.
**Food:** Shoots, buds, seeds and insects.
**Range:** From Alps, through mountains to Greece and mountains of central Italy.
**Movements:** Resident.

**Breeding:** Eight to fourteen brown-blotched buffy eggs are laid in a hollow, among vegetation, and incubated by the female for 24–26 days. The active, downy young fly after just 7–14 days.
**Confusing Species:** Chukar Partridge.

## Red-legged Partridge *(Alectoris rufa)*

A typical partridge with a rotund shape, short tail and rounded wings, the Red-legged Partridge is resident in western Europe and introduced to Britain. The upperparts are brown, with grey flanks barred with series of bold black, chestnut and white vertical stripes.

**Size:** 33–35cm (13–14in).
**Wing:** 152–169mm.
**Bill:** 12–15mm.
**Weight:** 391–547g.
**Voice:** Loud *chuk-chuk-chukar.*
**Habitat:** Heaths, dry fields, hillsides.
**Food:** Shoots, buds, seeds, insects.
**Range:** Endemic to Iberia, France, Corsica and northwestern Italy. Introduced Britain.
**Movements:** Resident.
**Breeding:** Ten to sixteen red-spotted yellowish eggs are laid in a hollow and

*The white bib of the Red-legged Partridge (left) is enclosed by a black line bordered by multiple black spots forming a streaked necklace around neck and chest.*

incubated by the female. A second clutch may be incubated by the male. Incubation lasts 23–25 days and the active, downy chicks fly after 10 days.
**Confusing Species:** None of the other 'red-legged' partridges has a streaked necklace below the bib.

J F M A M J J A S O N D

## Grey Partridge *(Perdix perdix)*

**Size:** 28–33cm (11–13in).
**Wing:** 151–166mm.
**Bill:** 11–14mm.
**Weight:** 320–433g.
**Voice:** A rasping *kirrick*, plus a chattering *kri-kri-kri-kri*.
**Habitat:** Heathland and fields.
**Food:** Seeds, shoots, insects.
**Range:** Resident across most of Europe from the Atlantic coast, eastwards to central Siberia, except for Mediterranean coasts, most of Iberia, Scandinavia and northern Russia.
**Movements:** Resident.
**Breeding:** Nine to twenty olive-brown eggs are well hidden on the ground and incubated by the female for 23–25 days. The active, down-covered chicks fly after 16 days.

*In flight, the Grey Partridge has broad chestnut corners to the tail. When at rest, these are visible only as thin streaks along the side of the tail.*

Europe's most widespread partridge, the Grey Partridge is similar in shape to other partridges, but different in coloration. The upperparts are streaked in black, browns and buff, and the underparts are grey with a chestnut horseshoe on the belly. The face is a dull orange. It is usually found in small flocks (coveys) and flies with rapid wingbeats before gliding on bowed wings low over the ground.

J F M A M J J A S O N D

## Common Pheasant *(Phasianus colchicus)*

The numbers of Pheasant are kept artificially high for sport. The male is golden brown with a metallic bottle-green head and a red eye wattle. The long tail is heavily barred black.

**Size:** 52–89cm (20–35in).
**Wing:** 255–266mm.
**Bill:** 25–27mm.
**Weight:** 1040–1200g.
**Voice:** Loud and resounding *kok-kok*.
**Habitat:** Fields, woods, heaths, coverts, marshes.
**Food:** Berries, shoots, seeds.
**Range:** Natural range is Middle East to China. Introduced recently in North America, Australia and New Zealand, and more than 1000 years ago in Europe, where it is now well established in

J F M A M J J A S O N D

Britain, France, Germany and elsewhere.
**Movements:** None.
**Breeding:** Seven to fifteen olive-brown eggs are laid in a hollow in the ground and incubated by the female for 23–27 days. The active downy chicks are self-feeding and fly after 12–14 days.

*The female Pheasant (right) is mottled buffy brown. This plumage provides suitable camouflage for any ground-nesting bird.*

*Although the Common Quail rarely takes to the air, preferring to run into cover, it does migrate to central Africa for the winter.*

A dainty little gamebird, the Common Quail is seen at rest only rarely and is usually noted only when it flies away on long wings low over the ground. It is streaked brown above and buffy below, with a short tail and prominent head markings, more obvious in male than female. The dumpy shape, combined with long pointed wings, are the best field marks when flushed.

**Size:** 15–18cm (6–7in).
**Wing:** 107–118mm.
**Bill:** 8–10mm.
**Weight:** 75–155g.
**Voice:** Repeated *wet-me-lips*, or plaintive *nana*.
**Habitat:** Grasslands.
**Food:** Seeds and insects.
**Range:** Summer visitor across Eurasia to eastern Siberia and southwards to northern India. Winters India, North

Africa and Sahel zone. Resident southern Africa and Madagascar. In Europe, breeds across continent, but only sparsely in Britain and Scandinavia. European birds winter in the Sahel and southern Africa.
**Movements:** Migrates on a wide front across the Mediterranean and Sahara, with large numbers stopping off along North African coasts in autumn.
**Breeding:** Seven to twelve brown-spotted creamy eggs are laid in a depression among grass or cereal crops. Incubation by the female takes 16–21 days and the active downy chicks fly after about 19 days. A pair may occasionally raise two broods.

---

An aquatic bird that spends most of its time deep inside dense vegetation, the Water Rail is laterally compressed enabling it to pass easily between growing stems. The upperparts are rust and black, with grey on face, breast and belly and white barring on black flanks. The red eye and long, red bill are obvious features, and frequent tail flicking exposes white undertail coverts. The strong legs and feet are pinkish.

*Water rails can move surprisingly quickly through the densest reedbeds by virtue of being laterally compressed (thin).*

**Size:** 25–28cm (10–11in).
**Wing:** 110–132mm.
**Bill:** 34–45mm.
**Weight:** 74–190g.
**Voice:** Shrill squeals and grunts.
**Habitat:** Freshwater marshes, waterside reedbeds.
**Food:** Amphibians, invertebrates, vegetation.
**Range:** Breeds right across temperate Eurasia. In Europe widespread as far north as Norway, though absent from northern Scandinavia and Russia. Resident in the west, but birds east of Italy are only summer visitors.
**Movements:** Eastern birds move

westwards to winter, some making considerable journeys. Hard winter weather produces more extensive westerly movements.
**Breeding:** Six to ten red-spotted, cream-coloured eggs are laid in a cup of reeds above water and are incubated mainly by the female for 19 or 20 days. The active, downy chicks fledge after 20–30 days.
**Confusing Species:** All other members of the rail-crake group have short bills.

## Spotted Crake (Porzana porzana)

A seldom seen inhabitant of marshes that is often heard after dark. The upperparts are mottled black and brown, the underparts greyish. It is spotted white on face and breast and barred black and white on the flanks.

The delicate spots and stripes that give this bird its name are seen at close quarters only by the extremely patient and extraordinarily lucky observer.

**Size:** 23–25cm (9–10in).
**Wing:** 100–118mm.
**Bill:** 18–23mm.
**Weight:** 60–126g.
**Voice:** A clear *quip quip quip* repeated for considerable periods, usually after dark and with ventriloquial effect.
**Habitat:** Freshwater marshes with masses of emergent vegetation.
**Food:** Invertebrates and vegetation.
**Range:** Summer visitor to most of temperate Europe to western Siberia. Winters India, South and East Africa.
**Movements:** A large movement through the Nile Valley occurs in autumn, though spring passage is more obvious elsewhere in North Africa.
**Breeding:** Eight to twelve red-blotched, buff-coloured eggs are laid in a cup of

grasses suspended over water. The 18–21 days of incubation are shared and the active, downy chicks fly after 25 or more days.
**Confusing Species:** Little and Baillon's Crakes lack white spots on the face.

J F M A M J J A S O N D

## Baillon's Crake (Porzana pusilla)

This is a tiny, highly secretive, summer visitor to densely vegetated freshwater marshes. The upperparts are mottled brown and black, the underparts are grey, with bold barring on rear flanks.

The bunched primary feathers of Baillon's Crake are virtually covered by the tertial feathers to form a rounded wing.

**Size:** 17–18cm (7in).
**Wing:** 87–97mm.
**Bill:** 15–18mm.
**Weight:** 28–52g.
**Voice:** Creaking and rasping notes.
**Habitat:** Freshwater marshes with much emergent vegetation.
**Food:** Invertebrates and plants.
**Range:** Summer visitor to Europe extending eastwards across central Siberia to Japan and China. Resident Africa, southern Asia, Australia and New Zealand. In Europe, highly localized but probably overlooked in many areas.
**Movements:** European birds probably winter in Ethiopia and Sudan. Eastern birds winter India and Southeast Asia.
**Breeding:** Six to eight buffy eggs, spotted with brown, are laid in a cup,

hidden among emergent vegetation. Incubation is shared and lasts 20 or 21 days. The chicks are active and downy.
**Confusing Species:** Little Crake has red base to bill, green legs, less flank barring and long primary projection.

J F M A M J J A S O N D

## Little Crake (Porzana parva)

The male is brown and black above and grey below, with barring on the flanks and undertail. The female is buffy below. Both male and female show long primary feathers. The bill is green with a red base.

Although the Little Crake spends much time wading among dense vegetation, it may also walk around in the open, unconcerned by humans.

**Size:** 18–20cm (7–8in).
**Wing:** 99–111mm.
**Bill:** 16–20mm.
**Weight:** 30–72g.
**Voice:** A *quek-quek-quek* trill.
**Habitat:** Freshwater marshes and lagoons with emergent vegetation.
**Food:** Invertebrates and vegetation.
**Range:** Summer visitor to temperate Europe. More widespread in east.
**Movements:** Winters in Pakistan and the Upper Nile marshes.
**Breeding:** Seven or eight, brown-spotted, yellowish eggs are laid in a cup hidden among emergent vegetation and are incubated by both sexes for 20 or 21 days. The chicks are active and downy.
**Confusing Species:** Baillon's Crake has bolder flank barring and no red base to the green bill.

J F M A M J J A S O N D

## Corn Crake (*Crex crex*)

Seldom seen, but often heard, this secretive inhabitant of grasslands and cereal crops was once widespread and common, but is now scarce. The upperparts are mottled black and buff, and the underparts barred chestnut and cream. It has a greyish face, stout yellowish bill and pinkish legs. In flight, it shows chestnut wings and trailing legs.

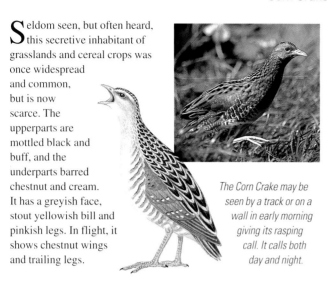

*The Corn Crake may be seen by a track or on a wall in early morning giving its rasping call. It calls both day and night.*

**Size:** 25–28cm (10–11in).
**Wing:** 130–150mm.
**Bill:** 19–25mm.
**Weight:** 128–197g.
**Voice:** Harsh, repeated *crek-crek*.
**Habitat:** Hay fields and cereal crops.

J F M A M J J A S O N D

Early harvesting and repeated silage cuts destroy many nests and young, accounting for the species' decline.
**Food:** Invertebrates, seeds.
**Range:** Summer visitor in Europe across Russia to Siberia. In Europe, absent from Iberia, much of Scandinavia and coasts of Mediterranean. Winters in areas of southeast Africa.
**Movements:** Population migrates to Africa, from Kenya to South Africa, and many birds cross deserts non-stop.
**Breeding:** Eight to twelve brown-blotched, greenish eggs are laid in grass nests on the ground. Incubation, by the female, lasts 15–18 days and the active, downy chicks fly after about 35 days.
**Confusing Species:** No other crakes or rails inhabit grasslands.

## Moorhen (*Gallinula chloropus*)

This widespread waterbird inhabits a variety of fresh waters, often alongside man. A red frontal shield and yellow tip to the red bill are the most obvious features.

*The adult Moorhen (above left) is black above and dark blue below, with white undertail coverts. The juvenile (left) has a similar pattern, but is a dull, sooty colour and lacks the red frontal shield.*

**Size:** 30–35cm (12–14in).
**Wing:** 169–194mm.
**Bill:** 23–28mm.
**Weight:** 186–493g.
**Voice:** A loud, rolling *kik kik kik*.
**Habitat:** Fresh waters, from city ponds to wild marshes.
**Food:** Insects, molluscs, seeds, plants.
**Range:** In Europe, absent only from northern Scandinavia, northern Russia and major mountain ranges.
**Movements:** Birds from areas east of Germany move south and west.
**Breeding:** Five to eleven purple- or brown-spotted, grey-buff eggs are laid in a nest on or near the ground close to water. Incubation, by both sexes, lasts 19–22 days and the active, downy, swimming chicks fly after 42–50 days.

J F M A M J J A S O N D

## Common Coot (*Fulica atra*)

A large, familiar dumpy waterbird, the adult coot is black with a metallic sheen above and below. It is is marked by a white bill and white frontal shield. The legs are strong, the feet lobed and grey-green in colour. It is a buoyant swimmer that dives well and pops back up to the surface like a cork.

*Young Coots are overall greyish and lack the white frontal shield.*

**Size:** 35–40cm (14–16in).
**Wing:** 197–229mm.
**Bill:** 26–32mm.
**Weight:** 300–1200g.
**Voice:** Explosive, hard *klukuuk*.
**Habitat:** Fresh waters and shorelines.
**Food:** Plants, insects, molluscs and other invertebrates.
**Range:** In Europe resident in west, summer visitor elsewhere.
**Movements:** Large migration of eastern birds westwards to rest of Europe.
**Breeding:** Six to nine grey eggs are lightly spotted black and laid in a large nest anchored to vegetation. Both sexes share the 21–24 days of incubation and the downy, active, swimming chicks fly after 42–56 days.
**Confusing Species**: Red-knobbed Coot of Spain has red head blobs in summer.

J F M A M J J A S O N D

# Crane *(Grus grus)*

J F M A M J J A S O N D

**Size:** 107–117cm (42–46in).
**Wing:** 522–629mm.
**Bill:** 97–119mm.
**Weight:** 3000–6100g.
**Voice:** Loud, rolling, trumpeting calls, especially in flight and display.
**Habitat:** Freshwater marshes and arable fields.
**Food:** Omnivorous.
**Range:** Breeds across northern Eurasia in the boreal zone. Winters western Europe, Sudan, India and China.
**Movements:** A migrational divide takes large numbers of birds to Hungary or northern France in autumn. Most move on to Turkey and Spain respectively, along traditional routes with stop-overs.
**Breeding:** Two brown-blotched grey, brown or buff eggs are laid on a platform of vegetation in a marsh or bog and incubated by both sexes for 28–30 days. The active, downy chicks fly after 65–70 days and accompany their parents on migration.
**Confusing Species:** Demoiselle Crane is smaller and confined to the southeast of Europe.

*The Crane's courtship display involves loud trumpeting and a great deal of strutting and parading.*

This huge, grey, gregarious bird nests and roosts in wetlands, but often frequents arable fields. It makes daily flights to and from roosts in noisy goose-like formations. The whole plumage is grey, with cascading grey plumes at the rear and a long neck marked with black and white. In the air, the black flight feathers contrast with grey coverts, and neck and legs are extended. The juvenile lacks head and neck markings.

# Demoiselle Crane *(Anthropoides virgo)*

Though still a large bird, this species is significantly smaller than the Crane. It is similarly grey, with grey plumes at the rear end that are tipped with black. The neck is black and white, the black being rather more extensive than in the Crane and forming a distinct plume on the breast. The Demoiselle Crane is gregarious outside the breeding season.

J F M A M J J A S O N D

*The Demoiselle Crane clearly shows the contrast between black flight feathers and grey coverts as it commutes to its roosts, often in V formation.*

**Size:** 89–100cm (35–39in).
**Wing:** 440–516mm.
**Bill:** 58–71mm.
**Weight:** 1985–3060g.
**Voice:** High-pitched, grating calls in flight and display.
**Habitat:** Grassy steppes with adjacent marshes and other wetlands.
**Food:** Vegetation and invertebrates.
**Range:** Breeds from southern Ukraine and eastern Turkey, across southern Siberia to western China. Winters in India and the Sudan.
**Movements:** Flies to winter quarters in Sudan; rare west of breeding range.
**Breeding:** Two red-spotted grey or buff eggs are laid in a hollow near water and incubated for 27–29 days, mainly by the female. The active, downy young fly after 55–65 days.
**Confusing Species:** Common Crane lacks black breast plumes.

## Little Bustard *(Tetrax tetrax)*

**Size:** 40–46cm (16–18in).
**Wing:** 238–259mm.
**Bill:** 16–19mm.
**Weight:** 525–975g.
**Voice:** An abrupt 'raspberry' *prrt*.
**Habitat:** Grasslands and cereal crops.
**Food:** Insects, invertebrates, vegetation.
**Range:** Widespread resident Iberia and more localized in southern France, Sardinia and Italy. Summer visitor to much of western France.
**Movements:** The French breeding birds winter in the south and in Spain.

**Breeding:** Three or four greenish brown eggs are laid on the ground and incubated by the female for 20 or 21 days. The chicks are active and downy.
**Confusing Species:** Great Bustard is huge in comparison.

A grassland bird that forms large winter flocks. It is mottled buff and brown above and white below. In flight, the shallow wingbeats reveal a large area of white in the wing.

*During courtship, the male Little Bustard (right) shows bold black and white neck feathers. The female (above), juveniles and males in winter are much drabber.*

## Great Bustard *(Otis tarda)*

The heaviest terrestrial flying bird in Europe, the Great Bustard is buff and black above and white below, the female being somewhat duller.

*When displaying, the male Great Bustard turns its wings inside out and puffs up its white throat, taking on the appearance of a white puffball, visible at vast distances.*

**Size:** 75–104cm (29–41in).
**Wing:** 475–633mm.
**Bill:** 27–40mm.
**Weight:** 3260–18,000g.
**Voice:** Mostly silent.
**Habitat:** Grasslands and crop fields.
**Food:** Omnivorous.
**Range:** Breeds locally in Iberia and Hungary, through Ukraine and southern Siberia. Eastern birds winter in China.
**Movements:** Some Ukrainian birds migrate to Turkey and the Middle East.
**Breeding:** Two or three brown-blotched greyish eggs are laid on the ground and incubated for 25–28 days by the female. The active, downy young fly after 28 days.
**Confusing Species:** Little Bustard is tiny in comparison.

## Stone-curlew *(Burhinus oedicnemus)*

This large, long-legged inhabitant of dry stony areas is well camouflaged and will stand still to avoid detection. The upperparts are heavily streaked and flecked brown and cream, while the

large rounded head is marked by a large yellow eye. The long legs are yellowish.

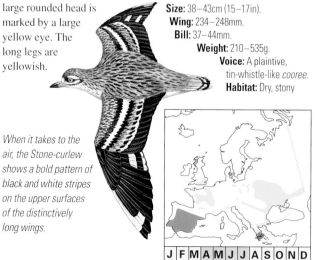

*When it takes to the air, the Stone-curlew shows a bold pattern of black and white stripes on the upper surfaces of the distinctively long wings.*

**Size:** 38–43cm (15–17in).
**Wing:** 234–248mm.
**Bill:** 37–44mm.
**Weight:** 210–535g.
**Voice:** A plaintive, tin-whistle-like *cooree*.
**Habitat:** Dry, stony lowlands, semi-desert, dry river beds.
**Food:** Insects and other invertebrates.
**Range:** Breeds right across temperate Europe and the Mediterranean to the Ukraine, Turkey and the Middle East, to India and Southeast Asia. Resident in Iberia, North Africa and India. Temperate European populations are summer visitors.
**Movements:** European birds move southwest on a broad front, many to winter in North Africa, though some may cross the Sahara.
**Breeding:** Two brown-blotched creamy eggs are laid on bare ground and incubated by both sexes for 25–27 days. The active, downy young fly after about 42 days.
**Confusing Species:** The female Little Bustard has a longer neck.

## Oystercatcher *(Haematopus ostralegus)*

A chunky shorebird, the Oystercatcher may form huge, high-tide flocks at roosts. It is marked by a long orange bill and pink legs and feet. The black upperparts extend over head and breast in summer.

*A bold white wingbar is seen in flight at all times. In winter, a white neck strap may be obvious.*

**Size:** 40–46cm (16–18in).
**Wing:** 252–276mm.
**Bill:** 61–87mm.
**Weight:** 300–745g.
**Voice:** Loud, yelping *kleep-a-kleep*.

**Habitat:** Largely coastal in winter but in summer breeds on inland fresh waters.
**Food:** Worms and particularly molluscs.
**Range:** Iceland, Britain across Baltic to Ukraine. Local in Mediterranean.

**Movements:** Eastern birds migrate westwards to winter around North Sea.
**Breeding:** Three black-blotched buffy eggs are laid in a scrape and incubated by both sexes for 24–27 days. Active, downy young fledge after 34–37 days.

## Black-winged Stilt *(Himantopus himantopus)*

As its name implies, this is the longest legged of all shorebirds. It is black above and white below, with a white head and neck in female, white-flecked black crown in male. Needle-like, long bill. Legs are pink and trail in flight.

*In summer, the male has a dark crown (left, above) that extends around the eye in winter (left, below). The female (above) lacks the crown.*

**Size:** 35–40cm (14–16in).
**Wing:** 222–255mm.
**Bill:** 56–68cm.
**Weight:** 142–289g.
**Voice:** A repeated, shrill *kee-uk*.
**Habitat:** Saline lagoons, fresh marshes.

**Food:** Insects.
**Range:** Summer visitor to much of temperate Europe, though local, and largest numbers found along Mediterranean coasts. Cosmopolitan.
**Movements:** Winters in savanna Africa, though evidence is lacking for the precise route of the trans-Sahara migration, as well as southern Spain and North Africa.
**Breeding:** Four black-spotted buffy eggs are laid in a scrape with no more than a gesture of a lining. They are incubated by both sexes, which have to virtually crash down as their long legs collapse beneath (and behind) them. Incubation lasts 25 or 26 days and the active, downy chicks take 28–32 days to fledge.

## Avocet *(Recurvirostra avosetta)*

This large, pied wader has long legs and an upswept, thin bill. The upperparts are white, marked with broad black lines. The underparts are white, extending to the head; crown and nape black. Long, blue-grey legs trail in flight, when black wing tips and shoulders form a bold pattern.

*The typical feeding action of the Avocet is to wade through shallow water, sweeping its bill from side to side through the mud (left) to search for small shrimps.*

**Size:** 40–46cm (16–18in).
**Wing:** 219–231mm.
**Bill:** 72–91mm.
**Weight:** 228–435g.
**Voice:** A yelping *klueet*.
**Habitat:** Shallow lagoons, estuaries.
**Food:** Insects and crustaceans.
**Range:** Summer visitor across Eurasia that winters in southern Europe, North Africa and in Pakistan and China. In Europe, scattered distribution around North, Mediterranean and Black Seas, and along Danube river system.
**Movements:** Passes along European coasts to Portugal and North Africa.
**Breeding:** Four black-blotched and spotted buffy eggs are laid in a bare scrape and incubated by both sexes for 22–24 days. The active, downy chicks fly after about 42 days.

149

## Collared Pratincole *(Glareola pratincola)*

*In flight, the Collared Pratincole shows rusty underwing coverts, though these may be difficult to see, and a white trailing edge to the secondaries. These features separate it from the otherwise similar Black-winged Pratincole.*

A long-winged, tern-like bird in the air, the Collared Pratincole effectively disappears on the ground. The upperparts are uniformly sandy buff, with black wing tips and a long, deeply forked tail. The short, stubby bill and creamy chin are enclosed by a black line. The creamy underparts fade to white on the belly.

J F M A M J J A S O N D

**Size:** 25–28cm (10–11in).
**Wing:** 184–211mm.
**Bill:** 13–16mm.
**Weight:** 62–95g.
**Voice:** A Sandwich Tern-like *kerrick*.
**Habitat:** Dried-out wetland margins and islands.
**Food:** Insects taken in flight.

**Range:** Summer visitor through the Mediterranean and Middle East to western central Asia. Winters across savanna Africa, where it is also a widespread resident.
**Movements:** Migrates on a broad front across the Sahara, with some concentrations in the Nile Valley. Most European birds are believed to winter in the Sahel zone.
**Breeding:** Three black-blotched creamy eggs are laid in a hollow in drying mud and incubated by both sexes for 17–18 days. The active, downy chicks fly after 22 days. Loosely colonial.
**Confusing Species:** Black-winged Pratincole lacks white trailing edge to the wings.

## Black-winged Pratincole *(Glareola nordmanni)*

Very similar to the Collared Pratincole, with similar tern-like flight and calls, the Black-winged Pratincole replaces the former north and east of the Black Sea. It is darker overall than the Collared Pratincole, but has a similar creamy throat bordered with black. The underwing is black, but in poor light it may be difficult to distinguish it from the rufous underwing of the Collared Pratincole.

*In flight, the underwing coverts are black, not rufous, but this is difficult to discern. This species can be differentiated from the Collared Pratincole by the lack of a white trailing edge to the inner wing.*

J F M A M J J A S O N D

**Size:** 23–25cm (9–10in).
**Wing:** 183–213mm.
**Bill:** 13–15mm.
**Weight:** 87–105g.
**Voice:** Like Collared Pratincole, utters a *kerrick*, but lower pitched.
**Habitat:** Steppes, dried-out marshes and salt flats near water.
**Food:** Insects.

**Range:** Summer visitor from Black Sea to west-central Asia. A few may breed in northeastern Romania. Winters southern Africa and in West Africa. Vagrant to most of western Europe.
**Movements:** Crosses Mediterranean and Sahara at high altitude to reach West African wintering grounds. Most

continue southwards to winter in Namibia, Botswana and South Africa.
**Breeding:** Lays four olive, black-blotched eggs in hollow, in small to huge colonies. No information on incubation or accurate fledging period.
**Confusing Species:** Collared Pratincole as above.

## Little Ringed Plover *(Charadrius dubius)*

Unlike the larger Ringed Plover, this species is seldom seen on coasts or estuaries. The upperparts are sandy brown with a distinctive black breast band and head markings, which, in the adult, show a diagnostic yellow eye-ring. The white line that runs above the black eye mask continues over the crown. The bill is black, and the legs yellowish. In flight it lacks a wingbar.

**J F M A M J J A S O N D**

*The juvenile Little Ringed Plover lacks the yellow eye-ring and is easily confused with the Ringed Plover.*

**Size:** 13–15cm (5–6in).
**Wing:** 112–121mm.
**Bill:** 12–14mm.
**Weight:** 33–48g.
**Voice:** A brief *peeoo*.
**Habitat:** Stony river and lake margins, gravel pits.
**Food:** Insects and molluscs.
**Range:** Summer visitor right across Eurasia from Britain to Japan, southwards to Southeast Asia and India, where it is resident. Winters Southeast Asia to New Guinea and in Sahel Africa.
**Movements:** European birds migrate across the Sahara on a broad front, although they seem to avoid the western Atlantic seaboard.
**Breeding:** Lays four brown-spotted buffy eggs in a scrape. They are incubated by both sexes for 24–26 days and the active, downy chicks are self-feeding and fledge after 21–24 days. Sometimes rears a second brood.
**Confusing Species:** Ringed Plover lacks bold yellow eye-ring.

## Ringed Plover *(Charadrius hiaticula)*

The standard 'banded' plover of Europe, this dumpy shorebird alternates running with standing. In flight, it shows distinctive white wingbar.

*If the nest is approached, the adult Ringed Plover will flutter as if it has a broken wing. Once the intruder is lured from the nest, the bird flies to safety.*

**Size:** 18–20cm (7–8in).
**Wing:** 124–144mm.
**Bill:** 13–15mm.
**Weight:** 56–74g.
**Voice:** Melodic *tor-lee*.
**Habitat:** Breeds tundra and mountain marshes, lakes, rivers, seashores and coastal marshes.
**Food:** Invertebrates.
**Range:** In Europe, breeds Iceland, Britain and Ireland, Scandinavia and northern Russia. Winters temperate Western Europe and savanna Africa.
**Movements:** European birds winter Britain and Atlantic coasts south to Spain and Portugal. Northern and eastern birds migrate to Africa, many crossing the Sahara.

**Breeding:** Four brown-spotted buffy eggs, laid in a scrape, are incubated by both sexes for 23–26 days. The active and downy young fly after 25 days.
**Confusing Species:** Little Ringed Plover has a bold yellow eye-ring.

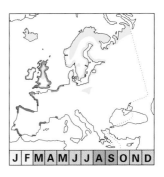

**J F M A M J J A S O N D**

## Kentish Plover *(Charadrius alexandrinus)*

A small, sandy coloured relative of the Ringed Plover, the Kentish Plover is found on all the world's great landmasses except Australasia. The adult is sandy above with a black mark at the sides of the breast. The male has a gingery crown, with a black mask and crown bar. The female has a black eyestripe. In flight the Kentish Plover shows a narrow, white wingbar.

*The juvenile has a brown smudge on the sides of its breast where the adults have a black mark.*

**Size:** 15–18cm (6–7in).
**Wing:** 108–117mm.
**Bill:** 14–17mm.
**Weight:** 38–69g.
**Voice:** A melodic *choo-wit*.
**Habitat:** Marshes, estuaries, shorelines, salt pans. In many areas coastal.

**J F M A M J J A S O N D**

**Food:** Insects, other invertebrates.
**Range:** Cosmopolitan except Australasia. In Europe, breeds along most temperate coasts from Jutland southwards through the Mediterranean, extending eastwards through the Black Sea and across Eurasia.
**Movements:** Highly complex, with significant local wintering as far north as Brittany, France. Some European birds move along the coasts of Africa as far as the Gulf of Guinea.
**Breeding:** Three black-spotted buffy eggs are laid in a hollow and incubated by both sexes for about 24 days. The active, downy chicks fledge after about 25 days. Raises two broods.
**Confusing Species:** Beware juvenile Ringed and Little Ringed Plovers, though these have darker facial markings.

## Dotterel (*Charadrius morinellus*)

A delightful little plover, the Dotterel is well marked in the adult female in summer. The upperparts are grey, mottled with buff, the head has distinct supercilia that meet on the nape, and the grey breast terminates in a narrow black and white breast band, with chestnut below. The male is a more sober version.

J F M A M J J A S O N D

**Size:** 20–23cm (8–9in).
**Wing:** 144–161mm.
**Bill:** 14–18mm.
**Weight:** 86–130g.
**Voice:** A soft *peep-peep* in flight.
**Habitat:** Bare mountain plateaux, bare tundra, bare steppes.
**Food:** Insects.
**Range:** Breeds across Eurasia at highest latitudes, as well as in mountains to south. In Europe, breeds

Scotland, Scandinavia and northern Russia, and locally in Italy, Austria and Romania. Exceptionally, at sea level on bare Dutch polders.
**Movements:** Whole population winters in marshes of Middle East and North Africa, with eastern Siberian birds making prodigious flights of 10,000km (6214 miles) or more.
**Breeding:** Three black-spotted buff eggs are laid on the ground and incubated by the male alone for 21–26 days. The active, down-covered chicks fly after about 28 days.
**Confusing Species:** Drabber juvenile similar to several rare European visitors.

*It is the female Dotterel (right) that takes the lead in displays, while the male (left) incubates the eggs and cares for the young.*

## European Golden Plover (*Pluvialis apricaria*)

This summer visitor to northern Europe is a widespread winter visitor farther south, occurring in huge flocks at favoured locations. Adult in summer is spangled gold and black above, with black underparts extending to the face. Upper- and underparts are separated by a narrow white line. In winter, upperparts less golden, underparts white with streaking on buffy breast. May be confused with Grey Plover in winter, particularly in poor light.

*Northern Golden Plovers (far left), from Iceland and Arctic Europe, show more black in summer on face, chest and belly than do British ones (left).*

J F M A M J J A S O N D

**Size:** 25–28cm (10–11in).
**Wing:** 181–203mm.
**Bill:** 20–24mm.
**Weight:** 140–205g.
**Voice:** A whistled *tlui*.
**Habitat:** Mountain plateaux and open tundra, hills and moors. Winters on grasslands and marshes.
**Food:** Worms and insects.
**Range:** Summer visitor to Iceland, Scotland and Scandinavia, Russia and adjacent western Siberia. Winters mostly in northwestern Europe and locally throughout the Mediterranean.
**Movements:** Often migrates at night to France, Britain and Holland, which are major wintering grounds.
**Breeding:** Four brown-blotched buff eggs are laid in a scrape among rough grasses and incubated for 27 or 28 days mainly by the female. The active and downy chicks fly after about 28 days.
**Confusing Species:** The Grey Plover has black axillaries.

## Grey Plover *(Pluvialis squatarola)*

A chunky bird, the Grey Plover is a winter visitor to many coastal areas of Europe. In summer, the black underparts and face are separated from the grey-spangled upperparts by a narrow white line. In winter, the underparts are white, with fine streaking on breast and flanks. In flight, it shows black axillaries.

*In summer, the Grey Plover has similar markings to the Golden Plover, but with a grey-spangled back.*

**Size:** 28–30cm (11–12in).
**Wing:** 185–212mm.
**Bill:** 27–34mm.
**Weight:** 223–310g.
**Voice:** Whistled *tee-oo-ee*.
**Habitat:** Breeds on barren tundra; winters on estuaries and open shorelines. Essentially marine and seldom seen inland.
**Food:** Invertebrates, worms.
**Range:** Circumpolar at highest northern latitudes. In North America is known as Black-bellied Plover. In Europe, breeds only in northernmost Russia. Winters on coasts throughout the world.
**Movements:** Though most migrate along coastlines there is evidence that some Siberian birds may fly across the continents to Africa. Large numbers of

J F M A M J J A S O N D

birds winter on north European coasts.
**Breeding:** Four dark-spotted buffy eggs are incubated for 26 or 27 days by both sexes. The chicks are active and downy.
**Confusing Species:** Winter Golden Plover lacks black axillaries.

## Lapwing *(Vanellus vanellus)*

A widespread plover, the Lapwing has adapted to a variety of open landforms, but has recently declined due to changing farming techniques.

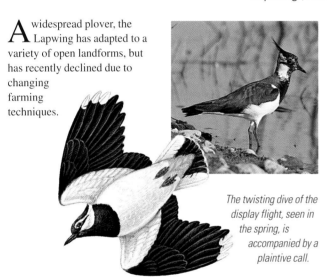

*The twisting dive of the display flight, seen in the spring, is accompanied by a plaintive call.*

**Size:** 28–30cm (11–12in).
**Wing:** 214–240mm.
**Bill:** 22–26mm.
**Weight:** 128–330g.
**Voice:** A plaintive *pee-wit*.
**Habitat:** Fresh and salt marshes, floods, damp grasslands and arable fields, both in summer and winter.
**Food:** Invertebrates.
**Range:** Breeds from Europe across Eurasia to Sea of Japan. Winters China, India and Europe. In Europe, absent most of Mediterranean region and virtually the whole of Italy.
**Movements:** Vast movements westwards across Europe, starting as early as June and continuing through autumn. Winters low countries, France, Britain and Iberia, but liable to make

hard weather movements at any time.
**Breeding:** Four black-blotched buff eggs are laid in a neat cup hidden by grass and incubated mainly by the female for 24–29 days. The active, downy chicks fledge in about 33 days.

J F M A M J J A S O N D

## Sociable Plover *(Chettusia gregaria)*

The Sociable Plover forms flocks inside and outside the breeding season. It is largely confined to eastern Europe, though vagrant individuals may turn up as far west as Britain.

J F M A M J J A S O N D

**Size:** 25–28cm (10–11in).
**Wing:** 197–220mm.
**Bill:** 26–32mm.
**Weight:** 180–252g.
**Voice:** A shrill whistled call.
**Habitat:** Dry plains and steppes, dried-out marshes, sometimes near water, farmland in mountains and at higher altitudes Also sometimes seen near coasts.
**Food:** Insects.
**Range:** Confined to the eastern Ukraine and adjacent parts of Siberia in summer. Winters in the eastern Sahel zone of Africa and across the Middle East to northern India.
**Movements:** Migrations are little known, but definite concentration west of the Caspian.
**Breeding:** Four black-spotted buffy

*The boldly marked head and breast are clear identification features in the summer.*

eggs are laid in a hollow and incubated by both sexes for about 25 days. The downy, active young fledge after 35–40 days. Colonial.
**Confusing Species:** Juvenile Dotterel in winter has superficially similar plumage, but noticeably darker legs.

## Knot (Calidris canutus)

A winter visitor and passage migrant that occurs in huge flocks at favoured feeding grounds, the Knot is absent from apparently similar areas nearby. It is a chunky wader that resembles an overlarge Dunlin with a shorter bill and white supercilium. In winter, the upperparts are grey, and the underparts are white, marked with streaks on the chest and chevrons on the flanks. In summer plumage, seen in Europe only in May and June, the upperparts are chestnut, black and grey with pure chestnut underparts. In flight, a narrow, white wingbar and grey rump can be seen.

*Winter plumage is grey and white (left) in contrast to the 'red' of summer.*

J F M A M J J A S O N D

**Size:** 24–27cm (9–10in).
**Wing:** 162–181mm.
**Bill:** 30–36mm.
**Weight:** 93–215g.
**Voice:** A low, grunted *knut.*
**Habitat:** Breeds high tundra, winters estuaries and shorelines.
**Food:** Molluscs, crustaceans, worms.
**Range:** North circumpolar, but only at highest of latitudes and most barren tundra deltas and oases. Winters from Scotland and North Sea to Africa.

**Movements:** Mostly along coasts, although Siberian birds fly across Asia to Australia.
**Breeding:** Four brown-spotted greenish eggs are laid in a lined hollow and are incubated by both parents for 21–22 days. The female leaves after hatching, and the male raises the active, downy young, which fledge after 18–20 days.
**Confusing Species:** Dunlin in winter plumage, but Dunlin is smaller with a longer bill.

## Sanderling (Calidris alba)

This dainty little wader is best known for its habit of running up and down beaches at the edge of the breaking waves. It is Europe's palest wader, with grey upperparts and white underparts, marked by a black patch at the bend of the wing. The bill is short and straight. In summer plumage, seen in Europe only in May and June, upperparts are spangled black and chestnut, and the head and breast are streaked chestnut and black. In this plumage, it could be confused with Little Stint.

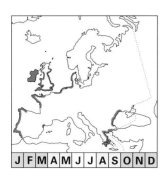

J F M A M J J A S O N D

*The upperparts change from grey in winter (above) to spangled black and chestnut in summer (right). In this plumage, Sanderling can be confused with other waders.*

**Size:** 18–20cm (7–8in).
**Wing:** 120–134mm.
**Bill:** 21–27mm.
**Weight:** 44–75g.
**Voice:** A chattering *quit-quit.*
**Habitat:** Breeds high-Arctic tundra; winters coasts and estuaries.
**Food:** Molluscs and crustaceans.
**Range:** Circumpolar in northernmost ice-free land; in central Siberia, Greenland and Arctic Canadian archipelago. Winters coasts throughout the world. In Europe, is a passage migrant and winter visitor to Atlantic and North Sea coasts.
**Movements:** Many North Sea birds seem to breed in Siberia, while many Irish Sea and Atlantic birds head for Greenland. Capacity for huge non-stop migratory flights recorded in South Africa by weighing for fat deposits.
**Breeding:** Four brown-spotted greenish eggs are laid in lined hollow and incubated by both sexes for 23–24 days. The active, downy young will take a similar period to fledge. Poor weather on breeding grounds may prevent breeding.
**Confusing Species:** None in winter; Little Stint in summer plumage, but this is paler and smaller.

## Little Stint *(Calidris minuta)*

Tiny, Dunlin-like shorebird, whose size is only obvious when compared side by side with that species. Mostly a passage migrant in Europe, with autumn juvenile the dominant plumage. Adult in winter is grey above, white below, with light streaking on the breast. Its small size and short, straight bill are identification features. Summer plumage is heavily scalloped in chestnut and black above, with brown streaking on head and breast. Juvenile is similar, but with double white 'V' on back.

J F M A M J J A S O N D

*Although adult Little Stints are brown in summer and grey in winter, the plumage most commonly seen is the juvenile during the autumn period (above). Warm buff-brown upperparts are marked by a bold, white double 'V' shape on the back.*

**Size:** 13cm (5in).
**Wing:** 93–104mm.
**Bill:** 17–20mm.
**Weight:** 21–40g.
**Voice:** A sharp *tyit*.
**Habitat:** High-Arctic tundra pools and marshes. Winters shorelines, estuaries and inland lakes and floods, as well as sewage works and salt pans.
**Food:** Molluscs, crustaceans and worms.
**Range:** Confined to northernmost Scandinavia and Siberian tundra. Winters Africa and India and in Middle East and Mediterranean to Portugal.
**Movements:** Regularly flies huge distances to winter over most of savanna Africa. In Europe, a regular double-passage migrant to most parts, usually most abundant in autumn juvenile plumage.
**Breeding:** Lays four brown-speckled, olive-coloured eggs in a cup of grasses on the ground. The chicks hatch active and downy, but the incubation and fledging periods are unknown.
**Confusing Species:** Size and short, straight bill shared only with greyer, less scalloped Temminck's Stint, which is essentially a freshwater species with yellow-green, not blackish, legs.

## Temminck's Stint *(Calidris temminckii)*

Temminck's Stint is a small wader that can easily be confused with the Little Stint, but it resembles a tiny Common Sandpiper rather than a Dunlin. In winter it is olive-grey above, with only narrow dark margins to its feathers. Its underparts are white, with olive-grey streaking ending abruptly on the breast. The legs are yellowish green. In summer, the upperparts have brown-margined black feathers. In contrast to the robust probing of the Little Stint, Temminck's Stint feeds by delicate picking.

*Temminck's Stint closely resembles a Common Sandpiper. In contrast, the Little Stint resembles a short-billed Dunlin.*

J F M A M J J A S O N D

**Size:** 13–15cm (5in).
**Wing:** 95–105mm.
**Bill:** 16–18mm.
**Weight:** 15–36g.
**Voice:** A *trrr-trrr*.
**Habitat:** Arctic tundra. On passage and in winter fresh waters and marshes.
**Food:** Insects.
**Range:** Breeds from Scandinavian mountains across tundra Russia to the Bering Strait. Winters China, South-east Asia, India and Sahel Africa.
**Movements:** Regular double passage migrant through Europe. Small numbers winters in Italy and Greece.
**Breeding:** Four brown-speckled pale olive eggs are laid in a hollow.
**Confusing Species:** Little Stint.

# Curlew Sandpiper *(Calidris ferruginea)*

A slim, more elegant, longer-winged and longer-necked version of the Dunlin, which is only a passage migrant through Europe in spring and autumn. In winter plumage, it is grey above, white below with faint breast streaking. In summer, upperparts are spangled chestnut and black and the entire underparts are a rich chestnut. Juvenile has neatly scalloped greyish upperparts and creamy-buff neck and breast. In all plumages, the long neck, rounded head, slim body and long decurved bill (and, in winter plumage in flight, the square white rump) are the best fieldmarks.

*In winter the russet summer plumage (left) becomes grey above and white below, with a clear square, white rump, most visible in flight.*

**Size:** 18–20cm (7–8in).
**Wing:** 125–139mm.
**Bill:** 33–42mm.
**Weight:** 44–102g.
**Voice:** A soft and faint *chirrup* when in flight.
**Habitat:** High-Arctic tundra and, on passage, fresh and salty marshes, sewage works, salt pans and areas of short grass.
**Food:** Molluscs, crustaceans, insects, and especially worms.
**Range:** Breeds in northeastern Siberia. Winters coasts of India to Australia and throughout savanna Africa, especially by lakes.
**Movements:** Migrates vast distances over land and sea between Siberia and winter quarters. Many pass through Europe in spring and autumn, presumably to and from West Africa. Birds that winter in South Africa pass over Middle East.
**Breeding:** Three or four brown-blotched olive eggs are laid in a hollow and the chicks hatch active and downy. Incubation period, role of sexes and fledging remain unknown.
**Confusing Species:** Dunlin, though the latter has a straighter bill, squatter body and shorter legs.

J F M A M J J A S O N D

---

# Purple Sandpiper *(Calidris maritima)*

Although it breeds inland in mountains and the tundra, this is a marine wader. In winter, the upperparts are a dull, uniform dark grey that extends over the face. The white underparts are streaked on the breast, with chevrons along the flanks. In summer, the upperparts are spangled black and chestnut, and the underparts heavily marked with chevrons. The dumpy structure and short legs create a robust impression.

*No other wader has plumage as noticeably dark as the Purple Sandpiper.*

**Size:** 21cm (8in).
**Wing:** 124–136mm.
**Bill:** 26–34mm.
**Weight:** 59–86g.
**Voice:** Occasional *weet-weet*.
**Habitat:** Mountain plateaux, tundra pools and marshes; and rocky shorelines in winter.
**Food:** Molluscs and crustaceans.
**Range:** Northern circumpolar, though with a gap either side of Bering Strait. In Europe, breeds Iceland, the Scandinavian mountain chain, and on Russian Arctic islands. Winters along Norwegian coast to Britain, Ireland and northwestern France and Spain.
**Movements:** Migration across North Sea and along Atlantic coasts.
**Breeding:** Four brown-blotched greenish eggs are laid in a lined hollow and incubated by the male for 21 or 22 days. The active, downy young fledge after 21–28 days.

J F M A M J J A S O N D

## Dunlin (Calidris alpina)

The Dunlin is the most widespread and abundant of all European small waders and is, therefore, the 'standard' from which all other species must be separated. In summer, it has chestnut and black spangled upperparts and a black belly. The juvenile is similar, but with black spots on belly. In winter upperparts are grey, underparts white, with streaking on breast.

J F M A M J J A S O N D

**Size:** 15–20cm (6–8in).
**Wing:** 105–124mm.
**Bill:** 23–36mm.
**Weight:** 36–48g.
**Voice:** A nasal *schreep*.
**Habitat:** Marshes, moors, mountains and tundra in summer. In winter, estuaries, floods, marshes, lakes, sewage works, lagoons.
**Food:** Molluscs, crustaceans, and insects.
**Range:** Northern circumpolar. In Europe, breeds Iceland, Britain, Ireland, through Scandinavia to northern Russia. Winters European coasts, particularly in Britain, North Sea and Atlantic France.

*No other wader has a black belly in summer, though in winter plumage it is easy to mistake the Dunlin for rarer waders of about the same size.*

**Movements:** Movements to Mediterranean, mostly along coasts.
**Breeding:** Four brown-blotched green eggs laid in a hollow are incubated by both sexes for 21 or 22 days. The downy, active young fledge after 25 days.
**Confusing Species:** Winter plumage Curlew Sandpiper, Knot, Little Stint and others.

## Ruff (Philomachus pugnax)

The difference in size between male and female led to the name of Reeve for the smaller female. In winter, both sexes are scaly brown above and buffy white below. In summer, the upperparts are richer, in buff and chestnut, with a broadly barred breast below, and the males at this time are adorned by head and neck plumes in chestnut, black and white that are erected in display.

*The adult male in breeding plumage (left) has neck and head plumes that are lacking at other times.*

J F M A M J J A S O N D

**Size:** 20–30cm (8–12in).
**Wing:** 173–200mm.
**Bill:** 29–37mm.
**Weight:** 72–230g.
**Voice:** A *chuck-chuck*.
**Habitat:** Marshes and floods in temperate and tundra zones in summer and, in winter, freshwater marshes and floods.
**Food:** Insects and other small invertebrates.
**Range:** Breeds right across Eurasia and winters in India and savanna Africa. In Europe, breeds from Holland eastwards through Russia and Scandinavia.
**Movements:** Some birds remain in western Europe during the winter, but the vast majority are trans-Saharan migrants, including those that breed near the Bering Strait and which make a 15,000km migration around the world to winter in Africa.
**Breeding:** Males gather like grouse at leks to display and mate with visiting females. Four brown-blotched olive eggs are laid in a hollow and incubated for 20 or 21 days by the female. The chicks hatch downy and active.

157

This brown and cream streaked wader has a very long, straight, probing bill. The spangled upperparts are marked by a bold double V. It has a heavily streaked breast, the streaks becoming chevrons on belly and flanks. The head is boldly striped and the long straight bill is some two and a half times the length of the head. The short, stout legs are yellowish. In flight, the rounded tail shows white margins. When disturbed the bird towers high into the sky in escape flights.

*The male Snipe performs diving displays with tail feathers outstretched, which produces a drumming sound.*

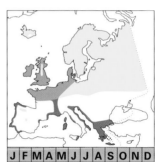

J F M A M J J A S O N D

**Size:** 24–28cm (9–11in).
**Wing:** 129–140mm.
**Bill:** 62–73mm.
**Weight:** 72–169g.
**Voice:** A harsh *scarp*.
**Habitat:** Bogs, marshes and floods.
**Food:** Worms and insects.
**Range:** Found on all the world's great landmasses save Australasia. In Europe, is a summer visitor to the northern half from Iceland through Britain, France, Germany and Scandinavia to Russia. Winters in the northwest and the southeast.
**Movements:** Huge numbers leave Eurasia on a broad front to winter in India and Southeast Asia and in sahel Africa. Large numbers also winter in Denmark, northern Germany, France and Britain, but these are mostly Scandinavian breeders.
**Breeding:** Four brown-blotched pale green eggs are laid in a grass-lined hollow and incubated by the female for 18–20 days. The active and downy young fly after 19 or 20 days.
**Confusing Species:** Jack Snipe and Great Snipe, which must be distinguished with care from this, the more common and widespread species.

A Dunlin-sized, snipe-like wader, the Broad-billed Sandpiper is decidedly scarce in Europe, breeding only in the Scandinavian mountains. Adult in summer is very dark above, with pale feather margins creating a scaly effect, and white below, with a heavily streaked breast and a few chevrons on the flanks. The striped crown and long bill, slightly decurved towards the tip, are diagnostic features. In winter, the bird is grey above, and only lightly streaked on the sides of breast below; it retains the grey head pattern.

**Size:** 15–18cm (6–7in).
**Wing:** 102–114mm.
**Bill:** 28–36mm.
**Weight:** 32–44g.
**Voice:** A trilled *tir-eek*.
**Habitat:** Bogs in mountains and tundra pools in summer. On passage prefers freshwater marshes and pools, but frequently winters along shorelines.
**Food:** Worms and insects, seeds.
**Range:** Breeds through mountains and hills of Scandinavia and adjacent Russia, and at three widely separated sites in northern and eastern Siberian tundra. Winters Southeast Asia and India.
**Movements:** Siberian birds winter in Asia. Scandinavian birds move southwards across the Black Sea and eastern Mediterranean to Aden and then on to unknown wintering grounds, presumably in Africa. Some have been found in Namibia.
**Breeding:** Four brown-speckled buffy eggs are laid in a marshy tussock and incubated for 21 days by both sexes. The young are active and downy.

J F M A M J J A S O N D

*The Snipe-like head pattern, coupled with size and downcurved bill, are clear fieldmarks.*

## Great Snipe *(Gallinago media)*

A chunky relative of the Common Snipe, the Great Snipe has upperparts spangled chestnut and cream, with a triple, creamy V across the back and wings. The underparts are streaked on breast and barred on flanks and undertail.

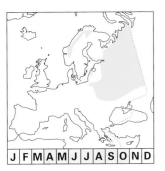

*The white outertail feathers are visible (left), and the characteristic male display posture (above).*

**Size:** 28cm (11in).
**Wing:** 139–151mm.
**Bill:** 54–69mm.
**Weight:** 153–225g.
**Voice:** Mostly silent, few croaking calls.
**Habitat:** Woodland bogs and marshes.
**Food:** Molluscs, insects and worms.
**Range:** Summer visitor to Scandinavia eastwards across Russia to adjacent Siberia. Winters in savanna Africa.
**Movements:** Migrates on a broad front across eastern Europe.
**Breeding:** Males display at lekking grounds. Four brown-speckled buffy eggs are laid in a tussock and incubated for 22–24 days by the female. The downy chicks fly after 21–28 days.
**Confusing Species:** Common Snipe has pointed wings and longer bill.

## Jack Snipe *(Lymnocryptes minimus)*

A tiny version of the Common Snipe, the Jack Snipe has a much shorter bill and a brief, low escape flight. The upperparts are spangled in browns and buffs, and marked by creamy lines forming a double V, very similar to the pattern of Common Snipe. The underparts are white, with streaking on breast and flanks; striped crown. The bill is less than one and a half times the length of the head. When flushed, it flies low and alights nearby, showing no white in the wedge-shaped tail.

*The Jack Snipe relies on camouflage for safety (above left). The bill (left) is shorter than that of the similarly marked Common Snipe.*

**Size:** 18–20cm (7–8in).
**Wing:** 105–119mm.
**Bill:** 36–42mm.
**Weight:** 33–77g.
**Voice:** Usually silent.
**Habitat:** Breeds on bogs in boreal zone; winters among floods and marshes with emergent vegetation in which to hide.
**Food:** Molluscs, worms and insects.
**Range:** Breeds Scandinavia to northern Siberia. Winters temperate Europe and sahel Africa, Middle East and India.
**Movements:** Apparent broad front migration southwest across Europe.
**Breeding:** Lays four brown-blotched greenish eggs in a lined cup on the ground. Female incubates for 24 days and the chicks hatch active and downy.
**Confusing Species:** Common Snipe.

## Woodcock *(Scolopax rusticola)*

This tubby, round-winged wader is totally orientated to a woodland existence. In flight, the head and bill are held pointing distinctly downwards.

*The Woodcock has superb camouflage (below) and rounded wings (right).*

**Size:** 30–35cm (12–14in).
**Wing:** 182–218mm.
**Bill:** 62–88mm.
**Weight:** 144–420g.
**Voice:** A clear *tissick* is uttered by the male during territorial flight in the late evening.
**Habitat:** Damp woodlands and woods with marshy pools and patches.
**Food:** Worms and molluscs.
**Range:** Breeds from Britain across Eurasia to Japan, mainly in temperate woodlands, but also in the boreal zone. Winters from western Europe and Mediterranean across India, Southeast Asia and China. In Europe, absent most of Iberia and Mediterranean.
**Movements:** Most European birds move west and south to winter in northwest and western Europe.
**Breeding:** Four brown-blotched creamy eggs are laid in a leaf-lined hollow and incubated for 20–23 days by the female. Young fledge after 15–20 days.
**Confusing Species:** Common Snipe.

# Black-tailed Godwit *(Limosa limosa)*

A slim, elegant wader, the Black-tailed Godwit is marked by long legs and a long bill. In summer, a pale pinkish chestnut on head and neck extends to the breast, with dark chevrons forming bands along flanks. Upperparts are spangled chestnut and black. The bill is twice the length of the head. In winter, the plumage is grey, with unstreaked back. In flight, it shows a white bar across mainly black wings, black band to tail and feet that extend well behind.

*In flight, the Black-tailed Godwit shows a clear white wingbar and black tail.*

**Size:** 38–43cm (15–17in).
**Wing:** 194–231mm.
**Bill:** 81–122mm.
**Weight:** 160–500g.
**Voice:** A loud *reeka-reeka-reeka*.
**Habitat:** Floods and grassy marshes in summer; floods, marshes, estuaries and shorelines in winter.
**Food:** Worms, molluscs and insects.
**Range:** Summer visitor to Iceland, locally to Britain and France and commonly from Holland eastwards across Russia and Ukraine to central Siberia. Some isolated populations in eastern Siberia and China. Winters in Europe as far north as Britain, but also in Sahel Africa, India, Southeast Asia and as far as Australia.
**Movements:** Huge migration across Europe, the Mediterranean and Sahara to wintering grounds in Sahel, mostly in the west. Some indication of a more easterly return route in spring.
**Breeding:** Four brown-blotched green eggs laid in a neatly lined cup on the ground are incubated by both sexes for 22–24 days. The active and downy young fly after 28 days.
**Confusing Species:** Bar-tailed Godwit has shorter legs and bill, no wing bar and a streaked back.

J F M A M J J A S O N D

# Bar-tailed Godwit *(Limosa lapponica)*

Close relative of the Black-tailed Godwit, the Bar-tailed replaces it in the tundra zone of Eurasia. It is slightly smaller than the Black-tailed, with shorter legs, a shorter upturned bill, heavily streaked upperparts and no white wingbar. In summer, head, neck and underparts are rich chestnut. In winter, it is streaked brown on head, neck, breast and back. The barred tail may be seen in flight, though the lack of a wingbar is clearer.

**Size:** 35–40cm (14–16in).
**Wing:** 203–230mm.
**Bill:** 72–107mm.
**Weight:** 195–447g.
**Voice:** A strong *kirrik-kirrik*.
**Habitat:** Breeds among tundra pools and marshes; winters exclusively on estuaries and shorelines.
**Food:** Molluscs and worms.

**Range:** Breeds from northern Scandinavia across Siberian tundra to Bering Strait and westernmost Alaska. Winters western Europe, Africa, Middle East, Pakistan, China to Australasia.
**Movements:** Vast migrations across the continents to Southern Hemisphere wintering grounds. Scandinavian and Russian birds move through Baltic to Britain and along coasts to Mauritania. Dramatic flocks move eastwards along the English Channel in the spring.
**Breeding:** Four brown-blotched olive eggs are laid in a grass-lined hollow and incubated by both sexes for 20 or 21 days. The chicks are active and downy.
**Confusing Species:** Black-tailed Godwit.

*The lack of a broad white wing bar in flight (right) easily separates this bird from Europe's other godwit, the Black-tailed Godwit. In its winter plumage (right) the bird has grey underparts and brown upperparts streaked with black.*

J F M A M J J A S O N D

## Whimbrel *(Numenius phaeopus)*

The Whimbrel, which resembles a small, short-billed Curlew, is a summer visitor to northern Europe, and a passage migrant elsewhere. The upperparts are streaked brown, the underparts have chevrons extending to the flanks. Head has a clear pattern of dark stripes and the bill is decurved towards the tip. The legs are silver-grey. In flight it shows no wingbar, but the white rump extends up the back in a V.

*In flight, the Whimbrel gives a series of whistles, often seven in number.*

**J F M A M J J A S O N D**

**Size:** 38–43cm (15–17in).
**Wing:** 229–273mm.
**Bill:** 72–94mm.
**Weight:** 268–600g.
**Voice:** Shrill, rippling whistles.
**Habitat:** Breeds on marshes, bogs and moorland in boreal zone and among treeless hills. Winters coasts and estuaries.
**Food:** Molluscs, crustaceans, and insects.
**Range:** Circumpolar in the north, though with significant gaps in Siberia, Canada and Greenland. Winters in the tropics and in Southern Hemisphere as far south as Cape Town and Tasmania. In Europe, breeds Iceland, Scotland, Scandinavia and across northern Russia.
**Movements:** Long-distance migrations across the continents to tropical wintering grounds. Few known autumn stop-overs, but large spring concentrations in Hungary, inland Belgium, and Holland and England.
**Breeding:** Four, brown-blotched olive eggs laid in a hollow and incubated by both sexes for 24–28 days. The down-covered chicks fledge at 42 days.
**Confusing Species:** Curlew is larger, lacks crown stripes and has longer and more evenly down-curved bill.

## Curlew *(Numenius arquata)*

**J F M A M J J A S O N D**

*The Curlew watches for a worm to come to the surface to eject its cast, then plunges its bill into the mud before the worm can retreat.*

This large brown wader has a long, decurved bill. The upperparts are streaked brown and buff, and the underparts are buffy streaked on the breast and marked with black chevrons on the belly. The head and neck are streaked. The bill is decurved from its base. Females have longer bills than males, and juvenile Curlews have shorter bills than adults. In flight, the white on the rump extends in a V up the back.

**Size:** 51–61cm (20–24in).
**Wing:** 276–333mm.
**Bill:** 107–168mm.
**Weight:** 500–1360g.
**Voice:** A clear *coor-lee*, and a more bubbling call in summer.
**Habitat:** Summer visitor to marshes, moorland and clearings in the boreal zone and, in winter, to shorelines, estuaries and adjacent fields.
**Food:** Molluscs, crustaceans and worms.
**Range:** Breeds across Europe to eastern Siberia. Winters along most coastlines as far as South Africa and Sumatra. Also inland in Niger Inundation Zone and Rift Valley lakes. In Europe, absent in summer from Iberia and the whole Mediterranean region. Winters west of a line from Jutland to Bosphorus, mainly around North Sea.
**Movements:** Most European breeders move westwards to winter inland. Western Asian breeders may cross the Sahara diagonally.
**Breeding:** Four brown-blotched olive-green eggs are incubated mainly by the female for 26–30 days. The active, downy chicks fledge after 35–42 days.
**Confusing Species:** The Whimbrel is smaller and has a less decurved bill.

## Spotted Redshank *(Tringa erythropus)*

Slim and elegant, the Spotted Redshank is a wader which in most of Europe is no more than a double-passage migrant. In winter, it has a grey back, slightly darker and barred on the wings, with a lightly streaked breast. In summer, it is black with a white wedge in the centre of the back. In all plumages, red legs and a red-based bill can be confused with Common Redshank, but that bird is brown with shorter legs.

**Size:** 28–33cm (11–13in).
**Wing:** 162–174mm.
**Bill:** 52–65mm.
**Weight:** 121–205g.
**Voice:** Clear *chu-wit*.
**Habitat:** Breeds Arctic tundra marshes. Winters on marshes and estuaries.

**Food:** Molluscs and crustaceans.
**Range:** Summer visitor from northern Scandinavia and Russia across Siberian tundra to Bering Strait. Winters China, Southeast Asia to India, the Middle East and Sahel Africa.
**Movements:** Regular migrant, with autumn moulting grounds on the Dutch Waddenzee and in Hungary and Greece. A few winter around the Mediterranean and as far north as Britain.
**Breeding:** Four black-blotched olive eggs are laid in a hollow and incubated by the male, which also cares for the active and downy chicks.
**Confusing Species:** Common Redshank in winter plumage has a heavier build and shorter legs and bill.

The summer plumage of the Spotted Redshank is a stunning black, lightly spotted white, which contrasts with the red legs and bill.

J F M A M J J A S O N D

## Common Redshank *(Tringa totanus)*

A widespread breeder over much of temperate and northern Europe, this bird is marked by the long red legs that give it its name. The adult in summer is spangled brown above and heavily streaked below. The bill is red with a black tip. In flight, it shows a white trailing edge to the wings.

**Size:** 25–33cm (10–11in).
**Wing:** 149–167mm.
**Bill:** 34–44mm.
**Weight:** 85–155g.
**Voice:** A yelping *tyew-yew-yew* and a hard *tuek*.
**Habitat:** Freshwater marshes and damp fields in boreal and temperate zones in summer. In winter, floods, fields, estuaries and shorelines.
**Food:** Worms, molluscs and crustaceans.
**Range:** Breeds right across Eurasia to Sea of Japan and on the central Asian plateau. Winters China, Southeast Asia and India, through the Middle East and Mediterranean to Atlantic and North Sea coasts. In Europe, sporadic through Mediterranean and France in summer. Winters mainly in Britain, France and Holland.
**Movements:** Large concentrations at favoured estuaries with total European winter population of about 150,000. Large numbers of Scandinavian and Russian birds fly overland to reach the Mediterranean.
**Breeding:** Four blackish-blotched olive-green eggs are laid in a hollow and incubated by both sexes for 23 or 24 days. The active, downy chicks can fly after about 30 days.
**Confusing Species:** Spotted Redshank and Ruff in winter plumage.

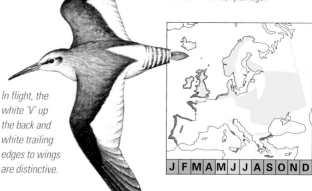

In flight, the white 'V' up the back and white trailing edges to wings are distinctive.

J F M A M J J A S O N D

## Marsh Sandpiper *(Tringa stagnatilis)*

This tall, slim, elegant wader has long legs and is similar to the larger Greenshank, but the small, rounded head and needle-like bill pick it out. In winter, the plumage is grey above with a dark area at the bend of the wing. The underparts are white with grey wash over crown. The legs are green, but are longer than those of the similar Greenshank. In summer, the bird is spangled and spotted black above, and the breast is streaked.

**Size:** 23cm (9in).
**Wing:** 136–148mm.
**Bill:** 37–45mm.
**Weight:** 55–90g.
**Voice:** Clear *tu* and *tchik*.
**Habitat:** Marshes and floods in the temperate zone, also on rivers in winter quarters and sometimes around sewage treatment works.

**Food:** Insects, molluscs and crustaceans.
**Range:** Temperate zone Russia and Ukraine eastwards across central Siberia. Winters in savanna Africa, India and Southeast Asia.
**Movements:** Migrates on a broad front across eastern Europe, Mediterranean and Sahara to winter in Sahel zone. In Europe, regular visitor only in eastern areas, but a few as far west as Spain.
**Breeding:** Four brown-speckled buffy eggs are laid in a depression hidden in grass and incubated by both sexes. The chicks are active and downy.
**Confusing Species:** Heavier build and longer, stouter bill of Greenshank should avoid confusion.

J F M A M J J A S O N D

*The Marsh Sandpiper's legs extend much further beyond the tail when seen in flight, and the white V on the back is longer.*

## Greenshank *(Tringa nebularia)*

A grey wader, the Greenshank has long green legs and a long, slightly upturned bill. In winter, the plumage is grey above and white below with fine streaking on the neck. In summer, the back is spangled grey and black, with darker neck streaking. In flight, it has a uniform grey wing, with a white V extending from rump up the back.

*Similar to the Marsh Sandpiper with a white V on the back and feet extending beyond the tail.*

**Size:** 28–30cm (11–12in).
**Wing:** 185–200mm.
**Bill:** 51–61mm.
**Weight:** 129–245g.
**Voice:** Clear *tu-tu-tu*.
**Habitat:** Moors and marshes in the boreal zone in summer. Winters on marshes, floods, estuaries and rivers.
**Food:** Insects, molluscs and crustaceans, small fish.
**Range:** Breeds across northern Eurasia from Scotland and Scandinavia to Kamchatka. Winters in savanna Africa,

coastal Arabia, India and from China south to Australia.
**Movements:** Small numbers winter in Britain, Ireland and Spain. Most are migrants to Africa, making a broad movement over Europe and the Sahara.
**Breeding:** Four brown-blotched eggs are laid in a hollow, often near a rotting branch, and are incubated by the female for 24 or 25 days. The downy, active chicks fly after about 28 days.
**Confusing Species:** The Marsh Sandpiper is slimmer and smaller.

J F M A M J J A S O N D

## Green Sandpiper *(Tringa ochropus)*

**D**ark and solitary, the Green Sandpiper can be confused with the Wood Sandpiper in flight. It is a dark olive-brown above, lightly speckled white, with white underparts, streaked on neck and breast. It has a moderately long bill and shortish green legs. In flight, the wings are dark and the rump square cut and white.

**Size:** 20–23cm (8–9in).
**Wing:** 140–151mm.
**Bill:** 32–38mm.
**Weight:** 53–105g.
**Voice:** A sharp *huit-weet-weet.*
**Habitat:** Bogs and marshes in boreal zone; winters marshes and channels.
**Food:** Insects, molluscs, crustaceans.
**Range:** Breeds across Eurasian boreal zone. Winters northwest Europe, savanna Africa, and Turkey to China.
**Movements:** Migrates on a broad front across the Sahara.

*In flight, the black underside of the wings contrasting with the white body is a clear fieldmark.*

**Breeding:** Lays four red-spotted olive eggs in a low tree. They are incubated for 20–23 days. The downy chicks leap to the ground and fly at 28 days.
**Confusing Species:** Wood Sandpiper is paler and more elegant.

J F M A M J J A S O N D

## Wood Sandpiper *(Tringa glareola)*

**T**his is a delicate small wader of freshwater marshes. The upperparts are brown, spangled white, and the underparts white with streaking on the neck and breast. A white supercilium extends beyond the eye, and the legs are long and yellow. In flight, the dark upperwing contrasts with a bold white rump.

**Size:** 18–20cm (7–8in).
**Wing:** 121–137mm.
**Bill:** 26–32mm.
**Weight:** 51–89
**Voice:** A fast *chi-chi-chi.*
**Habitat:** Breeds marshes of boreal zone, winters freshwater marshes.
**Food:** Insects, molluscs, crustaceans.
**Range:** Breeds right across boreal Eurasia and winters in sub-Saharan Africa, Middle East, and from India to China and Australia. European birds cross the Sahara on broad front.

*In flight, the Wood Sandpiper shows dark brown wings, body and head, with a square white rump, barred tail and trailing legs.*

**Breeding:** Four brown-blotched pale green eggs are laid in a hollow and incubated mainly by the female for 23 days. The chicks are active and downy.
**Confusing Species:** The Green Sandpiper is darker and stouter.

J F M A M J J A S O N D

## Common Sandpiper *(Actitis hypoleucos)*

**T**his small wader, bobs its whole body continuously and flies with flickering wingbeats, broken by brief glides. The upperparts, head and breast are olive with dark streaks. The white wedge between breast and wing is the best field mark. The underparts are white and the legs green. In flight it shows a wingbar and white sides to the tail.

J F M A M J J A S O N D

*Flies on broad wings with shallow, fluttering beats.*

**Size:** 18–20cm (7–8in).
**Wing:** 107–116mm.
**Bill:** 23–27mm.
**Weight:** 33–67g.
**Voice:** Whistled *swee-swee-oo.*
**Habitat:** Fast-flowing rivers and streams, freshwater marshes, estuaries.
**Food:** Insects, molluscs, crustaceans.
**Range:** Breeds across boreal and temperate Eurasia from Ireland and Spain to Kamchatka. Winters westernmost Europe, sub-Saharan Africa, and through Asia to Australia.
**Breeding:** Four brown-speckled buffy eggs are laid in a depression and incubated for 20–23 days. The active, downy chicks fly by 21 days.
**Confusing Species:** Wood Sandpiper does not bob as continuously.

## Terek Sandpiper *(Xenus cinereus)*

An eastern species that breeds in Russia, the Terek Sandpiper passes through eastern Europe on passage. The orange legs and long, upturned bill prevent confusion. In winter, the upperparts are grey with a dark area at the bend of the wing, and the underparts are white, with streaks on the sides of the breast. In summer, the breast is more heavily streaked with black 'braces' on the back.

*Crabs are a favourite food (left), being snapped up with darting movements. Top: Winter plumage.*

**Size:** 23cm (9in).
**Wing:** 128–140mm.
**Bill:** 43–52mm.
**Weight:** 58–108g.
**Voice:** Whistling *wik-wik-wik*.

**Habitat:** Marshes in the boreal zone. Winters estuaries and lagoons.
**Food:** Invertebrates and seeds.
**Range:** From Finland across the Eurasian boreal zone to Bering Strait. Winters coasts from West Africa, through Asia to Australia. In Europe, confined to head of Gulf of Bothnia and from Baltic States across Russia.
**Movements:** Most winter in Asia, but some reach Africa via Volga river system and the Middle East. Scarce in eastern Europe and Scandinavia and vagrant farther west.
**Breeding:** Four brown-blotched buff-coloured eggs are laid in a hollow and incubated by both sexes for 23 or 24 days. Chicks are active and downy.

JFMAMJJASOND

## Turnstone *(Arenaria interpres)*

A chunky, robust shorebird, the Turnstone uses its short, slightly upturned bill to turn over pebbles and other shoreline material, seeking its food beneath them. It will eat virtually anything. In summer, its upperparts form a pattern of chestnut and black, and the head and breast a mosaic of black and white. The short bill is black, the legs orange. In winter, much chestnut is lost, but the head pattern is clear if less well defined. In flight, shows a white wingbar and rump and bold braces. Usually flies in chattering flocks.

*The Turnstone uses its short bill to lift stones (right) and patches of seaweed, exposing invertebrates. Far right: Summer plumage.*

JFMAMJJASOND

**Size:** 20–23cm (8-9in).
**Wing:** 145–165mm.
**Bill:** 21–24mm.
**Weight:** 79–149g.
**Voice:** Chattered *tuk-a-tuk*.
**Habitat:** Arctic and tundra coasts in summer and virtually all types of coasts and estuaries in winter.
**Food:** Invertebrates, carrion.
**Range:** Circumpolar in the north from Scandinavia as far as ice-free land exists. Winters on coasts in most parts of the world. In Europe, breeds all Scandinavian coasts to northern Russia. Winters North Sea and Atlantic coasts, but not northern Mediterranean.
**Movements:** Mostly follows coasts, but central Siberian birds will head across the Caspian Sea towards the Middle East. Birds head westwards in autumn and eastwards in spring.
**Breeding:** Four brown-blotched green eggs are incubated by both sexes for 22 or 23 days and the chicks are active and down covered.

## Red-necked Phalarope *(Phalaropus lobatus)*

A delicate little wader, the Red-necked Phalarope spends its summers on shallow Arctic pools and its winters in large flocks on the open oceans. In summer, the female is brown above, with a creamy double V. The female's head and neck are grey, with rufous colouring from eye to breast. The male is duller. In winter, the bird has a grey and black spangled back, with a white double V, white head and black comma over the ear coverts. The juvenile is similar to the winter adult.

*The adult bird has grey upperparts with white below during the winter (below). During the breeding season, the female has a rufous neck and breast (left).*

**J F M A M J J A S O N D**

**Size:** 15–18cm (6–7in).
**Wing:** 104–117mm.
**Bill:** 19–23mm.
**Weight:** 20–40g.
**Voice:** A soft *ti-it.*
**Habitat:** Tundra. Winters at sea.
**Food:** Insects, planktonic crustaceans.
**Range:** Circumpolar tundra. Winters off Arabia, Peru and East Indies.
**Movements:** Passage migrant to the Persian Gulf, scarce in western Europe.
**Breeding:** Four brown-blotched green eggs are laid in a neat cup, incubated by the male for 18–20 days. The active, downy, young fly after 22 days.
**Confusing Species:** Grey Phalarope has a heavier bill.

## Grey Phalarope *(Phalaropus fulicarius)*

A compact little wader, the Grey Phalarope spends most of its life swimming, either among tundra marshes, or in the richest of the world's oceans. The adult in summer is black and buff, with rufous-chestnut underparts and a white face surrounded by black. In winter, it is uniformly pale grey above, with a smudgy mask. The juvenile is black and buff above, with a black eye patch.

*In summer the female has a brilliant plumage of reddish brown, while the male is rather duller.*

**J F M A M J J A S O N D**

**Size:** 18–20cm (7–8in).
**Wing:** 124–143mm.
**Bill:** 19–24mm.
**Weight:** 36–77g.
**Voice:** A high *twit.*
**Habitat:** Breeds on tundra pools and marshes. Winters at sea.
**Food:** Insects, molluscs, crustaceans.
**Range:** Circumpolar in north tundra zone. In Europe, breeds only in Iceland and is otherwise a passage migrant. Winters on western coasts of South

America and West and South Africa.
**Movements:** Migrates almost entirely over the sea and in Europe along Atlantic coasts.
**Breeding:** Four brown-blotched greenish eggs are laid in a marshy tussock and incubated by the male alone. The active, downy chicks hatch after 19 days and fly 21 days later.
**Confusing Species:** Juvenile easily confused with juvenile Red-necked Phalarope, but lacks 'V's on back.

## Pomarine Skua *(Stercorarius pomarinus)*

In size and bulk, this bird falls between the Great and Arctic Skuas, though it most closely resembles the latter, having two distinct colour phases. The dark phase is uniform dark brown, with bold white wing flashes. The pale phase is similar, but with creamy underparts marked by a dark breast band. The juvenile is heavily barred. In all plumages, a thick-set appearance is the best fieldmark.

*The Pomarine Skua is heavily built, with a deep chest, a breast band and, unless damaged, long central tail feathers.*

J F M A M J J A S O N D

**Size:** 40–53cm (16–21in).
**Wing:** 334–379mm.
**Bill:** 37–44mm.
**Weight:** 542–917g.
**Voice:** Silent at sea.
**Habitat:** Breeds high-Arctic tundra. Winters on coasts and open seas.
**Food:** Fish, but small mammals are important in summer.
**Range:** Circumpolar. Winters over southern oceans.
**Movements:** Migrates along North Sea and Atlantic coasts of Europe.
**Breeding:** Two brown-spotted buffy eggs are incubated for 28 days. The downy chicks fly after 35 days.
**Confusing Species:** Its heavy build distinguishes it from the Arctic Skua.

## Arctic Skua *(Stercorarius parasiticus)*

The most widespread and common of the four skuas regularly found in Europe, the Arctic Skua occurs in two distinct colour phases. The dark phase is uniformly dark brown with white wing flashes. The pale phase is similar, but with pale underparts marked by dark smudges at the sides of the breast. The juvenile is heavily barred with a pale belly. In summer, two central tail feathers extend in points. In all plumages, this bird is lighter in build than the otherwise similar Pomarine.

**Size:** 35–48cm (14–19in).
**Wing:** 306–353mm.
**Bill:** 29–34mm.
**Weight:** 301–644g.
**Voice:** A raucous *kee-ow*.
**Habitat:** Coastal moors and Arctic tundra pools and marshes. Winters far out at sea.

**Food:** Mammals in summer, particularly lemmings, and fish in winter, often obtained by robbery from other seabirds.
**Range:** North circumpolar. In Europe breeds Iceland, Scotland, coastal Scandinavia and northern Russia. Winters over the major oceans of the world, as far south as Cape Town and New Zealand.
**Breeding:** Two brown-blotched green eggs are laid on the ground and incubated for 24–28 days by both sexes. The helpless, downy chicks fly after about 30 days.
**Confusing Species:** Pomarine Skua has similar plumage but has a deeper chest and is heavier in build.

*Arctic Skuas show white wing flashes in flight. The pale phase bird has pale underparts while in the dark phase the plumage is all-dark.*

J F M A M J J A S O N D

Most lightly built of the skuas, the Long-tailed Skua is seen less often than the others, since it migrates farther out to sea. The adult is pale brownish above and creamy white below, with a dark cap. The shafts of the outer primaries are seen to be white at close range. The tail is long and wedge shaped; in summer its central feathers are greatly extended. The juvenile Long-tailed Skua is similar to a juvenile Arctic Skua, but shows white-shafted primaries.

*Dark wings, lacking the white flashes of other skuas, and a pale body are good field marks.*

**Size:** 38–53cm (15–21in).
**Wing:** 292–323mm.
**Bill:** 26–31mm.
**Weight:** 218–352g.
**Voice:** Brief *kreck*.
**Habitat:** Mountain plateaux and arctic tundra pools and moors. Winters at sea.
**Food:** Fish; small mammals in summer.
**Range:** Circumpolar in north, winters south Pacific and Atlantic. In Europe, breeds Scandinavian mountain chain and across northern Russia.
**Movements:** More pelagic than other skuas and relatively seldom seen from land. Passage to and from Siberia presumed to pass north of Norway.
**Breeding:** Two brown-blotched olive-green eggs in a hollow; incubated by both members of the pair for 25–28 days. Downy, helpless chicks fledge after 25 days. Dependent on lemming population for successful breeding. When these small mammals are absent, the birds may not even make an attempt.
**Confusing Species:** May be confused with pale phase and immature Arctic Skuas – a factor that may, at least partly, explain its apparent rarity.

J F M A M J J A S O N D

---

Largest and most powerful of the skuas, this bird is not easily confused with others. It has brown plumage, liberally flecked with white and marked by bold white wing patches in flight, when the wedge-shaped tail is apparent. It has a bulky build with a deep chest, small bill and broad-based wings.

**Size:** 56–61cm (22–24in).
**Wing:** 367–428mm.
**Bill:** 47–53mm.
**Weight:** 1210–1630g.
**Voice:** A harsh *uk-uk-uk* and nasal *skew*.
**Habitat:** Breeds on moors near seabird colonies, which it raids to feed its young. Winters at sea.
**Food:** Fish, smaller birds, eggs. A highly successful pirate that is quite capable of downing and robbing even large birds, such as Gannet.
**Range:** Breeds in Scotland, Iceland and in small numbers in Norway, Russia and on other northern islands. Large increase in numbers from 10 pairs on Shetland in 1774 to 5400 today. Several similar related species (opinions differ as to exact number) breed around Antarctic continent and may move northwards to European waters. In winter, ranges into central Atlantic Ocean.
**Movements:** Ranges right across North Atlantic from Spitzbergen to West Africa, eastern Canada and Brazil.
**Breeding:** Two brown-spotted olive eggs are laid on the ground and incubated by both sexes for 28–30 days. The helpless, down-covered chicks fly after 42–49 days.

*In threat displays, a Great Skua raises its wings, bristles its neck feathers and calls loudly.*

J F M A M J J A S O N D

## Mediterranean Gull (Larus melanocephalus)

This is a pale gull, marked by a black hood in summer. Summer adults are pale grey above, white below, with a black (not brown) hood, a broken white eye-ring and a scarlet bill. The whiteness of the wings can be startling. In all adult plumages, there are white wing tips without spots. In winter, the adult loses the dark head, which is replaced by a dark smudge behind the eye and streaking on the rear of the head. In all plumages, the large drooping bill is a major feature.

J F M A M J J A S O N D

*First-winter birds (left) have extensive black on primaries, greater coverts and secondaries, leaving a pale mid-wing panel. The adult summer plumage (above) is white with unmarked wing tips and a black head.*

**Size:** 35–38cm (14–15in).
**Wing:** 295–320mm.
**Bill:** 30–36mm.
**Weight:** 300-400g.
**Voice:** Plaintive *kee-ow*.
**Habitat:** Breeds among lakes and marshes. Winters mainly on coasts and estuaries, but also inland.
**Food:** Invertebrates, molluscs and fish.
**Range:** Breeds at only a few locations in Mediterranean and Black Seas and along the Danube river system. Recent colonization in Germany and Britain in small numbers. Winters Mediterranean and Atlantic and North Sea coasts. Largest numbers in Black Sea.
**Movements:** A definite movement from the Balkans northwest across Europe in autumn. Otherwise no more than a dispersal from breeding zones.
**Breeding:** Three black-speckled cream-coloured eggs are laid in a hollow near water, often among nests of other gulls. The eggs are incubated for 23–25 days by both sexes and the active and downy chicks fledge after 35–40 days.
**Confusing Species:** Paler even than Black-headed Gull and with white wing tips. Immatures more closely resemble immature Common Gull, but with longer, drooping bill.

## Little Gull (Larus minutus)

This is the smallest European gull and it frequently behaves like a Marsh Tern, picking food from the water's surface in flight. In summer, the adult is pale grey above, with white wing tips and a black hood. In flight, it shows a dark underwing. In winter, the black hood is lost and replaced by a black spot behind the eye. Like an immature Kittiwake, immature birds show a black W across the wings in flight, but are much smaller and lack the nape band of that species.

J F M A M J J A S O N D

*The black W across the wings in flight is a feature of the immature Little Gull.*

**Size:** 25–28cm (10–11in).
**Wing:** 204–237mm.
**Bill:** 20–23mm.
**Weight:** 93–150g.
**Voice:** Repeated *ka-eee*.
**Habitat:** Breeds among freshwater marshes with islands and emergent vegetation. Winters lakes, coasts and estuaries.

**Food:** Invertebrates, insects, small fish.
**Range:** Scarce and local breeder in western Europe, with colonies in Holland, Denmark, Sweden and the Baltic states and from Finland eastwards across Russia to central and eastern Siberia. Winters Mediterranean and Black Seas, Baltic and North Seas, as well as locally in eastern Canada. Frequently some distance from land.

**Movements:** Down-Channel movements noted in autumn, with large concentrations particularly in Holland and Belgium.
**Breeding:** Three black-blotched pale olive eggs are laid in a nest of reeds or rushes in a marsh and incubated by both sexes for 23–25 days. The active and downy chicks fledge after 21–24 days.
**Confusing Species:** Kittiwake.

## Black-headed Gull *(Larus ridibundus)*

In summer, the adults have a brown hood and upperparts are grey with black tips to the folded wings. The underparts are white with dusky colour on the inner primaries. Slender bill and legs are red. All plumages show a white leading edge on the outer wing. Immatures have brown and black across the wings and a black tail band.

J F M A M J J A S O N D

**Size:** 33–38cm (13–15in).
**Wing:** 282–323mm.
**Bill:** 30–37mm.
**Weight:** 190–400g.
**Voice:** A harsh *kee-arr*.
**Habitat:** Freshwater marshes, lakes, ponds, rivers, coasts, estuaries, gravel pits, rubbish tips, fields and grasslands.
**Food:** Invertebrates, seeds, carrion, waste foods.

**Range:** Breeds right across temperate Eurasia. Winters western Pacific coasts as far as Borneo and in the North Atlantic, Mediterranean, Black and Red Seas and Persian Gulf. In Europe, absent as a breeding bird from northern Scandinavia, most of Iberia and the Mediterranean. Winters inland across Britain, France, Germany, Jutland and southern Sweden, and around all coasts.
**Movements:** Migrates westwards from Russia and central Europe to western seaboards and inland areas. Some European birds may never see the sea.
**Breeding:** Three black-blotched buffy grey eggs are laid in a cup of vegetation; incubated by both sexes for 21–27 days; active, downy chicks fly after 35–42 days.
**Confusing Species:** Mediterranean and Slender-billed Gulls.

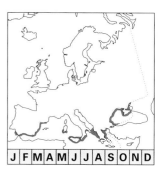

*The dark head fades in winter, but the white leading edge of the wing remains.*

## Slender-billed Gull *(Larus genei)*

Adult is grey above, white below and is marked in flight by a white forewing very similar to that of the Black-headed Gull. The head lacks dark markings at all times. Immature has a dark smudge behind the eye, dark greyish markings across the wing and a black tail band.

**Size:** 40–46cm (16–18in).
**Wing:** 279–321mm.
**Bill:** 36–46mm.
**Weight:** 223–275g.
**Voice:** Various nasal yelpings.
**Habitat:** Marshes, lakes and sea coasts.
**Food:** Fish and invertebrates.
**Range:** Breeds in Mauritania, Spain, France, Sardinia and Italy, Greece and from the Black Sea to Kazakhstan and the Middle East. But almost all colonies are isolated. Winters around the Mediterranean, Black, Caspian and Red Seas and in the Persian Gulf. Fewer than 1000 pairs breed in western Europe.
**Movements:** Local spread to wintering areas. Vagrant elsewhere.
**Breeding:** Two or three black-blotched creamy eggs are laid in a depression, usually on an island, and incubated by both sexes for 22 days. The chicks are down covered and active.
**Confusing Species:** Black-headed Gull.

*In all plumages the long neck, sloping forehead and long, thin bill of this elegant gull are the best identification features.*

J F M A M J J A S O N D

## Audouin's Gull *(Larus audouinii)*

This is a Mediterranean gull with a scattered distribution which is seemingly increasing in numbers. Grey above and white below, marked by extensive black wing tips with white 'mirrors'. The legs are grey, the bill is large, drooping and red, with a black band. Immatures are brown, with a very broad black tail band and a 'U'-shaped rump. In flight, in all plumages, the pointed wings and the elongated head and droopy bill, create an unmistakable shape.

*One of the best fieldmarks in flight is the relatively narrow outer wing.*

**Size:** 48–51cm (19–20in).
**Wing:** 384–423mm.
**Bill:** 40–52mm.
**Weight:** 580–770g.
**Voice:** Various braying calls.
**Habitat:** Breeds rocky islands, coasts, deltas and coastal marshes.
**Food:** Fish.

**Range:** Breeds along coasts of North Africa and Spain, the Balearics, Corsica and Sardinia, the Aegean and Cyprus. Winters near breeding sites and wanders locally.
**Movements:** Numbers along the Atlantic coast of Morocco may be either definite migration or wandering.

**Breeding:** Two or three black-blotched buff-coloured eggs are laid in a lined hollow and incubated by both sexes for 21–25 days. The active and downy chicks fledge after 35–40 days.
**Confusing Species:** Beware Yellow-legged and Mediterranean Gulls, especially immatures. Shape is crucial.

## Common Gull *(Larus canus)*

A neat grey and white gull, darker than the Herring Gull, with extensive black wing tips and white 'mirrors'. The white head is neatly rounded, marked with a dark eye and a gentle expression. The bill is short, tapered and, like the legs, yellow-green in colour. Immature has a grey mantle and a central wing panel in flight.

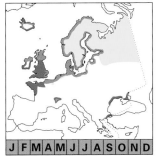

*In winter, the head and nape of an adult Common Gull are boldly speckled brown.*

**Size:** 40–43cm (16–17in).
**Wing:** 321–380mm.
**Bill:** 27–38mm.
**Weight:** 300–552g.
**Voice:** High-pitched *kee-arr*.
**Habitat:** Lakes, even in city centres, marshes, moors and, in winter, coasts, estuaries, reservoirs and fields.
**Food:** Invertebrates, insects and molluscs.
**Range:** Breeds right across Eurasia from Iceland to the Bering Strait in the boreal zone and in northwestern North America. In Europe, in Iceland, northwestern Britain and Ireland, along North Sea coasts to the Baltic and Scandinavia and across Russia. Winters on adjacent seas.
**Movements:** Large numbers migrate westwards to winter at the entrance to the Baltic and North Seas. Large numbers reach Britain.
**Breeding:** Three brown-blotched greenish eggs are laid in a lined hollow on the ground, often near the coast or on moorland. Eggs are incubated by both sexes for 22–27 days. The active and downy chicks fly after 30–35 days.
**Confusing Species:** Kittiwake, which has similar benign look and yellow bill. Herring Gull is larger, with pink legs.

171

## Lesser Black-backed Gull *(Larus fuscus)*

The adult bird is dark grey above, white below, and has black wing tips with white 'mirrors', a red-spotted yellow bill and yellow legs.

**Size:** 51–56cm (20–22in).
**Wing:** 377–446mm.
**Bill:** 40–57mm.
**Weight:** 545–908g.
**Voice:** Loud *kyow-kyow* and *kee-aa*.

**Habitat:** Moorlands, flat islands; winters estuaries, fields, salt pans.
**Food:** Omnivorous.
**Range:** Breeds across northern Eurasia; winters Baltic Sea to Africa.

*Young Lesser Black-backeds (right) are darker than young Herring Gulls and lack pale inner primaries.*

**Movements:** Migrates on coasts.
**Breeding:** Three black-blotched olive eggs in a hollow; incubated by both sexes for 24–27 days; active, downy young fly at 35–40 days.
**Confusing Species:** Great Black-backed Gull is larger.

---

## Herring Gull *(Larus argentatus)*

The standard large gull over most of coastal northern Europe. It is pale grey above and white below, marked by black wing tips with white 'mirrors'. The powerful bill is yellow with a red spot, and the legs are pink.

*The red spot and yellow bill of the adult Herring Gull attract the chicks to peck, which in turn prompts the adult to regurgitate food.*

**Size:** 53–59cm (20–23in).
**Wing:** 391–476mm.
**Bill:** 46–60mm.
**Weight:** 690–1495g.
**Voice:** Loud, laughing *kyow-kyow*.
**Habitat:** Cliffs, seaside buildings, moors coasts, estuaries, marshes, reservoirs.
**Food:** Omnivorous.
**Range:** North Atlantic, Iceland to Britain and Ireland, Atlantic Iberia, North Sea coasts to Scandinavia, and Russia.
**Movements:** Russian and Scandinavian birds move southwest to Britain, France.
**Breeding:** Two or three brown-blotched pale green eggs in a cup of vegetation; incubated mainly by the female for 28–30 days; active, downy young fly after 40 days.
**Confusing Species:** Yellow-legged Gull, resident in the Mediterranean.

---

## Yellow-Legged Gull *(Larus cachinnans)*

This bird is very similiar to the Herring Gull and it has only recently been recognized as a separate species. In contrast to the Herring Gull, it has darker grey upperparts and larger, more

squared-off black wing tips. It has a yellow bill with a red spot, but its legs are yellow, not pink.

**Size:** 51–59cm (20–23in).
**Wing:** 395–428mm.
**Bill:** 47–55mm.
**Weight:** 800–1300g.
**Voice:** Ringing *kyow-kyow*.
**Habitat:** Cliffs, marshes, shores, lakes.

**Food:** Omnivorous.
**Range:** Breeds in Mediterranean and Black Seas, extending inland along the Danube. Local dispersal in winter.
**Movements:** The occurrence of these birds in northwestern Europe in late summer indicates a northwards movement, probably along the Danube.
**Breeding:** Two or three brown-blotched pale green eggs are laid on a cliff ledge or among marshes; incubated mainly by the female for 25–33 days; active, downy chicks fly after 35–40 days.
**Confusing Species:** Herring Gull.

*In flight, the yellow legs are hidden (above right), but the bird differs from the Herring Gull in having larger black wing tips and a generally darker back.*

## Great Black-backed Gull *(Larus marinus)*

A fearsome, dark gull with a massive head and bill, this bird breeds around the coasts of northern Europe and is a winter visitor to Baltic and North Sea coasts. The bird will scavenge on dead sheep and prey upon birds as big as Puffins and mammals as large as rabbits. The adult has a black back and wings with white 'mirrors' at their tips. It has a large head, red-spotted yellow bill and pinkish legs. The immature is paler than that of other gulls, with dark markings on white.

*In first-winter plumage, the Great Black-backed Gull has black outer primaries and a clear black tail band.*

| J | F | M | A | M | J | J | A | S | O | N | D |

**Size:** 64–79cm (25–31in).
**Wing:** 453–521mm.
**Bill:** 54–71mm.
**Weight:** 1140–2273g.
**Voice:** Harsh *owk*.
**Habitat:** Coastal cliffs and stacks in summer. All coasts, including estuaries, and rubbish tips in winter.
**Food:** Offal, fish, birds, rubbish.
**Range:** Temperate and Arctic North

Atlantic. Winters coastal and pelagic Europe and North America. In Europe, breeds from Iceland, Britain and Ireland, northwestern France and Jutland through Scandinavia to Spitzbergen and northwest Russia. Winters locally and southwards to Portugal.
**Movements:** Far northern Scandinavian and Russian birds migrate around North Cape of Norway to southern North Sea.

**Breeding:** Two or three brown-speckled olive eggs laid in a large nest of seaweed on the ground or an island or stack; incubated by both members of the pair for 26–30 days. Active, downy chicks fly after 50–51 days.
**Confusing Species:** Lesser Black-backed Gull is smaller and paler.

## Iceland Gull *(Larus glaucoides)*

This is a regular, if scarce, winter visitor to extreme northwestern Europe from Greenland and Canada. Adults, like Glaucous Gulls, have pale grey upperparts, white underparts and white wing tips. The major differences are structural, with Iceland Gulls having a small, more rounded head and a smaller red-spotted, yellow bill; these combine to produce a gentle expression. The wing tips extend well beyond the tail at rest.

*The adult (top right) is pure white, but the immature (right) is spotted buffy, with white wing tips.*

| J | F | M | A | M | J | J | A | S | O | N | D |

**Size:** 51–56cm (20–22in).
**Wing:** 386–443mm.
**Bill:** 37–48mm.
**Weight:** Unknown.
**Voice:** Shrill *kyow*.
**Habitat:** Arctic cliffs and islands sheltered in deep fjords in summer. In winter frequents coasts.
**Food:** Fish, invertebrates.
**Range:** Confined to Greenland and adjacent eastern Canadian archipelago in summer. Winters across the North

Atlantic, including Iceland, southwards as far as northern Britain and Ireland. Regular along Norwegian coast.
**Movements:** Mostly disperses locally and movements to Europe are probably no more than extended wandering.
**Breeding:** Lays two or three eggs – nothing else known of breeding routine.
**Confusing Species:** Larger Glaucous Gull is distinguishable by its fierce expression, which is created by a larger head and bill and prominent pale eye.

173

## Glaucous Gull (*Larus hyperboreus*)

| J | F | M | A | M | J | J | A | S | O | N | D |

**Size:** 56–69cm (22–27in).
**Wing:** 422–496mm.
**Bill:** 53–69mm.
**Weight:** 1280–2125g.
**Voice:** Harsh *kyow*.
**Habitat:** Breeds on cliffs and islands in high-Arctic tundra. Winters coasts and estuaries, sometimes rubbish tips.
**Food:** Fish, invertebrates and carrion.
**Range:** Northern circumpolar at the highest latitudes. In Europe, breeds Iceland, Spitzbergen and northernmost Russia. Winters northern ice-free coasts southwards to southern North Sea and Britain and Ireland.
**Movements:** Large numbers move south to winter in Faeroe Islands; few

make it as far as Britain and Holland.
**Breeding:** Two or three black-blotched pale olive eggs are laid in a nest of available vegetation placed on a sea cliff, stack or marshy island. Incubation, which is shared, lasts for 27–30 days and the active, downy chicks fly after about 40–50 days.
**Confusing Species:** Iceland Gull has 'white wings', but is smaller and has a smaller head and bill and more benign expression.

This large 'white-winged' gull breeds in Iceland and Russia, but is a scarce winter visitor to temperate Europe. Adult is pale grey above and white below, marked by white wing tips visible at rest and in flight. The bill is large and yellow with a red spot; legs are pink. The pale eye gives it a very fierce expression. In winter the head and neck are spotted buff. Immatures are spotted buff with whitish wing tips.

*The lack of black wing tips in a pale Herring Gull-like bird precludes confusion with all except the Iceland Gull.*

## Kittiwake (*Rissa tridactyla*)

Europe's only truly oceanic gull, this dainty bird breeds in vast seacliff colonies and spends the year wandering the oceans. It is grey above and white below, with black wing tips, which lack the white 'mirrors' seen in other species, black legs and a delicate yellow bill. It flies gracefully on long narrow wings.

| J | F | M | A | M | J | J | A | S | O | N | D |

**Size:** 38–43cm (15–17in).
**Wing:** 279–326mm.
**Bill:** 31–38mm.
**Weight:** 305–525g.
**Voice:** A repeated *kitti-wake*.
**Habitat:** Seacliffs in summer. Winters at sea.
**Food:** Fish.
**Range:** Circumpolar in north. In Europe, breeds Iceland, Britain, locally in France, Portugal and Spain, Jutland and coastal Norway and Russia. Winters over

oceans southwards to western Mediterranean.
**Movements:** Wanders the oceans.
**Breeding:** Two brown-speckled creamy eggs are laid in a neat cup of seaweed placed on a narrow cliff ledge and are incubated by both sexes for 25–30 days. The active, down-covered chicks fly after 43 days.

*Juvenile shows an inverted black 'W' across wings in flight and a black nape bar.*

## Gull-billed Tern *(Gelochelidon nilotica)*

This large pale tern often hawks for insects over dry land. Upperparts are the palest of greys, underparts are white. In summer the bird has a clear-cut black cap that extends to the nape. This is replaced in winter by a black mark. In flight, the long wings are broadly based. Its large head and thick black bill add to its 'bull-necked' appearance.

*In winter, a black mark from eye to nape (above) replaces the black cap of summer (above right).*

**Size:** 35–38cm (14–15in).
**Wing:** 307–341mm.
**Bill:** 35–42mm.
**Weight:** 204–292g.
**Voice:** Harsh *ak-ak*.
**Habitat:** Margins of drying lagoons in summer, mostly coastal in winter, though also along river systems.

**Food:** Insects and, occasionally, small mammals.
**Range:** Cosmopolitan, but highly localized in many areas. In Europe, breeds Spain, at one place in France, four areas in Italy, five or six spots in Greece, a few places in Jutland and sporadically through the Black Sea to central Asia. Winters on Mediterranean and Atlantic coasts, in Sahel Africa, India and the Far East to Australia.
**Movements:** Very rare as a migrant along Atlantic and Channel coasts to and from Danish breeding grounds. Migration in numbers through Tunisia in autumn indicates trans-Saharan flight to Chad. The reverse migration in spring is even more evident, with large numbers passing through Italy.
**Breeding:** Three brown-speckled cream eggs laid in a scrape and incubated by both sexes for 22 or 23 days. The active, downy chicks fly after 28–35 days.
**Confusing Species:** Sandwich Tern is equally pale grey, but has a longer, thinner bill with easily missed yellow tip, and is not thick-necked.

## Caspian Tern *(Sterna caspia)*

**Size:** 48–56cm (19–22in).
**Wing:** 387–441mm.
**Bill:** 62–79mm.
**Weight:** 560–760g.
**Voice:** Loud *kraa*.
**Habitat:** Breeds on low rocky islands in sea or lakes. Winters mainly coasts, but also inland on large floods and lakes.
**Food:** Fish.
**Range:** Cosmopolitan except South America. In Europe, strangely scattered range, with birds in Baltic and Black Seas extending across central Asia to China, Australia and New Zealand. Winters southern Europe, but mainly in Africa and the Middle East.
**Movements:** European Baltic breeders move southwards across the continent via large river systems to the Mediterranean Sea before crossing the Sahara Desert to winter at Niger Inundation Zone, Lake Chad and coasts to the south.
**Breeding:** Two or three black-speckled cream eggs are laid in a hollow and incubated by both sexes for 20–22 days. The young hatch active and downy and fly after 25–30 days.

The Caspian is a gull-sized tern marked by a massive red bill. It is pale grey above and white below, with a black cap that terminates in a ragged crest. The head and red bill are the best field marks, although in flight, the dark primaries and neatly notched tail are useful. The immature has a dark-tipped tail and a grey band across the inner wing. The bird frequently loafs with other terns and stands taller than any other species.

*The Caspian Tern's huge red bill is obvious at all times.*

## Sandwich Tern *(Sterna sandvicensis)*

Significantly larger and paler than Common and Arctic Terns, this medium-sized bird forms dense breeding colonies that it abandons for no apparent cause. Adult is pale grey above, white below, with a black cap terminating in a ragged crest. The bill is black, tipped yellow, and the legs black. In winter the black cap is mostly lost.

*Immature Sandwich Tern (above) is heavily barred above, creating a distinctive scaly pattern.*

**Size:** 35–43cm (14–17in).
**Wing:** 294–320mm.
**Bill:** 49–58mm.
**Weight:** 198–291g.
**Voice:** A rasping *keerick*.
**Habitat:** Low-lying coastal islands and lagoons in summer. Winters along coasts.
**Food:** Fish, obtained by aerial diving.
**Range:** In Europe, breeds from Ireland to the Baltic, at a few spots in the Mediterranean and along the northern shores of the Black Sea. Winters Arabia and West African coasts south to the Cape. Some winter in Mediterranean.
**Movements:** Apparently follows coasts, with Black Sea birds exiting the Mediterranean via Gibraltar.
**Breeding:** Two brown-speckled buff-coloured eggs are laid in a scrape and incubated by both sexes for 20–24 days. The young are active and downy and fly after 35 days.
**Confusing Species:** Gull-billed Tern is equally pale and has a black bill.

J F M A M J J A S O N D

---

## Common Tern *(Sterna hirundo)*

This most common European tern is a summer visitor to coasts and inland waters. Adult in summer is grey above and whitish below, marked by a black cap and red legs and bill, the latter tipped black. The tail is deeply forked, but streamers do not extend beyond tips of folded wings. In winter, the black cap is confined to the rear crown. In flight, inner primaries are translucent. Immature has dark leading and trailing edges to the wing, creating a pale mid-wing panel in flight.

**Size:** 28–35cm (11–14in).
**Wing:** 244–290mm.
**Bill:** 32–40mm.
**Weight:** 80–165g.
**Voice:** Harsh, scolding *key-arr*.
**Habitat:** Low-lying coasts and islands, large rivers, lakes and lagoons. Winters along coasts.
**Food:** Fish, obtained by aerial diving, and insects picked from the water's surface.
**Range:** Circumpolar in the northern temperate zone. In Europe, the species breeds from Ireland and France eastwards to the Urals, though it is absent from the tundra zone and from most of Iberia. The birds winter to the south as far as Cape Town.
**Movements:** Birds from central and eastern Europe cross the continent to the Mediterranean and then head westwards to join birds from the north and so reach coasts of West Africa.
**Breeding:** Two or three black-blotched creamy eggs are laid in a scrape. They are incubated for 20–23 days, mainly by the female, and the young fly after 28 days. May occasionally raise two broods of young in a season.

*Immature has a black leading edge to the wing, forming a distinctive patch at the bend of the wing.*

**Confusing Species:** Arctic Tern is very similar but, in summer, is greyish below, has dark red bill lacking the black tip, and the tail streamers extend well beyond the folded wings.

J F M A M J J A S O N D

## Arctic Tern *(Sterna paradisaea)*

**Size:** 28–38cm (11–15in).
**Wing:** 238–290mm.
**Bill:** 29–35mm.
**Weight:** 87–119g.
**Voice:** Harsh *kee-rr*.
**Habitat:** Low-lying coasts and marshes, tundra pools and lakes in summer. Winters at sea.

J F M A M J J A S O N D

**Food:** Fish.
**Range:** Northern circumpolar. In Europe, a summer visitor from Iceland, to Britain and Ireland, North Sea, Scandinavia to tundra Russia. Winters southern oceans to Antarctica.
**Movements:** Vast coastal movements in Atlantic, with even North American birds crossing to coastal Iberia before heading south. Rare in Mediterranean.
**Breeding:** Two brown-blotched buffy eggs laid in a bare scrape and incubated by both sexes for 20–22 days. The active, down-covered chicks fly after 20–22 days.
**Confusing Species:** Common Tern has black tip to bill and short tail streamers.

Major differences between the Common Tern and this summer visitor to northern Europe and the Arctic are the Arctic Tern's blood-red (not orange-red) black-tipped bill, greyish underparts with white below crown, tail streamers that extend beyond the folded wings and translucent wings.

*Immatures have dark (not boldly black) forewing and prominent white trailing edge to the wing.*

## Roseate Tern *(Sterna dougallii)*

A scarce and localized summer visitor to Atlantic Europe, this tern survives at a few well-established colonies. Adult in summer is a paler grey than both Common and Arctic Terns, with white underparts washed pinkish. The bill is black, often showing a reddish base, the legs red. Long tail streamers that extend well beyond the folded wings are particularly obvious in flight. Despite its measurements, this is a smaller-looking bird than Common and Arctic Terns.

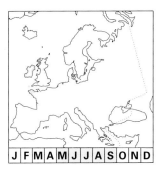

J F M A M J J A S O N D

**Range:** Widespread in Atlantic America, Europe, East Africa, Arabia, India, Southeast Asia to Australasia. In Europe, it is confined to Britain and Ireland and northwest France. Winters in West Africa.
**Movements:** Coastal migration around the bulge of Africa to winter quarters, mostly off Ghana, where many are trapped for food and sport.
**Breeding:** One or two brown speckled creamy eggs are laid in a hollow, often protected by low vegetation. Incubation by both sexes lasts 21–26 days and the active and downy chicks fly after 27–30 days.
**Confusing Species:** Arctic and Common Terns.

*Adult Roseate Tern has extended tail streamers that are longer than those of any other tern.*

**Size:** 30–38cm (12–15in).
**Wing:** 225–242mm.
**Bill:** 35–40mm.
**Weight:** 92–133g.
**Voice:** Loud *kee-ar*.
**Habitat:** Coastal islands and lagoons. Winters coasts and offshore.
**Food:** Fish.

## Little Tern *(Sterna albifrons)*

**Size:** 23–25cm (9–10in).
**Wing:** 164–187mm.
**Bill:** 27–33mm.
**Weight:** 49–63g.
**Voice:** Chattering *kitti-kitti.*
**Habitat:** Shorelines of shingle, also rivers and lakes. Winters along coasts.
**Food:** Fish, crustaceans and insects.
**Range:** Virtually cosmopolitan. In Europe, breeds along most temperate coasts and large river systems, but absent from Iceland, Norway, Biscay and much of inland Europe. Winters on coasts of Africa and inland at Niger Inundation Zone and in Nigeria.
**Movements:** Most birds move along coasts, but some follow major rivers and other overland routes. No evidence of trans-Saharan migration.

**Breeding:** Two or three, brown-blotched olive-green eggs are laid in a scrape and incubated by both sexes for 19–22 days. The downy, active young fly after 19 or 20 days.
**Confusing Species:** Other terns are noticeably larger.

In flight (far left) the dark outer primaries are obvious. At rest (left), the white forehead is a prominent feature.

A tiny, narrow-winged tern, the Little Tern is a summer visitor to coasts and large river systems. In summer the adult is grey above, white below, with a black cap marked by a prominent white forehead. The legs and bill are yellow, the latter tipped black. In flight the narrow wings are beaten fast and show a black forewing to the primaries. The immature bird has scaly plumage across back and wings.

## Whiskered Tern *(Chlidonias hybridus)*

A well-marked, grey marsh tern, the Whiskered Tern is easily confused with Black and White-winged Black Terns in winter and immature plumages. The adult in summer is grey above and darker grey below, with a wedge of white on the cheeks below a black cap. The bill and legs are dark red. In winter, the underparts are white and the wings grey. The immature has a black 'saddle' and a white tail with a dark tip.

The black and white head of the summer plumage is like that of other terns. The nest (below) floats on shallow bodies of fresh water.

**Size:** 25–28cm (10–11in).
**Wing:** 228–250mm.
**Bill:** 26–33mm.
**Weight:** 83–92g.
**Voice:** A nasal *knech.*
**Habitat:** Marshes, rice fields, lakes in summer and winter.
**Food:** Insects.
**Range:** Breeds right across the Old World. Winters Africa, India and Far East to Australia. In Europe, a summer visitor to Mediterranean and south temperate zones, from Spain and France to Balkans and eastwards to the Volga. Although generally scarce, it is locally abundant.
**Movements:** Western European birds wintering in Sahel Africa probably cross the Sahara.

**Breeding:** Three brown-spotted pale blue, grey or buff eggs are laid on a floating platform of aquatic vegetation and incubated by both parents for 18–20 days. The active, downy young fly after some 23 days.
**Confusing Species**: Black and, especially, White-winged Black Terns.

## White-winged Black Tern *(Chlidonias leucopterus)*

An apparition in gorgeous black and white summer plumage that breeds only in eastern Europe, the White-winged Black Tern is no more than a brief passage migrant to the west. In summer, its whole body is black, with a white undertail and contrasting white wings. The tiny bill is black, and the legs red. The immature has a dark back, forming a 'saddle' between grey wings and the white rump and tail.

**Size:** 23cm (9in).
**Wing:** 203–221mm.
**Bill:** 23–28mm.
**Weight:** 50–80g.
**Voice:** A clear *keer*.
**Habitat:** Marshes and lakes with emergent vegetation. In winter at lakes, rivers and salt pans, but seldom over the sea.

*The summer plumage (left) is striking in the air (right) with white wings, rump and tail contrasting with black head, body and underwing coverts.*

**Food:** Insects.
**Range:** Breeds across Eurasia from Hungary through Russia and the Ukraine to western Siberia, and again in eastern Siberia. Winters sub-Saharan Africa and in China and the Far East.
**Movements:** Most European birds migrate across the Sahara to reach their winter quarters. Abundant on the Rift Valley lakes of East Africa.
**Breeding:** Three brown-blotched buffy eggs are laid on a floating platform of aquatic vegetation in a marsh and incubated mainly by the female for 18–22 days. The active downy chicks fly after 24 or 25 days.
**Confusing Species:** Black Tern and Whiskered Tern.

J F M A M J J A S O N D

## Black Tern *(Chlidonias niger)*

A small, graceful, dark grey and black marsh tern, the Black Tern is most often seen flying low over water, delicately picking insects from the surface. In summer, the body is black with a white undertail and dark grey wings. The juvenile is similar to the winter adult, but is barred on the back and inner wings.

*The summer plumage (left) varies between dark grey and black. The nest (right) is made up of a mass of vegetation attached to strong reeds.*

J F M A M J J A S O N D

**Size:** 23–25cm (9–10in).
**Wing:** 201–226mm.
**Bill:** 25–30mm.
**Weight:** 56–88g.
**Voice:** A high *kik*.
**Habitat:** Freshwater marshes and lagoons. Winters mostly on coasts, sometimes along major rivers.
**Food:** Insects.
**Range:** Summer visitor to Europe, eastwards to central Asia, and across North America. In Europe, breeds sparsely in the west and more commonly from Holland through Germany to

Russia. Absent from Britain. Winters on African coasts.
**Movements:** Mainly follows coasts as far south as Namibia, but also passes overland in some areas. Huge autumn movements through English Channel.
**Breeding:** Three brown-spotted buff eggs are laid on an anchored platform of

aquatic vegetation in a marshy lagoon and incubated mainly by the female for 21 or 22 days. The active, down-covered young fly after 19–25 days.
**Confusing Species:** In winter plumage, must be distinguished from White-winged Black and Whiskered Terns with care.

This locally abundant, cliff-nesting auk spends most of its life at sea. It has slate-brown upperparts with white underparts, and is marked by a white wingbar.

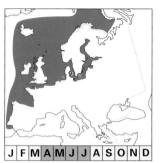

*In winter the breast, sides of the neck and face become white.(below). In summer the face is black (left).*

**Size:** 40–43cm (16–17in).
**Wing:** 190–225mm.
**Bill:** 43–51mm.
**Weight:** 490–853g.
**Voice:** Moaning and growling calls.
**Habitat:** Breeds sea cliffs and stacks. Winters at sea.
**Food:** Fish, crustaceans and molluscs.
**Range:** Breeds North Pacific and North Atlantic and winters over nearby seas. In Europe, breeds Iceland, Britain and Ireland, northern France, locally in Iberia, and locally in the Baltic and along the coasts of Norway and Russia.
**Movements:** Dispersive movements rather than definite migrations.
**Breeding:** A single blotchy egg is laid on a cliff ledge, often shared with other pairs in large colonies. The egg is incubated by both sexes for 28–35 days and the helpless, down-covered young is able to fly after 18–25 days.
**Confusing Species:** Brünnich's Guillemot and Razorbill.

Brünnich's Guillemot is very similar to the Common Guillemot, but it is found at higher latitudes and has a shorter, broader bill with a white mark at the gape. The bird's upperparts, extending over the neck and head, are slate brown, and its feet are flesh coloured.

**Size:** 40–43cm (16–17in).
**Wing:** 208–223mm.
**Bill:** 35–44mm.
**Weight:** 810–1206g.
**Voice:** Various growls.
**Habitat:** Breeds on Arctic cliffs, choosing narrower ledges than Common Guillemot. Winters in Arctic seas.
**Food:** Fish, crustaceans and molluscs.
**Range:** Breeds North Atlantic and North Pacific. Ranges over adjacent seas in winter. In Europe, it is confined to Iceland, Sptizbergen, northern Norway and northern Russia. Some wander as far south as Bergen in Norway and the Faeroe Islands. Vagrant to Britain.
**Movements:** Local dispersal.
**Breeding:** A single spotted creamy egg is laid on a narrow ledge, apart from other pairs. Incubation, by both sexes, lasts 28–35 days and the helpless, downy chick flies after 18–25 days.
**Confusing Species:** Common Guillemot is found at lower latitudes.

*In winter, the breast, neck and face are white (left), but white does not extend over the eye as in Common Guillemot.*

## Razorbill (Alca torda)

**Size:** 38–43cm (15–17in).
**Wing:** 201–216mm.
**Bill:** 32–39mm.
**Weight:** 372–890g.
**Voice:** Growling and grumbling notes.
**Habitat:** Sea cliffs, where it usually breeds among boulders. Winters at sea.
**Food:** Fish, crustaceans and molluscs.
**Range:** Breeds both sides of the Atlantic. In Europe, breeds from Iceland to Britain and Ireland, northwest France and the coasts of Scandinavia. Winters over adjacent seas.
**Movements:** European Razorbills range much farther from their natal colonies than Guillemots, reaching the coasts of southern Morocco and extending into the western Mediterranean in winter. Such flights of more than 1500km (938 miles) rank as true migrations rather than dispersal.
**Breeding:** A single brown-blotched egg is laid in a rock crevice or cliff hole and incubated by both sexes for 32–39 days. The helpless, down-covered young fledges after 14–24 days.
**Confusing Species:** Common Guillemot.

The Razorbill (top) has a much heavier bill than the Guillemot (middle) and a much narrower bill than the Puffin (bottom).

Similar to Common and Brünnich's Guillemots, with which it often associates at breeding cliffs, the Razorbill has black, rather than dark brown upperparts. It has a white wingbar and a very broad bill, marked by a white vertical line. In winter, its neck and face are white. The length of its head and depth and shape of its bill make it easy to identify.

## Black Guillemot (Cepphus grylle)

A sedentary auk that breeds around northern seacliffs, the Black Guillemot seldom wanders far south. In summer, its whole plumage is glossy black, marked by large, oval white wing patches. The feet are red. In winter, it is mottled grey above and plain grey below, but oval white wing patches remain.

Winter plumage (left) is grey with oval white wing patches, in contrast to its mostly black summer plumage (right).

**Size:** 33–35cm (13–14in).
**Wing:** 152–182mm.
**Bill:** 28–36mm.
**Weight:** 304–466g.
**Voice:** Varied whistles.
**Habitat:** Breeds at the foot of cliffs among rocky screes; winters close inshore beneath cliffs.
**Food:** Fish, molluscs and crustaceans.
**Range:** Circumpolar in north. In Europe, breeds from Iceland to Ireland, northern Britain and Scandinavia and also northern Russia. Resident as far north as ice-free coasts permit.
**Movements:** Only local wandering.
**Breeding:** Two black-speckled white eggs are laid in a hole or crevice among rocks and incubated by both sexes for 21–25 days. The helpless, downy young fly after 35–40 days.

**Size:** 20–22cm (8in).
**Wing:** 116–127mm.
**Bill:** 13–17mm.
**Weight:** 134–192g.
**Voice:** A trilled *kri-ri-ri-kikiki-ki-ki.*
**Habitat:** Breeds among mountain screes. Winters at sea.
**Food:** Crustaceans.
**Range:** High-Arctic North Atlantic, from Greenland to islands of central Siberia as far north as ice-free land extends. Winters across northern North Atlantic as far as North Sea.
**Movements:** Definite movements southwards as indicated by regular late autumn 'wrecks' of storm-driven birds, particularly along North Sea coasts. Winters as far north as the sea remains ice free.
**Breeding:** Breeds in vast mountain colonies numbering tens or hundreds of thousands. Lays a single brown-spotted bluish egg in a hole among rocks. Incubation by both sexes lasts 28–31 days and the helpless, downy chicks fly after 21–28 days.
**Confusing Species:** No other small auks exist in Europe.

This tiny black and white auk flies on long, pointed whirring wings, often in large flocks. It is one of the prime candidates for the title of the world's most abundant bird. The plumage is black above and white below with, in summer, the black head and neck forming a distinct breast band. In winter, white extends over the neck to the face. The bill is tiny and stubby. It enters European waters in the winter when pack ice covers its favoured feeding grounds in the Arctic Ocean.

*The Little Auk's small size and fast wingbeats preclude confusion with all of the other auks found in Europe.*

A somewhat comical, medium-sized auk, the Puffin is known to a wide audience from film and television. The adult in summer is black above and white below, with a large conical bill of brightly coloured stripes. The white face has a dark eye with more than a hint of eye-liner. Puffins stand upright, often in small cliff-top groups, and fly low over the water on fast-whirring wings. The large-headed appearance is clear even at long range.

*In winter the face is dark and the bill colours duller.*

**Size:** 28–30cm (11–12in).
**Wing:** 146–174mm.
**Bill:** 41–51mm.
**Weight:** 308–565g.
**Voice:** A purring *arr-arr.*
**Habitat:** Breeds on cliff tops and particularly on grassy landslips below cliff tops. Winters at sea.
**Food:** Fish, crustaceans and molluscs.
**Range:** Confined to North Atlantic. In Europe, breeds Iceland, Britain and Ireland, northwest France and along coasts of Norway and adjacent Russia. Winters over North Sea and Atlantic.
**Movements:** Coastal, southwards as far as the Canary Islands and into the western Mediterranean.
**Breeding:** A single white egg is laid in a burrow and incubated by the female for 40–43 days. The downy, helpless chick fledges after 47–51 days.

## Black-bellied Sandgrouse (Pterocles orientalis)

One of only two regular European sandgrouse, the Black-bellied lives in dry, open, stony countryside and flies regularly to water at dawn and dusk, but is otherwise difficult to locate. The male is brown, spotted dull orange above, with a grey head, orange throat and pinkish breast, bordered above by a narrow black line. The underparts are black. The female is finely spotted and barred black on buff above, but has a similar breast and belly pattern. In flight, the black belly of both sexes contrasts with white wing linings and black flight feathers.

*The black belly is by far the most important identification feature in flight and at rest.*

**Size:** 33–35cm (13–14in).
**Wing:** 221–224mm.
**Bill:** 12–16mm.
**Weight:** 395–550g.
**Voice:** A bubbling call.
**Habitat:** Dry stony plains, semi-deserts.
**Food:** Mainly seeds.
**Range:** Breeds through Mediterranean region, where resident, through Turkey and the Middle East to Caspian steppes, where it is a summer visitor. Winters Pakistan and Rann of Kutch.

**Movements:** None, except between trans-Caspia and Pakistan as above.
**Breeding:** Two or three brown-blotched buffy eggs are laid in a hollow and incubated for 21 or 22 days by both sexes. The young are active and downy. Two broods are regularly reared, perhaps even three on occasion.
**Confusing Species:** The only other European sandgrouse, the Pin-tailed, has a white belly with white wing linings and black flight feathers.

## Pin-tailed Sandgrouse (Pterocles alchata)

**Size:** 30–38cm (12–15in).
**Wing:** 201–214mm.
**Bill:** 13–14mm.
**Weight:** 225–290g.
**Voice:** Loud *gee-tar*.
**Habitat:** Dry, stony wastes and semi-deserts.
**Food:** Seeds.
**Range:** Breeds Iberia and Camargue (France), in North Africa and the Middle East and on the central Asian plateau. European birds are resident, eastern birds are partial migrants.
**Movements:** Some Middle East birds move southwards to central Arabia, and central Asian birds to Pakistan and northwest India.
**Breeding:** Three brown-speckled buffy eggs are laid in a hollow and incubated by both sexes for 19–21 days. The active, down-covered young fly after about 28 days. Occasionally has two broods in a season.
**Confusing Species:** The only other fast-flying, torpedo-shaped European sandgrouse, the Black-bellied, has a bold black belly.

A ground-dwelling, well camouflaged bird of dry, stony regions, the Pin-tailed Sandgrouse is easily distinguished from the Black-bellied Sandgrouse, the only other European species. The male is olive-green, spotted pale green above, with orange head, green neck and a pinkish breast outlined with narrow black lines. The belly is white and in flight it merges with the white wing linings to contrast with the black flight feathers. The long tail extends to a point in flight.

*The long, pointed, tail combined with the white belly, separate this bird from the closely related Black-bellied Sandgrouse.*

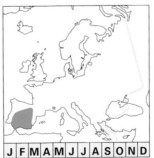

## Great Spotted Cuckoo *(Clamator glandarius)*

A long-tailed bird with pointed wings, the Great Spotted Cuckoo is a summer visitor to several parts of southern Europe. The adult is a warm grey above, liberally spotted with white. The head is grey, with a crest extending from the hind crown. The underparts are white, washed yellowish on the neck and breast. In flight, the long grey tail is prominent and is margined white.

*The juvenile is brown above, spotted white, and has a black cap. Bright rufous wings are visible in flight.*

**Size:** 38–40cm (15–16in).
**Wing:** 202–228mm.
**Bill:** 28–34mm.
**Weight:** 139–192g.
**Voice:** A harsh, raucous chattering.
**Habitat:** Parkland, olive or almond groves, open woodland.
**Food:** Hairy caterpillars form a significant part of its insectivorous diet.
**Range:** Summer visitor through the Mediterranean and to southern Africa. Resident across Sahel Africa, southwards through the savannahs of the east. In Europe, breeds Iberia, where some overwinter in Andalucia, and in southern France, western Italy and on the Greek-Turkish border.
**Movements:** Resident population of savannah Africa is joined in winter by birds that migrate from Europe and South Africa. An interesting, if not unique, colonizing tactic.
**Breeding:** Lays up to 18 brown-spotted, pale bluish eggs that mimic those of the host species, usually Magpie, occasionally Carrion Crow, Raven, Jay or Azure-winged Magpie. The hosts incubate for 12–14 days and the youngsters fledge after about 24 days.

J F M A M J J A S O N D

## Common Cuckoo *(Cuculus canorus)*

A well-known, summer visitor, the Common Cuckoo's characteristic calls are widely regarded as a harbinger of summer. The adult is dove-grey above with grey head and breast and a marked yellow eye. The underparts are white and heavily barred grey. The wings are very long and pointed, the tail long and rounded. The scarce hepatic, or rufous-phase, female is rich chestnut, and heavily barred black. The juvenile is much darker brown, barred black above and barred brown on white below. Juveniles may also show the rufous plumage, but this may fade with age.

*When perched, the Common Cuckoo always seems to have problems folding its wings comfortably.*

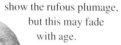

J F M A M J J A S O N D

**Size:** 30–33cm (12–13in).
**Wing:** 195–230mm.
**Bill:** 25–31mm.
**Weight:** 106–133g.
**Voice:** Far-carrying *cuc-coo*, repeated several times.
**Habitat:** Hillsides, moorland, marshes, woodland, parks, fields and hedgerows.
**Food:** Insects, particularly hairy caterpillars in late summer.
**Range:** Summer visitor right across Eurasia, southwards into Middle East and China. Winters southeast Asia and southern Africa. In Europe, breeds everywhere except Iceland and northernmost Norway.
**Movements:** All European birds and most of those from Siberia migrate to southern Africa. In autumn, birds overfly the Mediterranean and Sahara to Sahel Africa. But in spring they miss the Sahel and fly direct across it and the Sahara and the Mediterranean – a vast non-stop flight.
**Breeding:** Eight to twelve highly variable eggs that mimic host species (such as Meadow Pipit, Hedge Accentor, Reed and Garden Warblers, Robin and Pied Wagtail) are laid singly in various nests. They hatch after 12 days and the naked chick ejects other eggs or young from the nest. It flies after 20–23 days.
**Confusing Species:** Easily mistaken for a Kestrel in flight.

## Rock Dove *(Columba livia)*

It is doubtful if any truly pure-bred Rock Doves exist in Europe owing to interbreeding with Feral Pigeons, themselves escaped descendants of domesticated Rock Doves. Nevertheless, Rock Dove-type birds do still live a traditional wild existence among the remote mountains and coastlines of the continent. This is a typical, tubby dove, pale grey above, darker below, marked by an iridescent green flash on the nape, double black wingbar and square white rump.

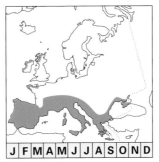

The Rock Dove is the ancestor of the Feral Pigeon. The white rump and bold black wingbars distinguish it from the Stock Dove.

**Size:** 30–33cm (12–13in).
**Wing:** 211–235mm.
**Bill:** 17–20mm.
**Weight:** 200–325g.
**Voice:** A repetitive *oo-roo-oo*.
**Habitat:** Wild birds breed in gorges, mountain cliffs and on coasts. Feral birds nest on buildings and bridges.
**Food:** Seeds.
**Range:** Impossible to delimit natural range due to introductions worldwide.
**Movements:** Unknown.
**Breeding:** Two white eggs are laid on a skimpy platform of vegetation placed in a cliff crevice; incubated by both sexes for 17–19 days. The helpless, downy chicks fledge after 30–35 days. Double or even triple brooded.
**Confusing Species:** Stock Dove.

## Stock Dove *(Columba oenas)*

Similar to the Feral Pigeon, so often overlooked. With a close approach, the grey plumage is seen to be washed with metallic pink on the breast and metallic green on the nape. There are two tiny black bars visible on the folded wing and the bird lacks the white rump of the Rock Dove. It is identifiable in flight when the wing can be seen to be broadly outlined in black.

In flight, the black margins to the wings separate this species from all other European pigeons, but at rest identification is not so clear.

**Size:** 30–33cm (12–13in).
**Wing:** 208–228mm.
**Bill:** 18–21mm.
**Weight:** 242–340g.
**Voice:** Monotonous *coo-roo-oo* calling.
**Habitat:** Open forests and woodland, fields and heaths.
**Food:** Seeds and leaves.
**Range:** Breeds across temperate Europe and Russian steppes. Western and southern populations are resident, but birds from Germany eastwards move westwards to winter.
**Movements:** Influx of eastern birds, mainly to France and Iberia, on a broad front in autumn.
**Breeding:** Two white eggs are laid in a

tree hole or rock crevice and incubated for 16–18 days by both sexes. The helpless, downy young fly after 27 or 28 days. Double or triple brooded.
**Confusing Species:** Rock Dove and Feral Pigeon.

## Wood Pigeon *(Columba palumbus)*

In many regions, this is the most common European pigeon. Upperparts are grey, with a green and white neck slash and a white line at the bend of the wing. This line becomes a broad white band across the wing in flight and is the best field mark of the species. The breast is a deep pink and the belly white. The large size and broad wings of this bird preclude confusion with other European species.

Wood Pigeons fly fast and straight, often in flocks, and displays aerially with glides and wing claps.

**Size:** 38–43cm (15–17in).
**Wing:** 240–263mm.
**Bill:** 19–24mm.
**Weight:** 471–566g.
**Voice:** Repeated *coo-coo-coo-cu-coo*.
**Habitat:** Woodlands and forests with adjacent fields; cities and parks.
**Food:** Seeds and leaves.
**Range:** Breeds throughout Europe, except Iceland and northern Scandinavia and Russia, eastwards to the Middle East and central Asian plateau. Birds eastwards of Germany are summer visitors.
**Movements:** Vast autumn migration southwestwards across Europe, avoiding long sea crossings, to France and Iberia, but also through southern England. Huge numbers pass through

the Jura Mountains and Pyrenees, where they are hunted.
**Breeding:** Two white eggs are laid on a platform of twigs in a tree; incubated for 17 days by both sexes. Downy, helpless young fledge after 29–35 days. Regularly rears three broods.

185

## Collared Dove *(Streptopelia decaocto)*

J F M A M J J A S O N D

The most successful European landbird of the twentieth century, the Collared Dove has spread right across the continent from its base in the Balkans, to colonize as far as the Faeroes and Portugal. The upperparts are buff; underparts and head pinkish with a black (white-bordered) neck slash. The longish tail shows white margins above and a broad white band below. Usually seen in pairs around towns and villages, but in large flocks where food is abundant.

**Size:** 28–30cm (11–12in).
**Wing:** 173–188mm.
**Bill:** 15–18mm.
**Weight:** 112–260g.
**Voice:** A repeated *coo-cooo-coo* and a plaintive *weer*.
**Habitat:** Towns, gardens, parks, fields.
**Food:** Seeds, particularly grain crops, and leaves.
**Range:** Resident over most of Europe though, so far, only at isolated spots in Iberia and northern Scandinavia. Absent Iceland, but for how long?
**Movements:** Autumn dispersal accounts for colonization.
**Breeding:** Lays two white eggs, on a flimsy platform of twigs placed in a tree, which are incubated by both sexes for about 14 days. The downy and helpless young fly after about 18 days. The bird's ability to rear two to five broods during a long breeding season has also played a role in its spread north and west.
**Confusing Species:** Turtle Dove has a chestnut-brown back and a narrow white tip to the tail.

*In flight, the boldly marked tail is usually held closed, but it is fanned out during the spectacular display flight.*

## Turtle Dove *(Streptopelia turtur)*

A fast-flying dove that is a summer visitor to the whole of temperate Europe, the Turtle Dove is, sadly, shot in huge numbers during its passage through the Mediterranean. The upperparts are broadly scalloped with rich chestnut; the underparts are pinkish and the neck has a bold black and white slash. The tail is black, narrowly tipped white.

*Although the plumage shown at rest (above) may resemble that of a Kestrel, the shape of the bird in flight (left) and its flight pattern are quite distinctive.*

J F M A M J J A S O N D

**Size:** 25–28cm (10–11in).
**Wing:** 167–185mm.
**Bill:** 15–19mm.
**Weight:** 100–208g.
**Voice:** A purring *roor-rr*, a characteristic sound of summer.
**Habitat:** Woods and forests, fields and hedges.
**Food:** Seeds and leaves.
**Range:** Summer visitor across much of Eurasia, from Britain and Iberia eastwards across Europe and Russia as far as central areas of Siberia. Winters Sahel zone of Africa. In Europe, absent Iceland, Ireland and Scandinavia.
**Movements:** Broad front migration across Mediterranean and Sahara to winter quarters in the Sahel zone of Africa, just south of the Sahara. Concentrations occur as the birds move through the Mediterranean, attracting large numbers of human hunters, many of them killing the birds illegally.
**Breeding:** Two white eggs are laid on a platform of twigs in a tree and incubated by both sexes for 13 or 14 days. The downy, helpless chicks fly after 19–21 days. Usually double brooded, though success depends on dry weather.
**Confusing Species:** Similar-sized Collared Dove is plain buff above.

186

## Barn Owl *(Tyto alba)*

*Though they mostly hunt by quartering open landscapes, Barn Owls sometimes perch (below) and pounce on prey.*

A pale, orange-buff owl that frequently hunts during daylight, the Barn Owl is declining in numbers in several parts of its European range. The large head, with a white facial disc, is prominent at all times, even in flight. The upperparts are orange-buff, spotted and barred black and white. The underparts are white in British and Irish birds; and black-spotted orange-buff in European birds. The rounded wings are silvery white below. It regularly quarters fields like a harrier.

**Size:** 33–36cm (12–14in).
**Wing:** 279–300mm.
**Bill:** 30–33mm.
**Weight:** 290–480g.
**Voice:** Shrieks, hisses and snoring notes.
**Habitat:** Rough, open grassland, marshy edges, neglected fields, hedgerows.
**Food:** Small mammals caught by pouncing from low flight.
**Range:** Resident in all the world's major landmasses, though absent from Scandinavia to the Bering Strait. In Europe, breeds as far east as the Volga.
**Movements:** Dispersal of young birds.
**Breeding:** Lays four to seven white eggs in a hole in a tree, a barn loft, a church tower, or specially erected nest box. The eggs are laid at intervals of two or three days, so the first chicks in a brood may hatch up to ten days before the last. The eggs are incubated for 32–34 days by the female and the naked and helpless young fledge after about 60 days. Sometimes double brooded.
**Confusing Species:** Snowy Owl, seen from below, is much larger and bulkier and significantly rarer.

## Snowy Owl *(Nyctea scandiaca)*

A tundra-breeding owl that extends southwards through the mountains of Scandinavia, the Snowy Owl occasionally erupts southwards to temperate Europe. The male is significantly smaller than the female and pure white with no more than a few odd spots of black on the wings. The female is heavily spotted black above and barred black below. Both sexes have plain white faces with yellow eyes and a tiny black bill. In flight, the large wings and short tail are apparent.

*The Snowy Owl may appear heavily streaked and barred when young (above), gradually becoming a purer white with age. The female (below) remains darker than the male, to help with camouflage when on the nest.*

**Size:** 53–66cm (21–26in).
**Wing:** 400–460mm.
**Bill:** 40–48mm.
**Weight:** 395–471g.
**Voice:** Occasional barking and mewing calls.
**Habitat:** Bare, open tundra and high mountain plateaux.
**Food:** Small mammals, up to rabbit size, and birds.
**Range:** Northern circumpolar. In Europe, breeds along Scandinavian mountain chain and across northern Russia.
**Movements:** Though some birds move southwards every year, occasionally large numbers erupt into areas where they are otherwise unknown, usually linked with the lemming population. Such movements led to the unique breeding in the Shetland Islands between 1967 and 1975.
**Breeding:** Four to ten white eggs are laid in a bare scrape, usually on a knoll with good views, and incubated by the female alone for 32–37 days. The helpless, down-covered young fledge after 43–50 days.
**Confusing Species:** Barn Owls of paler, western form.

## Scops Owl *(Otus scops)*

Only slightly larger than a House Sparrow, the Scops Owl is a summer visitor to southern and temperate Europe. It has yellow eyes and is mottled and streaked black on either grey or reddish brown. Two ear tufts accentuate the surprised look. It is often heard, but seldom seen as it is strictly nocturnal.

*While some birds are mainly grey (far left), others have a rusty, reddish colour (left), the 'rufous phase.'*

**Size:** 18–20cm (7–8in).
**Wing:** 154–167mm.
**Bill:** 18–20mm.
**Weight:** 58–127g.
**Voice:** A hollow *poo-p.*
**Habitat:** Woodlands, groves, orchards and villages.
**Food:** Insects.
**Range:** Summer visitor across North Africa and Eurasia to eastern Siberia. Winters Sahel Africa. In Europe, breeds from Iberia, to Russia.
**Movements:** Migrates across the Mediterranean and Sahara.
**Breeding:** Four or five white eggs are

J F M A M J J A S O N D

laid in a tree or building and incubated by the female for 24 or 25 days. The downy young fly after 21–29 days.
**Confusing Species:** Little Owl is larger and round-headed. Pygmy Owl is smaller and lacks ear tufts.

## Little Owl *(Athene noctua)*

A small, largely diurnal owl that often perches openly, the Little Owl has brownish grey upperparts, with large white spots on its back and wings. Its underparts are white and heavily streaked. A well-marked facial disc, with pale eyebrows over yellow eyes, and dark marks below, combine to produce quite a fierce expression.

J F M A M J J A S O N D

*The Little Owl flies with deeply bounding movements (left) on rounded wings.*

**Size:** 20–23 (8–9in).
**Wing:** 158–173mm.
**Bill:** 19–22mm.
**Weight:** 99–197g.
**Voice:** A plaintive *kee-oo.*
**Habitat:** Woods, fields and towns.
**Food:** Insects, small mammals, birds.
**Range:** Resident in Eurasia from Spain to the Sea of Japan. Absent from Scandinavia and northern Russia.
**Movements:** Local, post-breeding dispersal.
**Breeding:** Lays three to five white eggs in a hole in a tree or building. The female incubates the eggs for 28 or 29 days. The helpless, downy young fly after 28–35 days. Perhaps double brooded in some parts of its range.
**Confusing Species:** Other small owls.

## Pygmy Owl *(Glaucidium passerinum)*

This tiny owl, about the same size as a House Sparrow, has grey-brown upperparts with white spots and underparts that are white streaked with brown. Its size and rounded head make it easy to identify, and it has piercing yellow eyes and two distinct facial rings.

*A ferocious hunter, the Pygmy Owl will attack birds as large as itself, such as the House Sparrow (right).*

**Size:** 15–19cm (6–7in).
**Wing:** 93–109mm.
**Bill:** 13–16mm.
**Weight:** 47–79g.
**Voice:** Repeated *du-du-du-du* note.
**Habitat:** Conifer forests in the boreal zone and among the higher mountains farther south.
**Food:** Small birds and voles.
**Range:** Resident from Scandinavia across the Eurasian boreal zone to Japan. In Europe, it is found eastwards across the Baltic and northern Russia, as well as in the Alps, Carpathians and mountains of Slovenia and the hills of southern Germany.
**Movements:** Some local dispersal,

and eruptions occasionally occur.
**Breeding:** Four to six white eggs are laid in a tree hole and incubated by the female for 28–30 days. The helpless and downy young fly after 27–34 days.
**Confusing Species:** Scops Owl has ear tufts and different habitat.

J F M A M J J A S O N D

# Hawk Owl *(Surnia ulula)*

A ferocious owl of the northern conifer forests, the Hawk Owl frequently hunts by day, and may be seen perched on a prominent branch or post. It has grey upperparts with white-spotted wings and pale scapulars, which form bold white 'braces' across the wings during flight. The white underparts are evenly and boldly broken by grey bars. The facial disc is made prominent by broad black sides and heavy 'eyebrows', which frame piercing yellow eyes. Together with the white supercilium, these give the owl a particularly fierce expression. The Hawk Owl has quite short, pointed wings and a long tail.

JFMAMJJASOND

**Size:** 33–40cm (13–16in).
**Wing:** 224–249mm.
**Bill:** 23–27mm.
**Weight:** 230–371g.
**Voice:** A rattling *ki-ki-ki.*
**Habitat:** Conifer forests with clearings and fresh growth.
**Food:** Small mammals and small birds.
**Range:** Circumpolar in the north. Breeds in Europe from Scandinavia across to northern Russia.
**Movements:** Occasional extensions of range southwards are dependent on the population of voles. There are also large-scale eruptions, though these seldom cross the Baltic Sea.
**Breeding:** Three to ten white eggs are laid in a tree hole and incubated, mainly by the female, for 25–30 days. The young are helpless and downy and fly after 23–27 days.

*A long tail, which is easily seen when it is flying (above left), makes the Hawk Owl easy to distinguish from other owls. It is largely diurnal and perches openly, keeping a lookout for its prey (far left).*

# Tawny Owl *(Strix aluco)*

Although the Tawny Owl is a widespread resident, the most abundant of its kind in many parts of Europe, its nocturnal habits make it difficult to see. The body is usually brown, with streaking and barring above and streaking below. Its facial disc is plain brown and it has large, dark eyes. In flight, it has a bull-necked, flat-faced appearance.

*The primary feathers of the Tawny Owl have very soft margins that assist silent flight as it approaches its prey.*

**Size:** 35–40cm (14–16in).
**Wing:** 259-287mm.
**Bill:** 28–34mm.
**Weight:** 310–650g.
**Voice:** Familiar *who-who-who-who* and sharp *kee-wick.*
**Habitat:** Woods and forests, heaths and fields, towns and even cities.
**Food:** Small mammals and, in some places, small birds.
**Range:** Breeds across Eurasia from Europe to China. In Europe, widespread resident and absent only from Iceland, Ireland and northern Scandinavia.
**Movements:** Only local, post-breeding dispersal.

**Breeding:** Two to four white eggs are laid in a hole in a tree or in a building and incubated by the female alone for 28–30 days. The helpless, down-covered chicks fledge after 32–37 days.
**Confusing Species:** The Ural Owl is much larger and greyer.

JFMAMJJASOND

189

An owl of the boreal forests, the Ural Owl is like a long, grey version of the closely related Tawny Owl. It is grey above, heavily streaked black, and heavily streaked white below. The most obvious feature is the large, plain facial disc, with small dark eyes. In flight, the long tail and rounded wings recall a hawk.

*At roost (left) the streaked chest is noticeable, but in flight (right) the strongly barred flight feathers become more obvious.*

**Size:** 61cm (24in).
**Wing:** 340–376mm.
**Bill:** 38–45mm.
**Weight:** 451–1020g.
**Voice:** A deep, hooting *hoo-oo hoo-hu-hoo-hoo* that increases in volume.
**Habitat:** Forests, especially mixed or deciduous, but seldom seen in pure stands of conifers.
**Food:** Variety of birds and small mammals.
**Range:** Breeds across Eurasia to Japan, with outliers in northeastern China. In Europe, breeds in a broad band from Scandinavia across Russia, as well as in the Carpathians and among the mountains of Yugoslavia.
**Movements:** Resident, even in poor years for small mammals.
**Breeding:** Three or four white eggs are laid in a tree hole or rock crevice and incubated by the female for 27–29 days. The young are downy and helpless and take 24–35 days to fledge.
**Confusing Species:** Tawny Owl is considerably smaller and has a shorter tail. Great Grey Owl is larger. Short-eared Owl has noticeably narrower wings in flight.

JFMAMJJASOND

A huge grey owl of the boreal forest, the Great Grey Owl attempts to drive off intruders with intimidating, head-on dives. The entire plumage, both above and below, is dark grey, heavily streaked and barred in black. The head is large and rounded, with a series of concentric rings around each of the yellow eyes, which are separated by white 'spectacle marks' on the 'nose'. The large, flat face is visually dramatic, especially when seen head on. In flight, the wings are broad

and rounded. Unlike many other owls, it frequently hunts by day. The flight is distinctive among owls, having long, slow wingbeats interrupted by lengthy glides.

JFMAMJJASOND

**Size:** 66–72cm (26–28in)
**Wing:** 430–467mm.
**Bill:** 38–45mm.
**Weight:** 490–1900g.
**Voice:** A deep *ho-ho-ho* repeated eight to twelve times.
**Habitat:** Boreal forests.
**Food:** Predominantly voles.
**Range:** Circumpolar in the northern boreal zone. In Europe, breeds from the head of the Gulf of Bothnia across northern Russia into Siberia.
**Movements:** Frequent wandering at the end of the breeding season and, perhaps, through the winter, but always within the conifer forests.
**Breeding:** Three to five white eggs are laid in an old nest of another species in a tree and incubated by the female alone for 28–30 days. The helpless, downy young fledge after 60–65 days.
**Confusing Species:** The Eagle Owl has longer wings.

*The face (left) is distinctive with concentric circles around the eyes, a dark chin and a white moustache. At rest (right), the large head is particularly noticeable.*

## Eagle Owl *(Bubo bubo)*

The Eagle Owl is the largest and most powerful of the nocturnal predators. It is a formidable bird, quite capable of killing hares, foxes and even dogs. The brown plumage is heavily barred above and streaked below. The large facial disc surrounds big, piercing orange eyes. The prominent ear tufts are usually held nearly horizontal. In flight, the huge wings contrast with a short tail. The Eagle Owl is most active early in the morning and late in the evening.

**Size:** 60–75cm (24–29in).
**Wing:** 430–513mm.
**Bill:** 49–58mm.
**Weight:** 1160–3260g.
**Voice:** A low, deep repeated *ooo-hoo.*
**Habitat:** Forests, mountain gorges and cliff ranges.

**Food:** A huge variety of birds and small mammals.
**Range:** Resident right across Eurasia to India, China, the Middle East and even Saharan Africa. In Europe, somewhat disjointed distribution and absent from Britain and Ireland, as well as much of lowland France, Germany and Poland, probably as a result of deliberate persecution.

**Movements:** No more than post-breeding dispersal.
**Breeding:** Two or three white eggs are laid in a cave, crevice or in the old nest of another species. They are incubated by the female for 34–36 days and the helpless, downy young fly after 50–60 days.
  **Confusing Species:** Browner than other large owls.

*While roosting (above left), the large orange eyes seem almost to glow in the dark light of the forest. When hunting (above right) the Eagle Owl flies fast and low, interrupting steady wingbeats with lengthy glides. Prey, such as rabbits, are pounced on at speed.*

## Tengmalm's Owl *(Aegolius funereus)*

A well-marked, small owl of conifer forests, Tengmalm's Owl is called the Boreal Owl in North America. It is grey-brown above, marked by large white spots on the wings and whitish 'braces' over the back. The underparts are white with large brown spots. The most obvious feature is the large head, with yellow eyes set in a heart-shaped facial disc.

**Size:** 25–28cm (10–11in).
**Wing:** 167–182mm.
**Bill:** 19–23mm.
**Weight:** 98–215g.
**Voice:** A soft, repeated *po-po-po.*
**Habitat:** Conifer forests in mountains, hills and boreal zone.
**Food:** Voles.
**Range:** Northern circumpolar. In Europe, in a huge swathe from Scandinavia across Russia, southwards through the European mountains and forested hills of France, Germany and Belgium.
**Movements:** Eruptive movements in boreal zone are dependent on the population of its main prey. In central Europe, some dispersive movements, mainly of juveniles, but occasional lengthy flights by re-locating adults.
**Breeding:** Three to six white eggs are laid in a tree hole, often the old nest of a Black Woodpecker. Incubation, by the female alone, takes 26–36 days and the helpless, downy young fly after 30–36 days.

*During the day the owl roosts (far left). Its liking for abandoned woodpecker nest holes means Tengmalm's Owl takes readily to suitable nestboxes (left).*

One of the most widely distributed of European owls, yet one of the least frequently observed. Its well-marked brown plumage is liberally streaked above and below. The oval facial disc is warm buff-orange and the piercing eyes are a deep orange-red. There are prominent ear tufts. The Long-eared Owl sits upright, especially when being observed. It is essentially nocturnal and unwilling to fly during the day, even when disturbed by humans.

J F M A M J J A S O N D

The body posture, ear tufts and facial disc are highly mobile, depending on mood. At rest, the owl appears dumpy with a rounded face (above), but when alert (right), it stands tall and thin with a narrow face and erect ear tufts.

**Size:** 33–35cm (13–14in).
**Wing:** 282–310mm.
**Bill:** 26–30mm.
**Weight:** 151–370g.
**Voice:** A low *oo-oo-oo*. Nestlings have a unique call that sounds like a door with a rusty hinge being opened.
**Habitat:** Coniferous and deciduous woodland, belts and copses, also heaths and broken landscapes with trees.
**Food:** Small mammals.
**Range:** Circumpolar in the northern boreal and temperate zones. Winters mainly in southern parts of breeding range, but also well to the south in United States and Mexico, and in China. In Europe, resident over most of Europe, though birds in northern Scandinavia and Russia are summer visitors.
**Movements:** Migrants from northern parts of range move south and west in Europe to winter in France, Spain and Britain. Forms communal roosts in winter quarters.
**Breeding:** Four or five white eggs are laid in an old nest of a different species in a tree and incubated by the female alone for 25–30 days. The helpless, downy young fly after 23 or 24 days.
**Confusing Species:** The Eagle Owl is considerably larger.

A northern owl of marsh, moorland and tundra, the Short-eared Owl hunts by day, quartering the ground like a harrier. It is heavily streaked brown and buff above, with white streaked underparts. The head, which always seems large, has a prominent plain facial disc and bright yellow eyes. A close approach may reveal very short ear tufts. In flight, long, round-tipped wings have a creamy patch at the base of the primaries and a dark carpal patch on the underwing.

J F M A M J J A S O N D

**Size:** 35–38cm (14–15in).
**Wing:** 304–331mm.
**Bill:** 16–18mm.
**Weight:** 260–425g.
**Voice:** A high-pitched *kee-aw* and a low *boo-boo-oo*.
**Habitat:** Moorland, hills, tundra, marshes and woodland clearings; in winter mostly marshes.
**Food:** Small mammals.
**Range:** Northern circumpolar, but also resident in West Indies and South America. In Europe, mainly a summer visitor to the north, but with resident populations in Iceland, Britain and Low Countries and across the Ukraine.
**Movements:** Exodus of Scandinavian and Russian birds across northwestern Europe mainly to north Germany, Holland, France, Britain and Ireland.
**Breeding:** Lays four to eight white eggs in a hollow on the ground which are incubated by the female for 24–28 days. The helpless, downy young fly after 22–27 days. An occasional second brood is reared.

When hunting in daylight for its favoured prey of voles, the bird glides and hovers low over the ground, rather like a harrier. The abundance of voles dictates how many owls are present in an area.

Acamouflaged, ground-nesting, nocturnal summer visitor that is easily located by its song, the European Nightjar is always difficult to see well. An intricate pattern of streaking and barring in shades of grey and brown makes the Nightjar one of the best camouflaged of all birds, and the chances of seeing one on the ground are remote. In the air, the long pointed wings and long tail are easily recognized, but its nocturnal hunting offers only the briefest of viewing opportunities. It flies on silent wings and is often curious about intruders. The male has white patches in the wing and tail.

*When resting on the ground, camouflage plumage makes the bird almost invisible. In flight (above), the tiny bill opens into a huge gape to form an insect trap.*

J F M A M J J A S O N D

**Size:** 23–28cm (9–11in).
**Wing:** 184–202mm.
**Bill:** 8–10mm.
**Weight:** 61–88g.
**Voice:** A distinctive, prolonged churring that rises and falls.
**Habitat:** Heaths, open forests and woodland margins, and clear-felled areas of woods.
**Food:** Insects, mostly moths, taken in the air.
**Range:** Summer visitor across temperate Europe to east-central Siberia. Whole population winters in savanna Africa. In Europe, breeds from Ireland to Iberia, eastwards through southern Sweden and Finland to Russia and the Ukraine.
**Movements:** Broad front migration across Mediterranean and Sahara seems likely, though solid evidence for this is lacking.
**Breeding:** Two white eggs, lightly spotted with brown, are laid in a depression on the ground among leaves, broken sticks or branches. The eggs are incubated by both sexes for about 18 days. The active, downy chicks fly after 16–18 days. Double brooded.
**Confusing Species:** Red-necked Nightjar where species ranges overlap.

Very similar to the European Nightjar, the Red-necked has more rufous plumage, particularly around the neck, and two white areas on the chin. The male has white patches in wing and tail. The rufous barring on the underparts is almost impossible to see. A birdwatcher's best chance is to drive down quiet tracks and roads through suitable habitat after dark, when birds often sit quite openly.

*The Red-necked Nightjar (top) has rufous markings around the eye, chin and neck, as well as white patches on the chin and throat; these distinguish this species from the otherwise similar European Nightjar (above).*

J F M A M J J A S O N D

**Size:** 30cm (12in).
**Wing:** 198–214mm.
**Bill:** 10–12mm.
**Weight:** Little information.
**Voice:** Repetitive *ko-tok, ko-tok, ko-tok*, distinctive and quite dissimilar to European Nightjar's churring.
**Habitats:** Dry, sandy heaths and scrub.

**Food:** Insects, mainly moths.
**Range:** Endemic to western Mediterranean, breeds in Iberia and in North Africa from Morocco to Tunisia. Winter distribution inadequately known, though has been known to occur in the Niger Inundation Zone.
**Movements:** Migrates on a broad front across the Mediterranean and the Sahara to West Africa.
**Breeding:** Lays two creamy white eggs, with yellowish mottling, in a hollow on the ground. Virtually nothing else is known of its breeding routines.
**Confusing Species:** European Nightjar lacks rufous neck and white chin.

193

## Common Swift *(Apus apus)*

One of the world's most aerial birds, the Common Swift probably lands only when breeding. It has a torpedo-shaped body with a forked tail and long, sickle-like wings. A close approach reveals sooty plumage with a tiny white throat.

*This bird spends most of its life in flight (right). Its weak legs and feet are able only to cling to rough surfaces (left).*

**Size:** 15cm (6in).
**Wing:** 164–180mm.
**Bill:** 6–7mm.
**Weight:** 31–55g.
**Voice:** High-pitched screams, mostly from groups.
**Habitat:** Breeds in towns and villages, but also along cliff-girt coastlines.
**Food:** Aerial insects.
**Range:** Summer visitor across Eurasia and the Middle East to northern China. Winters exclusively in Africa south of the Equator.
**Movements:** Huge trans-Saharan migration by European breeders to the southern half of Africa. Even birds that breed as far away as northern China migrate to Africa.

J F M A M J J A S O N D

**Breeding:** Three white eggs are laid on a bed of leaves or feathers placed in a hole and are incubated by both sexes for 19–24 days. The helpless and naked young fly after 35–56 days.
**Confusing Species:** Pallid Swift paler.

## Pallid Swift *(Apus pallidus)*

Very similar in size and plumage to the Common Swift, the Pallid Swift is restricted to Mediterranean coastlines. It has the same torpedo shape and sickle-like wings as the Common Swift,

but is generally paler brown than that species. Although it looks black at any distance, reasonable views reveal the pale colour, particularly the paler inner wing. A bold white throat is a sure identification feature, when visible. It arrives at breeding grounds earlier in the season than Common Swift.

*Because of its close similarity to the Common Swift, the Pallid Swift is frequently overlooked and under-recorded as a result.*

**Size:** 15cm (6in).
**Wing:** 167–178mm.
**Bill:** 6–7mm.
**Weight:** 32–44g.
**Voice:** Screams when in groups.
**Habitat:** Breeds in holes in buildings or in caves.
**Food:** Aerial insects.
**Range:** Summer visitor through the Mediterranean to Arabia and Pakistan. Winters Nile Valley and Sahel Africa.
**Movements:** Migrates across the Sahara.
**Breeding:** Lays two white eggs on a bed of leaves in a hole. Incubation by both

sexes lasts 14–20 days, and the young fly after 44–48 days. It usually raises two broods, so arrives before and leaves after the Common Swift.
**Confusing Species:** Common Swift has darker plumage.

J F M A M J J A S O N D

## Alpine Swift *(Apus melba)*

*Similar in shape to other swifts, the Alpine Swift is instantly recognizable by its white belly and dark breast band.*

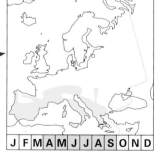

J F M A M J J A S O N D

**Size:** 20cm (8in).
**Wing:** 214–240mm.
**Bill:** 8–10mm.
**Weight:** 76–145g.
**Voice:** Loud chittering calls.
**Habitat:** Mountain cliffs and gorges, but also in towns.

Significantly larger and more bulky than the Common Swift, the Alpine Swift has longer wings. It flies fast and forms hunting flocks and sometimes enormous colonies.

**Food:** Aerial insects.
**Range:** Summer visitor to the Mediterranean through Turkey and the Middle East, south-central Asia and India, where it is resident. Winters east and southern Africa, where it also breeds. In Europe, breeds in Iberia, southern France, the Alps northwards to southern Germany, Italy, and Greece.
**Movements:** Alpine Swifts leave Europe for Africa on a broad front across the Mediterranean and Sahara.
**Breeding:** Three white eggs are laid on a bed of wind-blown materials in a hole in a cliff or building and are incubated by both sexes for 17–23 days. The young hatch naked and helpless and take 45–55 days to fly.
**Confusing Species:** Other swifts are smaller.

## Common Kingfisher (*Alcedo atthis*)

A blue and red jewel of a bird, this is Europe's only kingfisher. The upperparts are bright, metallic blue, and are most often seen as the bird flies away low over the water. The underparts are rich orange-red. The head has bold patches of blue, orange and white, and the bill is long, stout and, in the female, marked by an orange-red lower mandible. The bird perches alongside rivers and ponds before hovering and diving for its prey, which is caught in the bill under water.

*Both sexes of Common Kingfisher have similar plumage, but the female has an orange-red base to the lower bill. Younger birds have similar colours, but are noticeably duller, especially in sunlight.*

**Size:** 13–15cm (5–6in).
**Wing:** 76–87mm.
**Bill:** 30–36mm.
**Weight:** 34–43g.
**Voice:** Hard, metallic *cheek* or *chee-kee* often repeated as a chatter.
**Habitat:** Rivers, lakes, ponds and sheltered sea bays and harbours.

J F M A M J J A S O N D

**Food:** Fish.
**Range:** Breeds from Ireland to Japan and south to India and New Guinea. Resident in many areas, but northern populations do migrate. In Europe, absent from Iceland, most of Scandinavia, northern Russia and major mountain ranges.
**Movements:** Eastern European birds migrate south and west to join residents, as well as heading farther south to Mediterranean islands.
**Breeding:** Six or seven white eggs are laid at the end of a tunnel which the birds excavate in a river bank. They are incubated by both sexes for 19–21 days and the naked, helpless chicks fly after 23–27 days. Double brooded.

## Roller (*Coracias garrulus*)

**Size:** 28–30cm (11–12in).
**Wing:** 198–208mm.
**Bill:** 41–45mm.
**Weight:** 110–160g.
**Voice:** Harsh, crow-like *kraak-ak*.
**Habitat:** Scrub, open woodland, groves and orchards.
**Food:** Insects, taken by pouncing to the ground.
**Range:** Summer visitor to Europe, Turkey, the Middle East and western Siberia and the central Asian plateau. Winters in southeast Africa and, to a

A summer visitor to southern and eastern Europe, the Roller brings a splash of colour to a day's birding. A thick-set, chunky bird, with a large head and strong black bill, the Roller is marked in varying shades of pale blue on body, wings and head. The back is chestnut, the flight feathers black.

*Colourful enough at rest (above) the Roller has a stunning display flight (right). In this courting behaviour, the bird climbs into the air before tumbling and rolling downwards, displaying its gorgeous plumage. The Roller's blue feathers are especially beautiful as they are iridescent when seen in sunlight.*

J F M A M J J A S O N D

lesser extent, in West Africa. In Europe, breeds in Iberia, southern France, Italy and from former Yugoslavia northwards to St Petersburg and eastwards across Russia and the Ukraine.
**Movements:** Apparently migrates southwards on a broad front across the Mediterranean and Sahara, though details are lacking. Larger numbers wintering in East Africa probably reflect the larger breeding population of eastern Europe.
**Breeding:** Four or five white eggs, laid in a tree hole and incubated by both sexes for 18 or 19 days. The naked, helpless chicks fledge after 26–28 days.

195

## European Bee-eater *(Merops apiaster)*

An extremely colourful bird that is a summer visitor to Europe, the European Bee-eater is often seen in large flocks or colonies. Patches of colour mark the entire plumage. The tail has extended central streamers.

*In the air (left), the bird shows long, pointed wings; while at rest (far left) the yellow throat and blue underparts are good fieldmarks.*

**Size:** 28cm (11in).
**Wing:** 140–159mm.
**Bill:** 34–47mm.
**Weight:** 48–60g.
   **Voice:** Highly vocal: liquid *quip-quip*.
   **Habitat:** Parks, orchards, sand pits.
   **Food:** Insects, especially bees and dragonflies.
   **Range:** Summer visitor to southern and eastern Europe, the Middle East, southwestern Siberia and North Africa. Winters in West Africa and also in South Africa, where it breeds.
   **Movements:** Migrates across the Mediterranean and Sahara, with western birds flying to the bulge of Africa, and eastern birds to South Africa.
**Breeding:** Four to seven white eggs are laid in a tunnel in a sandy bank. They are incubated for 20 days by both sexes. The naked young fledge after 20–25 days.

J F M A M J J A S O N D

## Hoopoe *(Upupa epops)*

This summer visitor is, in most European languages, named after its call. It has a sandy body and bold black and white wings and crest.

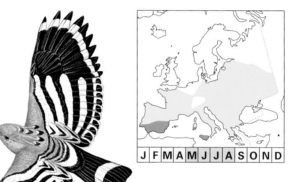

*The black and white wings seen at rest (far left) are more obvious in flight (left), as is their 'ping-pong bat' shape. However, the bird spends most of its time on the ground.*

J F M A M J J A S O N D

**Size:** 25–28cm (10–11in).
**Wing:** 142–153mm.
**Bill:** 41–57mm.
**Weight:** 47–80g.
**Voice:** Soft, far-carrying *poo-poo-poo*.
**Habitat:** Orchards, gardens, woodlands.
**Food:** Insects.
**Range:** Summer visitor across Eurasia from Portugal to Sea of Japan, but small numbers winter southern Spain. Absent from Britain (occasionally breeds), and from Germany and northern Russia.
**Movements:** European birds migrate on a broad front across the Sahara.
**Breeding:** Five to eight grey eggs are laid in a tree hole, rock crevice or hole in a building and are incubated for 16–19 days by the female. The helpless, downy chicks fledge after 20–27 days.

## Wryneck *(Jynx torquilla)*

This is the only member of the woodpecker family that is a long-distance migrant. Highly camouflaged, it is easily overlooked, being mottled, barred and streaked in browns, greys and buffs.

*The grey stripe running from the crown and nape to the centre of the back is a clear field mark (above), as is the long tail.*

**Size:** 15cm (6in).
**Wing:** 86–93mm.
**Bill:** 15–17mm.
**Weight:** 23–52g.
**Voice:** A repeated, loud, far-carrying *kee-kee-kee*, only uttered soon after arrival on breeding grounds.
**Habitat:** Heaths, woods, groves, orchards, parkland.
**Food:** Insects, especially ants.
**Range:** Summer visitor from Spain across Eurasia to Japan. Winters in Asia from India to China, and in Sahel Africa. In Europe, breeds right across the continent, though absent from Iceland and from Britain, where it formerly bred.
**Movements:** Birds west of the Urals migrate on a broad front across the Mediterranean and Sahara to winter, though long sea crossings may be avoided. Migrational divide in central Europe seems well established.
**Breeding:** Lays seven to ten white eggs in a hole in a wall, tree or nestbox. They are incubated for 12–14 days, mainly by the female. The naked and helpless young fly after 19–21 days.

J F M A M J J A S O N D

## Grey-headed Woodpecker *(Picus canus)*

Very similar to the Green Woodpecker in shape and coloration, the Grey-headed has a distinct preference for uplands; where it does inhabit lowlands it prefers damp, marshy areas. The upperparts are green with a bright yellow rump, and the underparts and head grey.

*Though otherwise similar, the female (above) and the male (left) can be distinguished easily: the female does not have a red forehead.*

**Size:** 25cm (10in).
**Wing:** 145–151mm.
**Bill:** 36–41mm.
**Weight:** 122–160g.
**Voice:** A flutey *ku-ku* repeated several times.
**Habitat:** Conifer and other upland forests, as well as damp lowland forests and copses.
**Food:** Insects, including ants, taken on the ground.
**Range:** Resident from France across Eurasia to Japan, and southwards to Southeast Asia. In Europe, breeds in central and highland France eastwards to Russia and the Ukraine.
**Movements:** Only local dispersal.
**Breeding:** Four or five white eggs are laid in a self-excavated tree hole and

J F M A M J J A S O N D

incubated by both sexes for 14 or 15 days. The naked, helpless young fly after 24 or 25 days.
**Confusing Species:** The Green Woodpecker is larger, with bigger, better defined head markings in red and black.

## Green Woodpecker *(Picus viridis)*

A large woodpecker, this bird is green above, paler below, and is marked by a distinctive red crown, black face and a moustachial streak, which is red and black in the male. The rear flanks show faint barring, and the juvenile is heavily barred on neck and underparts.

*Seen on the ground (above) more than other woodpeckers, the Green Woodpecker uses its long sticky tongue to extract insect grubs (right).*

**Size:** 28–33cm (11–13in).
**Wing:** 156–170mm.
**Bill:** 42–49mm.
**Weight:** 130–217g.
**Voice:** Loud, laughing *keu-keu-keu*.
**Habitat:** Deciduous woods, heaths and groves.
**Food:** Insects, particularly ants taken on the ground.
**Range:** Virtually endemic to the Western Palearctic. Breeds from Britain to Portugal, eastwards across temperate Europe to southern Scandinavia and Russia, and from Turkey to the adjacent Middle East.
**Movements:** Only local dispersal.
**Breeding:** Five to seven white eggs are laid in a nest hole in a tree which the birds excavate. Incubation, by

J F M A M J J A S O N D

both sexes, takes 18 or 19 days and the helpless and naked young fledge after 23–27 days.
**Confusing Species:** Grey-headed Woodpecker is smaller, with a plainer grey face.

## Three-toed Woodpecker *(Picoides tridactylus)*

Quite different from other pied woodpeckers in being black above without white barring or patches, the Three-toed Woodpecker has bold dark barring on the flanks and a prominent white rump in flight. The black wings and complete white stripe along the back are diagnostic.

*The head pattern (left) is black marked by white, rather than white with black markings as in other similar woodpeckers. The male (above) has a dirty yellow crown, which can be rather difficult to see in field conditions.*

**Size:** 21cm (8in).
**Wing:** 120–128mm.
**Bill:** 29–35mm.
**Weight:** 57–74g.
**Voice:** Quiet *tuk-tuk* and drumming on dead branch.
**Habitat:** Coniferous forests.
**Food:** Insects.
**Range:** Circumpolar in the north. Resident in Europe in the Alps, Carpathians and other mountains of the south (except the Pyrenees), and from Scandinavia eastwards through the boreal zone of Russia to Siberia.
**Movements:** No more than local dispersal, although Siberian birds do make regular southerly flights beyond their breeding range.
**Breeding:** Four or five white eggs are laid on a bed of wood chips in a

J F M A M J J A S O N D

self-excavated hole in a conifer. The eggs are incubated by both parents for about 11 days. The naked and helpless chicks fly after 22–25 days.
**Confusing Species:** Blacker on the upperparts than most other woodpeckers.

197

# Great Spotted Woodpecker *(Dendrocopos major)*

O ne of several black and white woodpeckers that should be distinguished with care and attention to plumage

details. The upperparts are black, marked with two large white ovals on the folded wings, and white bars across the primaries. The underparts are creamy white, with bold red undertail coverts.

*The face pattern (left) consists of a black moustache that runs around the ear coverts to the crown; this helps to distinguish it from other pied woodpeckers. The female (far left) lacks any red on its nape.*

**Size:** 20–23cm (8–9in).
**Wing:** 138–147mm.
**Bill:** 26–31mm.
**Weight:** 70–100g.
**Voice:** A loud, high-pitched *chick*; drums on dead branches.
**Habitat:** Woods and forests.
**Food:** Arboreal insects.
**Range:** Resident across Eurasia from Britain to Japan and China. In Europe, it is absent from Iceland, Ireland, far north of Scandinavia and most of Greece.
**Movements:** Mainly local dispersal.
**Breeding:** Four to seven white eggs are laid in a self-excavated tree hole and incubated by the female for 10–13 days. The chicks fly after 20–24 days.
**Confusing Species:** Other European pied woodpeckers are similar.

---

# Syrian Woodpecker *(Dendrocopos syriacus)*

T he Syrian Woodpecker is similar to the Great Spotted Woodpecker, but it is less confined to woods and can live around villages. It lacks the black line around the ear coverts that joins moustache to crown.

*Unlike the male (left), the female (right) lacks a red patch on the crown. In both sexes, the black moustachial streak does not connect with the black of the crown.*

**Size:** 23cm (9in).
**Wing:** 129–137mm.
**Bill:** 29–33mm.
**Weight:** 70–83g.
**Voice:** Loud *schik*; drums on dead branches.
**Habitat:** Groves, orchards, shelter belts, especially around villages.
**Food:** Insects.
**Range:** Breeds from central eastern Europe through to the Balkans and Turkey, Iran and Israel. Local in Syria, despite its Latin and common names.
**Movements:** Post-breeding dispersal is responsible for its colonization of eastern Europe as far north as Poland.
**Breeding:** Four to seven white eggs are laid in a tree hole and incubated by both sexes for 9–14 days. The naked young fledge after 24 days.
**Confusing Species:** Great Spotted Woodpecker and smaller, red-crowned Middle Spotted Woodpecker.

---

# Middle Spotted Woodpecker *(Dendrocopos medius)*

A lthough it is slightly smaller than the Great Spotted Woodpecker, the

Middle Spotted Woodpecker has similar white ovals on its back. It has lightly streaked flanks and pinkish, not red, undertail coverts, and does not have a black moustache.

*Both male and female birds have a red crown, and are difficult to separate.*

**Size:** 20cm (8in).
**Wing:** 124–134mm.
**Bill:** 23–28mm.
**Weight:** 50–80g.
**Voice:** A *que-que* repeated four to six times; drumming on hollow branches.
**Habitat:** Deciduous forests, particularly of mixed oak and hornbeam; avoids mountains in central Europe, but is found in mountains in the south.
**Food:** Insects.
**Range:** Found in many areas of the Western Palearctic. Resident from the mountains of northern Spain across lowland France, eastwards to Russia, and the Balkans to Turkey. Absent from Britain, Scandinavia and northern Russia.
**Movements:** Post-nuptial dispersal, but of no great distance.

**Breeding:** Four to eight white eggs are laid in a self-excavated tree hole and incubated by both sexes for 11–14 days. The naked and helpless chicks fledge after 22 or 23 days.
**Confusing Species:** Great Spotted and White-backed Woodpeckers.

## White-backed Woodpecker (Dendrocopos leucotos)

This is the largest and rarest pied woodpecker. It has white bars across the folded wings, and the white back is seen in flight. The red crown, streaked flanks and pinkish undertail of the male resemble the Middle Spotted, but the White-backed has a black moustache.

The female (left and above) has a black crown, whereas the male has a red crown. Both have a black and white 'ladder' back.

**Size:** 23–25cm (9–10in).
**Wing:** 144–152mm.
**Bill:** 35–41mm.
**Weight:** 99–116g.
**Voice:** A juk-juk; drumming.
**Habitat:** Mature deciduous and mixed forests with plentiful fallen trees and lack of tidiness.
**Food:** Insects.
**Range:** Resident across Eurasia from the Pyrenees, Alps, Italian mountains and Balkans, across temperate eastern Europe to Japan.
**Movements:** Some local dispersal that may take it outside its normal range. May also be eruptive, though low numbers make it difficult to assess individual wanderings.
**Breeding:** Three to five white eggs

J F M A M J J A S O N D

are laid in a self-excavated hole in a rotten tree and are incubated by both sexes for 10 or 11 days. The naked, helpless young fly after 24–28 days.
**Confusing Species:** Other pied woodpeckers are similar.

## Lesser Spotted Woodpecker (Dendrocopos minor)

A tiny, sparrow-sized woodpecker that flies directly, not with an undulating motion like other species, and forages among the thin branches of the tree canopy. It has black upperparts, with a white ladder-back; underparts are white and lightly streaked.

The male (left) has a red crown, whereas the female (right) has a dirty white one.

**Size:** 13–15cm (5–6in).
**Wing:** 87–94cm.
**Bill:** 16–18mm.
**Weight:** 20–27g.
**Voice:** A high-pitched repetitive kee-kee-kee.
**Habitat:** Woodland, hedgerows, heaths, parkland and gardens.
**Food:** Insects.
**Range:** Resident across Eurasia from Spain and Britain to Japan. In Europe, breeds in Spanish mountains and from France and Britain across most of Europe, wherever trees are found.
**Movements:** Post-breeding dispersal and perhaps some

J F M A M J J A S O N D

eruptive movements in the far north and east of its range.
**Breeding:** Four to six white eggs are laid in a tree hole and incubated by both sexes for 11 or 12 days. The naked and helpless young fledge after 18–20 days.

## Black Woodpecker (Dryocopus martius)

This is the largest European woodpecker. Its whole plumage is black, with a long tail and broad wings and with a patch of red on the crown, larger in the male than the female.

J F M A M J J A S O N D

The male Black Woodpecker usually excavates a nest chamber (left) and then attracts a mate. If the chamber is not complete, the female will help to finish it. Hollowing out the nest hole may take three weeks.

**Size:** 46cm (18in).
**Wing:** 229–242mm.
**Bill:** 55–69mm.
**Weight:** 200–374g.
**Voice:** Distinctive, laughing kwee-kwee.
**Habitat:** Conifer forests with occasional deciduous trees for excavating nests.
**Food:** Insects.
**Range:** Breeds across the boreal zone of Eurasia from Spain to Japan and southwards, in mountains, to Balkans and northern China. In Europe, absent from most of Spain and Italy; completely absent from Britain and Ireland.
**Movements:** Post-breeding dispersal.
**Breeding:** Four to six white eggs are laid in a self-excavated hole, usually in a deciduous tree, and are incubated by both sexes for 12–14 days. The naked young fledge after 24–28 days.

## Calandra Lark *(Melanocorypha calandra)*

This heavily-built lark is resident around the Mediterranean, but may wander to temperate Europe. The upperparts are streaked greyish buff-brown, and the underparts are white with faint streaking on the breast and a black half-moon forming a fore-collar. The bill is large, conical and horn coloured.

*At rest (left) the black neck patch is clearly visible, and in flight the diagnostic fieldmark of white trailing edges to wings become clear.*

**Size:** 18–20cm (7–8in).
**Wing:** 115–141mm.
**Bill:** 16–23mm.
**Weight:** 57–73g.
**Voice:** Variable sweet singing in circling flight, plus a nasal *kreet.*
**Habitat:** Grasslands and cereal fields.
**Food:** Seeds and insects.
**Range:** Breeds through the Mediterranean eastwards to the southern steppes of Siberia. Mostly resident, but some eastern birds migrate to areas outside the breeding range in the Balkans and Iran, and even westerly birds form large flocks that are somewhat nomadic outside the breeding season.
**Breeding:** Four or five brown-speckled, whitish eggs are laid in a cup on the ground and incubated for 16 days by the female alone. The downy, helpless young remain in the nest for 10 days, but the fledging period is unknown.
**Confusing Species:** No other European lark has large bill and wings.

## White-winged Lark *(Melanocorypha leucoptera)*

A well-marked, bird, the White-winged Lark has much chestnut in the adult plumage and more white in the wing than any other European lark. The adult has chestnut crown, ear coverts and wing coverts, with a white supercilium and streaking on the breast.

*Visible as white patches when the bird is on the ground (left), the broad white trailing edges of the wings are more noticeable in flight (right).*

**Size:** 18cm (7in).
**Wing:** 111–127mm.
**Bill:** 14–17mm.
**Weight:** 39–52g.
**Voice:** Song similar to Sky Lark's, but perhaps even more melodic.
**Habitat:** Grassy steppes at altitude, mostly uncultivated.
**Food:** Seeds and insects.
**Range:** Breeds across central, western steppes of the northern Caspian eastwards. Winters Ukraine and the Middle East.
**Movements:** Winter migration brings birds westwards into the Ukraine and to northern Romania. Decidedly rare outside this region.
**Breeding:** Lays five or six variably coloured and speckled eggs in a cup on the ground. Incubation is by the female for 12 or 13 days. The downy, but helpless young leave the nest before they can fly.
**Confusing Species:** Possible confusion with female Snow Bunting.

## Black Lark *(Melanocorypha yeltoniensis)*

A dark black, or black and grey, bird that breeds in the southeastern corner of Europe, the Black Lark is a winter visitor westwards. The male in summer is black, marked by fine white crescents, but in winter is heavily barred black. It has a stubby yellow bill. Immature birds are paler with black spots below.

*The male (far left) is the largest European lark. The female (left) is about 2cm smaller and has a greyish body, which is heavily barred above and below, and almost pure black wings.*

**Size:** 20cm (8in).
**Wing:** 117–142mm.
**Bill:** 15–21mm.
**Weight:** 51–76g.
**Voice:** Rich liquid song like Sky Lark's.
**Habitat:** Lowland grassy steppes.
**Food:** Seeds and insects.
**Range:** Breeds from northern Caspian eastwards over west Siberian Steppes. Winters to the south and southwest.
**Movements:** Migrates mainly westwards across the northern Black Sea to winter in the Ukraine, just reaches northernmost Romania.
**Breeding:** Lays five or six olive-blotched, pale blue or greenish eggs in a cup on the ground, often surrounded by animal droppings. The eggs are incubated by the female for 15 or 16 days before hatching.

## Short-toed Lark *(Calandrella brachydactyla)*

A torpedo-shaped, gregarious lark, the Short-toed Lark flies fast, often low over the ground. Flocks feed voraciously, hunched over the ground and are ever active. The upperparts are buff-brown, and the underparts white with a vertical smudge at the sides of the breast that is not easy to see. There is large colour variation according to location. A small conical bill and tertials that cover the primaries are fine identification points.

The eastern and western subspecies of this bird are best distinguished by the dark moustache, which extends down the side of the neck to become a broad smudge in the eastern bird (left), but which is thinner and less pronounced in the western race (right).

**Size:** 13cm (5in).
**Wing:** 86–102mm.
**Bill:** 13–15mm.
**Weight:** 16–25g.
**Voice:** Hard *chi-chirrp*.
**Habitat:** Dry, open, sandy ground, arable fields, semi-deserts.
**Food:** Seeds and insects.
**Range:** Breeds throughout the Mediterranean region eastwards across central Asia. Winters in the Middle East, on the Himalayan plateau and across much of Sahel Africa. In Europe, it is a summer visitor to Iberia, locally in France, Italy, the former Yugoslavia and along the Black Sea coasts. Some birds may winter in Greece.
**Movements:** European birds migrate on a broad front across the Mediterranean and Sahara. In spring, many stop over on Mediterranean islands.
**Breeding:** Three to five, brown-marked buffy eggs are laid in a cup on the ground and incubated mainly by the female for 12 or 13 days. The downy, helpless young fledge often after 11 or 12 days. Double brooded.
**Confusing Species:** Lesser Short-toed Lark is similar in shape, but has a more streaked breast and the primary feathers project visibly.

## Lesser Short-toed Lark *(Calandrella rufescens)*

Similar to the Short-toed Lark, this bird is decidedly scarce and localized in Europe. The upperparts are buffy to olive-brown and the underparts white, with a lightly streaked breast and flanks. The primaries extend beyond the tertials. Though the streaked breast would seem to be a straightforward distinguishing feature, when actively feeding birds turn their heads the effect is often to ruffle the feathers so as to produce a smudge similar to that of the Short-toed Lark.

**Size:** 13–15cm (5–6in).
**Wing:** 80–93mm.
**Bill:** 12–13mm.
**Weight:** 19–25g.
**Voice:** A rolling *prrt*.
**Habitat:** Dry, stony, semi-deserts.
**Food:** Seeds and insects.
**Range:** Breeds right across southern Eurasia from Spain to Korea. Winters northern China, Pakistan and Middle East and throughout the Mediterranean. In Europe, resident Spain and a summer visitor from the Crimea eastwards.
**Breeding:** Three or four brown-speckled creamy eggs, laid in a cup on the ground, are incubated by the female. The young hatch downy and helpless, but leave the nest after just 9 days.
**Confusing Species:** Short-toed Lark lacks streaked breast.

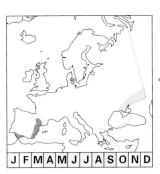

Very similar to the Short-toed Lark, this bird can be distinguished only with care in its arid Iberian range (above). It lacks the black moustache of the Short-toed Lark, and has pronounced streaking along the breast (left).

201

## Crested Lark *(Galerida cristata)*

*The spiked crest and large bill, together with the light streaking on the chest, are important field marks.*

widespread and common resident throughout much of temperate and southern Europe, the Crested Lark is easily identified by its spiky crest. In Iberia, the remarkably similar Thekla Lark should be identified with great care. The Crested Lark is streaked buff and brown above, with a well marked face and crest. The underparts are buffy white, and lightly streaked on the breast. The short tail shows rufous margins in flight, which is noticeably fluttery.

**Size:** 15–18cm (6–7in).
**Wing:** 97–111mm.
**Bill:** 18–21mm.
**Weight:** 40–52g.
**Voice:** A pleasant, whistled *wee-weeoo*.
**Habitat:** Fields, grasslands, sandy or stony dry areas.
**Food:** Seeds and insects.
**Range:** Resident across most of temperate Eurasia from Spain to Korea, southwards into the Sahara and Sahel zone, and through Arabia to India. In Europe, it is absent from the British Isles, Scandinavia, much of Russia and most of upland France and Italy.
**Movements:** Russian and Siberian birds are mostly summer visitors, though their winter quarters are largely within the breeding range to the south.
**Breeding:** Three to five, buff-spotted white eggs are laid in a cup on the ground and incubated by the female for 12 or 13 days. The young are helpless and downy and fledge after 15 or 16 days. Regularly double-brooded, may occasionally rear a third.
**Confusing Species:** Thekla Lark has a more ragged crest and a clearly shorter, blunter bill.

## Thekla Lark *(Galerida theklae)*

esident in southern Iberia, the Thekla Lark has a range overlapping that of the Crested Lark, from which it must be distinguished with great care. Although basically all but identical to the more abundant Crested Lark, the Thekla is slightly smaller in overall size. It has a crest that is ragged, rather than forming a single spike; a bill that is shorter and blunt tipped, rather than long and pointed; and a breast that is heavily streaked, rather than lightly streaked.

*The differences in facial and neck markings between the Thekla and Crested Larks appear clear on paper, but are difficult to see in the field.*

**Size:** 15cm (6in).
**Wing:** 92–108mm.
**Bill:** 17–20mm.
**Weight:** 25–37g.
**Voice:** A liquid *wee-weeoo*.
**Habitat:** Rocky, stony hillsides and uplands, overlapping Crested Lark, but also in areas where that, more lowland orientated, species is not found.
**Food:** Seeds and insects.
**Range:** Endemic resident of Western Palearctic, confined to North Africa, and Iberia and adjacent southern France.
**Movements:** Resident, though Spanish birds may descend from higher mountain ranges in winter.
**Breeding:** Three to six buff-speckled whitish eggs are laid in a cup on the ground. The helpless, downy young leave the nest after 9 days and fly 15 days after hatching. Raises two broods.
**Confusing Species:** Crested Lark.

## Wood Lark (Lullula arborea)

The upperparts are streaked brown and buff, with bold white supercilia that meet on the nape. A small, but bold, black and white mark at the bend of the wing is diagnostic.

*Inconspicuous when on the ground (below) the Wood Lark is most often seen perched on a branch (right).*

**Size:** 15cm (5–6in).
**Wing:** 91–101mm.
**Bill:** 14–16mm.
**Weight:** 23–35g.
**Voice:** Flute-like, descending *too-loo-eet* in rolled repeats.
**Habitat:** Open wooded heaths, groves, orchards.
**Food:** Insects and seeds.
**Range:** Breeds from Iberia to southern Scandinavia and across temperate Europe to Russia and Turkey. In south and west is largely resident, but from Poland eastwards is a summer visitor.
**Movements:** Eastern birds migrate to southern parts of breeding range, but are never obvious.

**Breeding:** Three or four brown-spotted buff eggs are laid in a cup on the ground and incubated for 12–16 days by the female. The downy, helpless chicks fly after about 10–13 days.
**Confusing Species:** Sky Lark.

## Sky Lark (Alauda arvensis)

Once widespread, the Sky Lark has suffered a decline as a result of new farming methods. Heavily streaked buff and brown above, it has a chestnut crest on the hind crown and white outertail feathers.

*In flight, the Sky Lark shows a long tail with white outer feathers.*

**Size:** 15–18cm (6–7in).
**Wing:** 99–123mm.
**Bill:** 14–17mm.
**Weight:** 34–41g.
**Voice:** Liquid *chirrup*, warbling notes during song flight.
**Habitat:** Arable and grasslands.
**Food:** Seeds and insects.
**Range:** Breeds across Eurasia from Ireland to the Bering Strait. Southern and western birds are resident. Winters China, Middle East and western Europe.
**Movements:** Eastern and northern birds migrate along coastlines to western Europe and may be seen in huge numbers in October.
**Breeding:** Three or four brown-blotched greyish eggs are laid in a neat cup of grasses on the ground and are incubated

by the female alone for 11 days. The young are helpless and downy and fly after 20 days.
**Confusing Species:** All larks are superficially similar, but this is the only species with a crest from the rear crown.

## Shore Lark (Eremophila alpestris)

A distinctively marked lark that breeds at high latitudes or high altitudes in Europe, the Shore Lark is otherwise only a scarce winter visitor to the shores of the North Sea. The adult is buffy above and white below, with a yellow face and black fore-collar, eye mark and horns. Immatures and winter birds have less bright markings.

*The summer head pattern (left) of black and yellow markings with small 'horns' fades in winter (above), and the 'horns' are reduced.*

**Size:** 15–18cm (6–7in).
**Wing:** 100–116mm.
**Bill:** 14–15mm.
**Weight:** 34–48g.
**Voice:** A *seep* or *tseep-seep*.
**Habitat:** High-Arctic tundra and mountain plateaux. Winters on bare grasslands and along shingle coasts.
**Food:** Seeds and insects.
**Range:** Circumpolar in the north, extending southwards throughout North America. In Eurasia, is a summer visitor across the tundra and resident 1000 kilometres to the south from Greece to northern China. Tundra birds winter within this southern range. In Europe, confined to the Scandinavian mountain chain, Russian tundra and the mountains of the Balkans.

**Movements:** Scandinavian birds winter along the shores of the North Sea.
**Breeding:** Four brown-speckled green eggs are laid in a cup on the ground and incubated by the female for 10–14 days. The downy and helpless chicks fledge after 16–18 days. Raises two broods.

203

## Sand Martin (Riparia riparia)

A highly gregarious little swallow, the Sand Martin is a summer visitor to most of Europe and nests in dense colonies in sand banks and cliffs. The upperparts are uniformly brown; the underparts are white, marked by a narrow brown breast band. Away from colonies, it forms feeding flocks, often over water, and roosts communally in reedbeds.

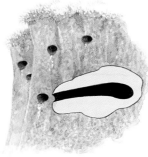

*The exterior of a burrow (left) is a simple hole, but within (above) it is a lengthy tunnel with a nest chamber at the end.*

**Size:** 13cm (5in).
**Wing:** 99–111mm.
**Bill:** 9–11mm.
**Weight:** 10–19g.
**Voice:** Continuous harsh twittering.
**Habitat:** Breeds in sandy banks and cliffs, feeds over water.
**Food:** Insects taken in the air.
**Range:** Circumpolar from boreal to temperate zones, where it is a summer visitor. Resident in high central Asia. In Europe, breeds from southern Spain to northern Norway and is absent only from Iceland and higher mountain and hill areas. Winters savanna Africa.

**Movements:** European and western Siberian birds migrate to savanna Africa on a broad front, though western birds seem to avoid the worst of the Sahara by concentrating in Iberia and Morocco. Return journey across the Sahara involves many casualties.

**Breeding:** Four to six white eggs are laid at the end of a tunnel, which the birds excavate themselves in a sandy bank or cliff. The eggs are incubated by both sexes for 14 or 15 days and the downy, helpless chicks fly after 19 days. Double brooded.

**Confusing Species:** The Crag Martin is larger and lacks a breast band.

## Crag Martin (Ptyonoprogne rupestris)

This chunky bird is a resident or summer visitor to rocky gorges and cliffs. Like the Sand Martin, it is of uniformly brown appearance, with greyish brown upperparts. The underparts are slightly warmer brown than the upperparts, with dark coverts on pale grey-brown underwings. The tail is notched and shows a row of dull white spots when spread. The bird glides on broad-based, pointed wings.

*The nest (left) is a well-built, deep cup of mud, which is plastered to a cave wall or rock hole in a cliff, or to a building.*

**Size:** 15cm (6in).
**Wing:** 126–136mm.
**Bill:** 11–12mm.
**Weight:** 20–27g.
**Voice:** High-pitched chirruping.
**Habitat:** Cliffs and gorges in mountains and hills.
**Food:** Insects.
**Range:** Breeds throughout the Mediterranean, Turkey and Middle East to south-central Asia. In Europe, breeds across Spain, through the mountains of France, where it is only a summer visitor, Italy and the Balkans, where it is resident only in the south.

**Movements:** Many birds move southwards to winter in southern Spain and cross into Morocco. Some of them may be French birds, but others doubtless originate in Iberia.

**Breeding:** Four or five red-spotted white eggs are laid in a cup of mud. They are incubated for 14 days by the female. The young are downy and helpless and fly after 24–27 days.

**Confusing Species:** Sand Martin has breast band.

## Swallow *(Hirundo rustica)*

Widespread and abundant, the Swallow is a familiar summer visitor to almost the whole of Europe and is widely regarded as a herald of spring. The adult is metallic blue above, and cream to warm pinkish below, with a crimson face edged dark blue. The wings are long and pointed, the tail deeply forked with tail streamers that are longer in the male than the female. The juvenile lacks tail streamers.

*Nests (far left) are made of mud shaped into a cup and stuck to a ledge or shelf on the inside of outbuildings, old chimneys or derelict buildings.*

**J F M A M J J A S O N D**

**Size:** 15–20cm (6–8in).
**Wing:** 118–129mm.
**Bill:** 11–13mm.
**Weight:** 14–24g.
**Voice:** A twittering trill.
**Habitat:** Suburbs, villages, farms, barns and over marshes and other waters.
**Food:** Insects caught in flight.
**Range:** In Europe, absent Iceland, Scandinavian mountains and tundra. Winters Africa, from Sahel southwards.
**Movements:** Migrates on a broad front across the Mediterranean and Sahara.
**Breeding:** Four or five red-spotted white eggs are incubated by the female for 14–16 days. The young are helpless and downy and fledge after 17–24 days.
**Confusing Species:** Red-rumped Swallow has pink rump and throat.

## Red-rumped Swallow *(Hirundo daurica)*

This summer visitor to the Mediterranean is gradually spreading northwards. The underparts are lightly streaked and the face and chin pale. The tail streamers turn inwards.

*In flight the bird has a less blue back than the Swallow, with a pink rump and neck.*

**Size:** 18cm (7in).
**Wing:** 118–128mm.
**Bill:** 10–13mm.
**Weight:** 19–27g.
**Voice:** Soft *chirrup.*
**Habitat:** Rivers, streams and marshes.
**Food:** Insects taken in the air.
**Range:** Summer visitor from the Mediterranean eastwards through the Middle East to China and Japan. Resident and winters in India and across savanna Africa.
**Movements:** Apparent migrational divide in Europe to avoid the central Sahara. Exact winter range undetermined because of local breeding.
**Breeding:** Three to five white, finely speckled red, eggs are laid in a

**J F M A M J J A S O N D**

flask-shaped nest of mud built under a bridge or in a cave. They are incubated by both sexes for 14 or 15 days and the downy, helpless young fly after 22–26 days. Two broods are usually raised.
**Confusing Species:** Swallow.

## House Martin *(Delichon urbica)*

A locally abundant summer visitor which constructs its domed nests of mud under the eaves of houses. It is metallic blue-black above, with a white rump and neatly forked tail. The underparts are white.

*The neat nest (above) is fixed to an overhanging beam or roof. The white underparts, uninterrupted by a breast band, contrast with the blackish back, wings and tail.*

**Size:** 13cm (5in).
**Wing:** 105–116mm.
**Bill:** 9–11mm.
**Weight:** 15–22g.
**Voice:** Abrupt *chirrup.*
**Habitat:** Towns, suburbs, villages, bridges, cliffs and rocky areas.
**Food:** Aerial insects caught in flight.
**Range:** Summer visitor right across temperate Eurasia from Ireland to Japan. Winters Himalayan foothills and Southeast Asia and in savanna Africa.
**Movements:** European birds migrate southwards, without westerly or easterly bias and presumably cross the Mediterranean and Sahara. Wintering grounds not accurately determined. It seems that migrating birds stop over in the nests of other House Martins along the way for bed and breakfast.

**J F M A M J J A S O N D**

**Breeding:** Four or five white eggs are laid in a domed nest of mud. In some large colonies nests virtually overlap. Incubation, by both sexes, lasts 13–19 days and the downy, helpless young fledge after 19–25 days. Regularly double or triple brooded.

## Tawny Pipit *(Anthus campestris)*

A tall, slim wagtail-like pipit, this is a summer visitor to the Mediterranean and temperate zones of Europe. The adult is warm buff above, with a neat line of large dark spots across the wing coverts. The line of dark spots is less obvious in young birds because of other dark markings. The underparts are white, with a moustachial streak, but no breast streaking.

The long tail accentuates the wagtail image, as does the fact that it walks wagtail-like on long legs and has a call like that of some wagtails.

| J | F | M | A | M | J | J | A | S | O | N | D |

*During the first winter, juveniles (left) are darker than the adults (above right) and have streaking on the back and upper breast.*

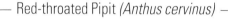

**Size:** 15–18cm (6–7in).
**Wing:** 84–101mm.
**Bill:** 17–21mm.
**Weight:** 20–32g.
**Voice:** Distinctive *tseep*.
**Habitat:** Dry, sandy and stony areas.
**Food:** Insects.
**Range:** Summer visitor from Portugal to eastern Siberia. Winters India, Middle East and across Sahel Africa. In Europe, widespread in Spain and along Mediterranean and Black Sea coasts. More scattered distribution across temperate central and eastern Europe, but then more widespread through Russia. Absent Iceland, Britain and Ireland and most of Scandinavia.
**Movements:** European birds winter in Sahel Africa, probably crossing the margins of the Sahara rather than making a direct crossing of the centre.
**Breeding:** Four or five brown-blotched white eggs are laid in a cup of vegetation on the ground and incubated by the female, perhaps with some help from the male, for 13 or 14 days. The downy, helpless young fly after 12–14 days, and the species raises two broods.
**Confusing Species:** Beware confusing first-winter birds with Richard's Pipit.

## Red-throated Pipit *(Anthus cervinus)*

This small, well-marked pipit is a summer visitor to the Eurasian tundra. The adult in summer is boldly streaked buff and brown above; the underparts are white, boldly streaked black on the flanks, but with a clear rust-red throat and face. In winter, it is heavily streaked above and below, with a pale throat. Many birds may still show a pinkish throat in autumn and even in their winter quarters.

*In the summer, the plumage has a rusty blush over the throat and head (above). In winter, this is replaced by a brown head and white throat (left).*

| J | F | M | A | M | J | J | A | S | O | N | D |

**Size:** 15cm (6in).
**Wing:** 82–90mm.
**Bill:** 14–16mm.
**Weight:** 17–24g.
**Voice:** A distinctive thin *tseez*.
**Habitat:** Breeds among tundra marshes, winters marshes and lake margins.
**Food:** Insects.
**Range:** Breeds from northern Scandinavia eastwards across the Siberian tundra to the Bering Strait and just into western Alaska. Winters Southeast Asia and Sahel Africa south to Kenya. In Europe, summer visitor to northern Norway, Sweden and Finland and across the Russian tundra.
**Movements:** Most European birds move southeastwards through eastern Europe to winter in East Africa, smaller numbers farther west may cross central Sahara. Decidedly scarce outside the European breeding range, save in Turkey and Cyprus, where common in spring.
**Breeding:** Five or six brown-speckled grey-buff eggs are laid in a cup on the ground and incubated for 11–14 days by the female alone. The young are helpless and downy and fledge after 12 or 13 days.
**Confusing Species:** Other heavily streaked pipits in winter.

## Water Pipit *(Anthus spinoletta)*

This bird spends the breeding season in the mountains of Europe and winters among lowland marshes. In summer, it has grey-brown, unstreaked upperparts and white underparts, with a warm rufous wash over the breast. In winter, the upperparts are uniformly brown, but the underparts are white, streaked black on breast and flanks. The supercilium and black legs aid identification.

*In winter plumage (right) the Water Pipit has clear streaking on its breast and a white throat. In summer, the streaking is replaced by rufous colouring on the breast.*

**Size:** 15–18cm (6–7in).
**Wing:** 82–96mm.
**Bill:** 16–18mm.
**Weight:** 18–29g.
**Voice:** A clear *jee-eet.*
**Habitat:** Breeds high, open mountain tops; winters on well-vegetated freshwater marshes, often among watercress beds.

**Food:** Insects.
**Range:** Breeds over most high mountains from central Spain and Pyrenees to Alps and Carpathians, and eastwards to Middle East and Siberia. Winters across lowlands of western and southern Europe into North Africa.
**Movements:** A general dispersal in winter, not only to lower levels, but with definite migrations southwards to North Africa and northwards as far as Britain.
**Breeding:** Four to six brown-spotted white eggs are laid in a neat cup in a rock crevice and incubated by the female for 14 days. The helpless, down-covered young fly after 16 days. Sometimes double brooded.
**Confusing Species:** This is the only regular European pipit with a plain brown back.

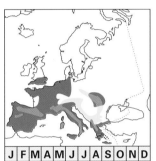

J F M A M J J A S O N D

## Rock Pipit *(Anthus petrosus)*

Darkest of the regular pipits, with greyish upperparts, streaked black, and paler underparts, also streaked. The legs are dark, the outer tail feathers grey. Scandinavian birds, *A.p.littoralis,* have greyish underparts; British birds, *A.p.petrosus,* are whitish. Both are heavily streaked.

*The two subspecies are similar, but can be distinguished by details of plumage. The Scandinavian bird is regularly seen in small numbers on the southern coasts of Britain.*

**Size:** 15–18cm (6–7in).
**Wing:** 82–93mm.
**Bill:** 17–19mm.
**Weight:** 21–32g.
**Voice:** Clear *weest.*
**Habitat:** Breeds rocky coastlines; winters in similar areas, as well as among estuarine marshes.
**Food:** Insects.
**Range:** Breeds along most Scandinavian coasts eastwards to adjacent Russia, and along coasts of Britain and Ireland and northern and western France. Winters in same areas, where conditions are not too severe.
**Movements:** More northerly birds may migrate as far as Britain and Portugal, in the former joining up with birds that have migrated within that country.
**Breeding:** Four to six brown-spotted grey eggs are laid in a cup placed in a rock crevice or beneath a tussock and are incubated by the female for 14 days. The helpless, downy young fly after 16 days. Single or double brooded.
**Confusing Species:** Dark Meadow Pipits, which share its winter habitat, have pink legs.

J F M A M J J A S O N D

A summer visitor to open woodland over most of Europe, the Tree Pipit is similar to the Meadow Pipit, but is always cleaner in its markings. The upperparts are olive-buff, streaked brown. The underparts are white, with a light yellowish wash over the breast and black streaking on the breast and flanks. The long legs are pinkish and the outertail feathers white. The bird sings over its territory, climbing high into the sky, then singing as it parachutes down to perch in a tree or bush.

J F M A M J J A S O N D

**Size:** 13–15cm (5–6in).
**Wing:** 79–90mm.
**Bill:** 14–16mm.
**Weight:** 18–29g.
**Voice:** Song is a descending trill with a drawn-out ending. Call a harsh *tees.*
**Habitat:** Open woodland and well-treed heaths.
**Food:** Insects.
**Range:** Breeds across temperate Eurasia, from northern Spain to eastern Siberia. In Europe, widespread, though absent from southern Spain and from Mediterranean coasts, as well as from Iceland and Ireland. Winters in savanna Africa and India.
**Movements:** Major movements of European birds westwards to Portugal before flying around the western edge of the Sahara, but some still cross the Sahara, particularly when heading north in spring.

**Breeding:** Four to six brown-speckled eggs of variable colour are laid in a cup on the ground and incubated by the female for 12–14 days. The downy, helpless young fly after 12 or 13 days. Single or double brooded.
**Confusing Species:** The similar Meadow Pipit never quite looks as clean or elegant.

*A male Tree Pipit performs its display song (above) in the spring as it marks out its breeding territory. The nest (left) is a simple cup-shaped affair, built on the ground.*

---

Common and widespread during the summer in northern Europe and during the winter in southern and western Europe, this is the standard pipit from which all others must be separated. The upperparts are variably streaked on a clean olive-buff to a dark buff-brown background. The underparts are whitish, with extensive breast and flank streaking. The legs are pinkish and the tail has white outer feathers. Dark birds can be confused with Rock Pipit, and pale birds with Tree Pipit.

J F M A M J J A S O N D

*At rest (above) the Meadow Pipit can look undistinguished and is difficult to identify. The white outertail feathers (right) are distinctive.*

**Size:** 15cm (6in).
**Wing:** 74–85mm.
**Bill:** 14–15mm.
**Weight:** 15–22g.
**Voice:** High-pitched *tissip* or *eest*; an accelerating trill produced in song flight, which ends in a parachuting descent.
**Habitat:** Mountains, moorland, tundra, marshes, estuaries and coasts.
**Food:** Insects.
**Range:** Virtually endemic from eastern Greenland to just beyond the Urals in northern Siberia, and southwards to Italy and the Black Sea. Absent from most of the Mediterranean, Iberia and southeastern Europe. Winters from Iberia to Scotland and Denmark and through the Mediterranean.
**Movements:** Birds from Scandinavia and from eastern Germany eastwards migrate south and west to winter as far as North Africa and the Middle East. Vast numbers fly westwards through England in autumn.
**Breeding:** Three to five brown-spotted eggs of variable colour are laid in a neatly lined cup on the ground and incubated by the female for 11–15 days. The helpless, downy young fledge after 10–14 days. Double brooded.
**Confusing Species:** Tree Pipit.

208

## Grey Wagtail (*Motacilla cinerea*)

Largest of the European wagtails, the Grey Wagtail has an extremely long tail and distinctive yellow and grey plumage. It is associated with running water more than any other species. The adult male in summer is grey above, with a black bib and a black tail with white outer feathers. The female and winter male are similar, but lack the bib, and the yellow is confined to the undertail. It bobs its tail continuously as it scours the edges of fast-running streams.

*In summer, the sexes have distinct plumages. The male (left) has a black bib and brighter yellow underparts.*

**Size:** 18–20cm (7–8in).
**Wing:** 81–89mm.
**Bill:** 16–17mm.
**Weight:** 14–25g.
**Voice:** A metallic *tzi-tzi*.
**Habitat:** Running waters, such as streams and boulder-strewn rivers, waterfalls, weirs.
**Food:** Insects.
**Range:** Breeds across Eurasia from the Azores to Kamchatka, southwards through the Middle East, Himalayas, China and Japan, but is curiously absent from most of Scandinavia, European Russia and the Ukraine. Winters widely across the Far East and in Arabia and East Africa, as well as in most areas of western Europe.
**Movements:** The migrant population of Scandinavia and eastern Europe moves southwest or southeast. In the west many birds move south to Portugal, France and Britain.
**Breeding:** Four to six grey-mottled buffy eggs are laid in a cup placed close to rapidly moving water and are incubated mainly by the female for 11–14 days. The downy, helpless chicks fledge after about 13–14 days. The birds occasionally rear a second brood.
**Confusing Species:** Yellow Wagtail.

## Pied Wagtail (*Motacilla alba*)

Two distinct subspecies of this bird occur in Europe. The Pied Wagtail *M.a.yarrellii* breeds in Britain, Ireland and northern parts of France, while the White Wagtail *M.a.alba* breeds over the rest of the continent. The male Pied Wagtail is black above and white below, with a greyish wash over the flanks, a white face and a bold black bib that joins the black upperparts. The female is sooty black above. The White Wagtail has a black bib and black cap that do not meet, and the upperparts are a pale grey.

*The European White Wagtail has a grey back and a small black bib that is extended in summer.*

*The black bib of the Pied Wagtail extends round the neck to reach the black cap.*

**Size:** 15–18cm (6–7in).
**Wing:** 85–96mm.
**Bill:** 15–17mm.
**Weight:** 17–26g.
**Voice:** A clear *chis-ick*.
**Habitat:** Freshwater lakes and ponds, rivers, streams, tundra pools, marshes and estuaries, but also away from water in towns, cities and villages.
**Food:** Insects.
**Range:** Breeds right across Eurasia and just into North America, from Iceland to Alaska and southwards to the Middle East and China. Winters southern and western Europe, Africa south to Kenya, Middle East, India and Southeast Asia.
**Movements:** Western birds are resident or partial migrants, moving south to the Mediterranean.
**Breeding:** Five or six brown-speckled grey eggs are laid in a cup on the ground, or on a ledge on a building, and incubated mainly by the female for 12–14 days. The young are helpless and downy and fly after 13–16 days. Two broods are raised.

A summer visitor to most of Eurasia, the Yellow Wagtail winters over much of sub-Saharan Africa and Asia. It can be divided into a number of distinct subspecies, each of which has its own Latin name, as well as a common name in most European languages. The males differ more than females, mostly in the colour, or pattern, of the head. Subspecies mostly have discrete breeding ranges, but interbreed freely where they meet or overlap. As a result, hybrids occur widely, showing a confusing array of plumages, some of which closely resemble subspecies found hundreds, or even thousands of kilometres away. In Europe there are eight subspecies and others may occur from time to time.

Males are green above and yellow below, with a long white-bordered tail. The legs and bill are black. Females are dull olive-green above, with a yellow wash on the underparts.

The head colours of males vary from pure yellow to pure black according to subspecies, though most have blue or blue-white elements. The British

*Top:* flavissima *male. Above left:* iberiae *male. Above right:* feldegg *male.*

Yellow Wagtail, *M.f. flavissima*, has a yellow face and supercilium with a green crown. The Continental Blue-headed Wagtail, *M.f. flava*, has a blue head with a white supercilium, a black eyestripe and a yellow chin, while the Iberian, *M.f. iberiae*, is similar, but with dark ear coverts and a white chin. The Scandinavian *M.f. thunbergi* has black ear coverts, a grey crown and yellow chin, whereas the largely Italian *M.f. cinereocapilla* has a paler grey head and a white chin. The Greek Black-headed Wagtail, *M.f. feldegg*, has a black head and yellow chin.

*The variety of types has led some scientists to believe that the Yellow Wagtail is in the process of evolutionary change.*

| J | F | M | A | M | J | J | A | S | O | N | D |

**Size:** 16–17cm (6–7in).
**Wing:** 75–89mm.
**Bill:** 15–17mm.
**Weight:** 15–22g.
**Voice:** An explosive *tsee-ip.*
**Habitat:** Breeds on freshwater marshes and floods, around cattle ponds and among market garden crops. Winters around ponds, rivers and floods.
**Food:** Insects, mainly taken on the ground where the bird walks easily.
**Range:** Breeds right across Eurasia from Portugal to the Bering Strait and into western Alaska. It winters across most of sub-Saharan Africa, in the Caucasus and from India to Southeast Asia and China. In Europe, it is absent from mountain areas, as well as Iceland, Ireland and most of Scotland.
**Movements:** Whole of population breeding east of Urals migrates across Europe, the Mediterranean and Sahara to winter in Africa. In spring, vast numbers gather at the Sahel wetlands prior to crossing the desert to the north, seemingly taking a different route from that followed in autumn.
**Breeding:** Five or six brown-speckled greyish eggs are laid in a cup on the ground and incubated for 12–14 days mainly by the female. The helpless, downy young fly after 17 days. Sometimes rears two broods.
**Confusing Species:** Darker backed males similar to female Grey Wagtail, though latter has a longer tail.

## Waxwing *(Bombycilla garrulus)*

The Waxwing breeds among boreal forests, occasionally erupting westwards and southwards in a movement known as irruption. The plumage is pinkish buff, darker above than below. The head has a prominent crest and there is a black eyestripe and chin patch that give an angry appearance. The black primaries are tipped yellow with red, waxy protrusions across the folded wing.

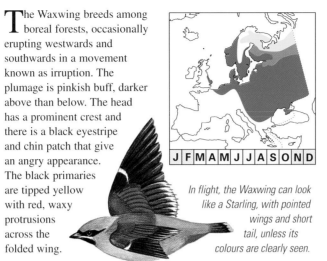

| J | F | M | A | M | J | J | A | S | O | N | D |

*In flight, the Waxwing can look like a Starling, with pointed wings and short tail, unless its colours are clearly seen.*

**Size:** 17–19cm (7in).
**Wing:** 114–125mm.
**Bill:** 17–19mm.
**Weight:** 50–83g.
**Voice:** A tinkling trill.
**Habitat:** Boreal forests.
**Food:** Berries.
**Range:** Circumpolar in the north. In Europe, breeds from northern Sweden eastwards across northern Russia.
**Movements:** Irruptions every ten or so years dependent on population levels and berry crop. At times the birds may reach as far west as Britain, birds in Ireland may be of trans-Atlantic origin.
**Breeding:** Five black-spotted blue eggs are laid in a cup in a conifer and incubated by the female for 13–14 days and young fledge after 15–17 days.

## Dipper *(Cinclus cinclus)*

An unmistakable bird of rushing hill and mountain streams, the Dipper swims and wades under water and is most often seen bobbing atop a

torrent-washed boulder. It is largely brown-black with white chin and breast bordered dark chestnut in British subspecies, but brown-black in Continental birds. The rounded wings and short, often cocked tail give the impression of an over-large Wren.

| J | F | M | A | M | J | J | A | S | O | N | D |

*The domed nest is built under tree roots or in a crevice or hole close to running water. It may be used by a pair of dippers to raise up to three broods of chicks in a year.*

**Size:** 17–19cm (7in).
**Wing:** 82–99mm.
**Bill:** 20–23mm.
**Weight:** 50–70g.
**Voice:** High-pitched *zit-zit*.
**Habitat:** Fast moving rivers and streams. Often winters at weirs.
**Food:** Aquatic insects.
**Range:** Breeds Europe from Spain and Ireland eastwards to Russia and Turkey. Mainly resident.
**Movements:** Migration of Scandinavian birds southwards to winter in Finland, the Baltic States and Jutland.
**Breeding:** Five white eggs are laid in a domed nest and incubated by the female for 15–18 days. The helpless, downy young fly after 19–25 days.

## Wren *(Troglodytes troglodytes)*

One of the smallest of European birds, the Wren is also one of the most common, with up to 20 million in Britain alone. All other species of wrens are confined to the New World. This tiny

brown bird is deep brown barred black above, and creamy below, barred with brown on the flanks. There is a strong, buffy supercilium and speckled ear coverts. The short, brown-barred tail is frequently cocked.

| J | F | M | A | M | J | J | A | S | O | N | D |

*The Wren's size and camouflage means that it relies on its song to defend territory.*

**Size:** 9–10cm (3–4in).
**Wing:** 45–52mm.
**Bill:** 12–15mm.
**Weight:** 8–12g.
**Voice:** Very loud warbling song, ending with a rapid trill.
**Habitat:** Woods, forests and groves, gardens, parks, moors and sea cliffs.
**Food:** Insects.
**Range:** Across Eurasia from Europe through the Himalayas to Japan.
**Movements:** Complex pattern of resident, partial and full migrant, but difficult to tell migrants from residents.
**Breeding:** Five to eight red-speckled white eggs are laid in a domed nest and incubated by the female for 15–20 days. The downy, helpless young fly after 15–20 days.

**Size:** 13–15cm (5–6in).
**Wing:** 66–74mm.
**Bill:** 14–16mm.
**Weight:** 15–25g.
**Voice:** A jingling warble.
**Habitat:** Woods, hedges, gardens, scrub, groves.
**Food:** Insects and berries.
**Range:** Breeds across temperate Europe, largely avoiding the Mediterranean, as far north as northern Scandinavia and sub-tundra Russia. Absent from Iceland, southern Russia and most of the Ukraine, but present in the Caucasus. It is resident from Germany westwards.
**Movements:** Scandinavian and Russian birds move south and west to the Mediterranean and Turkey, but do not reach North Africa.
**Breeding:** Four or five blue eggs are laid in a cup in a small tree or bush and incubated for 12 or 13 days by the female. The helpless, down-covered young fly after 12 days. Rears two, occasionally three, broods in a season.
**Confusing Species:** Alpine Accentor has similar behaviour and structure.

*Male and female Hedge Accentors are similar in appearance. During the breeding season, male Hedge Accentors indulge in communal singing and wing waving.*

Otherwise known as the Dunnock, this is the only accentor to have abandoned the mountains to take up a widespread, virtually endemic existence in western Eurasia. This is a ground-dwelling, shuffling little bird with a horizontal carriage. The upperparts are streaked black and brown, the underparts are dull grey, extending over the face, with a dirty white belly and brown-streaked flanks.

A high-altitude bird, similar in structure and shuffling movement to the Hedge Accentor, the Alpine Accentor descends to the valleys to avoid the worst of the winter. The upperparts are streaked brown and black and marked by two narrow white wingbars. The head and breast are grey, with a distinctive black and white spotted gorget. The flanks are heavily streaked with chestnut. Though it spends much time among low vegetation, it also perches openly on top of rocks.

**Size:** 15–20cm (6–8in).
**Wing:** 95–110mm.
**Bill:** 17–18mm.
**Weight:** 33–42g.
**Voice:** A liquid *chirrup*.
**Habitat:** High mountain tops and bare screes; lower hillsides in winter.
**Food:** Insects and seeds.
**Range:** In Europe, local through mountains of Spain, the Alps, Carpathians and Yugoslavia, Bulgaria and Greece. Extends eastwards through Turkey, Iran, Himalayas and China to eastern Siberia and Japan.
**Movements:** Largely resident, but much more widespread in Spain and Yugoslavia in winter than purely local movements would account for. Some movement detected through Pyrennean passes and Gibraltar.
**Breeding:** Three or four blue eggs are laid in a cup built into a rock crevice and incubated by both sexes for 15 days. The helpless, downy chicks fly after 16 days. Double brooded.
**Confusing Species:** The similar Hedge Accentor is rarely found in the mountains.

*The brightly marked Alpine Accentor has become a familiar bird to those who take skiing holidays; it is increasingly tame around ski lifts as it forages for food scraps.*

## Rufous Scrub-robin *(Cercotrichas galactotes)*

A well-marked, attractive summer visitor, this bird has suffered a variety of name changes, ranging from Rufous Warbler to Rufous Bush Robin, but has many African relatives that are called scrub-robins. The upperparts are a warm, sandy colour, with a creamy supercilium and black eyestripe. The underparts are creamy white. A major feature is the long rufous tail, which is often cocked or jerked up and down to reveal the black and white tipped corners.

J F M A M J J A S O N D

*In display, the male perches on a prominent post or branch, droops its wings and fans its tail. The tail is then jerked up and down as the bird sings its melodic, if rather disjointed, song.*

**Size:** 15cm (6in).
**Wing:** 81–92mm.
**Bill:** 18–22mm.
**Weight:** 19–28g.
**Voice:** A harsh *tek-tek* and a sweetly warbling song.
**Habitat:** Thickets, especially of oleanders, in shingly river beds.
**Food:** Insects.

**Range:** Breeds throughout the Mediterranean to Turkey and the Middle East to beyond the Caspian. Winters in Sahel Africa, where it is also resident. In Europe, summer visitor to southern Iberia, Greece and some parts of the western Balkans.
**Movements:** Definite western and eastern populations that may, in autumn, avoid the worst of the Sahara by migrating around its margins to (probably) distinct wintering grounds in the Sahel. The spring passage indicates that some birds, at least, do cross the Sahara at that season.
**Breeding:** Four or five brown-speckled, white eggs are laid in a cup in a bush and incubated for 13 days by the female. The naked, helpless young fledge after 12 or 13 days. May raise two broods.

## Robin *(Erithacus rubecula)*

This widespread and relatively common resident or summer visitor to Europe, has become a tame garden bird in parts of its range. The adult is khaki-brown above and buffy below, with an orange-red face and breast. The juvenile is speckled brown above and barred with crescents below. It stands and perches upright, cocking its tail frequently.

J F M A M J J A S O N D

*The juvenile bird lacks the red breast of the adult and is mottled in shades of brown.*

**Size:** 13–15cm (5–6in).
**Wing:** 68–76mm.
**Bill:** 14–16mm.
**Weight:** 13–23g.
**Voice:** A thin, warbling song and a hard *tic-tic-tic*.
**Habitat:** Woodland margins and clearings, hedges, gardens and parks.
**Food:** Insects.
**Range:** Breeds right across temperate, Mediterranean and boreal Europe to beyond the Urals and locally in northern Iran. Winters in the Middle East, North Africa and within the breeding range. Absent from Iceland.
**Movements:** Western and southern birds are residents or partial migrants,

birds north and east of Austria are summer visitors. However, the situation is complex because of partial migration and differences in migratory pattern between the sexes. Many northern birds appear to fly southwards to winter in North Africa.

**Breeding:** Five or six reddish-speckled white eggs are laid in a cup hidden on the ground, or a bank, or tree stump and are incubated by the female for 12–15 days. The helpless, downy young fledge after a similar period. Regularly raises two broods, and sometimes a third.

## Thrush Nightingale *(Luscinia luscinia)*

**Size:** 15cm (6in).
**Wing:** 84–94mm.
**Bill:** 16–18mm.
**Weight:** 21–30g.
**Voice:** Varied and melodious song, lacking the crescendo of Nightingale.
**Habitat:** Damp habitats, such as flooded forests, waterside thickets and copses.
**Food:** Insects.
**Range:** Summer visitor from Jutland and southern Scandinavia eastwards across Poland and Slovakia to Russia and the Ukraine as far as south-central Siberia. Winters in eastern Africa.
**Movements:** Whole population flies south in the autumn, where it is locally abundant. Crosses eastern Mediterranean and many birds follow the Nile.

**Breeding:** Four or five reddish-mottled eggs are laid in a cup hidden on or near the ground. They are incubated for 13 or 14 days and the helpless, downy young fly after 11 or 12 days.
**Confusing Species:** Nightingale.

Although their ranges overlap, this species replaces the Nightingale in eastern Europe and is regularly referred to as the Sprosser. It is much less rufous than the Nightingale, with dull brown upperparts, a greyish mottled breast and a less reddish tail. It is similarly shy and secretive, seldom perching openly, even when singing.

*The Thrush Nightingale is paler and more mottled than the Nightingale.*

## Nightingale *(Luscinia megarhynchos)*

The Nightingale is the greatest of all European songbirds, its achievements being highlighted by regular after-dark performances on summer evenings. Its upperparts are warm brown, with a narrow, creamy eye-ring, and it has buffy underparts and a bright rufous tail. It shows its reddish tail prominently as it flies.

*Generally a skulking bird that prefers to perch deep within thickets when it sings. It is the rich, flute-like song which usually gives away the presence of this elusive bird.*

**Size:** 15–18cm (6–7in).
**Wing:** 78–87mm.
**Bill:** 16–18mm.
**Weight:** 16–36g.
**Voice:** Wonderfully melodic concerto of variable, liquid phrases that ends with a crescendo.
**Habitat:** Open woodlands with ground cover, thickets and heaths, copses and groves.
**Food:** Insects.

**Range:** Summer visitor to western and central Europe, extending east to the Black Sea and to south-central Siberia. Winters in the Sahel zone of Africa.
**Movements:** General southwesterly orientation across Europe to northern coasts of Mediterranean in autumn. Thereafter flies across that sea and the Sahara in a non-stop flight to winter across the Sahel zone.
**Breeding:** Four or five reddish-mottled eggs are laid in a cup on the ground, hidden among ivy or other vegetation, and are incubated by the female for 13 or 14 days. The helpless, down-covered young fly after 11 or 12 days.
**Confusing Species**: See Thrush Nightingale for differences.

214

## Bluethroat (Luscinia svecica)

This Robin-like chat, marked with a bright blue breast in the summer male, occurs in two subspecies: red-spotted and white-spotted. The male in summer is grey-brown above, buff below with a white supercilium. The female lacks the bold blue breast, but has a dark moustache which widens into an incomplete necklace. In all plumages a red base to the tail sides is diagnostic. Hides in ground cover, but cocks tail, showing red base to the sides.

**Size:** 13–15cm (5–6in).
**Wing:** 73–79mm.
**Bill:** 15–17mm.
**Weight:** 15–26g.
**Voice:** Melodic warbling that is highly mimetic of other species: a hard *tic-tic*.
**Habitat:** Marshland margins with bushes, trees and reeds.
**Food:** Insects.
**Range:** Breeds right across temperate Eurasia from Spain to the Bering Strait and locally in Alaska, extending southwards into central Asia. Winters Sahel zone of Africa, Middle East, India and Southeast Asia. In Europe, red-spotted subspecies breeds from Scandinavia eastwards; while the white-spotted subspecies breeds from France across central Europe.
**Movements:** Migrates across Europe to southwest or southeast, with a migrational divide in Scandinavia. Western birds cross the Mediterranean and Sahara on a wide front, but eastern birds winter in Pakistan and India.
**Breeding:** Five to seven, red-spotted green eggs are laid in a cup on the ground and incubated by the female for 14 or 15 days. The helpless, downy young fly after 14 days. Sometimes has two broods.

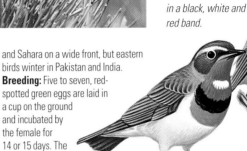

*Both Red- and White-spotted subspecies have blue throats ending in a black, white and red band.*

## Red-flanked Bluetail (Tarsiger cyanurus)

**Size:** 13–15cm (5–6in).
**Wing:** 73–84mm.
**Bill:** 13–15mm.
**Weight:** 12–18g.
**Voice:** Loud, whistled song of mournful quality; hard *seep-seep*.
**Habitat:** Boreal forests with dense undergrowth and mixed woods, often with water.
**Food:** Insects, often taken in trees and shrubs and in the air.
**Range:** Breeds from Finland and Estonia (locally), across boreal Russia and Siberia to Japan and, separately, in Himalayan region. Winters Japan, China and Southeast Asia.
**Movements:** Huge migration of European birds southeastwards to the Far East. Vagrant to western Europe, seldom overshooting.
**Breeding:** Five to seven white eggs, lightly spotted brown, are laid in a cup hidden among tree roots on the ground. They are incubated by the female and the young fledge after 15 days.
**Confusing Species:** Juvenile looks like a juvenile Robin with a blue tail.

An east Siberian species which has spread westwards across northern Russia and is now a localized breeder in Finland. The male is blue above and white below, marked by bright orangey chestnut flanks and a blue tail, that is often cocked. In fresh autumn plumage a bold whitish supercilium is apparent. The female is brown above, with a white bib, brown breast, rufous flanks and a blue tail.

*The female Red-flanked Bluetail (above) has a rufous patch at the bend of its wing and a blue tail.*

215

## Black Redstart (*Phoenicurus ochruros*)

**Size:** 15cm (6in).
**Wing:** 83–91mm.
**Bill:** 14–16mm.
**Weight:** 14–20g.
**Voice:** Brief *sip* or *tissic*; brief, high-pitched, weak warbling.
**Habitat:** Rocky hillsides with scrub, gullies with shade, cities, towns, gardens, parks and, in some areas, industrial and development sites.
**Food:** Insects.
**Range:** Breeds across temperate Europe, from southern England and Portugal to the Baltic States and the Ukraine; locally through the Middle East to central southern Asia. Winters south and west Europe, North and East Africa to India.
**Movements:** Most European breeders winter in the Mediterranean basin, migrating on a broad front. Abundant in Spain in spring, indicating that many winter in North Africa.
**Breeding:** Four to six white eggs are laid in a cup hidden in a hole or crevice and incubated by the female for 12–16 days. The helpless, down-covered young fly after 12–19 days. Double or triple brooded.

*The female (below) is grey where the male (far left) is black, but retains the red tail.*

A summer visitor or resident over most of temperate Europe, this bird prefers rocky hillsides and dark gulleys, but has spread into towns and even city centres in many areas. The male is black above, with a palish crown and a bold white wingflash. The underparts are sooty black, the shimmered tail bright rufous. The female is a dirty grey, with a rufous tail. Eastern subspecies have red, not black, underparts in the male.

## Common Redstart (*Phoenicurus phoenicurus*)

**Size:** 13cm (5in).
**Wing:** 75–84mm.
**Bill:** 14–16mm.
**Weight:** 10–20g.
**Voice:** Thin warbling; call a thin *hweet*.
**Habitat:** Open woodland of many types, wooded heaths, copses, hedgerows, parkland.
**Food:** Insects.
**Range:** Summer visitor from Britain and Spain across Europe, Russia and the Ukraine to well beyond the Urals. Winters in Sahel Africa.
**Movements:** Broad front migration across Mediterranean and Sahara in a single non-stop flight. In spring, many stop over in North Africa, where they are decidedly rare in autumn.
**Breeding:** Six or seven pale blue eggs are laid in a cup in a tree hole or bank and incubated by the female for 11–14 days. The downy, helpless young fly after 14–20 days. Double brooded.
**Confusing Species:** Female is browner than the female Black Redstart.

*The female (left) lacks the black mask of the male (above left), but it retains a dull version of the red markings.*

This is a summer visitor to open woodlands and heaths over most of Europe. The male is pale grey over the crown, back and wings with a black face extending to the chin marked by a white forehead. The underparts are a rich orange, the tail rufous. The bird perches among the lower branches of trees and feeds by pouncing to the ground.

## Whinchat *(Saxicola rubetra)*

This is a widespread summer visitor to open country that perches on top of a bush or on a stalk near the ground and is easily seen as a result. Both sexes are neatly mottled black and buff above, with an orange breast and whitish belly. Both show a distinctive whitish supercilium, and a white base to the outertail feathers. The male has dark brown ear coverts, a white moustachial streak and white innerwing patches in flight. It is more boldly coloured than the female at all times.

J F M A M J J A S O N D

**Size:** 13cm (5in).
**Wing:** 74–81mm.
**Bill:** 14–15mm.
**Weight:** 14–22g.
**Voice:** Song is a brief warble; hard *tic-tic*.
**Habitat:** Heaths, hillsides, scrubby downlands.
**Food:** Insects, taken with a perch-and-pounce technique.
**Range:** Summer visitor to most of temperate Europe extending eastwards to beyond the Urals. Largely absent from the Mediterranean. Winters in savanna Africa.
**Movements:** Migrates on a broad front, crossing the Mediterranean and Sahara to reach the western Sahel zone of Africa.

*The adult male (left) and juvenile (right) share the rufous breast and white supercilium, although the male is more strongly marked. Both also share the upright stance that makes the bird so noticeable.*

**Breeding:** Five to seven brown-speckled blue eggs are laid in a cup on the ground beneath a bush and incubated by the female for 13 or 14 days. The helpless, down-covered young fly after 17 days. One or two broods are reared in a season.
**Confusing Species:** Similarly brown-speckled Stonechat also perches openly, but lacks a supercilium in all plumages.

## Stonechat *(Saxicola torquata)*

A widespread Old World species, the Stonechat sits openly on bushes and is easily observed. The male is brown and black above, warm orange below, with a white belly and undertail. The head is black and is marked by a white half-collar. The female is similar, but lacks the white collar and has a brown speckled head. In flight, adults show a narrow white rump.

J F M A M J J A S O N D

**Size:** 13cm (5in).
**Wing:** 63–68mm.
**Bill:** 14–16mm.
**Weight:** 13–19g.
**Voice:** Song is a jingling warble; call a hard *chak chak*.
**Habitat:** Gorse and other prickly scrub thickets, hedges, clearings.
**Food:** Insects.
**Range:** Breeds across temperate Europe; also over most of temperate and boreal Eurasia, as far south as China, and over savanna Africa. In Europe, is absent from Scandinavia and much of Russia and is only a summer visitor from Germany eastwards. Winters in western Europe and the Mediterranean region.
**Movements:** Large migration to Iberia

*Adult males (left) are boldly marked, while the juvenile (above) has a speckled appearance.*

and Algeria indicates that many cross the Mediterranean, although there is a tendency to fly around, rather than over, mountain chains.
**Breeding:** Five or six brown-speckled blue eggs are laid in a cup hidden at the base of a bush and incubated by the female for 14 or 15 days. The downy, helpless chicks fly after 12 or 13 days. Rears two or three broods.
**Confusing Species:** Whinchat.

## Black-eared Wheatear *(Oenanthe hispanica)*

In Europe, there are two subspecies. The western male is sandy rufous, the eastern male is creamy white. Males of both subspecies are smaller than the Northern Wheatear and have either a black mask or a totally black face. Both males and females show a long-shanked black 'T' on a white tail.

J F M A M J J A S O N D

**Size:** 13–15cm (5–6in).
**Wing:** 86–92mm.
**Bill:** 16–18mm.
**Weight:** 12–22g.
**Voice:** Harsh, scratchy warbled song.
**Habitat:** Open rocky hillsides.
**Food:** Insects.
**Range:** Summer visitor to the Mediterranean extending eastwards to Turkey and adjacent Middle East. Winters in Sahel zone, Africa.
**Movements:** Crosses Sahara on a broad front and is more abundant in Mediterranean, on islands for example, in spring than in summer.
**Breeding:** Four or five brown-speckled blue eggs are laid in a cup placed in a rock crevice and incubated by the female for 13 or 14 days. The helpless, downy

*Some males of both subspecies have a solid black face (right), not the more usual mask (left).*

young fledge at 11 or 12 days. Probably has two broods.
**Confusing Species:** Female Northern Wheatear and both sexes of pale eastern subspecies with Pied Wheatear.

## Pied Wheatear *(Oenanthe pleschanka)*

This summer visitor to the eastern part of Europe has to be separated with care from the Black-eared Wheatear. The male has a black back and wings that are joined to a black face and bib. The underparts are white, variously washed with creamy buff. The female is brown above, creamy below.

J F M A M J J A S O N D

**Size:** 15cm (6in).
**Wing:** 90–99mm.
**Bill:** 16–18mm.
**Weight:** 16–25g.
**Voice:** Scratchy warbled song.
**Habitat:** Bare stony areas, often on hillsides.
**Food:** Insects.
**Range:** Summer visitor to Black Sea, eastwards across southern Asia. All populations winter in eastern Africa. In Europe, is a scarce breeder from Bulgaria to the Ukraine.
**Movements:** Migrates on a broad front, through eastern Turkey, Iran and the Persian Gulf, where it may be the most abundant migrant wheatear.
**Breeding:** Five or six reddish-spotted blue-green eggs are laid in a cup in a

*The black tail markings show a distinctive narrow terminal band and long shank.*

hole or rock crevice and incubated for 13 or 14 days. Young fledge at 13–14 days.
**Confusing Species:** Black-eared Wheatear of eastern subspecies.

## Black Wheatear *(Oenanthe leucura)*

This is a large wheatear, resident in the western Mediterranean and endemic to the Western Palearctic. Both sexes are black above and below with white undertail coverts, a white rump and white sides to the T tail pattern, which is characteristic of all wheatears.

*This is the only wheatear that is entirely black, apart from the white rump and tail.*

**Size:** 18cm (7in).
**Wing:** 92–105mm.
**Bill:** 20–23mm.
**Weight:** 38–44g.
**Voice:** A pleasant, fluty warble.
**Habitat:** Rocky hillsides, screes.
**Food:** Insects.
**Range:** In Europe, confined to Spain, with smaller populations in adjacent Portugal and southern France. Also found in North Africa from Morocco to Tunisia.
**Movements:** Local dispersal, but unconfirmed passage from Spain to Morocco in small numbers.
**Breeding:** Three to five brown-spotted blue eggs are laid in a cup placed in a rock crevice with a wall of small stones at the entrance. The eggs are incubated by the female for 14–18 days and the downy, helpless young fledge after 14 or 15 days.
**Confusing Species:** Immatures of the White-crowned Black Wheatear of North Africa are similar, but lack any hint of a black tip to the tail.

J F M A M J J A S O N D

218

## Northern Wheatear *(Oenanthe oenanthe)*

The world's most successful wheatear, this is a familiar bird in many hill and wilderness areas. The male is dove-grey from the crown to the back, with black wings and a black mask. The breast is buffy orange, fading to white on the belly. The tail is a broad inverted T in black and white.

**Size:** 15cm (6in).
**Wing:** 93–110mm.
**Bill:** 16–19mm.
**Weight:** 18–30g.
**Voice:** A brief scratchy warble, often in song flight.
**Habitat:** Open tundra to grassy heaths, shingle shorelines and semi-desert.
**Food:** Insects.
**Range:** Summer visitor across most of Europe, eastwards across Russia and the Middle East to the Bering Strait and Alaska. It is absent from central Canada, but breeds in the eastern archipelago to Greenland and Iceland.
**Movements:** Unlikely as it may seem, all Northern Wheatears migrate to Sahel and eastern Africa. Birds from Siberia and Alaska fly westwards, those from eastern Canada and Greenland fly eastwards. Both, doubtless, return along their original colonization routes. Birds from Greenland fly non-stop to Europe. Crosses the Mediterranean and Sahara on a broad front.
**Breeding:** Five or six pale blue eggs are laid in a cup placed in a ground hole or crevice and incubated mainly by the female for 14 days. The helpless, downy chicks fly after some 15 days. Sometimes rears a second brood.
**Confusing Species:** Female and young males may be confused with other wheatears, notably Isabelline Wheatear.

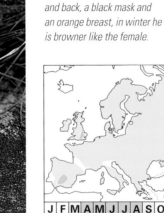

*Although the male in summer has a grey crown and back, a black mask and an orange breast, in winter he is browner like the female.*

## Isabelline Wheatear (Oenanthe isabellina)

An eastern wheatear in which the sexes are similar, this bird bears a strong resemblance to a female Northern Wheatear. The upperparts are a warm buff, and the underparts a rich creamy buff, with a white supercilium as the only distinguishing feature. Identification rests on large size, remarkably upright stance, long legs and a broad black tail band forming a short-shanked 'T'. The bird both runs and perches very erect.

**Size:** 15–18cm (6–7in).
**Wing:** 93–106mm.
**Bill:** 20–22cm.
**Weight:** 25–38g.
**Voice:** A fine, liquid warbling that includes much mimicry of other species and sounds.
**Habitat:** Dry open plains with rocks and other perches.
**Food:** Insects.
**Range:** Summer visitor from Greece through Turkey and the Ukraine to eastern Siberia. Winters Sahel Africa, Middle East and Pakistan. In Europe, breeds northern Greece, European Turkey and from the Crimea eastwards.
**Movements:** European birds migrate on a broad front crossing the eastern Mediterranean and Sahara, mainly to the eastern part of the Sahel zone.
**Breeding:** Five or six pale blue eggs are laid in a cup placed in a rodent burrow and incubated by the female alone for 12 days. The downy, helpless young leave the nest after 13–15 days, which is before they can fly.
**Confusing Species:** Female Northern Wheatear.

*Seen with the female Northern Wheatear (far left), the larger Isabelline Wheatear (left) stands more upright, with longer legs. These are fine points that are easily confused by the inexperienced birder.*

A decidedly scarce summer visitor to southern Europe, this bird, or the male at least, is colourful and easily identified. The male has a powder blue head, neck and mantle, which forms a clear breast band where it meets the orange-red underparts. The wings are black, the tail orange-red, and there is a smudgy white horseshoe-shaped rump. The orange-red tail is diagnostic.

*While the male (below) is bright and colourful, the female (right) is buffy brown, marked by dark crescents, and with a bright orange-red tail.*

**Size:** 18–20cm (7–8in).
**Wing:** 113–131mm.
**Bill:** 23–27mm.
**Weight:** 42–65g.
**Voice:** A loud warbling song; a harsh *chak*.
**Habitat:** Rocky mountain slopes, hillsides and gullies, often with scattered trees.
**Food:** Insects and berries.
**Range:** Summer visitor to southern Europe, eastwards through Turkey to the Middle East and south-central Asia as far as northern China. Winters in Sahel and East Africa. In Europe, widespread in Spain, through the Alps and Italy, the Balkans and the Carpathian Mountains.
**Movements:** European breeders cross the Sahara on a broad front, though there is evidence that they may concentrate on the central section.
**Breeding:** Four or five blue eggs are laid in a cup placed in a hole among rocks and incubated by the female for 14 or 15 days. The helpless, down-covered young fly after 14–16 days.
**Confusing Species:** Female Blue Rock Thrush lacks warm wash on the breast.

J F M A M J J A S O N D

This resident of the Mediterranean sits on large prominent rocks for long periods and resembles a Common Starling in flight. The male is dark blue with black wings and tail, but looks black at any distance. The female is dark grey, paler below, and heavily marked with crescents to form a scaly pattern all over. In flight, a shortish tail and pointed wings could cause confusion with the Common Starling or Spotless Starling.

*The male (right) has bold blue plumage, but the female (below) is dark and mottled.*

J F M A M J J A S O N D

**Size:** 20cm (8in).
**Wing:** 120–133mm.
**Bill:** 27–31mm.
**Weight:** 37–69g.
**Voice:** Fluty warble that resembles the song of the Blackbird.
**Habitat:** Rocky hillsides and gorges, but at lower altitudes in winter.
**Food:** Insects and seeds.
**Range:** From Mediterranean eastwards through the Himalayas to China and Japan. Mostly resident, with local dispersal and altitudinal movements.

**Movements:** Populations in Turkey and the Middle East and in northern China and Korea are migrants. European birds may be more migratory than assumed, merging with residents in North Africa. Birds that winter in the western Sahel are almost certainly of European origin. Middle East populations winter in Arabia and East Africa.

**Breeding:** Four or five pale blue eggs are laid in a cup placed in a hole or rock crevice and are incubated for 12 or 13 days by the female alone. The downy, helpless young fly after 17 days. It raises one or, sometimes, two broods.
**Confusing Species:** The female Rock Thrush has a clear warm wash on the underparts.

# Ring Ousel *(Turdus torquatus)*

Often termed the European mountain Blackbird, this bird is very similar in plumage and behaviour to that bird. The male is black, with a bold white crescent on the breast and flashes of silver in the wings, particularly obvious in flight. The female is browner, with a more subdued breast crescent, lightly scaled underparts and silvery wings.

**Size:** 23–25cm (9–10in).
**Wing:** 134–145mm.
**Bill:** 16–18mm.
**Weight:** 90–138g.
**Voice:** A repetitive warble of plaintive notes; call an explosive *chook-chook*.
**Habitat:** Rocky mountain slopes and upland pastures.
**Food:** Insects, worms, berries.
**Range:** Summer visitor to mountains and hills of Europe eastwards to the Middle East. Winters in the Mediterranean area and Iran. In Europe, breeds northern Spain, Britain and Ireland, Scandinavia, Alps, Apennines, Carpathians and the Balkans.
**Movements:** West European birds migrate to Spain and North Africa, but still maintain a hill and mountain habitat. Spring migration is farther west than autumn. Elusive, secretive, migrant through non-breeding areas.
**Breeding:** Four or five brown-blotched blue eggs are laid in a cup on the ground and incubated by both sexes for 13 or 14 days. The downy, helpless young fly after a similar period.
**Confusing Species:** Watch out for a silver-winged Blackbird.

*The male (left) has black plumage and a clear white collar. The female (above) is similar, but duller.*

J F M A M J J A S O N D

# Blackbird *(Turdus merula)*

A familiar, all-black thrush, the Blackbird is common and widespread in many parts of Europe. The male is black, with a yellow bill and yellow eye-ring; the female is dark brown above and mottled below, with a yellow base to the bill.

**Size:** 25–28cm (10–11in).
**Wing:** 116–132mm.
**Bill:** 16–18mm.
**Weight:** 70–148g.
**Voice:** Melodic, fluty warble; harsh cackle of alarm.
**Habitat:** Woods and forests, hedges, copses, gardens parks and groves.

**Food:** Worms, insects, berries.
**Range:** Breeds from Europe, through Turkey and the Middle East to India, the Himalayas and China. Introduced Australia and New Zealand. Birds of eastern Europe are summer visitors.

**Movements:** Huge migration of Scandinavian birds to Britain, Ireland and western France. Birds from Germany and eastwards migrate to France, Iberia and Italy. However, large numbers of birds also move from Britain to France and Ireland and a similar situation doubtless exists in other areas where the species appears to be resident but, in reality, individual birds move significant distances.
**Breeding:** Four or five brown-blotched bluish eggs are laid in a well-built nest of grass and mud placed in a tree or shrub and incubated by the female for 11–17 days. The downy, helpless young fly after 12–19 days. The species is often double or triple brooded.

*While the male blackbird (above) lives up to the species' name by having black plumage, the female (left) is brown with a mottled throat and chest, rather like a dark thrush.*

J F M A M J J A S O N D

221

This neatly proportioned, spotted thrush is a summer visitor to temperate Eurasia and resident in southern and western Europe. The upperparts are a warm brown, while the underparts are white, neatly spotted on breast and flanks and with a warm buffy wash on the breast. It flies fast and direct.

**Size:** 23cm (9in).
**Wing:** 111–119mm.
**Bill:** 13–15mm.
**Weight:** 61–107g.
**Voice:** Song consists of a variety of phrases, each repeated three or four times; call is a short *tsip.*
**Habitat:** Woods and forests, groves, orchards and gardens.
**Food:** Worms, insects, berries, snails.
**Range:** Breeds across Eurasia, from northern Spain to Scandinavia and east to Siberia. It is absent from Iceland, Mediterranean coasts, and most of Iberia and Greece. Birds from Germany eastwards are summer visitors.
**Movements:** Large numbers of northern and eastern birds migrate to Iberia and the Mediterranean, as well as to Britain, Ireland, France and North Africa.
**Breeding:** Four to six black-spotted blue eggs are laid in a cup lined with mud, placed low in a tree, and incubated by the female for 11–15 days. The downy, helpless young fledge after 12–16 days and the birds regularly lay a second, and sometimes a third, clutch.
**Confusing Species:** The larger Mistle Thrush is greyish brown.

*Song thrushes are unique in using an 'anvil', a convenient stone, on which to smash open snail shells.*

J F M A M J J A S O N D

Slightly smaller than a Song Thrush, this is a well-marked bird that breeds in the north, but is a widespread winter visitor or passage migrant over most of temperate Europe. It is brown above and white below, with rows of spots over the breast and flanks. A white supercilium is the best field mark. Flies fast and direct.

**Size:** 20–23cm (8–9in).
**Wing:** 110–121mm.
**Bill:** 13–16mm.
**Weight:** 47–80g.
**Voice:** Long warbling song with a melancholy opening followed by twittering; call is a clear *seeip.*
**Habitat:** Birches and mixed woods, often near water in boreal zone.
**Food:** Insects, worms, berries.
**Range:** Summer visitor from Iceland and Scandinavia to Poland and eastwards across Russia almost to the Bering Strait. It has colonized Scotland in the twentieth century. Winters throughout western and southern Europe, Turkey and the Middle East.
**Movements:** Whole population migrates westwards. Scandinavian birds fly the North Sea on a broad front to winter in Britain and Ireland, as well as France and Iberia. Birds from Eastern Europe winter from Germany westwards and southwards to Greece.
**Breeding:** Four or five brown-speckled blue eggs are laid in a cup placed on a branch right against a tree trunk. They are incubated by the female for 11–15 days. The helpless, downy young fly after 10–15 days. Often has two broods.
**Confusing Species:** Song Thrush.

J F M A M J J A S O N D

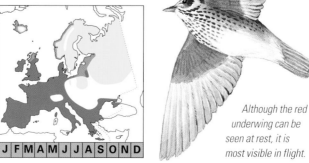

*Although the red underwing can be seen at rest, it is most visible in flight.*

# Fieldfare *(Turdus pilaris)*

*The clear line between the Fieldfare's grey rump and its black tail feathers is especially noticeable when the bird is seen from behind in flight.*

A large, well marked thrush which is a widespread European breeding bird in the north and east and a winter visitor to the south and west. The grey head and rump are separated by a brown back and wings. The underparts are white with a buffy wash over the breast, the whole heavily marked with chevrons.

**J F M A M J J A S O N D**

**Size:** 23–28cm (9–11in).
**Wing:** 136–152mm.
**Bill:** 14–17mm.
**Weight:** 76–128g.
**Voice:** Song consists of a quiet warbling with wheezy laughs; call is a harsh *chak-chak*.
**Habitat:** Breeds in a wide variety of woodland in the boreal and temperate zones, often with birches and rivers. Winters over fields, hedges, grasslands.
**Food:** Insects, berries and fruit, worms.
**Range:** Breeds from eastern France right across Eurasia to eastern Siberia. In Europe, breeds as far north as the North Cape of Norway. Winters right across Mediterranean and temperate Europe north to southern Finland.

**Movements:** Migrates south and west to winter as far as Iceland and Iberia, as well as within the breeding range. Hard-weather movements occur throughout the winter and birds do not seem faithful to particular wintering zones.
**Breeding:** Five or six pale blue eggs with reddish spots are laid in a cup placed in the fork of a tree and incubated by the female for 11–14 days. The helpless, downy young fledge after 12–16 days. It raises one or two broods.
**Confusing Species:** Mistle Thrush.

# Mistle Thrush *(Turdus viscivorus)*

Largest of the European thrushes, this bird has a strong similarity to the significantly smaller Song Thrush. Always paler and greyer than that bird, with grey-brown upperparts; white underparts, washed buffy on flanks and breast, and marked with lines of large black spots. The tail is long and marked with white corners, particularly obvious in flight, which is deeply undulating.

*In flight, the white tips to the tail feathers are not easily seen, but they do help to make an identification.*

**J F M A M J J A S O N D**

**Size:** 25–28cm (10–11in).
**Wing:** 147–162mm.
**Bill:** 14–17mm.
**Weight:** 100–167g.
**Voice:** Loud and shrill warbling song broken by pauses; a rattling call.
**Habitat:** Groves, orchards, open woodland, hedges, parks.
**Food:** Berries, worms and insects.
**Range:** Breeds from Europe in a broad swathe across central and southern Siberia, avoiding the open steppes.

In Europe, it is resident from Germany and the former Yugoslavia westwards and a summer visitor farther east. Winters south and west.
**Movements:** Northern and eastern birds move south and west to winter mostly within the breeding range, though some do make considerable migrations. Avoids making long sea crossings such as across the North Sea.
**Breeding:** Four or five blue eggs with reddish spots are laid in a cup placed in a major fork of a tree, often before the tree has foliage. They are incubated by the female for 12–15 days and the downy, helpless young fledge after about 20 days. It raises two broods.
**Confusing Species:** Song Thrush.

223

## Fan-tailed Warbler *(Cisticola juncidis)*

This tiny resident of the Mediterranean has expanded its range to the north and east over the past 40 years. It is the only European representative of one of the most confusing of Old World genera of warblers. In fact, there are 50 or so species spread across Africa and Asia. It is a heavily streaked black and buff bird, marked by a decurved bill and a short, rounded tail that is often cocked. It is usually seen in a song flight in which the bird utters a *zit* with every bounce.

*As its name suggests, this bird has a tail which can be held together or fanned out (below) to show its rounded shape and bold streaking. It is most often seen perched precariously on reeds and the long stems of grasses (left).*

**Size:** 7–10cm (3–4in).
**Wing:** 45–56mm.
**Bill:** 11–13mm.
**Weight:** 7–13g.
**Voice:** Repeated *zit-zit-zit* in song flight.
**Habitat:** Marshy margins and reedbeds and, increasingly, dry cereal fields.
**Food:** Insects.
**Range:** Resident in Mediterranean, sub-Saharan Africa, India and the Far East, and a summer visitor to China. In Europe, it has spread eastwards through the Mediterranean and northwards along the Atlantic coasts of France to the Channel coasts. Though a vagrant to England, it seems poised for colonization.
**Movements:** Post-breeding dispersal and occasional eruptive movements in some areas due to high populations and mild winters.
**Breeding:** Four to six pale blue eggs are laid in a purse-shaped nest in low vegetation and incubated by the female for 12 days. The downy, helpless young fledge after 14 or 15 days. The species may be double brooded.

J F M A M J J A S O N D

## Cetti's Warbler *(Cettia cetti)*

Distinctively dark, this is a resident of southern Europe that hides away in vegetation. The upperparts are rich, dark chestnut-brown with a clear grey-buff supercilium. The underparts are greyish white, with a wash of dirty buff along the flanks. The large, rounded, chestnut-brown tail is a major feature. It is the darkest of the plain brown marsh warblers.

*This highly secretive bird not only hides its nest in dense vegetation (right), but also sings from deep inside thickets.*

J F M A M J J A S O N D

**Size:** 13cm (5in).
**Wing:** 52–66mm.
**Bill:** 13–16mm.
**Weight:** 12–16g.
**Voice:** Explosive *chit chetti-chetti-chetti*, often delivered in an explosive burst. The call has nothing to do with its name, which comes from an 18th-century Italian naturalist.
**Habitat:** Marshland scrub, bushes along margins or amid reeds, bushy riverside thickets.
**Food:** Insects.
**Range:** Resident from western France, southern England and Iberia

through the Mediterranean to Turkey, the Middle East and Siberia beyond the Caspian Sea. Populations from Turkey eastwards are at least partial migrants, wintering in the southern parts of the breeding range and in Pakistan.
**Movements:** Post-breeding dispersal has been responsible for colonization

northwards during the twentieth century, but such populations are highly vulnerable to hard winters.
**Breeding:** Four or five reddish eggs are laid in an untidy cup, hidden among emergent vegetation, and incubated by the female for 16 or 17 days. The downy, helpless young fly after 14–16 days.

Without its distinctive, reeling song this summer visitor to temperate Europe could easily be overlooked. The upperparts are dull brown, streaked black; underparts buffy white, with fine streaking on breast and flanks. The tail is rounded and the undertail heavily streaked. This is a secretive, little brown bird that may perch openly to sing, but spends the rest of its time among dense, often aquatic, vegetation.

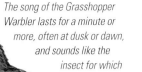

*The song of the Grasshopper Warbler lasts for a minute or more, often at dusk or dawn, and sounds like the insect for which the bird is named.*

**Size:** 13cm (5in).
**Wing:** 61–68mm.
**Bill:** 13–16mm.
**Weight:** 11–17g.
**Voice:** Reeling with bill open. Sounds like a fisherman's reel being wound in and lasts for a minute or more.
**Habitat:** Wetland margins, especially reedbeds; also heaths with young conifer plantations and among damp woodland thickets.
**Food:** Insects.
**Range:** Summer visitor to temperate Eurasia from Spain to central-southern Siberia. Winters India and locally in Sahel Africa.
**Movements:** European birds seemingly migrate southwest to avoid Sahara, but some do cross directly to the Sahel zone. Birds east of the Urals winter in India.
**Breeding:** Lays five or six brown-speckled white eggs in a cup on, or near, the ground and hidden by vegetation. Both parents share the incubation for 12–15 days and the downy, helpless young fledge after 10–12 days. Double, possibly triple, brooded.
**Confusing Species:** Savi's Warbler has a plain, warm brown back. Sedge Warbler has contrasting upperparts.

J F M A M J J A S O N D

---

This summer visitor to central Siberia crosses the Urals to breed in Russia and is a rare vagrant farther west. It is a seriously skulking warbler, which often behaves more like a rodent than a bird. It most closely resembles the Grasshopper Warbler, but has more strongly contrasting streaking above, is heavily streaked below and has a short tail. The juvenile, the most likely to wander, is less streaked and is thus an even better candidate for confusion with the Grasshopper Warbler.

J F M A M J J A S O N D

**Habitat:** Dense aquatic vegetation along wetland margins.
**Food:** Insects.
**Range:** Summer visitor from Russia west of the Urals, across Siberia to Japan. Winters in Southeast Asia.
**Movements:** Apparent movement along coasts of China, but problems of observation make it difficult to be certain about these movements. Vagrant westwards across Europe in autumn, with many being trapped for ringing.
**Breeding:** Lays three to five red-spotted pinkish white eggs in a well-hidden cup near the ground. Incubation, by the female, lasts 13 or 14 days.
**Confusing Species:** Grasshopper Warbler and other Asian vagrants.

*Although this bird spends most of its time scurrying about on the ground (above), males (left) will perch openly to sing.*

**Size:** 13cm (5in).
**Wing:** 53–62mm.
**Bill:** 12–14mm.
**Weight:** 10–13g.
**Voice:** Grasshopper Warbler-type reeling, but slower and with a pulsing quality that makes it even easier to confuse with crickets.

## River Warbler *(Locustella fluviatilis)*

This summer visitor utters a peculiar chuffing and reeling-type song. The upperparts are dull olive-brown, lacking streaking; the underparts are white with a buffy wash on streaked breast and flanks. The undertail coverts are distinctly barred and the face plain. The rather short bill is a useful identification feature in the field.

*The streaking on the sides of the neck, chest and the barred undertail are good field marks.*

**J F M A M J J A S O N D**

**Size:** 13cm (5in).
**Wing:** 69–80mm.
**Bill:** 15–16mm.
**Weight:** 12–17g.
**Voice:** A quiet, repeated *derr-derr-derr* sounds like a distant steam engine.
**Habitat:** Marshy thickets and other dense wetland vegetation.
**Food:** Insects.
**Range:** Summer visitor from eastern Germany across Poland and Russia to western Siberia, extending southwards to Slovenia. Winters in southeast Africa.
**Movements:** Little known, due to its skulking behaviour. Rarely identified west of breeding range. Has colonized Finland during the last quarter of the twentieth century.
**Breeding:** Five or six brown-speckled white eggs are laid in a well-hidden cup on the ground and incubated by both sexes for 11 or 12 days. The downy, helpless young fly after 14–16 days.
**Confusing Species:** All plain-backed warblers, but it is less rufous than most.

## Savi's Warbler *(Locustella luscinioides)*

A warm-coloured, plain-backed 'marsh' warbler, this summer visitor to temperate Europe produces a reeling sound, like a Grasshopper Warbler. The upperparts are warm brown, marked by a clear, but short, supercilium and a less dagger-like bill than a Reed Warbler. The underparts have a warm buff wash along the flanks. It has a rounded tail and pale legs. Sings from a reed top, showing a clear white throat.

**Size:** 13cm (5in).
**Wing:** 66–73mm.
**Bill:** 15–17mm.
**Weight:** 11–21g.
**Voice:** Reeling like a fisherman's reel being rewound, but lower pitched and in briefer runs than the otherwise similar song of the Grasshopper Warbler.
**Habitat:** Reedbeds.
**Food:** Insects.
**Range:** Localized summer visitor across Spain, France, southern England and Germany to Poland, Hungary, Romania and the Ukraine. Also beyond the Urals in western Siberia. Winters Sahel Africa.
**Movements:** General absence from Mediterranean in both spring and autumn suggests that migrants make long flights over both that sea and the Sahara. There is a migrational divide in central Europe.
**Breeding:** Four to six brown-speckled white eggs are laid in a cup constructed near the ground and incubated mainly by the female for 10–12 days. The downy, helpless chicks fledge after 11–16 days.
**Confusing Species:** Other plain-backed 'marsh' warblers, particularly Reed Warbler.

**J F M A M J J A S O N D**

*Though Savi's Warbler spends most of its time deep in the reedbeds (far left), it will climb to a prominent perch to sing (left).*

## Moustached Warbler *(Acrocephalus melanopogon)*

This well-marked 'marsh' warbler is resident in Mediterranean reedbeds and is a summer visitor to the north of the Black Sea and trans-Caspia. This species has often been described only by its differences from the Sedge Warbler, with emphasis on the white supercilium as the major means of distinction. In fact, it is a well-marked bird that precludes confusion if seen clearly. The upperparts are a warm, sandy rufous, with distinct black stripes over wings and back, but not the nape. The underparts are washed sandy rufous over the flanks. The head has a black eyestripe, a broad white supercilium that terminates squarely, and a dark cap.

*The clear head pattern (above), with a black eyestripe, broad white supercilium and dark cap identifies this bird.*

**Size:** 13cm (5in).
**Wing:** 56–62mm.
**Bill:** 14–16mm.
**Weight:** 9–17g.
**Voice:** Harsh chatter *chirri-chirri.*
**Habitat:** Reedbeds.
**Food:** Insects.
**Range:** Resident Mediterranean coasts of Spain, Balearics, locally in France, Italy and Greece, in Hungary, along the Danube valley, and across the Crimea to the Caspian Sea and beyond.
**Movements:** Birds from the Crimea eastwards winter in Pakistan and northern India, and there is some movement within Europe, with birds reaching Sicily and Greece, which are outside the breeding range. Only in the Balearics is this other than a scarce bird.
**Breeding:** Five or six greenish-speckled whitish eggs are laid in a cup among reeds over water, and incubated for 13 or 14 days, mainly by the female. The helpless, naked young fledge after 12–14 days. It raises two broods.
**Confusing Species:** The Sedge Warbler lacks a bold white supercilium.

J F M A M J J A S O N D

## Aquatic Warbler *(Acrocephalus paludicola)*

A scarce, localized and possibly endangered summer visitor to Europe, the Aquatic Warbler is a small, well-marked bird. It has alternate stripes of yellow-buff and black over the upperparts, which give it a rather zebra-like appearance. The underparts are whitish and the legs are pale.

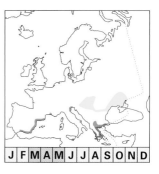

*The contrasting yellow-buff and black head stripes (above) are a clear field mark that can be seen in even the briefest glimpse among the reeds (left).*

J F M A M J J A S O N D

**Size:** 10–13cm (4–5in).
**Wing:** 60–66mm.
**Bill:** 13–15mm.
**Weight:** 10–15g.
**Voice:** Harsh, jarring song.
**Habitat:** Marshes with stands of sedges and reeds.
**Food:** Insects.
**Range:** Localized across Germany and Poland to Russia as far as the Urals, perhaps a little beyond. Tiny European population in eastern Germany, with several important sites in Hungary and a major stronghold in the Biebrza marshes of Poland, with good numbers elsewhere in that country. Winters Sahel Africa.
**Movements:** Although it is presumed to winter elsewhere, the only known wintering grounds are in the Niger Inundation Zone. Autumn migration, initially westwards, brings birds to southern England, but they may be overlooked elsewhere. Such movements presumably are followed by a trans-Saharan migration.
**Breeding:** Five or six buff-speckled white eggs are laid in a cup hidden among low vegetation and incubated by the female for 12–15 days. The downy, helpless young fledge after 13 or 14 days. Double brooded.

## Sedge Warbler *(Acrocephalus schoenobaenus)*

Widespread and locally common, this is a summer visitor to most of temperate Europe and a passage migrant elsewhere. This is the standard 'marshy' warbler, from which scarcer species must be separated. The upperparts are streaked black on brown, with an unstreaked rump. Underparts are white with a buffy wash along the flanks. The head has a dark cap, with a creamy supercilium and dark eyestripe. The juvenile has more contrasting stripes above and the hint of a pale centre to the crown.

*Though it usually sings from a perch (left), the Sedge Warbler may suddenly fly high into the air, to spiral down while singing loudly (right).*

**Size:** 13cm (5in).
**Wing:** 62–71mm.
**Bill:** 14–16mm.
**Weight:** 8–16g.
**Voice:** Song of repeated harsh phrases mixed with sweet notes.
**Habitat:** Reedbeds and

other well-vegetated marshy margins.
**Food:** Insects.
**Range:** Summer visitor across temperate Europe eastwards across Russia to central Siberia. Winters savanna Africa.
**Movements:** Huge migration on a broad front across the Mediterranean and Sahara after a mainly southwesterly movement across Europe.
**Breeding:** Four or five brown-speckled white eggs are laid in a cup among reeds and incubated by the female for 12 days. The downy, helpless young fledge after 12–14 days and a second brood is usually reared.
**Confusing Species:** Grasshopper and Moustached Warblers.

J F M A M J J A S O N D

## Marsh Warbler *(Acrocephalus palustris)*

This is a summer visitor to temperate Europe that, while preferring low-lying damp ground, is nowhere near as confined to wetlands as most other 'marshy' warblers. It must be compared carefully with the Reed Warbler, from which it differs in having olive-brown, not warm brown, upperparts; a paler supercilium; a steeper angled forehead; a long, but not dagger-like, bill; whiter underparts narrowly washed buffy on the flanks; and rather paler legs.

J F M A M J J A S O N D

**Size:** 13cm (5in).
**Wing:** 65–73mm.
**Bill:** 15–17mm.
**Weight:** 10–18g.
**Voice:** Song of harsh notes liberally laced with fine melodic phrases and consummate mimicry.
**Habitat:** Thickets among damp, reedy wetlands, as well as other drier thickets

and hedges and adjacent fields, often including nettles and meadowsweet.
**Food:** Insects.
**Range:** Summer visitor to temperate Europe from England across eastern France to the Balkans, and southern Scandinavia to just beyond the Urals. Winters in East Africa.

*It is necessary to distinguish this bird from the Reed Warbler with care. It has longer wings, with a greater primary projection (below). When singing (below left), its voice is less harsh and repetitive.*

**Movements:** Moves southeast across Europe and the Middle East to East Africa, avoiding the Sahara. Follows a similar easterly route in spring.
**Breeding:** Four or five pale blue eggs are laid in a well hidden cup and incubated by both sexes for 12–14 days. The helpless, naked young fledge after 10 or 11 days.
**Confusing Species:** Reed Warbler and Blyth's Reed Warbler.

## Reed Warbler *(Acrocephalus scirpaceus)*

This is a widespread and common summer visitor to reedbeds and reedy margins wherever they occur, though it is largely absent from the far north. It is an undistinguished buff and brown warbler, with warm-brown upperparts, a rusty rump and creamy underparts. A dagger-like bill is accentuated by a flat, sloping forehead.

J F M A M J J A S O N D

*Although similar to the Marsh Warbler, the Reed Warbler's wings are more rounded, with a shorter primary projection.*

**Size:** 13cm (5in).
**Wing:** 63–69mm.
**Bill:** 16–18mm.
**Weight:** 9–16g.
**Voice:** Song always has harsh repeated notes, *jag-jag, chirrug-chirrug,* etc.
**Habitat:** Reedbeds and reedy margins to lakes, canals and ditches.
**Food:** Insects.
**Range:** Summer visitor across Europe, though somewhat localized in the Mediterranean and absent from Scotland and northern Scandinavia and Russia. Also breeds in the Middle East and to beyond the Aral Sea. Winters in the Sahel and eastern Africa.

**Movements:** Southwest and southeast orientation of European birds indicates that crossing the Sahara is mainly avoided and that migration proceeds in short hops around the coastal edges rather than in a long continuous flight.

**Breeding:** Three to five olive-spotted green eggs are laid in a cup in reeds and hatch after 9–12 days. The helpless, naked young fledge at 9–13 days.
**Confusing Species:** Marsh Warbler and Blyth's Reed Warbler.

## Blyth's Reed Warbler *(Acrocephalus dumetorum)*

This summer visitor to eastern Europe is only a rare vagrant over most of Europe. It can be distinguished from the Reed and Marsh Warblers only with great care. The upperparts are grey-brown, with a tiny supercilium that does not extend beyond the eye. The underparts are pale grey-buff on the flanks; the legs are dark. The bill is less dagger-like than the Reed Warbler's. It frequently explores tangled and fallen trees and stumps on marshy ground.

J F M A M J J A S O N D

*Blyth's Reed Warbler has a longer tail and shorter primaries than the Marsh or Reed Warbler.*

**Size:** 13cm (5in).
**Wing:** 61–66mm.
**Bill:** 16–18mm.
**Weight:** 9–15g.
**Voice:** Song of varied, musical phrases, each repeated.
**Habitat:** Wet tangles of vegetation at margins of floods, lakes and marshes.

**Food:** Insects.
**Range:** Summer visitor from Finland and Baltic States across boreal Russia to central Siberia. Winters Indian sub-continent. In Europe, the population has increased and spread westwards through Finland to Sweden.
**Movements:** Moves southeast from western breeding grounds to overfly breeding range on its way to winter quarters in India.
**Breeding:** Four or five brown-spotted greenish eggs are laid in a cup placed low in a shrub and are incubated for 12–14 days by both sexes. The naked, helpless young fledge after 11–13 days.
**Confusing Species:** Reed and, especially, Marsh Warbler.

229

## Paddyfield Warbler *(Acrocephalus agricola)*

Decidedly rare, this bird migrates south and east in autumn and is a summer visitor to the southeast of Europe. It is a neat brown and buff warbler, with plain brown upperparts, warm buffy flanks and a white belly. The best recognition features are a broad, creamy supercilium and white chin. The wings are short, the tail is long and frequently raised, and the bill is shorter than that of most other similar species.

*Although it normally appears to have a relatively small head (above), the Paddyfield Warbler can raise its crest to give a large-headed appearance (left).*

**Size:** 13cm (5in).
**Wing:** 55–61mm.
**Bill:** 14–15mm.
**Weight:** 8–13g.
**Voice:** A continuous melodic chatter lacks harsh churring notes.
**Habitat:** Marshy margins, particularly in thin or isolated patches of reeds, often mixed with low thickets.
**Food:** Insects.
**Range:** Breeds from Romania eastwards across the Ukraine and the Caspian and Aral Seas to central Siberia. Winters India.
**Movements:** Migrates south and east across Asia to winter quarters. Decidedly rare westwards in Europe.
**Breeding:** Lays three to six greenish-blotched pale green eggs in a deep cup lashed to emergent vegetation. The eggs are incubated for about 12 days by the female. It may raise two broods.
**Confusing Species:** Reed and Marsh Warblers lack crest and supercilium, and have longer bills.

J F M A M J J A S O N D

## Great Reed Warbler *(Acrocephalus arundinaceus)*

A massive warbler, the size of a song thrush, this is a summer visitor to the reedbeds of south and temperate Europe. In form and coloration it is rather like the Reed Warbler, but it is almost twice the size. The upperparts are warm brown with a creamy supercilium. The underparts are creamy white, with a buffy wash over the flanks. The large tail is rounded, and the bill heavy, although not as long in comparison to the head as that of the Reed Warbler. The sheer size and direct flight of this bird precludes confusion with any other European warbler.

J F M A M J J A S O N D

*The song of the Great Reed Warbler, usually given from an isolated reed (right), is loud and carries for great distances. The churring and croaking of its usual song will give way to a sudden chattering if it is alarmed.*

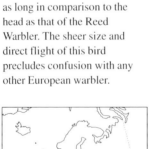

**Size:** 18–20cm (7–8in).
**Wing:** 89–101mm.
**Bill:** 22–25mm.
**Weight:** 24–44g.
**Voice:** Loud, strident, harsh calls, including a distinct *clak-iti-clak* fast repeated.
**Habitat:** Reedbeds and reedy margins.
**Food:** Insects.
**Range:** Summer visitor right across temperate Eurasia from Portugal to Japan. Winters central and southern Africa and in the Far East. In Europe, it is absent from Iceland, Britain and Ireland, most of Scandinavia and across large areas of northern Russia.
**Movements:** European birds migrate south to cross the Mediterranean and Sahara to reach their Sahel winter quarters. Also overflies East Africa.
**Breeding:** Four to six brown-spotted blue-green eggs are laid in a substantial cup suspended between reeds and are incubated by both sexes for 14 or 15 days. The naked and helpless young fly after about 12 days.

A yellow and olive-green, summer visitor to the eastern half of Europe, this bird forms a species pair with the more westerly Melodious Warbler. It is olive-green above, with a large bill, accentuated by a flat, sloping forehead. The underparts are yellow, and the legs are bluish. A short yellow supercilium extends beyond the eye.

J F M A M J J A S O N D

**Size:** 13cm (5in).
**Wing:** 75–83mm.
**Bill:** 16–17mm.
**Weight:** 10–15g.
**Voice:** Song of harsh notes mixed with melodic phrases.
**Habitat:** Thickets and heaths, open woodland.
**Food:** Insects.

*As with some other warblers, identification is clinched by the long primary projection (left and far left) and the pale mid-wing panel.*

**Range:** Summer visitor eastwards of a line from Cap Gris Nez in France to the Danube Delta in Romania. Localized in the former Yugoslavia and the Alps, absent from northern Scandinavia and Russia. Winters southern Africa.
**Movements:** Crosses central Sahara in non–stop sea and desert migration. In spring stops over on North African coast.

Eastern birds join this stream after passing through Caspian region.
**Breeding:** Four or five black-spotted pinkish eggs are laid in a cup placed in a shrub and incubated by both sexes for about 13 days. The naked, helpless young fledge after about 13 days.
**Confusing Species:** Melodious Warbler has shorter, rounded wings.

Melodious Warbler *(Hippolais polyglotta)*

This summer visitor to western Europe is absent from eastern Europe, where it is replaced by the Icterine Warbler. The upperparts are olive-green, and the underparts yellow, extending to the lores and above the eye in an ill-defined supercilium. It has a comparatively long bill, and a distinctly rounded head; The rounded wings show a short primary projection.

J F M A M J J A S O N D

*The Melodious Warbler is outwardly similar to the Icterine Warbler, but has a shorter tail and noticeably shorter, more rounded wings (left).*

**Size:** 13cm (5in).
**Wing:** 62–71mm.
**Bill:** 15–17mm.
**Weight:** 8–17g.
**Voice:** Song of repeated melodic phrases accelerating into a chattering.
**Habitat:** Thickets, copses, orchards and groves.
**Food:** Insects.
**Range:** Summer visitor west of a line that roughly follows the eastern frontier of France, through the northern Alps to Trieste and a little beyond. Absent from Britain and the Mediterranean islands. Also breeds North Africa east to Tunisia. Winters West Africa.
**Movements:** Migrates southwest through Iberia and Gibraltar following the west coast of Africa in order to avoid the exhausting long sea and desert crossings .
**Breeding:** Four, black-spotted pinkish eggs are laid in a cup placed in the fork of a bush and incubated by the female for 12 or 13 days. The naked, helpless young fly after 11–13 days. Occasionally double brooded.
**Confusing Species:** Icterine Warbler has sloping forehead, pale wing panel and bluish legs.

## Olivaceous Warbler *(Hippolais pallida)*

A summer visitor to Iberia, this bird is far more widespread in the Balkans. The upperparts are olive-grey and the long bill is accentuated by a flat, sloping forehead that peaks behind the eye.

*This bird has a tubby shape. The short, rounded wings have a short primary projection, and the primary feathers do not reach the tail coverts when folded.*

**Size:** 13cm (5in).
**Wing:** 67–74mm.
**Bill:** 17–19mm.
**Weight:** 8–16g.
**Voice:** A pleasant scratchy song, with subdued melodies.
**Habitat:** Thickets, scrubby gullies, orchards and groves, all with tall trees.
**Food:** Insects.
**Range:** Summer visitor to the eastern Mediterranean, ranging to beyond the Caspian. Local in Spain and on coasts of Croatia, more widespread from Greece to Romania.
**Movements:** Western populations cross Sahara on a broad front. Eastern birds migrate through the Middle East.
**Breeding:** Three or four black-spotted grey eggs are laid in a cup placed in a

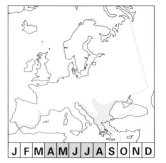

J F M A M J J A S O N D

bush and incubated by the female for 12 or 13 days. The naked, helpless young fly after 11 or 12 days. Double brooded.
**Confusing Species:** Pale, autumn Melodious and Icterine Warblers and larger Olive-tree Warbler.

## Olive-tree Warbler *(Hippolais olivetorum)*

Second in size among warblers only to the Great Reed Warbler, this bird is grey above and white below, with a faint wash of buffy yellow on its breast and flanks. A short and narrow white supercilium extends beyond the eye, but the best identification feature is the large yellow bill.

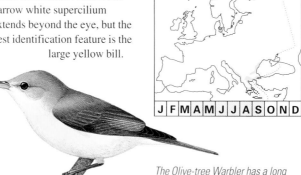

J F M A M J J A S O N D

*The Olive-tree Warbler has a long primary projection, a pale mid-wing panel and a huge yellow bill.*

**Size:** 15cm (6in).
**Wing:** 82–92mm.
**Bill:** 19–21mm.
**Weight:** 14–23g.
**Voice:** The deep, slowly delivered song has sweet notes interspersed with grating ones.
**Habitat:** Scrubby thickets, open woodland, groves, orchards.
**Food:** Insects.
**Range:** Breeds coasts of the Balkans and Turkey. Winters southeast Africa.
**Movements:** Little known, but probably makes long non-stop flights to Africa.
**Breeding:** Three or four black-speckled pinkish eggs are laid in a cup in a low tree and incubated for about 13 days.
**Confusing Species:** Smaller Olivaceous Warbler lacks big yellow bill.

## Booted Warbler *(Hippolais caligata)*

A small warbler, this bird is easily confused with any *Phylloscopus* warbler. The upperparts are greyish brown and the underparts whitish, with a buff wash on the breast sides. The bold supercilium is a useful feature for identifying this bird.

*The wings are short, with short primary projections at rest. The bill, too, is relatively short, but the tail is long with pale margins.*

**Size:** 10–13cm (4–5in).
**Wing:** 57–64mm.
**Bill:** 7–8mm.
**Weight:** 8–11g.
**Voice:** Song of melodic phrases, but with little variety. Call a sharp *chick*.
**Habitat:** Copses, riverside thickets, plantations, orchards, reedbeds.
**Food:** Insects.
**Range:** Summer visitor to European Russia almost as far west as the Finnish border, eastwards beyond the Urals and southwards to the Persian Gulf. Winters in India.
**Movements:** Whole population moves to Indian subcontinent, where it is a widespread and locally common winter visitor. Regular passage migrant through eastern Iran.
**Breeding:** Four to six blackish-spotted

J F M A M J J A S O N D

white eggs are laid in a cup on or near the ground and are incubated by both sexes for 12–14 days. The naked, helpless young fledge after 11–14 days.
**Confusing Species:** Olivaceous Warbler, but beware also of Bonelli's Warbler.

## Marmora's Warbler (Sylvia sarda)

Found only on islands of the western Mediterranean, this is an all-grey version of the Dartford Warbler, with similar habits and long tail. The male's upperparts are deep grey, and the underparts paler grey, becoming whitish on the belly.

The head is large, almost crested, with a bulging throat. It flits, on its short, rounded wings, among dense vegetation, but perches on shrubs to sing, often with its tail cocked. The female is similar, but with a pinkish wash on the underparts.

**Size:** 13cm (5in).
**Wing:** 51–59mm.
**Bill:** 12–13mm.
**Weight:** 8–13g.
**Voice:** Scratchy, high-pitched warble.
**Habitat:** Low, prickly Mediterranean scrub, usually lacking taller bushes.
**Food:** Insects.
**Range:** Breeds in the Balearics, Corsica, Sardinia and Pantelleria (Italian island southwest of Sicily). Visitor to Malta. Some birds winter in North Africa.
**Movements:** Partial migrant, with some birds migrating to Tunisia and adjacent Libya, but most remaining on breeding sites, even at higher altitudes.

J F M A M J J A S O N D

**Breeding:** Three or four reddish-spotted white eggs are laid in a cup at the base of a bush in dense scrub. They are incubated for 12–15 days, mainly by the female, and the naked, helpless young fledge after about 12 days. Raises two, or sometimes, three broods each season.
**Confusing Species:** Young Dartford Warblers are also grey below.

*While the adult bird (far left) is dark grey with red eyes, the juvenile bird (above) is browner on the upperparts and paler below.*

## Dartford Warbler (Sylvia undata)

This small, long-tailed warbler of dense thickets is largely resident throughout Italy, Iberia, western France and parts of southern England. The male is deep grey above and reddish brown below, with brownish wings and a long, white-tipped tail which is frequently cocked.

**Size:** 13cm (5in).
**Wing:** 51–58mm.
**Bill:** 12–14mm.
**Weight:** 8–11g.
**Voice:** A churring buzz and scratchy warbling song.
**Habitat:** Prickly thickets of Mediterranean scrub, and of gorse and heather farther north.
**Food:** Insects.
**Range:** Resident Iberia, northwards through southern and western France to southern England, and east via Corsica and Sardinia to Italy and North Africa.
**Movements:** Largely resident, with northerly populations suffering losses during hard winters. Other birds are

J F M A M J J A S O N D

*The adult male (left) is dark above and reddish-brown below, while the female is pinker below. The juvenile (below) is brown above and greyish below. All ages and both sexes cock their tails.*

partial migrants to North Africa.
**Breeding:** Three or four brown-spotted white eggs are laid in a cup hidden among dense vegetation near the ground and are incubated mainly by the female for 12 or 13 days. The naked, helpless young fledge after 11–13 days. Double or triple brooded.
**Confusing Species:** Marmora's Warbler.

233

Though frequently regarded as a diminutive version of the Common Whitethroat because of its rufous wings, this is, in fact, a distinctive little summer visitor to the Mediterranean. The male has a brown back, with bright orange-brown wings, and a grey head marked by a white moustachial streak and a white eye-ring set in a dark grey, almost black, face. The white underparts are washed pinkish on the flanks. The female lacks grey head and dark face and has a white throat.

J F M A M J J A S O N D

**Size:** 13cm (5in).
**Wing:** 53–59mm.
**Bill:** 12–13mm.
**Weight:** 9–12g.
**Voice:** Song is a pleasant, scratchy warble, call a harsh rattle.
**Habitat:** Very low ground vegetation on rocky hillsides and plateaux. Also among dried-out flood vegetation.
**Food:** Insects.
**Range:** Summer visitor to Cyprus, Israel and western Mediterranean. Winters North Africa. In Europe, breeds Spain, southern France, Corsica, Sardinia, Malta and southern Italy.

**Movements:** Whole European population migrates southward to winter northwest Africa, with a few penetrating deep into the Sahara.
**Breeding:** Four or five olive-speckled whitish eggs are laid in a cup well hidden in a bush and incubated by both sexes for 12–14 days. The naked, helpless young fledge after 12 or 13 days. Double, possibly triple brooded.
**Confusing Species:** Female similar to female Whitethroat, but with orange-brown wings.

*The nest (top) is difficult to find, being well hidden among dry scrub. The male (top) helps the female (above) with the nesting duties.*

J F M A M J J A S O N D

A typical scrub warbler, the male is a well marked and easily identified summer visitor throughout the Mediterranean. It is grey above and pinkish below, with a prominent red eye and distinctive, white moustachial streak. The female is much paler below and has a broader moustachial streak.

**Size:** 13cm (5in).
**Wing:** 57–63mm.
**Bill:** 12–13mm.
**Weight:** 7–15g.
**Voice:** Song is a scratchy chatter.
**Habitat:** Low scrub with adjacent trees on rocky hillsides.
**Food:** Insects.
**Range:** Summer visitor to all European Mediterranean coasts and inland through Iberia. Also to western Turkey and North Africa. Winters Sahel Africa.
**Movements:** Whole European population crosses Sahara on a broad front, with notable concentrations on Malta, but scarce at Gibraltar. Also common at Saharan oases.
**Breeding:** Three or four olive-buff-spotted white eggs are laid in a cup hidden among low vegetation among rocks and incubated by the female for 11 or 12 days. The helpless and naked young fly after a similar period. Double brooded.
**Confusing Species:** Tristram's Warbler when seen in Europe.

*The female is duller than the male, having buff-brown back and wings and lacking the rich orange chest.*

## Sardinian Warbler *(Sylvia melanocephala)*

This is the most common of the Mediterranean 'scrub' warblers. The male is grey above and white below, with a black cap, red eye and white throat. The female is brown above, buffy on the flanks and has a paler cap.

*The male (far right) is more boldly marked than the female (above); both skulk in dense cover.*

**Size:** 13 cm (5in).
**Wing:** 54–62cm.
**Bill:** 13–15mm.
**Weight:** 8–17g.
**Voice:** Harsh rattle and scratchy warble.
**Habitat:** Prickly scrub, also gardens and woods with low ground cover.

**Food:** Insects.
**Range:** Resident from Iberia, southern France and Italy to Greece and Turkey. Summer visitor to coastal Balkans.
**Movements:** Mainly resident, but some migration south to the central Sahara.
**Breeding:** Three or four brown-spotted white eggs are laid in a cup in dense vegetation and incubated by both sexes for 13 or 14 days. The helpless, naked young fly after 12 days. Double brooded.
**Confusing Species:** Orphean Warbler is much larger and has a yellow eye.

J F M A M J J A S O N D

## Orphean Warbler *(Sylvia hortensis)*

*The female (right) has a much greyer cap than the otherwise similar male (above).*

A widespread summer visitor to the Mediterranean, this is the largest of the 'scrub' warblers. The male is grey above, white below, marked by a black cap and a yellow eye. The female is similar, but has dark ear coverts. The legs are dark grey.

**Size:** 15cm (6in).
**Wing:** 74–86mm.
**Bill:** 17–19mm.
**Weight:** 15–30g.
**Voice:** Melodic warbling with a distinctly Nightingale-like quality; call is a harsh *tak-tak*.
**Habitat:** Prickly scrub, with thickets of taller bushes.
**Food:** Insects.
**Range:** Summer visitor to Mediterranean eastwards through Turkey, the Middle East to Afghanistan. Winters Sahel Africa, Arabia and Indian subcontinent. In Europe, breeds Spain eastwards to Greece and Turkey.
**Movements:** Western populations probably migrate on a broad front across the Mediterranean and Sahara.

J F M A M J J A S O N D

**Breeding:** Four or five brown-spotted white eggs are laid in a cup in a tree and incubated for 12–14 days by both sexes. The naked young fly after 12–13 days.
**Confusing Species:** Sardinian Warbler is smaller.

## Rüppell's Warbler *(Sylvia rueppelli)*

This small, long-tailed warbler is found in the eastern Mediterranean. The male is well marked with a black head and throat broken by a white moustachial streak. The female has a dark grey head with a whitish moustache, and a red eye-ring that is not as bold as that of the male.

*The clear song of the male (right) is rather harsh, and is repeated in short, sharp bursts.*

**Size:** 15cm (5–6in).
**Wing:** 65–74mm.
**Bill:** 14–16 mm.
**Weight:** 11–17g.
**Habitat:** Low, uniform maquis scrub, on gently rolling hillsides.
**Food:** Insects.
**Range:** Confined to southern Greece and south and west Turkey, where it is a summer visitor. Winters in eastern Sahel zone of Africa.
**Movements:** Large-scale movement through Egypt in the autumn, though more widespread in spring, when passage over Libya and Cyprus occurs in late March and early April.

J F M A M J J A S O N D

**Breeding:** Four or five heavily speckled whitish eggs are laid in a cup hidden low among dense scrub and incubated for 13 days by both members of the pair. The young are born naked and helpless.
**Confusing species:** Beware male Cyprus Warbler when not seen perfectly.

235

**Size:** 13cm (5in).
**Wing:** 63–69mm.
**Bill:** 12–14mm.
**Weight:** 10–15g.
**Voice:** Song is a clear bunting-like rattle; call a hard metallic *tak*.
**Habitat:** Scrubby heaths, open woodlands with plentiful undergrowth.
**Food:** Insects.
**Range:** Summer visitor from Britain south to northern Italy and eastwards across temperate and boreal Europe to eastern Asia, southwards to central Asian plateau. Winters from Sahel Africa, through Arabia to India.
**Movements:** All European birds migrate southeast to reach winter quarters via the eastern Mediterranean. Eastern populations head southwest to the same area and may continue on to winter in the Sahel.
**Breeding:** Four to six olive-spotted white eggs are laid in a cup low in a bush and are incubated by both sexes for 11–14 days. The naked, helpless young fledge after a further 10–11 days. Occasionally a second brood is reared.
**Confusing Species:** Common Whitethroat has reddish wings.

J F M A M J J A S O N D

*The female (above) is generally similar to the male (above left), but is less well marked, with a paler mask and brownish crown.*

This attractive summer visitor, despite its name, is quite different in appearance from the Common Whitethroat. The adult is grey above and white below, with a grey crown contrasting with black ear coverts that form a mask. The tail has white outer feathers. First-winter birds are browner than the adult and have a paler mask that blends into the crown.

---

**Size:** 13–15cm (5–6in).
**Wing:** 68–77cm.
**Bill:** 13–15mm.
**Weight:** 65–78g.
**Voice:** A scratchy, warbling song, often uttered in bouncy song flight. Call is a harsh *tac-tac*.
**Habitat:** Scrubby thickets, woodland clearings, hedgerows and gardens.
**Food:** Insects and berries.
**Range:** Summer visitor from Britain and Ireland to Spain, eastwards across Europe to the Urals and beyond. Winters savanna Africa.
**Movements:** Migrational divide in Scandinavia more or less along Norway-Sweden border, but birds still pass through the Mediterranean and cross the Sahara on a broad front.
**Breeding:** Four or five olive-speckled bluish eggs are laid in a neat cup near the ground and are incubated by both sexes for 11–13 days. The chicks hatch naked and helpless, and fly after 10–12 days. The species is habitually double brooded.
**Confusing Species:** Lesser Whitethroat and Spectacled Warbler.

J F M A M J J A S O N D

This widespread summer visitor to almost all of Europe has suffered a decline due to drought in the Sahel, where it winters. The adult male is grey on the head, with a prominent white throat, and brownish rust on the folded wing. The underparts are washed pinkish.

*The female (right) is similar to the male (above), but it has a brown, rather than a grey, crown.*

## Garden Warbler *(Sylvia borin)*

This warbler is a summer visitor to most of Europe, but it is decidedly local in the Mediterranean region and all but absent from Italy and Greece. Olive-grey above, and buffy below, with a plain face, it has a short, thickish bill and is generally more robustly built than other warblers.

**Size:** 13–15cm (5–6in).
**Wing:** 76–82mm.
**Bill:** 14–15mm.
**Weight:** 15–29g.
**Voice:** A sweet, melodic song that chatters quietly, but lacks variety.
**Habitat:** Open woodland with clearings, damp thickets and scrub.
**Food:** Insects, berries.
**Range:** Summer visitor throughout Europe, absent from much of Mediterranean and highest Scandinavian mountains. Winters savanna Africa.
**Movements:** Migrates southwest across Europe, stopping over in the Mediterranean before flying the Sahara.
**Breeding:** Four or five brown-spotted white eggs are laid in a cup placed in a bush and incubated by both sexes for 11 or 12 days. The naked, helpless young fly after 9 or 10 days. Double brooded.
**Confusing Species:** Olivaceous Warbler, but no other featureless warbler has such a short, stubby bill.

*With few obvious fieldmarks, this bird is best identified by its pale eye-ring and short, stout bill.*

## Blackcap *(Sylvia atricapilla)*

A common and widespread summer visitor and local resident over most of Europe, this is a large, chunky, grey warbler. It is marked by a neat crown, black in the male, that just reaches the eye.

*While the male (left) has a black cap, the female (above) has a russet cap.*

**Size:** 13–15cm (5–6in).
**Wing:** 70–80mm.
**Bill:** 14–15mm.
**Weight:** 14–30g.
**Voice:** A melodic warbling with considerable variety of phrases.
**Habitat:** Woods, heathlands, hedgerows, copses, gardens.
**Food:** Insects and berries.
**Range:** Summer visitor throughout Europe, although absent from Iceland, most of Scotland, northern Scandinavia and tundra Russia. Blackcaps winter in southern and western Europe and in North, West and East Africa.
**Movements:** Leap-frogging movements, with more northerly birds flying farther south. Definite trans-Saharan migration in spring and autumn.

**Breeding:** Four or five red-blotched white eggs are laid in a cup in a bush or tree and incubated by both sexes for 12 or 13 days. The naked, helpless young fledge after 10–14 days. The Blackcap usually has two broods.

## Barred Warbler *(Sylvia nisoria)*

This summer visitor to eastern Europe is well marked and easily identified in spring. The adult is grey above, extending to below the yellow eye. The entire underparts are boldly barred grey on white.

*In contrast to the adult (below) which has yellow eyes, the juvenile (right) has dark eyes.*

**Size:** 15cm (6in).
**Wing:** 87–94mm.
**Bill:** 17–19mm.
**Weight:** 21–34g.
**Voice:** Warbling with some harsh phrases; rattling calls.
**Habitat:** Woods and copses with plentiful undergrowth, as well as thickets, hedges and bushy hillsides.
**Food:** Insects and berries.
**Range:** Summer visitor from eastern Germany and northern Italy, eastwards across Romania, Ukraine and Russia to the Urals, and beyond into Asia. Entire population winters East Africa, mainly Kenya.
**Movements:** All birds pass through eastern Mediterranean countries, and possibly the Middle East as well, on their way to Kenya.

**Breeding:** Five or six grey- and brown-speckled white eggs are laid in a cup placed in a thorny bush. The eggs are incubated by both sexes for 12–15 days. The helpless and naked young fledge after 11–15 days. The species is thought to raise two broods on occasion.

## Bonelli's Warbler (Phylloscopus bonelli)

**B**onelli's Warbler has now been split into two distinct species: Eastern and Western. Both are similar to Chiffchaff, but have washed-out greyish or greyish brown head and back contrasting with bright yellow wing panel and yellow rump.

**Size:** 10–13cm (4–5in).
**Wing:** 58–67mm.
**Bill:** 11–13mm.
**Weight:** 6–12g.
**Voice:** Slow trill and a strong *choo-weet* in Western birds; a quicker, briefer trill and a soft *cheep* in Eastern birds.
**Habitat:** Deciduous and mixed woodland, but also pure conifer stands.

**Food:** Insects.
**Range:** Western birds breed across Spain, France, the Alps, Italy and Austria, and winter in western Sahel Africa. Eastern birds breed across the former Yugoslavia, Greece and Turkey, and winter in eastern Sahel Africa.
**Movements:** Trans-Mediterranean and Saharan migrations to southwest and southeast take most birds to western half of the Sahel by different routes.
**Breeding:** Four to six brown-speckled white eggs are laid in a domed nest on the ground and incubated by the female for 12 or 13 days. The downy, helpless young fly after 12 or 13 days.

J F M A M J J A S O N D

*The Eastern Bonelli's Warbler, P. orientalis (left) has brighter wings and a greyer head than the Western Bonelli's Warbler, P. bonelli (right) and shows a longer primary projection.*

## Wood Warbler (Phylloscopus sibilatrix)

**T**he Wood Warbler is a summer visitor to mature woodlands right across temperate Europe. Its upperparts are yellow-green, with a distinct yellow primary patch in the folded wing. Underparts are white, with a strong yellow wash over breast, face and bold supercilium. The legs are pinkish. It is far brighter than Willow Warbler and Chiffchaff and distinctly more arboreal.

*The Wood Warbler is the most colourful and cleanly marked of the Phylloscopus warblers.*

**Size:** 13cm (5in).
**Wing:** 72–79mm.
**Bill:** 12–14mm.
**Weight:** 8–14g.
**Voice:** A sibilant trill uttered in distinctive fluttering song flight immediately below a thick forest canopy; often preceded by a soft, plaintive, repeated *peu-peu-peu*.
**Habitat:** Mature deciduous forests with scanty undergrowth.
**Food:** Insects.
**Range:** Breeds from Britain and France eastwards across temperate Europe to

J F M A M J J A S O N D

the Urals and beyond. Absent from Iberia and Mediterranean coasts, northern Scandinavia and Russia; winters in forested western Africa.
**Movements:** Migrates southeast to south directly across Sahara to winter quarters. In spring, it is common on passage in the eastern Mediterranean.
**Breeding:** Five to seven white, red-spotted eggs are laid in a domed nest placed on the ground and are incubated for 12–14 days by the female. The downy, helpless chicks fledge after 11–13 days.

## Chiffchaff *(Phylloscopus collybita)*

This summer visitor to northern and temperate Europe undertakes lengthy migrations to the tropics. Recent taxonomic 'advances' have split off several separate species, including Canary Islands, Iberian, Mountain and Caucasian. The adult in spring is greenish brown above, buffy white below, with a hint of yellow in the plumage. Autumn birds are brighter, with olive-green upperparts and yellow-washed underparts.

*The Chiffchaff can be distinguished from the Willow Warbler by its darker legs, duller plumage and shorter supercilium.*

**Size:** 10cm (4in).
**Wing:** 53–65mm.
**Bill:** 10–12mm.
**Weight:** 7–10g.
**Voice:** Distinctive *chiff-chaff-chiff-chaff* repeated is a familiar sound of spring in woodlands. Its call is a soft *weet*.
**Habitat:** Mainly deciduous woodlands with plentiful undergrowth.
**Food:** Insects.
**Range:** Summer visitor right across Eurasia from Ireland and Portugal to eastern Siberia and southwards to the Caucasus (but see revised taxonomy, left). Winters in western Europe, Mediterranean and across Sahel Africa, Arabia, Iran and the Himalayas.

**Movements:** European birds winter in the Mediterranean and across Sahel Africa, although individual populations adopt different migratory tactics.
**Breeding:** Four to nine purple-spotted white eggs are laid in a domed nest on the ground and incubated by the female alone for 13 or 14 days. The downy, helpless young fly after 12–15 days. It has one or two broods each season.
**Confusing Species:** Willow Warbler has pinker legs.

## Willow Warbler *(Phylloscopus trochilus)*

*The Willow Warbler, in all plumages including first-winter (right), always looks more clean-cut than the Chiffchaff. Both can be quite yellow in first-winter plumage.*

The Willow Warbler is the most abundant summer visitor to temperate and boreal Europe and a widespread and common passage migrant elsewhere. The spring adult is olive-green above and lightly washed yellow below. A clear, pale yellow supercilium, which contrasts with a clear, dark eyestripe, extends farther beyond the eye than that of Bonelli's Warbler. Autumn birds are greener above and very yellow below. The legs are pale pink in all plumages.

**Size:** 10cm (4in).
**Wing:** 60–71mm.
**Bill:** 11–13mm.
**Weight:** 7–11g.
**Voice:** A melodic descending trill; call a two-syllabled *hoo-eet*.
**Habitat:** Wooded heaths, clearings in woodland with scrub.
**Food:** Insects.
**Range:** Summer visitor to Britain and Ireland, across France to the Carpathians, and northwards as far as the North Cape of Norway, eastwards across Russia to the Bering Strait. Winters savanna Africa.
**Movements:** Whole population makes huge migratory flights, across Mediterranean and Sahara in the west and across Eurasia in the east, to winter among the savannas of Africa and south to the Cape.
**Breeding:** Six or seven red-speckled white eggs are laid in a domed nest on the ground and are then incubated for 13 days by the female. The downy, helpless young fledge after 13–16 days. Sometimes has two broods.
**Confusing Species:** Chiffchaff lacks colour and cleanness of Willow Warbler, particularly in head pattern, and has dark, instead of pink, legs.

## Arctic Warbler *(Phylloscopus borealis)*

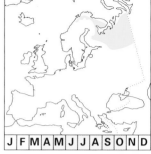

This typical *Phylloscopus* warbler is similar to the Chiffchaff and Willow Warbler, but is marked by a single narrow wingbar and a long, white supercilium that reaches the nape with a distinct upsweep. It has a bold, dark eyestripe, and a longish bill accentuated by a flat, sloping forehead.

*This bird closely resembles Greenish Warbler, but head markings and pale legs are clear features.*

**Size:** 13cm (5in).
**Wing:** 61–69mm.
**Bill:** 13–15mm.
**Weight:** 8–15g.
**Voice:** A repeated, musical trill, often compared with that of Cirl Bunting; Arctic Warbler's call is a harsh *zik*.
**Habitat:** Birch scrub among and at the margins of conifer forests.
**Food:** Insects.

**Range:** Breeds right across boreal Eurasia, from Lapland across northern Russia to the Bering Straits and western Alaska. Decidedly local west of European Russia.
**Movements:** Migrates east and then southeast to winter in southeast Asia. In spring migrates through China and thence westwards, being a late arrival in Europe.
**Breeding:** Six or seven reddish-speckled white eggs are laid in a domed nest on the ground and incubated by the female for 11–13 days. The downy, helpless young fledge after about 13 or 14 days.
**Confusing Species:** The Greenish Warbler has similar plumage.

## Greenish Warbler *(Phylloscopus trochiloides)*

The Greenish Warbler is a summer visitor to the Baltic eastwards that bears a close resemblance to the Arctic Warbler in plumage, but which is more like a Chiffchaff in shape. Its upperparts are olive-green with a single, narrow wingbar. Its underparts are white and its legs darkish. The head shows a bold, white supercilium and a dark eyestripe, but it has a shorter bill and steeper forehead than the Arctic Warbler.

*While the supercilium of the Greenish Warbler (above) is prominent, it does not sweep up so markedly at the nape as that of the Arctic Warbler.*

**Size:** 10cm (4in).
**Wing:** 55–65mm.
**Bill:** 11–13mm.
**Weight:** 6–9g.
**Voice:** Song is a brief, high-pitched trill that ends with a rattle; its call is a *see-wee*.
**Habitat:** Open conifer forests with good growth of deciduous birch and aspen.
**Range:** Breeds from the Baltic eastwards across Russia and southern Finland to Siberia, southwards to central Asia. Winters India and northern Southeast Asia.
**Movements:** Migrates eastwards and enters India via the northwest. Common in Nepal; scarce in western Europe.

**Breeding:** Lays four or five white eggs in a domed nest on the ground that are incubated for 12 or 13 days by the female. The downy, helpless young fly after 12–14 days.
**Confusing Species:** Arctic Warbler.

# Goldcrest *(Regulus regulus)*

**Size:** 9cm (3½in).
**Wing:** 50–57mm.
**Bill:** 9–12mm.
**Weight:** 4–8g.
**Voice:** Very high-pitched *zi-zi-zi*; song similar but terminating with a flourish.
**Habitat:** Open conifer forests, heaths with birch trees.
**Food:** Insects and spiders.
**Range:** Breeds across temperate and northern Europe to central Siberia and Japan, extending southwards to the mountains of Spain, Turkey and central Asia. Winters within and to the south of breeding range.
**Movements:** Apparently a general shift southwards, with many European birds moving to the Mediterranean, to be replaced by more northerly and easterly birds.

**Breeding:** Seven to ten brown-speckled white eggs are laid in a cup placed high on the outer branches of a conifer and incubated by the female for 14–17 days. The downy, helpless young fledge after 16–21 days. Double brooded.
**Confusing Species:** Firecrest.

*The Goldcrest's plain face, which lacks a supercilium and eyestripe, enables it to be distinguished from the similar-sized Firecrest.*

The Goldcrest, Europe's smallest bird, can be confused only with the better-marked Firecrest. It has olive-greenish upperparts, marked by black wings with two bold white wingbars. The underparts are whitish, washed yellow-buff on the flanks. The plain face has a thin moustachial streak and the crown has a golden central stripe, broadly bordered black.

# Firecrest *(Regulus ignicapillus)*

The Firecrest is endemic to the Western Palearctic and is similar in size to the closely related Goldcrest. The upperparts are yellow-green and are much brighter than in the Goldcrest. The wings are black with two bold, white wingbars, and a warm orange wash on the sides of the neck. The head pattern is bold and distinctive, with a moustachial streak, black eyestripe, white supercilium and orange-red crown stripe, bordered black. Both female and juveniles show some or all of these markings.

*Female and juvenile Firecrests have a subdued face pattern, but one that is nevertheless more pronounced than that of the Goldcrest.*

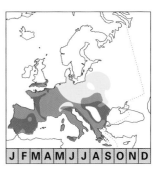

**Size:** 9cm (3½in).
**Wing:** 48–56mm.
**Bill:** 10–12mm.
**Weight:** 4–7g.
**Voice:** High-pitched *zi-zi-zi*; similar to that of the Goldcrest, ending abruptly.
**Habitat:** Conifer forests with tall understorey of deciduous trees and shrubs.
**Range:** Breeds across temperate and Mediterranean Europe, from northern Portugal to western Russia and southwards to Sicily and Crete.
**Movements:** Populations from Germany eastwards are summer visitors, but complex pattern of migrations takes birds to southern and western Europe, with some crossing the Channel to England, and others crossing the Strait of Gibraltar to North Africa.
**Breeding:** Seven to eleven brown-speckled white eggs are laid in a cup placed high in a tree, usually a conifer, and incubated by the female for 14 or 15 days. The downy, helpless young fledge after 19 or 20 days. Double brooded.
**Confusing Species:** Goldcrest.

## Spotted Flycatcher *(Muscicapa striata)*

The Spotted Flycatcher is a widespread and locally abundant summer visitor to virtually the whole of Europe. This is a brown flycatcher that perches openly and makes repeated aerial sallies in pursuit of flying insects, often returning to the same perch. The adult is brown above, marked by buffy margins to the flight feathers that form a pale mid-wing panel. Though an obvious feature, this is not as marked as with the contrasting white panel of the 'pied' flycatcher group.

In all plumages, underparts are white with buffy flanks and a lightly streaked breast, but the juvenile Spotted Flycatcher (above) is heavily spotted above and below, creating a scaly impression.

**Size:** 13–15cm (5–6in).
**Wing:** 83–90mm.
**Bill:** 14–17mm.
**Weight:** 10–21g.
**Voice:** A weak *tsee*.
**Habitat:** Groves, gardens, orchards, woodland edges.
**Food:** Insects.
**Range:** Summer visitor from Ireland and Iberia eastwards across Eurasia to eastern Siberia. Winters in savannah Africa. In Europe, absent only from Iceland, the French Alps, parts of Iberia, the higher Scandinavian mountains and the Russian tundra.
**Movements:** Migrates on a broad front, crossing the Mediterranean and Sahara, setting off at night. Arrives at its destination late in the spring.
**Breeding:** Four or five red-blotched very pale blue eggs are laid in a shallow cup placed on a ledge of a building, in a nestbox, or in the crotch of a tree. Eggs are incubated for 11–15 days by the female. The helpless, down-covered chicks fly after 12–14 days. Sometimes has two broods in a season.

J F M A M J J A S O N D

## Red-breasted Flycatcher *(Ficedula parva)*

The Red-breasted Flycatcher is a summer visitor to the damp woodlands of eastern Europe. It is easily identified in all plumages by the white sides to its frequently cocked tail. The adult male in summer is brown above, fading to grey on the head and marked by a clear white eye-ring. The black tail has prominent white sides that are broadly tipped in black, forming a T-shape, not unlike that of the Northern Wheatear. The male has white underparts and a distinctive red throat.

J F M A M J J A S O N D

The female (left) is greyish brown above, and lacks the red throat of the male (right).

**Size:** 10–13cm (4–5in).
**Wing:** 64–72mm.
**Bill:** 11–14mm.
**Weight:** 8–13g.
**Voice:** Call is sharp *zeet;* song a clear trill.
**Habitat:** Damp deciduous forests.
**Food:** Insects.
**Range:** Summer visitor from Germany, central Europe and the Balkans across Russia and the Ukraine eastwards through Eurasia to the Bering Strait. Winters India and Southeast Asia. In Europe, breeds eastern Germany, Austria, Hungary and the former Yugoslavia and farther north into central Sweden and southern Finland.
**Movements:** European birds migrate southeast to winter in India, and are no more than vagrant visitors westwards in both spring and autumn to Britain and France.
**Breeding:** Five or six reddish-spotted white eggs are laid in a cup in a tree hole, or on a low branch, and incubated for 12 or 13 days by the female. The downy, helpless young fledge after 12 or 13 days.

## Collared Flycatcher *(Ficedula albicollis)*

The adult male is black above with white patches in the wing and on the forehead, and is marked by a white collar and a greyish white rump.

*The male's summer black and white plumage is replaced in autumn by brown, much like that of the female.*

**Size:** 12–13cm (5in).
**Wing:** 77–88mm.
**Bill:** 11–14mm.
**Weight:** 9–19g.
**Voice:** A repeated *see-see-see see-oo.*
**Habitat:** Deciduous forests, often alongside rivers.
**Food:** Insects.

**Range:** A summer visitor from eastern France and central Italy eastwards across central Europe to the Urals. Winters southern East Africa.
**Movements:** Whole population winters Tanzania, Malawi, Zambia, Zimbabwe and Zaire, passing across the eastern Sahara. Regular passage through

Mediterranean islands. Spreading westwards, where there are nestboxes.
**Breeding:** Six or seven pale blue eggs in a tree hole; incubated for 12–14 days by the female. Helpless, downy young fly after 12–14 days.
**Confusing Species:** Semi-collared and Pied Flycatchers.

J F M A M J J A S O N D

## Semi-collared Flycatcher *(Ficedula semitorquata)*

The summer male resembles the Pied Flycatcher, with black upperparts and white underparts. It has more white in the wing and a larger white primary patch than the Pied, sometimes with a neat row of white spots across the median coverts. A white half-collar is distinctive, but of variable extent and shape. This bird generally has a larger white patch on its forehead than the Pied. The extent of white in the tail seems equally variable. Where present, the spotted median coverts are diagnostic.

*The white shoulder streak is the clearest identification mark of this otherwise confusing species.*

**Size:** 13cm (5in).
**Wing:** 75–86mm.
**Bill:** 6–8mm.
**Weight:** 13–17g.
**Voice:** Repeated *see-see-see see-oo* song, like Collared but faster.
**Habitat:** Deciduous forests among hills and along river banks.
**Food:** Insects.
**Range:** Summer visitor to Balkans, locally in Turkey and the Caucasus to the southern Caspian Sea. Winters East Africa.
**Movements:** Whole population apparently winters in Kenya and southern Sudan, migrating across the Mediterranean and the Sahara.
**Breeding:** Five or six pale blue

J F M A M J J A S O N D

eggs are laid in a tree hole and incubated by the female for 13 or 14 days. The downy, helpless chicks fly after 14–17 days.
**Confusing Species:** Collared and Pied Flycatchers.

## Pied Flycatcher *(Ficedula hypoleuca)*

The Pied Flycatcher is a widespread and locally common summer visitor to much of northern Europe, as well as to hilly regions to the south. The male is black and white, with a white wing patch, two small white dots at the base of the bill and a small white primary patch.

*Female (left) is brown above, whitish below, with a similar wing pattern to the male (right), although showing significantly less white.*

**Size:** 13cm (5in).
**Wing:** 75–84mm.
**Bill:** 11–14mm.
**Weight:** 8–19g.
**Voice:** *Zee-chee* song.
**Habitat:** Mixed woods.
**Food:** Insects.
**Range:** From Britain to Siberia. Absent from Iceland, Ireland, most of France, much of Spain, Italy and Balkans.
**Movements:** Whole population crosses the Mediterranean

and the Sahara in autumn, to West African forests.
**Breeding:** Five to seven blue eggs laid in a tree hole; incubated by female for 13–16 days; young fly after similar time.
**Confusing Species:** Collared and Semi-collared Flycatchers.

J F M A M J J A S O N D

243

## Long-tailed Tit *(Aegithalos caudatus)*

Long-tailed Tits are highly gregarious, occurring in flocks up to 20 strong. The very long tail, black with white margins, is a useful field mark.

The upperparts are black with a white crown stripe and pinkish scapulars. The underparts are dirty white, with a pinkish wash along the flanks.

**Size:** 14–15cm (6in); tail is 9cm (3½in).
**Wing:** 57–70mm.
**Bill:** 7–8mm.
**Weight:** 7–10g.
**Voice:** *Srrip* and *zee-zee-zee* calls between members of a flock.
**Habitat:** Woodland, heaths, hedgerows.
**Food:** Insects, spiders.
**Range:** Resident right across Eurasia from Ireland to Japan, extending southwards to the Middle East and northern and western China. In Europe, absent from Iceland, some Mediterranean islands and northern Scandinavia.
**Movements:** Local movements from hill areas to lowlands in winter.

**Breeding:** Eight to twelve white eggs are laid in a domed nest of moss and lichens. The nest is bound together with spiders' webs and is able to expand to accommodate the growing brood. The eggs are incubated mainly by the female for 12–14 days, and the naked and helpless chicks fly after 14–18 days. Sometimes has two broods.

A.c.caudatus *(behind), the northern subspecies, has a pure white head, whereas the Spanish A.c.irbii (front) has a pale grey back.*

## Bearded Tit *(Panurus biarmicus)*

A long-tailed brown bird that is confined to reedbeds. The wings show black, cream and white marks. The underparts are white, washed orange-buff on the flanks. The dumpy body and wings are similar to those of the Long-tailed Tit.

*Male (above right) is a warm orange-brown with a grey head and a black moustache. Female (left) is similar but lacks the grey head and moustache.*

**Size:** 15–18cm (6–7in).
**Wing:** 57–64mm.
**Bill:** 10–12mm.
**Weight:** 9–21g.
**Voice:** Clear, repeated *pting-pting.*
**Habitat:** Reedbeds.
**Food:** Insects and seeds.
**Range:** Patchily distributed across Eurasia from Spain, France and England to the Sea of Japan. In Europe, highly localized, though widespread in the east. May winter in non-breeding areas.
**Movements:** Autumn eruptions take birds to Iberia, England and elsewhere, though their origins are obscure save for ringed Dutch birds recovered in England.

**Breeding:** Five to seven brown-speckled white eggs are laid in a bulky nest among reed debris over water; incubated by both sexes for 12 or 13 days; naked, helpless young fly at 12 or 13 days. May raise two to four broods.

## Penduline Tit *(Remiz pendulinus)*

This bird is easily overlooked and is nowhere numerous. It builds its nest suspended from a tree over water. The male has a chestnut back, black wings edged white, and a distinctive black mask. The female is plainer, with a duskier brown head and upperparts and a dull chestnut back.

**Size:** 10cm (4in).
**Wing:** 54–59mm.
**Bill:** 10–12mm.
**Weight:** 9–12g.
**Voice:** A soft, plaintive, repeated *psee.*
**Habitat:** River and marsh margins with reed mace and overhanging trees.
**Food:** Seeds and insects.
**Range:** Summer visitor from Germany eastward. Resident in Mediterranean, the Middle East and from India to China.
**Movements:** Western European birds move south and west, while those farther east move south.
**Breeding:** Six to eight white eggs are laid in a penduline nest made up of plant fibres and wool and are incubated by the female for 13 or 14 days. The naked and helpless young fledge in 16–18 days. It may have two broods.

*The male has a bold black mask, while the female is plain faced.*

244

A neatly marked resident of woods and wooded heaths, the Marsh Tit forms a species pair with the Willow Tit, from which it should be distinguished with care. The upperparts are brown, with a shiny black cap, white cheeks and a small, neat black bib. The underparts are washed buffy.

*The Marsh Tit (left, back) does not have a pale wing panel like the Willow Tit (left, front); this is the main difference between the species.*

**Size:** 10–13cm (4–5in).
**Wing:** 61–69mm.
**Bill:** 10mm.
**Weight:** 9–14g.
**Voice:** Distinctive, repeated *pitchoo pitchoo*.
**Habitat:** Open woodland, treed heaths and hedgerows.
**Food:** Insects and seeds.
**Range:** Resident from northern Spain, Britain and southern Scandinavia eastwards across the whole of Europe almost to the Urals. Absent from Mediterranean coasts, Finland and much of Scandinavia and Russia. A separate population is resident in eastern Siberia.
**Movements:** Some local movements and dispersal, but basically resident.

J F M A M J J A S O N D

**Breeding:** Six to nine red-spotted white eggs are laid in a hole in rotten wood and incubated by the female for 13–17 days. The downy, helpless young fly after 16–21 days. May raise one or two broods in a season.
**Confusing Species:** Willow Tit has a dull, not shiny, black cap, a large black bib and a pale mid-wing panel.

---

## Willow Tit *(Parus montanus)*

Very similar to Marsh Tit, but generally more scruffy, the Willow Tit is resident across most of temperate and northern Europe. It prefers mountains in the south and arctic vegetation in the north. The upperparts are brown, marked by a dull black cap and a large scruffy bib. The underparts are dirty white, washed pale buff over the flanks. Northern birds of the subspecies *P.m. borealis* are paler grey above and white below.

J F M A M J J A S O N D

*Given a nestbox filled with polystyrene, the Willow Tit will excavate a hole as if digging out a nest in rotten wood (below left).*

**Size:** 10–13cm (4–5in).
**Wing:** 62–70mm.
**Bill:** 10–12mm.
**Weight:** 10–14g.
**Voice:** A harsh, buzzing *erz-erz-erz* and a high-pitched *zi-zi-zi*.
**Habitat:** Conifer forests, damp lowland woods of birch and boreal forest clearings with mixed woods.
**Food:** Insects and seeds.
**Range:** Breeds across Eurasia from Britain to Japan and the Bering Strait. In

Europe, resident from central France to northern Scandinavia eastwards and among the forested mountains of central Europe and the Balkans. Absent from Iberia and virtually absent in Italy.
**Movements:** Resident with only local dispersal, though some populations are definitely eruptive.

**Breeding:** Six to nine reddish-speckled white eggs are laid in a self-excavated hole in rotten wood and incubated by the female for 13–15 days. The helpless, downy chicks fledge after 17–19 days.
**Confusing Species:** The Marsh Tit has a shiny black cap, a smaller black bib and uniformly brown wings.

This bird is like the Willow Tit, but is larger, with a heavier bill. The upperparts are greyish brown with a brown-black cap, white cheeks and a large black bib. Underparts are white, washed pale buff on the flanks.

*The Sombre Tit (below left) has a much more extensive bib than the Willow Tit (above left), and its bill is significantly larger.*

**Size:** 13–15cm (5–6in).
**Wing:** 71–78mm.
**Bill:** 12–14mm.
**Weight:** 15–18g.
**Voice:** A hard *charr* and various chattering notes.
**Habitat:** Rocky hillsides and conifer woods with clearings.
**Food:** Insects and seeds.
**Range:** Resident from the former

Yugoslavia south and east through the Balkans to Turkey and the Middle East.
**Movements:** Local dispersal only.
**Breeding:** Five to seven, perhaps up to ten, reddish-speckled white eggs are laid in a hole in a tree and are incubated for 12 or 13 days by the female. The downy, helpless chicks fledge after 21 or 22 days. Usually has two broods.
**Confusing Species:** Willow and Marsh Tits overlap in range, but both are smaller, with smaller bills.

Though very similar to the Willow Tit and equally scruffy in appearance, this is a relatively simple bird to identify. It is a resident of the northern boreal forests. The upperparts and cap are black with a distinct brownish wash. A large, scruffy black bib encloses white cheeks. The white underparts are marked by bold rufous flanks, which form the best field mark.

*Typically, the Siberian Tit, along with several other species, frequently holds food in its foot (right).*

**Size:** 13–15cm (5–6in).
**Wing:** 64–71mm.
**Bill:** 11–12mm.
**Weight:** 11–13g.
**Voice:** A repeated, nasal *eez*.
**Habitat:** Conifer and birch forests.
**Food:** Insects, berries and seeds.
**Range:** Resident from Scandinavia

eastwards through the boreal zone as far as the Bering Strait and onwards into western Alaska. In Europe, breeds in high mountains of southern Norway and from central Norway across Sweden to Finland and northern Russia.
**Movements:** Resident, though some birds leave the harsher mountain areas

to descend to nearby woods in winter.
**Breeding:** Six to ten red-spotted white eggs laid in an excavated or natural tree hole are incubated by the female for 14 or 15 days. The helpless, downy young fledge after 19 or 20 days.
**Confusing Species:** Willow Tit is similarly scruffy, but lacks rufous flanks.

## Crested Tit *(Parus cristatus)*

*Seen at close quarters, the head of the Crested Tit (below) shows a distinct black eyestripe, which joins with a bold black line around the ear coverts, to form a 'hook' shape.*

The Crested Tit is one of the most distinctive of European tits. The upperparts are brown, with a black line surrounding the black and white patterned face. A heavily barred black and white crest covers the crown, and there is a small black bib. The underparts are washed buffy. The Crested Tit is generally gregarious and feeds high in conifers.

**Size:** 10–13cm (4–5in)
**Wing:** 61–70mm.
**Bill:** 11–12mm.
**Weight:** 10–13g.
**Voice:** A trilling *chirr-chirr-rr.*
**Habitat:** Mostly conifer forests, but also mixed woods, particularly in southern parts of the range.
**Food:** Seeds and insects.
**Range:** Resident virtually wherever there are stands of conifers, from southern Spain to northern Sweden, eastwards across Europe to the mountains of the Balkans. Absent from Britain (except for the Scottish Highlands), Italy and northernmost Scandinavia and Russia. Reaches just beyond the Urals.
**Movements:** Highly sedentary, with southern and western birds rarely moving more than a few miles. Some eastern birds may move up to 70km (45 miles) on exceptional occasions. Scottish breeders have been unable to colonize nearby suitable valleys.
**Breeding:** Four to eight purple-spotted eggs are laid in a hole in a rotting tree stump and incubated by the female for 13–18 days. The helpless, downy young fly after 17–21 days.

## Coal Tit *(Parus ater)*

This tiny tit is most often found among conifers, especially spruce, but also occurs in oak and mixed woods. It scours the upper branches in the manner of a nuthatch, often clinging to rough bark. The upperparts are grey-blue, the underparts buffy. The black cap shows a distinctive and diagnostic white nape and a scruffy bib encloses white cheeks. The wings have a bold white double wingbar.

*The Coal Tit will frequent deciduous forest but prefers to roost in conifers (above).*

**Size:** 10–13cm (4–5in).
**Wing:** 58–66mm.
**Bill:** 10–12mm.
**Weight:** 8–12g.
**Voice:** High-pitched *zee-zee-zee;* also a repetitive *wichoo wichoo wichoo* song, similar to Great Tit.
**Habitat:** Conifer woods, but also mixed and pure deciduous woods in some areas.
**Food:** Insects and seeds.
**Range:** Largely resident across Eurasia, from Portugal and Ireland to Japan, also southwards to western China. In Europe, absent from Iceland and northernmost Scandinavia. Winters within, and south of, breeding range.
**Movements:** Regular migrant in northern parts of range, though seldom making long-distance movements. Also highly eruptive from these areas, sometimes in large numbers. In France and Italy, it is widespread in winter in areas where it does not breed.
**Breeding:** Seven to nine red-spotted white eggs are laid in a tree hole and incubated for 14–18 days by the female. The downy, helpless young fly after 16–19 days. Has two broods.
**Confusing Species:** No other tits show a white nape patch.

## Blue Tit *(Parus caeruleus)*

This locally abundant bird is a frequent visitor to gardens through most of its range, especially where peanuts are provided, and it breeds readily in nestboxes. It has yellow

underparts and green-blue upperparts, with blue crown, wings and tail. The head is marked black and white.

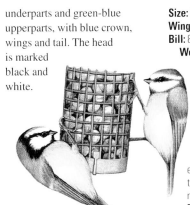

*The Blue Tit is particularly common where food is provided in winter.*

**Size:** 10–13cm (4–5in).
**Wing:** 62–71mm.
**Bill:** 8–10mm.
**Weight:** 9–13g.
**Voice:** Harsh *churr* and a *tsee-tsee-tsee*.
**Habitat:** Woodlands (especially deciduous) gardens, orchards, parks, groves, marshes.
**Food:** Insects, nuts and seeds.
**Range:** Virtually endemic to Western Palearctic, with breeding extending from the Mediterranean to central Scandinavia. Absent northern and northeastern Russia.
**Movements:** Basically resident, but with northern populations being eruptive, often in large numbers. Erratic movements, seemingly dependent on

population levels, head southwest.
**Breeding:** Seven to twelve red-spotted white eggs, laid in a cup of mosses in a tree hole or nestbox, are incubated by the female for 13–16 days. The downy, helpless young fledge in 15–23 days.

## Azure Tit *(Parus cyanus)*

A close relative of the Blue Tit, the Azure Tit overlaps only in central Russia, but replaces the Blue Tit eastwards. The upperparts are

*The plumage of male Azure Tit (above) is much whiter and bluer than its western relative.*

pale blue, with a white head, and a blue-black eyestripe. The wings are bright blue, with a broad white wingbar. The tail is blue with white outer feathers; the underparts are white.

**Size:** 13cm (5in).
**Wing:** 67–72mm.
**Bill:** 9–11mm.
**Weight:** 11–14g.
**Voice:** Blue Tit–like trill, and *tsirr–tsirr* churring.
**Habitat:** Deciduous woodland lying alongside streams and floods, especially stands of willow, as well as seasonal floods and marshland with intervening belts of trees.
**Food:** Insects and seeds.
**Range:** Resident from central Russia eastwards across Siberia to the Sea of Japan and southwards to beyond the Aral Sea.
**Movements:** Resident, with only a handful of sightings recorded farther west than the breeding range.

**Breeding:** Nine to eleven red-spotted white eggs are laid in a tree hole and incubated by the female for 13 or 14 days. The downy, helpless young fly after some 16 days. Occasionally has two broods in a season.

## Great Tit *(Parus major)*

*The male's breast stripe widens between its legs, unlike the female's, which is a uniform width.*

European birds are grey-green above and yellow below, with blue wings, a black cap and a black line around the ear coverts. A black bib extends to a broad band down the breast.

**Size:** 13–15cm (5–6in).
**Wing:** 73–82mm.
**Bill:** 12–13mm.
**Weight:** 14–22g.
**Voice:** A wide variety of calls and a clear *teecha-teecha-teecha* song.
**Habitat:** Woods and forests, parks and groves, orchards and gardens, hedgerows and heaths.
**Food:** Insects, berries, nuts.
**Range:** Eurasia. In Europe, it is absent only from Iceland and the Scandinavian mountain chain to northern Russia.
**Movements:** Largely resident, but occasional eruptions from northern and eastern populations.
**Breeding:** Eight to thirteen reddish-spotted white eggs are laid in a tree hole. The species readily takes to

nestboxes and has been much studied. The eggs are incubated by the female for 13 or 14 days. The helpless, downy chicks fly after 16–22 days.

## European Nuthatch (Sitta europaea)

The European Nuthatch has a long, heavily built and sharply pointed bill. The upperparts are pale blue, the underparts white, variably washed with rusty chestnut. The short tail has white outer feathers and a black eyestripe extends along the side of the nape almost to the wing.

**Size:** 13–15cm (5–6in).
**Wing:** 75–83mm.
**Bill:** 18–20mm.
**Weight:** 20–26g.
**Voice:** High-pitched *kee-kee-kee*; a ringing *chwit-chwit-chwit..*
**Habitat:** Deciduous woods and forests, parkland, groves and conifers.
**Food:** Insects, seeds and nuts.
**Range:** Eurasia. In Europe breeds across the continent, avoiding treeless coasts and islands. Absent Iceland, Ireland, Scotland and northern Scandinavia.
**Movements:** Resident, though first-year birds do wander in autumn.
**Breeding:** Six to nine red-spotted white eggs are laid in a tree hole with a mud-plastered entrance and incubated by the female for 14–18 days. The helpless, downy youngsters fly after 23–25 days.
**Confusing Species:** All other nuthatches.

| J | F | M | A | M | J | J | A | S | O | N | D |

*The most widespread of the world's nuthatches, this bird is found across Eurasia and southwards through Japan and China to India.*

## Western Rock Nuthatch (Sitta neumayer)

Virtually endemic to the Western Palearctic and, in Europe, confined to the Balkans. Occupies the niche among rocks occupied by the European Nuthatch among trees. Climbs among cliffs and fallen boulders as well as ruins.

Upperparts pale blue, greyer and paler than European Nuthatch, with white underparts lightly washed warm rufous on the flanks. The tail is pale blue and lacks any markings. Shares the prominent black eyestripe with the arboreal species.

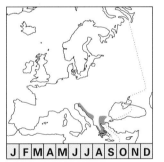

| J | F | M | A | M | J | J | A | S | O | N | D |

**Size:** 13–15cm (5–6in).
**Wing:** 78–85mm.
**Bill:** 24–25mm.
**Weight:** 30–35g.
**Voice:** Shrill piping notes on a descending scale.
**Habitat:** Canyons, cliffs, rocky slopes and screes, ruins.
**Food:** Insects.
**Range:** Resident in the former Yugoslavia, Greece and Bulgaria, extending eastwards through Turkey to the adjacent Middle East.
**Movements:** Some altitudinal movements to lower ground in winter, but otherwise resident.
**Breeding:** Six to ten red-speckled white eggs are laid in a gourd-shaped

*The nest is a gourd-shaped construction of mud, usually fixed in a rock crevice or under an overhang, where it is safe from predators.*

nest constructed of mud in a cave or overhang on a cliff or ruin. The eggs are incubated by the female for 15–18 days and the helpless, downy young fledge after 30 days.
**Confusing Species:** European Nuthatch as above, but habitat is the best key.

249

A small, well-marked nuthatch, which has pale blue-grey upperparts and white underparts. Like its close relative, the Corsican Nuthatch, it has a bold white supercilium separating a black eyestripe and a black crown. A rich chestnut breast band and chestnut undertail are diagnostic.

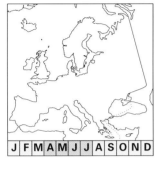

*Krüper's Nuthatch feeds like other nuthatches, running up and down tree trunks and branches.*

**Size:** 13cm (5in).
**Wing:** 69–78mm.
**Bill:** 13–14mm.
**Weight:** 10–14g.
**Voice:** Harsh rasping note, plus repetitive rippling *pi-pi-pi-pi.*
**Habitat:** Caucasian fir woodland.
**Food:** Insects, seeds.
**Range:** Confined to firs around the coasts of Turkey and nearby islands, extending into the Caucasus mountains.
**Movements:** Some local dispersal and altitudinal movements in Turkey.
**Breeding:** Five or six rusty-speckled whitish eggs are incubated in a tree hole by the female for 14–17 days. Downy, helpless young fledge at 16–19 days.
**Confusing Species**: Other nuthatches.

This is the only nuthatch found on Corsica and it is unique to that island. The upperparts are a deep greyish blue, and the underparts white with no more than a faint wash of buffy pink. The crown is black, separated from a bold black eyestripe by an equally bold white supercilium. The bill is a little shorter than that of other nuthatches. It behaves like the European Nuthatch and is an adept tree climber.

*The differences between the sexes of the Corsican Nuthatch are subtle and easy to miss in the field. The male has a black cap and black eyestripe, while the female has a slate-grey cap and charcoal-grey eyestripe.*

**Size:** 13cm (5in).
**Wing:** 70–76mm.
**Bill:** 17–19mm.
**Weight:** 12–14g.
**Voice:** A nasal *char-char* and a rippling *po-po-po-po.*
**Habitat:** Forests of pine in Corsica usually at some altitude.
**Food:** Seeds and insects.
**Range:** Resident Corsica.
**Movements:** Descends to valleys during poor weather.
**Breeding:** Five or six reddish-spotted white eggs are laid in a tree hole, which may be that of a Great Spotted Woodpecker or which may be self-excavated in rotten wood. Incubation is by the female alone for an unknown period and the downy, helpless young fly after 22–24 days. It may produce two broods during a season.
**Confusing Species:** Krüper's Nuthatch, but none on Corsica.

The upperparts are mottled and streaked in browns, buffs and black, with a white supercilium, and the underparts are white. The tail is pointed.

**Size:** 10–13cm (4–5in).
**Wing:** 59–68mm.
**Bill:** 15–21mm.
**Weight:** 8–13g.
**Voice:** A thin *tsee-tsee*.
**Habitat:** Strictly a woodland bird, preferring deciduous forests.
**Food:** Spiders and insects.
**Range:** Breeds right across Eurasia from Ireland to Japan. In

J F M A M J J A S O N D

*This dainty bird is easily overlooked, being perfectly camouflaged as it climbs the trunks of forest trees.*

Europe, absent from much of Iberia, France, the southern North Sea countries and Italy.
**Movements:** Resident in Europe. Wintering in Balkans is probably due to birds descending from hills.
**Breeding:** Five or six red-spotted white eggs are laid in a cup hidden behind the loose bark of a tree and incubated by the female for 14 or 15 days. The helpless, downy chicks fledge after 14–16 days. Single or double brooded.
**Confusing Species:** Short-toed Treecreeper is very similar, but a dirty white below, with buffy flanks, and less clean and contrasting upperparts.

This bird is very similar to the Common Treecreeper, and should be identified only with the greatest care. It tends to occupy less densely forested habitats. The ranges of the two species overlap in central Europe. The upperparts are brown, speckled and streaked buff and black, but with less contrast than in the Common Treecreeper. The underparts are dull, or dirty white, with a definite buffy wash along the flanks. The supercilium is dull buff or cream, rather than white as in the Common Treecreeper.

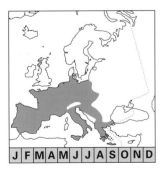

J F M A M J J A S O N D

*Where the two treecreepers overlap in range, they must be distinguished with the greatest of care and attention to finer points of plumage.*

**Size:** 10–13cm (4–5in).
**Wing:** 56–67mm.
**Bill:** 15–20mm.
**Weight:** 8–11g.
**Voice:** Clear *dit-dit-diddly-dit*.
**Habitat:** Woods, avenues, parks, conifer belts and forests. The species is generally found at lower altitudes, below around 1500m, while the Common Treecreeper is more numerous above such altitudes.
**Food:** Spiders and insects.
**Range:** This bird is found extensively throughout the region from Iberia through continental Europe to Poland, Slovakia, Serbia, Greece and Turkey.
**Movements:** Resident with no more than local dispersal. Birds recorded on the south coast of England may be the precursors of future colonists moving in from northern France rather than definite migrants.
**Breeding:** Six or seven reddish-spotted white eggs are laid in a cup placed behind loose bark and are incubated by the female for 13 or 14 days. The down-covered, helpless young fly after 15–18 days. The species may raise one or two broods each season.
**Confusing Species:** Common Treecreeper as outlined above.

251

# Wallcreeper *(Tichodroma muraria)*

The Wallcreeper is a highly localized bird of the high mountains, which descends to lowland cliffs and buildings in winter. It is one of the most elusive of all European birds. Basically grey above and below, the Wallcreeper is marked by bright crimson in the wings that are continually flicked open and closed. In the breeding season, the male has a black face and breast. It climbs rock faces with consummate ease and flies on rounded wings. The bill is long and decurved.

**Size:** 15–18cm (6–7in).
**Wing:** 94–104mm.
**Bill:** 30–39mm.
**Weight:** 17–19g.
**Voice:** A high-pitched *zee-zee-zee*.
**Habitat:** Mountain cliffs, especially gorges, and in winter old buildings.

**Food:** Insects.
**Range:** Breeds throughout main mountains of Europe, Turkey, the Caucasus, Himalayas and central Asian mountains. Winters at lower altitudes.
**Movements:** Though many birds are resident throughout the year, some

*The rarely seen Wallcreeper has large crimson patches on wings that are shaped like ping-pong bats, and its flight is not dissimilar to that of a butterfly.*

descend to nearby valleys, while others may migrate considerable distances to occupy the same winter territory year after year.
**Breeding:** Four or five white, lightly speckled reddish, eggs are laid in a deep rock cleft on a cliff, but often low down near water and spray. They are incubated for 19 or 20 days by the female, and the downy, helpless young fly after 29–30 days.

# Red-backed Shrike *(Lanius collurio)*

*Female has dull brown back, grey nape, dark mask and greyish rump and is heavily marked with dark crescents below.*

This summer visitor to Europe drops on its prey from a prominent perch and stores it in a thorny larder. The adult male has a rust-brown back, grey head with a black mask, a grey rump, and a black, white-margined tail. The chin and underparts are white. The juvenile is brown above, buffy below and heavily scaled.

**Size:** 15–18cm (6–7in).
**Wing:** 89–99mm.
**Bill:** 17–20mm.
**Weight:** 23–30g.
**Voice:** Harsh *chak-chak*.
**Habitat:** Heaths, scrub, rocky and bushy slopes.
**Food:** Insects, birds, reptiles.
**Range:** Summer visitor from northern Spain, northwards to southern Scandinavia and eastwards to central Siberia. Winters southern Africa. In Europe, absent or scarce northwest France, Belgium and Holland; has abandoned England.
**Movements:** Even western breeding birds migrate southeastwards in autumn, towards the eastern end of the Mediterranean, before heading south and west to Africa. Birds thus avoid crossing the Mediterranean, in the west at least, and the Sahara. Feeds on small migrant birds along the way.
**Breeding:** Five or six variably coloured eggs, spotted in shades of brown, are laid in a cup placed in a thorny thicket and are incubated by the female for 14–16 days. The helpless, naked chicks fledge after 12–16 days.
**Confusing Species:** Juvenile with juvenile Woodchat Shrike.

## Lesser Grey Shrike *(Lanius minor)*

The Lesser Grey Shrike is a summer visitor, mainly to eastern Europe, westwards through the Mediterranean to a few isolated areas in southern France and northeastern Spain. It is similar to the Great Grey Shrike, but smaller, with a pinkish wash over its breast in summer. The adult is grey above with long black wings and a long, white-margined black tail. A black facial mask extends over the forehead. The underparts are washed a warm pink, most noticeably on males in summer.

J F M A M J J A S O N D

*The immature Lesser Grey Shrike in its first-winter plumage (right) is similar to the adult, but heavily scaled with dark crescents above and over the flanks. The mask is dark, not black, and does not extend on to the forehead.*

**Size:** 18–20cm (7–8in).
**Wing:** 114–126mm.
**Bill:** 19–23mm.
**Weight:** 42–55g.
**Voice:** Various harsh rattling notes.
**Habitat:** Agricultural areas with large trees, groves and orchards and scrubby thickets.
**Food:** Birds, insects, small mammals.
**Range:** Summer visitor from central Poland southwards to the former Yugoslavia, east to central Siberia and south to the Middle East. Winters Namibia and adjacent Africa. In Europe, breeds locally Spain, France, Italy and through the Balkans and Ukraine.
**Movements:** Western birds migrate east and southeast through the eastern Mediterranean to reach Egypt before heading southwards, then southwest towards winter quarters. Amazingly numerous in Namibia in winter.
**Breeding:** Five or six brown-spotted greenish eggs are laid in a cup placed in a tree and are incubated mainly by the female for 12–15 days. The naked, helpless young fledge after 16–18 days.
**Confusing Species:** Great Grey Shrike is larger, has shorter wings and a longer tail, and a black mask that does not extend to its forehead.

## Great Grey Shrike *(Lanius excubitor)*

This substantial bird is either a resident, a summer visitor or a winter visitor over much of Europe. Some birders split it into two species, others see the types as being subspecies: the Great Grey, *excubitor*, is found to the north and east of central France, and the Southern Grey, *meridionalis*, in southern France and Iberia. Both are grey above with short black wings and a white-margined black tail. The black mask over the eye does not cover the forehead. The underparts are white, although the Southern Grey has a pinkish wash.

*The Great Grey Shrike often sits on top of a bush or post to sing (above right), showing off its clear white chest. The grey, black and white markings of the adult (right) are unmistakable.*

**Size:** 23–25cm (9–10in).
**Wing:** 108–118mm.
**Bill:** 22–24mm.
**Weight:** 48–81g.
**Voice:** Harsh *chek-chek*.
**Habitat:** Heaths, scrub, clearings, thickets, plantations.
**Food:** Birds, small mammals, reptiles and insects.
**Range:** Complex interrelationships between species and subspecies. Breeds across Eurasia from central western Sahara north to the North Cape of Norway; in a broad swathe across the Middle East to India; and as far north as the Russian taiga to the Bering Strait. In Europe, a summer visitor north of 60°N and a resident or winter visitor to the south. Few large areas (except Italy and Ireland) do not see this species, although it is not numerous.
**Movements:** Complex movements within Europe.
**Breeding:** Five to seven red-spotted white eggs are laid in a cup placed in a shrub and are incubated mainly by the female for 15–17 days. The helpless and naked young fledge after some 15–18 days.
**Confusing Species:** The Lesser Grey Shrike.

J F M A M J J A S O N D

253

This widespread and locally common summer visitor to Mediterranean Europe is also found across Germany to Poland. The adult is black above, marked by white oval wing patches, a white rump and white outertail feathers. The underparts are white, but the best recognition feature is a chestnut crown that extends to the nape. The juvenile is buffy with pale oval wing patches.

*Juveniles are buff-brown, covered with dark scaly markings.*

**Size:** 15–18cm (6–7in).
**Wing:** 97–103mm.
**Bill:** 18–20mm.
**Weight:** 21–41g.
**Voice:** Harsh chattering.
**Habitat:** Scrub, bushy wasteland, groves, orchards.
**Food:** Insects and small birds.
**Range:** Virtually endemic summer visitor to Western Palearctic. In Europe it breeds in Iberia, France northwards to central Germany, Italy, the Balkans and Greece. Also found eastwards through Turkey to adjacent areas of the Middle East during the summer months. Winters in Sahel Africa.
**Movements:** European birds move south to southwest on a broad front to

cross the Mediterranean and Sahara. Spring migration takes birds farther east than in autumn.
**Breeding:** Five or six brown-spotted greenish eggs are laid in a cup-shaped nest placed in a tree. The eggs are

incubated mainly by the female for 14 or 15 days. The naked and helpless young fledge after 15–18 days.
**Confusing Species:** Beware juvenile Red-backed Shrike, which lacks pale oval wing patches.

---

Masked Shrike *(Lanius nubicus)*

This is a highly localized summer visitor to the eastern Mediterranean. The adult is black above and white below, with a pale pinkish wash over the flanks. Like the Woodchat Shrike, it has white wing ovals, but the head is black, not chestnut, with a white forehead extending to a supercilium.

*The male (right) has clear black and white markings with rufous flanks. The female (above) is similar but with a grey wash over the black. The nest is neatly constructed in a cup shape and securely fixed among dense foliage on the branch of a tree.*

**Size:** 15–18cm (6–7in).
**Wing:** 87–96mm.
**Bill:** 17–20mm.
**Weight:** 15–23g.
**Voice:** Produces a scratchy, warbler-like song; call is a harsh *queer* repeated.
**Habitat:** Groves, orchards and parkland.
**Food:** Birds and insects.
**Range:** Breeds Greece, Bulgaria and Montenegro, as well as eastwards through Turkey to Middle East. Winters East Africa westwards through the Sahel.
**Movements:** Migrates across the eastern Mediterranean to the Nile Valley and East Africa. Common in Cyprus, but virtually unknown farther west.
**Breeding:** Four to six brown-blotched creamy eggs are laid in a cup placed in a tree and incubated for 14 or 15 days by the female. The naked, helpless young fledge after a similar period. Raises two broods.
**Confusing Species:** Woodchat Shrike.

## Eurasian Jay *(Garrulus glandarius)*

*Jays collect and hide hundreds of acorns each autumn, storing them for eating in the cold winter months.*

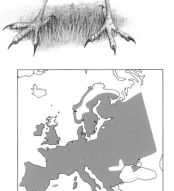

**Size:** 33–35cm (13–14in).
**Wing:** 175–196mm.
**Bill:** 30–36mm.
**Weight:** 138–180g.
**Voice:** Harsh *kaaa.*
**Habitat:** Both deciduous and coniferous forests.
**Food:** Nestlings, eggs, nuts, seeds, worms and insects.
**Range:** Resident Eurasia from Ireland to Japan, southwards through the Middle East to China and the Himalayas.
**Movements:** In Europe, resident with only post breeding dispersal. In the east, irregular eruptive movements take place across wide areas.
**Breeding:** Five to seven buff-speckled greenish eggs are laid in a well constructed cup placed in a tree fork and incubated by both sexes for 16 or 17 days. The naked, helpless young fledge after 19 or 20 days.

J F M A M J J A S O N D

A large bird that is resident in woodlands throughout Europe, the Jay may be difficult to see in many areas. The upperparts and underparts are pinkish brown, marked by black wings with prominent blue and black greater coverts that are visible in flight and when perched. It has a black tail and a prominent white rump. The crown is streaked and a black moustache crosses the white cheeks and chin.

## Siberian Jay *(Perisoreus infaustus)*

*In flight, the rufous wing patches, rump and outertail feathers are clear and obvious fieldmarks.*

**Size:** 30cm (12in).
**Wing:** 135–152mm.
**Bill:** 27–30mm.
**Weight:** 81–101g.
**Voice:** Harsh *chair* and *kook-kook* calls.
**Habitat:** Conifer forests.
**Food:** Omnivorous: eats birds, mammals, insects, berries, seeds.
**Range:** Resident from Scandinavia through the boreal zone of Russia and Siberia to northern Japan and the Bering Strait. In Europe, present in the Baltic States and Scandinavia, but absent from southern Sweden and southwest Norway, southern Finland and much of the mountain chain.
**Movements:** European birds are strictly resident. Some eastern Siberian birds move within the boreal forests.
**Breeding:** Three or four brown-blotched pale blue eggs are laid in a cup placed in a conifer and incubated for 19 days by the female. The helpless, naked young fledge after 21–23 days.

J F M A M J J A S O N D

R esident in the northern boreal forests, this bird is seldom seen elsewhere. The upperparts are pale grey, with rufous patches in the rounded wing, and a rufous rump and outertail. The underparts are rufous, fading to grey on the breast and grey-brown on the face. The rufous rump and outertail is a key field mark as the bird flies away.

Highly gregarious, this bird spends much of its time feeding with others on or near the ground, but it has the ability to melt into vegetation when approached. The body is a warm buff, marked by blue wings and a long, tapered blue tail. A black cap extends to the nape and well below the eye. These birds are reluctant to fly across open ground and instead spend much of their time moving along the underside of the canopy of small trees and bushes. There are no similar species in Europe.

**Size:** 33–35cm (13–14in).
**Wing:** 126–143mm.
**Bill:** 25–29mm.
**Weight:** 65–79g.
**Voice:** Repeated *shree shree* among noisy groups.
**Habitat:** Groves, orchards, woodland, conifer forests.
**Food:** Insects, seeds, berries that are picked up from the ground and from low bushes.
**Range:** Resident Iberia and, strangely, from northern China to Korea and Japan.

This extraordinary division between virtually identical populations would seem to indicate that the species was originally native to one of these areas, and was subsequently introduced to the other by humans. But this poses a problem. Were Iberian birds imported from China, or did the Chinese birds originate with imports from Spain?
**Movements:** Virtually none are known in Europe.
**Breeding:** Five to seven brown-spotted creamy eggs are laid in a cup-shaped nest placed in the fork of a tree. The eggs are incubated for 15 or 16 days by the female alone. The helpless and down-covered chicks fledge after about 14–16 days.

*Gathering in flocks of up to 100 birds, Azure-winged Magpies move through woodlands just under the canopy. They are shy, and a flock will drift out of view quickly if disturbed.*

J F M A M J J A S O N D

Magpie *(Pica pica)*

This large black and white bird is resident virtually throughout Europe and is well established in the folklore of many countries. The upperparts are black and the underparts white with the black of the head extending to form a distinctive breast band. The white ovals in the wing and a long, graduated black tail are distinctive.

J F M A M J J A S O N D

**Size:** 42–51cm (16–20in).
**Wing:** 183–213mm.
**Bill:** 37–44mm.
**Weight:** 160–268g.
**Voice:** Harsh *chak-chak*.
**Habitat:** Woods, hedgerows, copses, groves, parkland.
**Food:** Insects, seeds, carrion, nestlings and eggs.
**Range:** Resident across most of Eurasia and from Alaska through western North America. In Europe, absent from Iceland, northern Scotland, the highest Scandinavian mountains, tundra

*The Magpie's nest is a well constructed cup of twigs covered by a ragged canopy. The whole appears an untidy mess, like a squirrel's drey.*

Russia, the Alps and several islands in the Mediterranean.
**Movements:** Only local post-breeding dispersal.
**Breeding:** Five to eight olive-spotted bluish eggs are laid in a solid cup of sticks, usually with a stick canopy. The eggs are incubated by the female for 21 or 22 days. The chicks are naked and helpless and fly after 22–28 days.

Closely related and very similar to the Red-billed Chough, this species is more closely confined to the highest mountains. The plumage is entirely black, with red legs and a yellow bill that is noticeably shorter than that of its more widespread relative. It flies high among the tall, windswept crags with great agility.

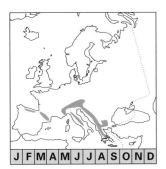

| J | F | M | A | M | J | J | A | S | O | N | D |

**Size:** 38cm (15in).
**Wing:** 251–254mm.
**Bill:** 20–24mm.
**Weight:** 191–250g.
**Voice:** High-pitched whistling *churrish*.

**Habitat:** Gorges, high mountain cliffs and adjacent meadows.
**Food:** Insect and worms.
**Range:** Resident from mountains of Atlas in North Africa to Pyrenees, Alps, Corsica, central Italy, northern Balkans and Greece. Also eastwards from Turkey and the Caucasus to the Himalayas and central Asia.
**Movements:** Some descend to lower altitudes in winter, which may bring birds to areas where they do not breed.
**Breeding:** Three to five brown-speckled whitish eggs are laid in a cup placed in a rock crevice and incubated by the female for 17–21 days. The helpless, downy chicks fly after 23–31 days.
**Confusing Species:** Red-billed Chough has a longer, red (not yellow) bill and is not as confined to high mountains areas.

*The bird flies on rounded wings with separated primaries showing at the wing tip, and is an aerial master.*

## Red-billed Chough *(Pyrrhocorax pyrrhocorax)*

Very similar in structure to Alpine Chough, this species is more widespread and less confined to high mountains. The plumage is black, washed with metallic green, particularly on the breast. The legs and feet are red and the bill, longer than the Alpine's, is red and distinctly decurved. This bird flies aerobatically on rounded wings, well waisted at the body and showing bold 'fingers' at the tips. The broad tail is shorter than the Jackdaw's, which sometimes occupies the same habitats.

*Seen in flight (right), the Red-billed Chough has broader wings and a shorter tail than the Alpine. On the ground (below), the red, decurved bill is obvious.*

**Size:** 35–40cm (14–16in).
**Wing:** 282–315mm.
**Bill:** 48–63mm.
**Weight:** 293–350g.
**Voice:** High-pitched, whistled *kee-arr*.
**Habitat:** Gorges and mountain cliffs, sea coast cliffs and quarries, adjacent meadows.
**Food:** Insects, worms and seeds. Apparently dependent on insects in cow pats for winter food.
**Range:** Resident right across temperate Eurasia, from Ireland and Portugal to Himalayas and northern China. In Europe, has a decidedly south and west distribution and is absent from northern and eastern mountain ranges. Widespread around the Mediterranean.
**Movements:** Resident, with only local movements from high hills to avoid the severest winter conditions.
**Breeding:** Three or four brown-spotted very pale greenish eggs are laid in a cup situated in a hole or crevice in a cliff and are incubated by the female for 17–23 days. The downy, helpless young fly after 31–41 days.
**Confusing Species:** Alpine Chough has short yellow, not red, bill.

| J | F | M | A | M | J | J | A | S | O | N | D |

*Despite the bright yellow and black of the adult male, and the green and white of the female, this bird is more often heard than seen.*

**Size:** 23–25cm (9–10in).
**Wing:** 146–160mm.
**Bill:** 26–30mm.
**Weight:** 51–79g.
**Voice:** Flute-like whistled notes.
**Habitat:** Woodlands and groves, particularly of figs and poplars.
**Food:** Insects, fruit and berries.
**Range:** Summer visitor across Eurasia to Turkey, central Siberia, and southwards to the Himalayas. Winters southern Africa and India. In Europe, widespread from Iberia and France eastwards. Absent from Iceland and almost all of Scandinavia, and is only a recent recolonist of eastern England.

A large, colourful, yellow and black bird, this is a summer visitor across the whole of temperate Europe, and it is surprisingly difficult to see satisfactorily. The male has a bright yellow body with black wings and tail. Both sexes have stout, red bills. These are long-winged birds that fly powerfully, but with a distinctive floppiness that, once familiar, can be picked out at long distance. They are also highly vocal and their presence in an area is often detected by song rather than by sight.

**Movements:** European birds head south or southeast in autumn to cross the Mediterranean and Sahara, with significant concentrations in the Red Sea. Probable migrational divide in the Pyrennean region.
**Breeding:** Three or four black-spotted white eggs are laid in a cup-shaped nest strapped hammock-like in a horizontal fork in a tree. They are incubated mainly by the female for 16 or 17 days and the downy, helpless young fly after a similar period. The species may raise two broods.

R esembling an overgrown Starling, the Nutcracker is wholly confined to extensive conifer forests, where it is highly gregarious but often strangely elusive. The body is dark slaty brown, evenly and boldly spotted white. The cap, wings and tail are black, while the undertail coverts are white. The bill is long and pointed, like that of a Starling.

*In flight, the short tail and broad wings are clearly visible, together with the white undertail coverts and white-edged tail.*

**Size:** 30–33cm (12–13in).
**Wing:** 178–198mm.
**Bill:** 46–55mm.
**Weight:** 100–197g.
**Voice:** A harsh *kror* among flocks.
**Habitat:** Conifer forests, both in the boreal zone and in the mountains and hills to the south.
**Food:** Seeds, berries and nuts.

**Range:** Resident right across Eurasia from southern Belgium and the foothills of the Alps eastwards through the Balkans and the Carpathians, and from southern Scandinavia through the Baltic states and Russia to the Bering Strait, China and the Himalayas.
**Movements:** Usually no more than local wandering through the adjacent forests. Occasionally it erupts south and west, sometimes for 1000km or more, at which times it may be seen in surprising and quite unsuitable habitats.
**Breeding:** Four or five brown-speckled blue eggs are laid in a cup placed in a conifer and are incubated by both sexes for 17–19 days. The downy, helpless young fly after 24 or 25 days.

## Jackdaw *(Corvus monedula)*

Smallest of the typical crows, the Jackdaw is highly gregarious throughout the year. It has learned to live happily alongside man and is a common sight in many European town centres, often around churches. The black plumage is broken by a grey nape, paler in the southeast, where it may appear almost white, and by a startling white eye. It has a shorter bill than other corvids. It often performs aerobatics in gorges and along cliffs, but lacks the mastery of choughs.

*In flight, Jackdaws have rounded wings with slight 'fingering'.*

**Size:** 30–35cm (12–14in).
**Wing:** 220–252mm.
**Bill:** 33–40mm.
**Weight:** 215–256g.
**Voice:** High-pitched and explosive *daw* or *kyee*.
**Habitat:** Extremely varied, from woods, copses and farms to coastal and mountain cliffs and town centres.
**Food:** Omnivorous.
**Range:** Breeds right across Europe to central Siberia. In the west, absent from Iceland and mountain Scandinavia. In northern Russia is only a summer visitor.
**Movements:** Northern and eastern birds move south and west to winter within resident range.
**Breeding:** Four to six brown-spotted blue eggs are laid in a hole in a tree, cliff, building or nestbox and incubated by the female for 17 or 18 days. The helpless, downy chicks fly after 28–32 days.
**Confusing Species:** Alpine and Red-billed Choughs have longer bills and more 'fingering' at the wing tips.

J F M A M J J A S O N D

## Rook *(Corvus frugilegus)*

A locally common bird of agricultural and grassland areas across temperate Europe, the Rook forms large, tree-top nest colonies in many villages and shelter belts. The adult is glossy black, with a thinner bill than the similar Carrion Crow. In bright sunlight the feathers have a silvery sheen.

*The adult (far right and below) has a patch of bare grey skin at the base of the bill. The juvenile (right) lacks the bare patch and has feathers at the base of the bill.*

J F M A M J J A S O N D

**Size:** 43–48cm (17–19in).
**Wing:** 297–335mm.
**Bill:** 55–67mm.
**Weight:** 325–600g.
**Voice:** A cawing *kaah*, repeated among flocks and colonies.
**Habitat:** Grasslands, agricultural land with copses or shelter belts, often around settlements.
**Food:** Worms, insects, seeds.
**Range:** Breeds across Eurasia, from Ireland to northern China and the Sea of Japan. Entire Siberian population is summer visitor. In Europe, patchy distribution in Britain, Ireland, France, Holland and Denmark; local occurrence in central Europe. Common in Danube Basin and from Poland eastwards.
**Movements:** Siberian and Russian populations move southwards within the breeding range.
**Breeding:** Four to six brown-spotted blue eggs are laid in a substantial cup of twigs placed very high in a tree alongside other nests. Colonies, called rookeries, may be used for up to 100 years. The eggs are incubated for 18–20 days by the female and the downy, helpless young fly after 28–35 days.
**Confusing Species:** Carrion Crow is robust; lacks pale patch at base of bill.

## Carrion Crow/Hooded Crow *(Corvus corone)*

Widespread and common, this bird is found throughout Europe and occurs as two distinct subspecies. The Carrion Crow is black; the Hooded Crow has a grey body with black head, breast, wings and tail. Both are robustly built, with heavy heads and bills. They fly somewhat laboriously on slowly flapped wings and usually occur singly or in pairs.

**J F M A M J J A S O N D**

*The Carrion Crow (far left) and the Hooded Crow (left) are subspecies of the European Crow species.*

**Size:** 46–48cm (18–19in).
**Wing:** 303–340mm.
**Bill:** 50–61mm.
**Weight:** 465–655g.
**Voice:** Hard, penetrating *kraa-kraa.*
**Habitat:** Woodland, hedgerows, heaths, farmland, estuaries, towns and cities.
**Food:** Omnivorous.
**Range:** Resident across Eurasia, from Portugal and Ireland to Bering Strait.
**Movements:** Northern populations are migratory, but winter in resident range.
**Breeding:** Four to six brown-speckled bluish eggs, laid in a nest of twigs and mud in a tree, are incubated by the female for 18–20 days. The helpless, downy young fledge after 28–35 days.
**Confusing Species:** Rook has bare grey skin at the base of the bill.

## Raven *(Corvus corax)*

Largest and most powerful of crows, the Raven enjoys a wide distribution, but is now confined to mountain and other wilderness areas. In flight, the long tail is wedge shaped.

*Ravens are solidly built with purple-glossed black plumage and a distinct ragged beard.*

**J F M A M J J A S O N D**

**Size:** 59–69cm (23–27in).
**Wing:** 400–452mm.
**Bill:** 71–83mm.
**Weight:** 980–1383g.
**Voice:** Hollow *pruk pruk,* or *kock-kock.*
**Habitat:** Mountains, moors, sea cliffs.
**Food:** Omnivorous, but carrion often particularly important.

**Range:** Resident right across Eurasia, southwards through the Middle East, to the Himalayas and western China. Also across North America to Greenland, southwards into Central America. In Europe, absent from much of Britain, France and Germany eastwards.
**Movements:** Post-breeding dispersal throughout Europe, but more northerly birds migrate longer distances, perhaps up to 500km (320 miles).
**Breeding:** Four to six brown-speckled greenish eggs are laid in a large cup placed in a tree or on a rocky ledge and incubated by the female for 20 or 21 days. The downy and helpless chicks fly after 35–42 days.
**Confusing Species:** Carrion Crow is smaller, with less massive bill, and lacks wedge-shaped tail.

## Common Starling *(Sturnus vulgaris)*

The Starling is widespread and common, and may be locally abundant. It walks easily with a distinctive swagger and is both gregarious and aggressive. It flies directly on sharply pointed wings and has a short tail. The juvenile is grey-buff, becoming spotted black during the summer.

**Size:** 20–23cm (8–9in).
**Wing:** 123–141mm.
**Bill:** 26–32mm.
**Weight:** 58–108g.
**Voice:** Chattering, wheezing calls.
**Habitat:** Estuaries, marshes, farmland, woods, towns, cities.
**Food:** Omnivorous.
**Range:** Breeds from the Pyrenees to Far-eastern Siberia. Winter visitor to Iberia and most Mediterranean islands.
**Movements:** Birds from Scandinavia eastwards perform migrations to Iberia, North Africa and Western Europe.

*In winter, the adult (left) is spotted buffy. In summer, it is iridescent black, spotted brown above (far left).*

**J F M A M J J A S O N D**

**Breeding:** Five to seven pale blue eggs are laid in a hole in a tree or building and incubated by both sexes for 12–15 days. The helpless, downy chicks fly after 20–22 days. May rear a second brood.
**Confusing Species:** Spotless Starling.

S imilar in size and behaviour to the Common Starling, the Spotless Starling is confined to the western Mediterranean. The bill is yellow and the legs are bright pink.

*During the winter, the plumage takes on faint spotting, while the bill gains a dark tip. In all plumages this bird appears darker than the Common Starling, even at a distance.*

JFMAMJJASOND

**Size:** 18–20cm (7–8in).
**Wing:** 126–138mm.
**Bill:** 27–32mm.
**Weight:** 80–115g.
**Voice:** Wide variety of wheezing calls.
**Habitat:** Towns, cliffs, parkland, groves.
**Food:** Insects, fruit and seeds.
**Range:** Resident Iberia and just into adjacent Mediterranean France; also Corsica, Sardinia, Sicily and parts of western North Africa.
**Movements:** Resident, though some southward post-breeding dispersal. Has expanded range eastwards.
**Breeding:** Four or five pale blue eggs, laid in a hole in a tree or building are incubated by both sexes for 10–15 days. The downy, helpless young fly after 21 or 22 days. A second brood is often reared in the same nest site, but only after a new nest is built.
**Confusing Species:** The Common Starling has more spotting in the plumage and darker pink legs.

*In its summer plumage, this bird is unmistakable, though the occasional biscuity juvenile Starling may cause some confusion.*

A n erratic summer visitor to southeast Europe, the Rose-coloured Starling regularly disperses westwards from its Ukrainian breeding quarters in the late summer and may then reach western Europe in small numbers. The entire body of the adult is pale pink, with a black head and breast, black wings and a black tail. The bill is pinkish and the legs dull reddish. Most aspects of its behaviour and flight are similar to those of the much more numerous Common Starling.

JFMAMJJASOND

**Size:** 20–23cm (8–9in).
**Wing:** 125–139mm.
**Bill:** 22–26mm.
**Weight:** 60–90g.
**Voice:** Variety of wheezing calls.
**Habitat:** Agricultural land and villages.
**Range:** Summer visitor to Bulgaria and Romania eastwards through the Ukraine to south-central Siberia. Winters India and southern Arabia.
**Movements:** Despite a southeasterly axis of migration, large flocks of these colourful starlings head south and west in early summer in apparent eruptive movements that may lead to colonization and breeding. Vagrant westwards as far as Britain.
**Breeding:** Five or six pale blue eggs are laid in an untidy nest in a crevice and incubated by the female for 11–14 days. The naked, helpless chicks fly after about 24 days.
**Confusing Species:** Juvenile similar to juvenile Common Starling.

Widespread, common and familiar, this resident of Europe is found wherever humans live. In parts of the Mediterranean it has cross-bred with the Spanish Sparrow to produce the 'Italian Sparrow'. The male is streaked rich chestnut and black above, with a chestnut nape. The underparts are dirty grey-buff and a grey cap, black eyestripe and bib enclose white cheeks. The female is streaked buff-brown above and plain buff-grey below, with a distinct pale supercilium.

*The 'Italian Sparrow' has a chestnut crown, white cheeks, and a larger black bib.*

**Size:** 13–15cm (5–6in).
**Wing:** 71–85mm.
**Bill:** 14–16mm.
**Weight:** 23–39g.
**Voice:** Clear *chirrup*.
**Habitat:** Cities, towns, villages, farms, hedges, fields.
**Food:** Seeds and insects.
**Range:** Resident across Eurasia from

Ireland to the Sea of Japan, south to India. Introduced North and South America, southern Africa, Australia and New Zealand. In Europe, absent from Iceland, the mountains of Scandinavia, tundra Russia, and Sardinia, where the Spanish Sparrow reigns supreme in glorious isolation.
**Movements:** Largely resident, with a little local wandering in search of food.
**Breeding:** Three to five grey-blotched white eggs are laid in an a nest placed in a hole in a building or high in a bush and are incubated by the female for 11–14 days. The naked, helpless young fly after 12–16 days. Double or treble brooded.
**Confusing Species:** Spanish and Tree Sparrows.

---

## Spanish Sparrow *(Passer hispaniolensis)*

Similar to the House Sparrow, with which it frequently associates and freely interbreeds, the Spanish Sparrow is locally abundant in southern Europe. The male is rich chestnut above, streaked black and buff, with a chestnut crown. The highly distinctive face pattern has a broken, narrow white line above the eye, bright white cheeks, and a black bib that extends to the breast, and to the flanks in streaked chevrons. The remaining underparts are white.

*The female (left) is similar to the female House Sparrow, but is paler greyish buff in colour with a prominent supercilium, yellowish bill, pale buffy 'braces' and lightly streaked flanks.*

**Size:** 13–15cm (5–6in).
**Wing:** 73–84mm.
**Bill:** 14–16mm.
**Weight:** 23–36g.
**Voice:** Variety of *chirrups*.
**Habitat:** Tendency to frequent more open countryside, including scrub-covered hillsides and fields, than House Sparrow, but also joins mixed colonies in buildings with nearby scrub and fields.
**Food:** Seeds and insects.
**Range:** Breeds from the Mediterranean eastwards through the Middle East to beyond the Aral Sea. Resident in the west, summer visitor further east.
**Movements:** Resident or partial migrant Iberia and Sardinia. Birds from the Balkans and Turkey winter across North Africa. Siberian birds winter in Pakistan and northern India. Makes lengthy sea crossings.
**Breeding:** Five or six greyish-blotched eggs are laid in a scrappy dome placed in a tree, tree hole, or a hole in a building or in the nest of a White Stork. They are incubated for 11–14 days by both sexes and the helpless, downy young fly after 11–15 days. It raises two or three broods in a season
**Confusing Species:** House Sparrow has grey crown and lacks flank chevrons.

## Tree Sparrow *(Passer montanus)*

**B**oth sexes of this bird are similar, with the upperparts streaked chestnut and black, and a brown crown. A small black bib encloses the white cheeks.

The best field mark, however, is the incomplete white neck ring. Confined to rural areas in Europe, in Asia it is a common town sparrow.

*Though similar to a male House Sparrow, the Tree Sparrow can be identified by the head markings. It has a chocolate-brown crown and bold black patch on white cheeks.*

J F M A M J J A S O N D

**Size:** 13–15cm (5–6in).
**Wing:** 66–74mm.
**Bill:** 12–14mm.
**Weight:** 17–29g.
**Voice:** Distinctive *cheep*.
**Habitat:** Belts of old trees, hedgerows, parkland, groves.
**Food:** Insects and seeds.
**Range:** Breeds right across Eurasia from Iberia and Britain as far north as the Kola Peninsula, eastwards to Japan and southwards through China to Southeast Asia. Birds from northern Russia and Siberia are only summer visitors. In Ireland it is present only as a highly localized species and in small numbers.
**Movements:** European birds are resident, or undertake only short-distance movements, though some do apparently cross the North Sea.
**Breeding:** Four to six brown-blotched, grey eggs are laid in a tree hole, rock crevice or nest box and are incubated by both sexes for 15–20 days. The helpless, naked young fledge after 12–14 days. Double or triple brooded.
**Confusing Species:** House Sparrow and especially the 'Italian Sparrow' type.

## Rock Sparrow *(Petronia petronia)*

**A** highly localized resident of the Mediterranean region, the Rock Sparrow resembles a female House Sparrow, but can be easily distinguished with good views. It is paler and sandier than the House Sparrow, with streaked upperparts, a large pale bill, and a distinctly striped head pattern with a pale crown stripe and an inconspicuous yellow throat patch. The underparts are creamy, with light flank streaking. The tail shows a row of pale spots near the tip that are obvious in flight.

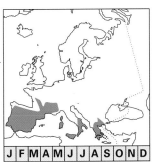

J F M A M J J A S O N D

*Male and female are similar, but the juvenile is generally paler and lacks the distinctive yellow throat spot.*

**Size:** 13–15cm (5–6in).
**Wing:** 91–103mm.
**Bill:** 15–19mm.
**Weight:** 26–39g.
**Voice:** A sharp *tut* and a plaintive *chwee*.
**Habitat:** Groves, hillsides, hill villages.
**Food:** Seeds and insects.
**Range:** Resident throughout the Mediterranean, though seldom common, eastwards through Turkey and the Middle East to central Asia. In Europe, resident Iberia, southern France, Italy,

Greece and Bulgaria and on western Mediterranean islands.
**Movements:** Post-breeding dispersal, but European birds make no long migrational journeys.
**Breeding:** Five or six brown-blotched white eggs are laid in a domed nest placed in a rock crevice and incubated for 11–14 days by the female, probably alone. The naked, helpless young fly after 16–21 days. Double brooded.
**Confusing Species:** Female House and Spanish Sparrows.

263

This may be a resident, summer visitor or winter visitor, depending on area. It is a familiar garden bird in many parts. The male has a grey crown, brown back, black wings marked with a bold, double white wingbar, and pink underparts. In flight, both sexes show white outertail feathers.

J F M A M J J A S O N D

*The female (left) lacks the bright colours of the male (right). It is brown and buff with whitish wingbars and a plain face.*

**Size:** 15cm (6in).
**Wing:** 81–95mm.
**Bill:** 14–16mm.
**Weight:** 19–28g.
**Voice:** Distinctive *pink*, but with local variations; song a pleasant warble ending in a flourish.
**Habitat:** Woodland margins, hedgerows, orchards and groves, often in gardens.
**Food:** Seeds and fruit.
**Range:** Resident right across Europe, but a summer visitor to Scandinavia and Russia, and beyond to the central boreal zone of Siberia.
**Movements:** Huge westerly and southwesterly movements of Russian and Scandinavian birds to Britain, France, Iberia and other more maritime regions of Europe.
**Breeding:** Four or five purple-scrawled bluish eggs are laid in a neat cup-shaped nest placed low in a bush. The eggs are incubated by the female for 11–13 days. The helpless, down-covered chicks fledge after 12–15 days. One or two broods are raised each year.

A well-marked relative of the Chaffinch, this is a summer visitor to Scandinavia and Russia and a winter visitor across much of temperate Europe. The male in summer is black above, with an orange breast and broad orange markings across the wings. In winter, the male closely resembles the summer female, with a scaly black and brown back and head, but still with more orange in the wings. The underparts are white, boldly spotted black on the flanks. In all plumages, it shows a white rump in flight. Bramblings feed in flocks on the woodland floor and among fields in winter.

**Size:** 13–15cm (5–6in).
**Wing:** 84–97mm.
**Bill:** 15–17mm.
**Weight:** 17–35g.
**Voice:** Harsh *swik* call; song a Greenfinch-like *dwee*.
**Habitat:** Birch and conifer woods in the boreal zone. In winter, it frequents woods, fields and hedgerows.
**Food:** Berries and seeds, particularly beechmast in winter.
**Range:** Breeds right across northern Eurasia, from Scandinavia to Kamchatka. Winters Japan, China, the Middle East and across most of Europe.
**Movements:** Large movements southwest across Europe from Scandinavia, where some birds winter in the south, and Russia as far as Spain, Portugal and Greece.

J F M A M J J A S O N D

**Breeding:** Five to seven reddish-blotched blue eggs are laid in a neat cup, usually placed in a pine near the trunk, and are incubated by the female for 11 or 12 days. The helpless, downy chicks fledge after 11–13 days.

*The female (far left) has a brown cap and orange cheeks, and a back that is buff with black scaling. It is, therefore, quite distinct from the summer male (left).*

**Size:** 10–13cm (4–5in).
**Wing:** 66–78mm.
**Bill:** 10–11mm.
**Weight:** 8–14g.
**Voice:** A musical twittering.
**Habitat:** Orchards, groves, farms, gardens.
**Food:** Seeds.
**Range:** Breeds across most of Mediterranean and temperate Europe from Portugal to western Russia and Ukraine. Birds from Holland and the Balkans eastwards are only summer visitors. It is a scarce colonizer in Denmark and southern areas of England.
**Movements:** Eastern birds move south and west to winter within other parts of the breeding range, but such movements are easily overlooked.
**Breeding:** Four brown-spotted pale blue eggs are laid in a neat cup-shaped nest placed in a bush. The eggs are incubated by the female for 13 days. The helpless, down-covered chicks fly after 13–18 days. Usually two broods are raised each year.

*The male (below), is more yellow than the female, and performs a territorial song flight.*

The European equivalent of the Canary, this native of the Mediterranean has spread northwards during the past 50 years. It is a compact little finch, with a rounded head and a stubby face. The male is heavily streaked brown on green above, with a yellow head and yellow rump. The head has a brown wash over the crown and ear coverts. The breast is yellow, and the underparts white, broadly streaked black. The female has much less yellow.

This European native is virtually confined to the high mountain ranges of Western Europe. The birds of the Corsican uplands descend to lower levels during the winter, while birds elsewhere remain at altitude all year round. The male is green above and has black and yellow wings with a double wingbar, a yellow rump and a grey crown and nape. The crown and nape are diagnostic. The female is duller, with less yellow over the face and breast. They are generally gregarious.

*The female (right) is considerably duller and less yellow than the male, especially around the face and chest, though retaining the yellow rump.*

**Size:** 13cm (5in).
**Wing:** 75–83mm.
**Bill:** 11–12mm.
**Weight:** 12–14g.
**Voice:** A sweet jingling song.
**Habitat:** Largely resident at the upper limits of the conifer tree level in mountain areas of southern Europe, particularly areas with scattered dwarf pines. In Corsica, may be found almost to sea level in open country with isolated stands of pine.
**Food:** Seeds.
**Range:** Breeds in mountains of north and central Spain, in the Massif Central and Alps of France into Switzerland and Austria, northwards to the Jura. Also in Corsica and Sardinia.
**Breeding:** Four or five red-spotted blue eggs are laid in a cup-shaped nest placed in a tree. The eggs are incubated by the female for 13 or 14 days. The helpless and down-covered young fledge after 15–18 days. The species usually produces two broods.
**Confusing Species:** Be aware of the similar European Serin.

265

# Greenfinch *(Carduelis chloris)*

Widespread, common and familiar, this garden or woodland bird is found in most of Europe, except the far north. The male is olive-green above, with bold yellow margins to the flight feathers that create a colourful wing panel. The underparts are yellowish. There is a dark area around the eye, and the bill is pale ivory. The female is broadly similar. The yellow in the wing identifies this species in all plumages.

**Size:** 13–15cm (5–6in).
**Wing:** 81–92mm.
**Bill:** 9–11mm.
**Weight:** 20–38g.
**Voice:** A nasal *skaar*, a jangling twitter in song flight.
**Habitat:** Gardens, orchards, groves, woodland margins, scrubby heaths, hedgerows and farmland.
**Food:** Seeds, berries.
**Range:** Breeds throughout Europe save for Iceland, northern and mountain Scandinavia and northern shores of the Black Sea. Largely resident, but birds of Sweden, Finland and Russia are summer visitors.
**Movements:** Most Greenfinches migrate some distance, but only within the species' breeding range. Many birds move to the milder coasts of southern and western Europe.
**Breeding:** Four to six black-spotted blue eggs are laid in a cup placed in a bush and incubated by the female for 12–14 days. The helpless, downy young fly after 14–18 days. Two or three broods are raised each year.
**Confusing Species:** No other green finch is so large.

At first sight very similar to the male, the female is browner with faint streaking on the flanks.

# European Goldfinch *(Carduelis carduelis)*

A dainty, colourful little finch, the Goldfinch utters a tinkling call and song, and feeds largely on thistle seeds. The adult has a fawny brown back with black wings heavily marked by bright yellow. The head is vertically banded in crimson, white and black. The juvenile has a plain face, but retains the yellow in the wing. Generally gregarious, this bird forms single species flocks, called 'charms', outside the breeding season.

*The male has crimson face markings that extend behind the eye, while those of the female end at the eye.*

**Size:** 13cm (5in).
**Wing:** 75–84mm.
**Bill:** 14–17mm.
**Weight:** 11–20g.
**Voice:** A pleasant tinkling call and song.
**Habitat:** Heaths, woodland margins, groves, orchards and gardens where thistles predominate.
**Food:** Seeds.

**Range:** Resident across southern and temperate Europe to Siberia beyond the Urals. Absent from Iceland, northern Scotland and most of Scandinavia. Birds from Finland and northern Russia are migrants.
**Movements:** Much winter wandering, but also definite migrations south and west within the breeding range. Most British birds move to continental Europe. Probably resident in the Mediterranean.
**Breeding:** Four to seven black-speckled blue eggs are laid in a delicate little cup placed near the outside of a shrub and are incubated by the female for 12–14 days. The helpless, downy chicks fledge after 13–16 days. It produces two broods each season.

## Siskin *(Carduelis spinus)*

The male is green above, heavily streaked black, with white underparts, streaked black on the flanks. The black cap and black bib are diagnostic.

*The female Siskin is similar to the male Siskin, but lacks the bib and has a mottled crown.*

**Size:** 13cm (5in).
**Wing:** 69–76mm.
**Bill:** 12–14mm.
**Weight:** 10–18g.
**Voice:** A nasal *tsu tsu-weet.*
**Habitat:** Forests of spruce and fir in summer. In winter, frequents alders.
**Food:** Seeds.
**Range:** Breeds from Scotland eastwards across Scandinavia and Russia to Japan. Elsewhere in Europe breeds in the Pyrenees and mountains of northern Spain, France, the Carpathians and southern Germany and Balkans.
**Movements:** Southerly and westerly migrations in winter bring Siskins to all of Europe.

J F M A M J J A S O N D

**Breeding:** Three to five red-spotted bluish eggs are laid in a cup placed high in a conifer and incubated for 11–14 days by the female. The helpless, down-covered young fly after 13–15 days.
**Confusing Species:** Greenfinch.

## Linnet *(Carduelis cannabina)*

This is a versatile finch that frequents a variety of open habitats. The male has a brown, unstreaked back, with a reddish crown and breast. The wings and tail are black, the latter with white outer feathers.

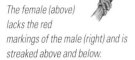

*The female (above) lacks the red markings of the male (right) and is streaked above and below.*

**Size:** 13–15cm (5–6in).
**Wing:** 76–85mm.
**Bill:** 12–14mm.
**Weight:** 12–24g.
**Voice:** A high-pitched twittering.
**Habitat:** Heaths, wasteland, hedgerows, groves, estuaries.
**Food:** Seeds.
**Range:** Breeds across Europe, but absent Iceland, northern Scotland, much of Scandinavia and northern Russia. Summer visitor to Scandinavia and from Poland eastwards to central Ukraine.
**Movements:** Migrates south and west within breeding range, with birds from eastern parts of range making lengthy journeys. Common in winter along western shorelines.
**Breeding:** Four to six red-speckled blue

J F M A M J J A S O N D

eggs are laid in a cup placed in a bush and incubated for 10–14 days by the female alone. The downy, helpless chicks fly after 14–17 days. Two or three broods are produced each year.
**Confusing Species:** Twite.

## Twite *(Carduelis flavirostris)*

*In its winter plumage (right) the Twite is slightly paler than in summer (above) and less heavily streaked, and the bill becomes pale yellow rather than greyish.*

This linnet-like bird replaces that species in the north and among southern mountains. It is a heavily streaked finch marked only by a pink rump. The upperparts are strongly streaked brown and buff, and the underparts black on white.

**Size:** 13–15cm (5–6in).
**Wing:** 73–80mm.
**Bill:** 11–12mm.
**Weight:** 12–19g.
**Voice:** Linnet-like twittering that is subtly harder in tone.
**Habitat:** Northern moors and hillsides; winters on coasts and other scantily vegetated landscapes.
**Food:** Seeds.
**Range:** In Europe, breeds mountains of western Ireland, Scotland, northern England and Norway. Also from eastern Turkey across southern Siberia to the Asian plateaux. Winters around the Baltic and North Seas.
**Movements:** Scottish birds may be resident, but Norwegian birds migrate to southern Sweden, Germany, Poland and Holland and the English east coast.

**Breeding:** Five or six red-spotted blue eggs are laid in a cup on the ground and are incubated by the female for 12 or 13 days. The helpless, downy chicks fly at 11 or 12 days. Usually raises two broods.
**Confusing Species:** Linnet, especially in ground-feeding, mixed winter flocks.

J F M A M J J A S O N D

# Common Redpoll *(Carduelis flammea)*

Small and heavily streaked, this finch could easily be confused with the Twite except that it is totally arboreal in its habits. The upperparts are streaked brown and black, the underparts streaked brown on white. The male has red on the crown, a tiny black bib and a rosy wash on the breast. It feeds in a tit-like manner among trees, particularly birches in winter.

*The female (below) has the distinctive red forehead, but lacks the other reddish markings of the male (left).*

J F M A M J J A S O N D

**Size:** 13cm (5in).
**Wing:** 71–78mm.
**Bill:** 11–13mm.
**Weight:** 10–18g.
**Voice:** A distinctly nasal buzzing trill in flight.
**Habitat:** Heaths and woods with conifers and birches.
**Food:** Seeds.
**Range:** Northern circumpolar in the boreal zone. In Europe, breeds Iceland, Britain and Ireland and from Scandinavia eastwards across northern Russia. Also locally across Central Europe. Winters throughout temperate Europe, reaching the Mediterranean only in southern France and Slovenia.
**Movements:** Though resident over much of their range, Redpolls perform lengthy migrations that take them thousands of kilometres to south and west. Tendency to eruptive movements from time to time.
**Breeding:** Four or five reddish-speckled blue eggs are laid in a cup-shaped nest and incubated by the female for 10–13 days. The helpless, downy chicks fly after 11–14 days. Sometimes rears a second brood.
**Confusing Species:** None of similar habits and habitat.

# Arctic Redpoll *(Carduelis hornemanni)*

The high-Arctic equivalent of the Common Redpoll, this bird replaces that species in the taiga and tundra zones. It is similar in plumage, but much paler, with brown streaking on a whitish buff background. It shows a red crown and small black bib, but no more than a rosy wash over the breast. The so-called Mealy Redpoll, a subspecies of the Common Redpoll, is intermediate in colour and may cause confusion.

*The diagnostic feature of the Arctic Redpoll (left), that distinguishes it from the Common Redpoll (far left), is the white rump, which is most visible in flight.*

J F M A M J J A S O N D

**Food:** Seeds.
**Range:** Resident north circumpolar. In Europe, confined to northernmost Scandinavia and Russia.
**Movements:** Regular movements southward to the boreal zone, reaching the southern Baltic. Occasional eruptions may take birds to more temperate zones, but this is far more exceptional than with other northern breeding passerines.
**Breeding:** Three or four red-spotted blue eggs, laid in a cup in a dwarf bush or tree, or on the ground, are incubated for 11 or 12 days by the female. The downy, helpless young fly after 10–12 days. May produce two broods.
**Confusing Species:** Common Redpoll.

**Size:** 13cm (5in).
**Wing:** 70–80mm.
**Bill:** 11–12mm.
**Weight:** 10–15g.
**Voice:** Rasping, nasal buzzing like Common Redpoll.
**Habitat:** Dwarf conifers among open tundra landscapes.

## Common Crossbill *(Loxia curvirostra)*

*The crossbills are identified by bill shape and size. Below: Parrot Crossbill (top), Scottish Crossbill (centre) and Common Crossbill.*

Substantial and chunky, this finch is confined to conifer forests. The male is red with black wings and tail. The female is olive-green with a paler, almost yellow-green rump. Both are easily overlooked among cone-laden conifers. The thickset appearance in flight and large, silvery bill are helpful identification features.

**Size:** 15–18cm (6–7in).
**Wing:** 94–102mm.
**Bill:** 21–25mm.
**Weight:** 31–49g.
**Voice:** Distinctive *chup.*
**Habitat:** Conifer forests, particularly of spruce, but also, in places, pines.
**Food:** Conifer seeds.
**Range:** Circumpolar in the north. In Europe, breeds among hills of Spain, France, the Alps, Germany, the Carpathians, Balkans and right across the boreal zones of Russia and Scandinavia; also locally in Britain and elsewhere in temperate lowland Europe, where commercial conifer plantations have been allowed to mature.
**Movements:** Local movements within forests are regular, but large-scale eruptions take place every few years, bringing birds to conifer forests where they do not breed.
**Breeding:** Three or four purplish-spotted bluish eggs are laid in a cup placed high in a conifer and incubated by the female for 13–16 days. The downy, helpless young fly after 17–22 days.
**Confusing Species:** Scottish and Parrot Crossbills must be distinguished with great care.

J F M A M J J A S O N D

## Scottish Crossbill *(Loxia scotica)*

The only bird species unique to Britain is found in the Old Caledonian forests of Scots pine in the Highlands. The male is red with black wing markings, and the female green. Easily confused with the Common Crossbill, which now breeds in Scotland, the Scottish can be distinguished from it only by its larger silver bill. Any crossbills feeding on Scots pines in the Highlands are likely to be this species.

J F M A M J J A S O N D

*The female (below and foreground far left) has green plumage, whereas the male (background, far left) has red.*

**Size:** 15–18cm (6–7in).
**Wing:** 92–105mm.
**Bill:** 21–25mm.
**Weight:** 39–49g.
**Voice:** Clear *chup.*
**Habitat:** Forests of Scots pine.
**Food:** Pine seeds.
**Range:** Scottish Highlands.
**Movements:** Resident.
**Breeding:** Three or four purple-spotted bluish eggs are laid in a cup high in a pine tree and are incubated by the female for 13–16 days. The helpless, downy chicks fly after 17–22 days.
**Confusing Species:** Common Crossbill and Parrot Crossbill.

## Parrot Crossbill *(Loxia pytyopsittacus)*

Although similar to the Common Crossbill, this species is larger and has a much heavier bill. Basically the male is red, and the female green. The parrot-like bill has parallel upper and lower mandibles that emerge from the flat head to give the impression of a complete lack of forehead. The cutting edges of both mandibles are pale ivory. Its heavy bill can tackle pine cones, but this bird also feeds on other conifers.

J F M A M J J A S O N D

**Size:** 15–18cm (6–7in).
**Wing:** 102–109mm.
**Bill:** 23–26mm.
**Weight:** 44–69g.
**Voice:** *Jup-jup.*
**Habitat:** Pines, as well as other coniferous trees in the boreal zone.
**Food:** Pine and other seeds.
**Range:** Breeds in the boreal zone of Europe, just creeping eastwards into the Urals. Winters within the breeding range. In Europe, breeds Scandinavia, Baltic States and Russia, but absent from much of Norway.
**Movements:** Some movements within forests in winter, but regularly erupts southwards, usually coinciding with eruptions of other crossbills. It may reach the Low Countries and Britain.
**Breeding:** Three or four purple-spotted bluish eggs are laid in a cup in a conifer and incubated for 14–16 days by the female. The downy, helpless young fly after 21–23 days.
**Confusing Species:** Common Crossbill is smaller.

*While the male (far left) is red and black, the female (left) is green and black with a yellow rump.*

## Two-barred Crossbill *(Loxia leucoptera)*

A close relative of the other crossbill species, the Two-barred Crossbill can be easily distinguished by its white wing markings. The male is red, like other crossbills, but it has two white bars across the wings and white tips to the tertials. The bill is crossed but is much thinner than that of any other crossbill. The female is green but has similar white markings on the wings and a thin bill.

J F M A M J J A S O N D

**Food:** Larch and spruce seeds.
**Range:** Circumpolar in northern boreal zone. In Europe, breeds across northern Russia from the Finnish border. Resident throughout its range.
**Movements:** Erratic, with up to 500 pairs in Finland in a good season, but often far fewer. Erupts south and west and may reach temperate Europe, though usually in small numbers.
**Breeding:** Three or four purple-spotted bluish eggs are laid in a cup placed high in a conifer and incubated for 14 or 15 days by the female. The downy, helpless chicks fly after 22–24 days.
**Confusing Species:** No other crossbills have white in the wing, but beware Pine Grosbeak which does.

*Like other crossbills, the male (above) is red, while the female (left) is green, but this species can be distinguished by a thin bill and white wingbars.*

**Size:** 13–15cm (5–6in).
**Wing:** 87–96mm.
**Bill:** 13–16mm.
**Weight:** 27–40g.
**Voice:** A clear *jip.*
**Habitat:** Conifer forests in the boreal zone, particularly of larch.

## Snow Finch *(Montifringilla nivalis)*

Living among the high mountains, this species has the unique distinction of being seen far more often by non-birdwatchers than by birders because it inhabits ski slopes and resorts in winter. In summer, it has a brown back and grey head, with black and white wings and tail. The underparts are pale and there is a small black bib beneath the conical black bill. In flight, the bird shows a huge amount of white in the wing and tail.

*In summer plumage (left) the bird has a small black bib and a grey beak, while in winter (above) the bill is yellow.*

J F M A M J J A S O N D

**Size:** 18cm (7in).
**Wing:** 113–127mm.
**Bill:** 16–18mm.
**Weight:** 35–45g.
**Voice:** A repeated *sitti-char*.
**Habitat:** Rocky slopes and screes in high mountains.
**Food:** Insects and seeds.
**Range:** Resident in highest mountains of Europe eastwards to the Asian plateaux. In Europe, breeds in northern Spain and the Pyrenees, the Alps, Italy and Corsica, Albania, Croatia, Serbia and Greece.
**Movements:** Some altitudinal movements, particularly in the east of the range, but most western birds do no more than drop down to the nearest ski resort, whether fashionable or not.
**Breeding:** Four or five white eggs are laid in a cup-shaped nest placed in a rock crevice and incubated by both sexes for 13 or 14 days. The helpless young fly after 20 or 21 days. This species will sometimes abandon incubation altogether if the temperature drops significantly.
**Confusing Species:** Snow Bunting has large amounts of white in the wing, but cannot otherwise be confused and the ranges do not overlap.

## Bullfinch *(Pyrrhula pyrrhula)*

**Size:** 13cm (5–6in).
**Wing:** 87–97mm.
**Bill:** 15–16mm.
**Weight:** 18–40g.
**Voice:** A soft *heu*.
**Habitat:** Deciduous and mixed forests, woodland margins, gardens, orchards.
**Food:** Seeds, particularly of ash, and buds.
**Range:** Breeds right across Eurasia from Ireland to Japan and Korea and southwards to Turkey. Mostly winters within breeding range. In southern Europe, confined to mountains, but is more widespread from France north as far as northern Scandinavia.
**Movements:** Mostly resident, but some local movements within the breeding range and some descent and wandering to lower altitudes in the south of the range.
**Breeding:** Four or five purple-speckled blue eggs are laid on a platform of twigs well hidden in a bush. The eggs are incubated by the female for 12–14 days. The helpless, down-covered young fly after 12–18 days. Sometimes rears a second brood.

J F M A M J J A S O N D

Chunky and thickset, this finch is invariably seen singly or in a pair. The male is bright pink below and grey above, marked by a black cap that extends to below the eye. The wings are black with a broad white bar; the tail black with a neat, square-cut white rump. The bill is black, thick and powerful.

*The female (above right and below) is duller than the male (above left) with a buffy chest and neck.*

Increasing in number and spreading northwards and westwards across Europe, this is a well-marked finch in the male, although the female is remarkably featureless and is easily overlooked as a result. The male is streaked brown above, with a double pink-washed wingbar. The head is bright red, extending to the breast, and the rump is also red. The underparts are white. The bill is silvery in both sexes. Juveniles are rather similar to females and, like the females, are best distinguished from sparrows by the double wingbar, featureless face and black eyes.

*The female (right) lacks all the red markings of the male (left) and is brown above, with a faint double white wingbar and a featureless face that, surprisingly, helps to distinguish it from similar-looking sparrows.*

J F M A M J J A S O N D

**Size:** 13–15cm (5–6in).
**Wing:** 80–88mm.
**Bill:** 13–15mm.
**Weight:** 17–30g.
**Voice:** A quiet *tu-ick*.
**Habitat:** Meadows with trees, fields and marshes.
**Food:** Seeds.
**Range:** Breeds from eastern Germany right across Eurasia to Kamchatka, extending southwards to Turkey, the Middle East, China and the Himalayas. In Europe, has spread westwards to Hungary and Slovenia in the south and to Denmark and Norway farther north.
**Movements:** Migrates to India and China in the winter, a movement which involves European birds heading southeast for several thousand kilometres. Inevitably, some individuals wander westwards, where they can be observed as rare vagrants.
**Breeding:** Five or six purple-black speckled, pale blue eggs are laid in a cup-shaped nest, which is built low in a bush or small tree. The eggs are incubated for 12–14 days by the female alone. The young fly after about 10–13 days.

J F M A M J J A S O N D

Large and chunky, this thickset finch is similar to a crossbill, but with a longer tail. It is confined to boreal forests, but frequently resorts to villages and towns in winter. The male is washed pink on head, breast and rump, with black wings marked by a double white bar. Although they do not undertake regular migrations, birds do move southwards in winter and may erupt from time to time.

**Size:** 20–23cm (8–9in).
**Wing:** 106–113mm.
**Bill:** 20–22mm.
**Weight:** 47–64g.
**Voice:** A whistled song and a high-pitched *tee-tee-tu*.
**Habitat:** Boreal forests but also thickets of birch, alder and juniper. In winter, often resorts to gardens where berries are abundant.
**Food:** Berries of a wide variety of species; buds, shoots and seeds.
**Range:** Northern circumpolar. In Europe, breeds in mountains of Scandinavia,

across Lapland and into boreal Russia.
**Movements:** Generally local, descending from mountains, but also moving southwards to areas beyond its breeding range.
**Breeding:** Three to five black-spotted pale blue eggs, laid on a platform of twigs placed in a tree, are incubated by the female for 13 or 14 days. The young fly after 13–18 days.

*The female (above) is just as distinctively marked as the male (above left), but she is a dirty orange where the male is pink.*

## Hawfinch (*Coccothraustes coccothraustes*)

Large, well built and short-tailed, this finch is essentially arboreal and highly elusive. Both sexes are brown above and pinkish brown below, with a broad white wingbar and a white-tipped tail. In flight, the short tail and large head create a no-necked chunky appearance, and the white wingbar shows well. Birds may form large winter flocks.

**Size:** 15–18cm (6–7in).
**Wing:** 110–118mm.
**Bill:** 21–25mm.
**Weight:** 52–78g.
**Voice:** A high-pitched *tic*, rather like that of a Robin.

**Habitat:** Woods, parks and gardens.
**Food:** Seeds, nuts and especially hard seeds that other species cannot crack.
**Range:** Breeds right across Eurasia, from Britain and Portugal eastwards to Japan. Winters over much of Europe and in Japan and northern China.
**Movements:** Russian birds head westwards to winter in Europe, while western birds make limited migrations. Localized winter concentrations may consist of hundreds of individuals.
**Breeding:** Three to five black-spotted blue eggs are laid in a cup of twigs placed in a tree or shrub and are incubated for 9–14 days by the female, with help from the male. The helpless, downy young fly after 10–14 days.

*Outstanding features are the large head and massive silvery bill. The powerful bill is used to crack open the toughest of seeds, even including cherry stones, to get at the nutritious kernel.*

J F M A M J J A S O N D

## Lapland Bunting (*Calcarius lapponicus*)

A tundra-breeding bunting, this bird migrates southwards to winter in more temperate, but far from warm, climates. In all plumages, the upperparts are a rich chestnut, boldly streaked black and buff, with buffy underparts heavily spotted in streaks on breast and flanks. The well-marked ear coverts, pale crown stripe and chestnut nape are the clearest identification features. The male in summer is distinguished by a black head and breast, broken by a bold white supercilium.

*The black markings of the summer male (right) are distinctive, but the female (above) and winter male are similar to other buntings.*

**Size:** 13–15cm (5–6in).
**Wing:** 85–99mm.
**Bill:** 11–15mm.
**Weight:** 19–20g.
**Voice:** A rolling *rrrp*.
**Habitat:** Rocky tundra in summer; winters steppes, plough, coastal marshes.
**Food:** Seeds.
**Range:** Northern circumpolar, from Scandinavia to the Bering Strait, Canada and Greenland. Winters south of the breeding range in the steppe zone of Ukraine and Siberia.
**Movements:** Birds from Scandinavia and Greenland move to the steppes of Ukraine and southern Russia, but also regularly to Denmark, Holland and eastern England. They are regular on passage in northwest Scotland.
**Breeding:** Five or six reddish-spotted green eggs are laid in a cup hidden on the ground and incubated by the female for 11–13 days. The helpless, downy young fledge after 11–15 days.
**Confusing Species:** Reed Bunting is very similar, but always has a dark, not yellow, bill.

J F M A M J J A S O N D

273

## Snow Bunting *(Plectrophenax nivalis)*

A chunky, little bunting, this bird breeds among the Arctic tundra as far north as ice-free land exists, and is a winter visitor to temperate Europe. In all plumages, the extent of white in the wing in flight is a good field mark. The summer male has a white head and body contrasting with black wings and tail. The female and juveniles are warm buff, with white underparts and black and white wings and tail. The birds are gregarious and feed in flocks, low on the ground.

*In flight, flocks of Snow Buntings tend to look like pieces of paper blown in the wind.*

**Size:** 15–18cm (6–7in).
**Wing:** 100–118mm.
**Bill:** 12–16mm.
**Weight:** 28–53g.
**Voice:** A loud *tsweep.*
**Habitat:** Open tundra with rocky slopes; winters steppes and shingle coasts.
**Range:** Northern circumpolar. In Europe, is resident Iceland, summer visitor to mountains of Scandinavia eastwards across high Russian tundra. Small isolated population Scottish Highlands. Winters Scotland, shores of North Sea, Denmark, southern Sweden, eastern Germany eastwards across Ukraine.
**Movements:** The origins of European wintering birds remains unknown, but there is some movement out of Iceland to Britain and southwards through Scandinavia to the southern North Sea.
**Breeding:** Four to six red-spotted bluish eggs are laid in a cup hidden among rocks and incubated by the female for 10–15 days. The helpless, downy young fly after 15–20 days. In a few areas it may raise two broods.

---

## Yellowhammer *(Emberiza citrinella)*

A widespread resident of heaths and farmland across most of Europe, the Yellowhammer has a song that is well known to the country dweller. The male is rusty, streaked black above with a rusty rump and a long tail. The head is boldly yellow with scanty black markings and the yellow underparts are streaked chestnut on breast and flanks.

*The female (above) has less yellow than the male (left), but more than the similar female Cirl Bunting.*

**Size:** 15–18cm (6–7in).
**Wing:** 79–96mm.
**Bill:** 12–16mm.
**Weight:** 81–97g.
**Voice:** Song a jingling *'little bit of bread and no cheese'*, with the accent on the rasping flourish.
**Habitat:** Heaths, groves, orchards, hedgerows.
**Food:** Seeds and berries.
**Range:** Breeds right across Europe to central Siberia. In Europe, absent from Mediterranean coasts and islands, as well as most of Iberia and from the harshest parts of northern Scandinavia.
**Movements:** Northernmost birds are only summer visitors, but many long-distance movements are hidden within the broad breeding range. Mostly a partial migrant.
**Breeding:** Three to five purple-spotted white eggs are laid in a cup low in a bush and are incubated by the female for 11–14 days. The helpless, downy chicks fly after 16 days. It raises two or three broods each year.
**Confusing Species:** Cirl Bunting has a more clear-cut face pattern and is less yellow.

274

## Cirl Bunting *(Emberiza cirlus)*

A well-marked bunting that is found across southern Europe. The male is rusty backed, with yellowish underparts, and has a clear black and yellow face pattern with a greenish crown and black bib. The facial markings are bolder than those of the male Yellowhammer and the rump is greyish, rather than a bold chestnut colour.

*The female (right) is similar to the male (below right), but with less yellow and less distinct facial markings.*

**Size:** 15–18cm (6–7in).
**Wing:** 74–86mm.
**Bill:** 13–15mm.
**Weight:** 20–29g.
**Voice:** Song like Yellowhammer's, but lacks the final flourish. Can be confused with rattle of Lesser Whitethroat.
**Habitat:** Hedgerows, orchards, groves.
**Food:** Seeds and berries.
**Range:** Resident Iberia, France, Italy, western Balkans, Greece, Bulgaria and northern and western Turkey, with smaller populations in the Alps and in Devon, England.
**Movements:** Some movements southwards away from more severe winters, but basically resident.
**Breeding:** Three or four brown-speckled white eggs are laid in a cup in a bush and incubated by the female for 11–13 days. The downy, helpless young fly after a similar time. It raises two or three broods each season.
**Confusing Species:** Yellowhammer.

JFMAMJJASOND

## Rock Bunting *(Emberiza cia)*

A hill and mountain bunting often associated with conifer forests, this bird is resident in the Mediterranean and is one of the easiest of all buntings to identify. The male has an orange-buff body, heavily streaked black above, with a greyish white head well marked with black lines, especially on the crown. The rather long tail is black, edged with white.

*The female (right) is very similar to the male (below right) but has less-distinct facial markings, with the eyestripe being speckled rather than solid.*

**Size:** 15cm (6in).
**Wing:** 72–87mm.
**Bill:** 11–15mm.
**Weight:** 20–29g.
**Voice:** A *zi-zi-zi.*
**Habitat:** Rocky slopes and undercliffs with large rocks, screes and hillsides, open conifer forests.
**Food:** Seeds and berries.
**Range:** Resident throughout the Mediterranean to Turkey and the adjacent Middle East, to the central Asian plateau and the Himalayas.
**Movements:** Largely resident, but birds breeding at higher altitudes descend to nearby coasts in winter. Birds that breed in western Germany are probably only summer visitors.
**Breeding:** Four to six black-lined grey eggs are laid in a cup well hidden in a rock crevice and are incubated for 12 or 13 days by the female alone. The young hatch helpless and downy and fly after 10–13 days. Regularly double brooded.
**Confusing Species:** No other bunting has such clear facial markings.

JFMAMJJASOND

## Ortolan Bunting *(Emberiza hortulana)*

A well-marked summer visitor to Europe, from the Mediterranean to beyond the Arctic Circle, the Ortolan Bunting is curiously absent from a swathe of countryside that extends from Britain to the Black Sea. The summer male is streaked chestnut and black above, and is a warm orange below, with a grey-green head marked by a yellow moustache and bib. The bill is pink. This bird may be confused with Cretzschmar's Bunting in all but male summer plumage.

*The female (left) lacks the grey-green head of the male (far left), but shows a yellow bib and moustache. The winter male is similar to the female.*

**Size:** 15–18cm (6–7in).
**Wing:** 77–96mm.
**Bill:** 12–15mm.
**Weight:** 19–28g.
**Voice:** Six or seven notes repeated and terminating on an odd one.
**Habitat:** Open landscapes, particularly hilly plateaux with scanty vegetation; on passage, mostly on ploughed fields.
**Food:** Seeds and insects.
**Range:** Summer visitor from Spain through the Mediterranean, and from eastern Germany across Russia and the Ukraine, with a wide gap between. Also from Sweden across northern Russia. Extends eastwards to central southern areas of Siberia.
**Movements:** Whole population winters in Sahel Africa. Spring passage much more obvious than autumn, with clear evidence of a trans-Saharan migration on a broad front. Common on Mediterranean islands at this time.
**Breeding:** Four to six blackish-spotted bluish eggs are laid in a cup on the ground hidden beneath a bush and incubated by the female for 11–14 days. The downy, helpless young fly after 10–15 days. Double brooded.
**Confusing Species:** Cretzschmar's Bunting.

| J | F | M | A | M | J | J | A | S | O | N | D |

---

## Cretzschmar's Bunting *(Emberiza caesia)*

A localized summer visitor to Greece and the eastern Mediterranean, this bird is similar to the Ortolan Bunting. Both sexes are streaked black and chestnut above. The male has a grey head, with an orange moustache and bib. The female has pale chestnut-streaked underparts. The bill is pink.

**Size:** 15–18cm (6–7in).
**Wing:** 77–88mm.
**Bill:** 12–15mm.
**Weight:** 20–25g.
**Voice:** Series of clear repeated notes, with the last note at a different pitch.
**Habitat:** Rocky, stony hillsides with prominent bushes, used as song posts.
**Food:** Seeds, berries and insects.
**Range:** Confined to eastern Mediterranean, where it is found in localized areas of Greece, Crete, Turkey, Cyprus and from Syria to Israel. Winters eastern Ethiopia.
**Movements:** Whole population moves southeast to winter quarters, with large numbers of birds passing through Cyprus and Israel.
**Breeding:** Four to six black-spotted grey eggs are laid in a cup-shaped nest on the ground. The eggs are incubated for 12–14 days by the female. The helpless and down-covered young fledge after 12 or 13 days. It frequently rears a second brood.
**Confusing Species:** Beware Ortolan Bunting in any plumage other than adult male in summer plumage.

| J | F | M | A | M | J | J | A | S | O | N | D |

*The female (below) is similar to the male (far left), but has more subdued head markings.*

## Yellow-breasted Bunting *(Emberiza aureola)*

A summer visitor to the far northeast of Europe, this species migrates southeast away from Europe and is, therefore, only a rare vagrant farther west. The male is a gem, with rich chocolate-brown upperparts marked by a white double wingbar and yellow underparts. The face is black and the bill ivory. The female is streaked buff grey and black above, grey or buff on the flanks, with a clear face pattern that includes enclosed ear coverts, a bold supercilium and a crown stripe.

J F M A M J J A S O N D

**Size:** 13cm (5in).
**Wing:** 72–81mm.
**Bill:** 14–15mm.
**Weight:** 17–28g.
**Voice:** Melodic high-pitched, more rapid version of song of Ortolan Bunting; call is a thin *zick*.
**Habitat:** Scrub and marshy thickets in the boreal zone, as well as some agricultural areas.
**Food:** Insects, seeds, berries.
**Range:** Summer visitor from Finland across boreal Eurasia to Japan. Winters Southeast Asia. In Europe, is increasing and spreading westwards through Finland, though population remains at only a few hundred pairs.

*While the male (left) has the yellow breast of the species name, the female (right) is streaked and well marked, with a hint of yellow on the sides of the neck.*

**Movements:** Migrates vast distances eastwards through Russia, Siberia and China to its wintering grounds in Southeast Asia.
**Breeding:** Four or five black-spotted grey eggs are laid in a cup in a bush and incubated by the female for 13 or 14 days. The helpless, downy young fly after 11–14 days. It probably raises two broods each year.
**Confusing Species:** Vagrant females and juveniles resemble several vagrant American sparrows.

## Rustic Bunting *(Emberiza rustica)*

*Although the female (right) has a similar crest to the male (left), it is speckled rather than black.*

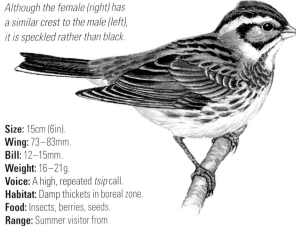

**Size:** 15cm (6in).
**Wing:** 73–83mm.
**Bill:** 12–15mm.
**Weight:** 16–21g.
**Voice:** A high, repeated *tsip* call.
**Habitat:** Damp thickets in boreal zone.
**Food:** Insects, berries, seeds.
**Range:** Summer visitor from Scandinavia eastwards through boreal

J F M A M J J A S O N D

A well-marked summer visitor to Scandinavia and northern Russia, this bird is scarce farther west and is seen only on passage. The male is streaked black and brown above, with a chestnut nape that extends to the breast to form a clear, but ill-defined breast band. Chestnut streaks extend along the white flanks. The head is black and distinctly crested. The supercilium and throat are both white.

Russia to the Bering Strait. Winters China and Japan. In Europe, breeds Sweden and Finland.
**Movements:** Even Scandinavian birds fly eastwards to winter in the Far East and in autumn they are locally common on the east coast of Sweden.
**Breeding:** Four or five brownish-spotted grey eggs are laid in a cup well hidden near the ground and incubated by the female for 12 or 13 days. The downy, helpless chicks fly after 9 or 10 days.
**Confusing Species:** No other European bunting shows a crest.

# Little Bunting *(Emberiza pusilla)*

**Size:** 13–15cm (5–6in).
**Wing:** 67–76mm.
**Bill:** 11–13mm.
**Weight:** 13–17g.
**Voice:** A thin *tic*.
**Habitat:** Damp tundra or taiga with shrubs along rivers.
**Food:** Insects, berries and seeds.
**Range:** Summer visitor from Lapland to the Bering Strait. Winters China, Korea.
**Movements:** Whole population heads eastwards to its Asian winter quarters.
**Breeding:** Four or five black-streaked green eggs laid in a cup on the ground and incubated by both parents for 12 days. Helpless, downy chicks fledge at 11 days. A second brood may be raised.
**Confusing Species:** Reed Bunting.

This small bunting resembles the female Reed Bunting. The upperparts are streaked black and brown, and the underparts are white with fine streaking on breast and flanks. The most obvious features are the peaked crown, pale crown stripe, clear, broad supercilium and a black outline to pinkish cheeks. The thin bill is grey.

*In summer plumage (right), the male is distinctive. The peaked crown tops chestnut cheeks that are clearly edged in black. In winter (top), the species is duller all over, with less extensive cheek colouring.*

J F M A M J J A S O N D

# Reed Bunting *(Emberiza schoeniclus)*

Widespread and common, this bird is a resident of wetlands over much of temperate Europe. It is a summer visitor to the north and east and a winter visitor to southern Europe and North Africa. The plumage of both sexes is streaked brown and black above, with white outertail feathers. The male has a black head and breast, broken by a white moustachial streak and backed by a white collar. The breast and flanks are streaked in the female, and only the flanks in the male. This bird is seen most frequently as it sits openly near the top of a reed.

*The female (right) has dark ear covers, pale supercilium and a prominent moustachial streak. Only the female Lapland Bunting shares all these features, but that bird has a yellow bill and a clear pale crown stripe.*

**Size:** 15–18cm (6–7in).
**Wing:** 70–87mm.
**Bill:** 6–8mm.
**Weight:** 15–27g.
**Voice:** A plaintive, weak little warble ending rapidly.
**Habitat:** Marshy margins, reedbeds and heaths.
**Food:** Insects and seeds.

**Range:** Breeds across Europe and Siberia to Japan. Birds from Scandinavia and Poland eastwards are summer visitors. Winters Europe, Japan, China and central southern Asia.
**Movements:** Much movement from north and east Europe to the south and west within the breeding range.
**Breeding:** Four or five black-speckled grey eggs are laid in a cup on or near the ground and incubated for 12–14 days mainly by the female. The helpless, downy chicks fledge after 10–13 days. Two or three broods may be raised.
**Confusing Species:** Over most of Europe, the female is the base species from which other female buntings must be distinguished.

J F M A M J J A S O N D

## Black-headed Bunting *(Emberiza melanocephala)*

This summer visitor to southeast Europe arrives late, but may then be locally abundant. The male has a chestnut back, black and buff wings and bright yellow underparts. A black crown extends to the eye and ear coverts. The female is greyish on the crown and back, with pale underparts washed yellow on the breast and undertail.

J F M A M J J A S O N D

*The female (right) is like other female buntings, but can be identified by a plain grey face and clear pale eye-ring.*

**Size:** 15–18cm (6–7in).
**Wing:** 86–101mm.
**Bill:** 16–18mm.
**Weight:** 23–33g.
**Voice:** Song a slow rendering of four or five notes.
**Habitat:** Open bushy country with tall trees, groves, orchards.
**Food:** Insects, seeds and berries.
**Range:** Summer visitor to parts of Italy, coastal Croatia, Albania, Greece and Bulgaria, extending eastwards to Turkey, Cyprus and the Middle East. Winters northwest India.
**Movements:** Arrives late and leaves early, spending only May to July in Europe. The whole population migrates through Iran and Pakistan to reach winter quarters.
**Breeding:** Four or five brown-speckled blue eggs are laid in a cup, well concealed in a thicket, and are incubated by the female with some help from the male for 10–14 days. The downy, helpless young fly after 13–16 days. Single brooded.
**Confusing Species:** Female can be confused with the female Cinereous Bunting, but this bird has a darker bill and faint spotting creates a scruffy look.

## Corn Bunting *(Miliaria calandra)*

**Size:** 18–20cm (7–8in).
**Wing:** 87–107mm.
**Bill:** 8–10mm.
**Weight:** 34–64g.
**Voice:** Repeated jangling rattle.
**Habitat:** Open fields with hedges and thickets, heaths.
**Food:** Seeds and berries.
**Range:** Resident from Britain, where it is highly localized, and Iberia eastwards across Europe to Turkey, the Middle East and beyond the Aral Sea. Absent from Ireland, Scandinavia and most of Russia.

**Movements:** Definite movements south and west within resident range, but longer-distance movements of birds that breed to north and east of resident range may also take place.
**Breeding:** Four to six greyish-spotted white eggs are laid in a cup on or near the ground and incubated by the female for 12–14 days. The helpless, down-covered chicks fly after 12 or more days. A second brood is sometimes raised.

*The rattle of the male's song can be heard at almost any season or time of day as an aggressive defence of the breeding territory.*

J F M A M J J A S O N D

Both sexes resemble streaked female buntings of other species, being heavily streaked black and greyish brown above, and finely streaked brown on cream below. The thick neck, large, stubby bill and propensity to sing with its head tilted back create an unmistakable shape. The species is regularly seen on wires and posts and frequently flies with legs dangling. It is locally abundant in southern Europe, forming winter flocks.

# ACCIDENTAL AND MARGINAL SPECIES

Accidentals are birds that have strayed from their normal breeding or wintering areas, or their migration routes, and have occurred at least once, but less than annually in Europe during the last 50 years.

These accidentals have not been included in the main part of the book and are listed below, along with marginal species that have a restricted range or occur in low numbers.

| | |
|---|---|
| White-billed Diver | *Gavia adamsii* |
| Pied-billed Grebe | *Podilymbus podiceps* |
| Black-browed Albatross | *Diomedea melanophris* |
| Wandering Albatross | *Diomedea exulans* |
| Southern Giant Petrel | *Macronectes giganteus* |
| Cape Verde Petrel | *Pterodroma feae* |
| Madeira Petrel | *Pterodroma madeira* |
| Soft-plumaged Petrel | *Pterodroma mollis* |
| Capped Petrel | *Pterodroma hasitata* |
| Bulwer's Petrel | *Bulweria bulwerii* |
| Cape Verde Shearwater | *Calonectris edwardsii* |
| Little Shearwater | *Puffinus assimilis* |
| Madeiran Storm-petrel | *Oceanodroma castro* |
| Swinhoe's Storm-petrel | *Oceanodroma monorhis* |
| Wilson's Storm-petrel | *Oceanites oceanicus* |
| Double-crested Cormorant | *Phalacrocorax auritus* |
| American Bittern | *Botaurus lentiginosus* |
| Least Bittern | *Ixobrychus exilis* |
| Green Heron | *Butorides virescens* |
| Western Reef Heron | *Egretta gularis* |
| Bald Ibis | *Geronticus eremita* |

**Bald Ibis**

| | |
|---|---|
| Lesser Flamingo | *Phoenicopterus minor* |
| Snow Goose | *Anser caerulescens* |
| American Wigeon | *Anas americana* |
| Falcated Duck | *Anas falcata* |
| Black Duck | *Anas rubripes* |
| Blue-winged Teal | *Anas discors* |
| Lesser Scaup | *Aythya affinis* |
| Redhead | *Aythya americana* |
| Ring-necked Duck | *Aythya collaris* |
| Canvasback | *Aythya valisineria* |
| Spectacled Eider | *Somateria fischeri* |
| Surf Scoter | *Melanitta perspicillata* |
| Bufflehead | *Bucephala albeola* |
| Bald Eagle | *Haliaeetus leucocephalus* |
| Pallas's Fish Eagle | *Haliaeetus leucoryphus* |
| American Kestrel | *Falco sparverius* |
| Golden Pheasant | *Chrysolophus pictus* |
| Lady Amherst's Pheasant | *Chrysolophus amherstiae* |
| Sora Rail | *Porzana carolina* |
| Purple Gallinule | *Porphyrio porphyrio* |
| Allen's Gallinule | *Porphyrula alleni* |
| American Purple Gallinule | *Porphyrula martinica* |
| Little Button-quail | *Turnix sylvatica* |
| American Coot | *Fulica americana* |
| Red-knobbed Coot | *Fulica cristata* |
| Sandhill Crane | *Grus canadensis* |
| Siberian White Crane | *Grus leucogeranus* |
| Houbara Bustard | *Chlamydotis undulata* |
| Cream-coloured Courser | *Cursorius cursor* |
| Oriental Pratincole | *Glareola maldivarum* |

| | |
|---|---|
| Semipalmated Plover | *Charadrius semipalmatus* |
| Killdeer | *Charadrius vociferus* |
| Lesser Sand Plover | *Charadrius mongolus* |
| Greater Sand Plover | *Charadrius leschenaultii* |
| Caspian Plover | *Charadrius asiaticus* |
| White-tailed Plover | *Chettusia leucura* |
| Great Knot | *Calidris tenuirostris* |
| Semipalmated Sandpiper | *Calidris pusilla* |
| Western Sandpiper | *Calidris mauri* |
| Red-necked Stint | *Calidris ruficollis* |
| Long-toed Stint | *Calidris subminuta* |
| Least Sandpiper | *Calidris minutilla* |
| White-rumped Sandpiper | *Calidris fuscicollis* |
| Baird's Sandpiper | *Calidris bairdii* |
| Pectoral Sandpiper | *Calidris melanotos* |
| Sharp-tailed Sandpiper | *Calidris acuminata* |
| Stilt Sandpiper | *Micropalama himantopus* |
| Buff-breasted Sandpiper | *Tryngites subruficollis* |
| Pin-tailed Snipe | *Gallinago stenura* |
| Short-billed Dowitcher | *Limnodromus griseus* |
| Long-billed Dowitcher | *Limnodromus scolopaceus* |
| Hudsonian Godwit | *Limosa haemastica* |
| Slender-billed Curlew | *Numenius tenuirostris* |
| Little Whimbrel | *Numenius minutus* |
| Upland Sandpiper | *Bartramia longicauda* |
| Greater Yellowlegs | *Tringa melanoleuca* |
| Lesser Yellowlegs | *Tringa flavipes* |
| Solitary Sandpiper | *Tringa solitaria* |
| Spotted Sandpiper | *Actitis macularia* |
| Grey-tailed Tatler | *Heteroscelus brevipes* |
| Willet | *Catoptrophorus semipalmatus* |
| Great Black-headed Gull | *Larus ichthyaetus* |
| Laughing Gull | *Larus atricilla* |
| Franklin's Gull | *Larus pipixcan* |
| Bonaparte's Gull | *Larus philadelphia* |
| Ring-billed Gull | *Larus delawarensis* |
| Ivory Gull | *Pagophila eburnea* |
| Ross's Gull | *Rhodostethia rosea* |

**Ross's Gull**

| | |
|---|---|
| Royal Tern | *Sterna maxima* |
| Lesser Crested Tern | *Sterna bengatensis* |
| Elegant Tern | *Sterna elegans* |
| Aleutian Tern | *Sterna aleutica* |
| Forster's Tern | *Sterna forsteri* |
| Bridled Tern | *Sterna anaethetus* |
| Sooty Tern | *Sterna fuscata* |
| Least Tern | *Sterna antillarium* |
| Brown Noddy | *Anous stolidus* |
| Ancient Murrelet | *Synthliboramphus antiquus* |
| Spotted Sandgrouse | *Pterocles senegallus* |
| Pallas's Sandgrouse | *Syrrhaptes paradoxus* |
| Rufous Turtle Dove | *Streptopelia orientalis* |

| | |
|---|---|
| Mourning Dove | *Zenaida macroura* |
| Rose-ringed Parakeet | *Psittacula krameri* |
| Oriental Cuckoo | *Cuculus saturatus* |
| Black-billed Cuckoo | *Coccyzus erythrophthalmus* |
| Yellow-billed Cuckoo | *Coccyzus americanus* |
| Marsh Owl | *Asio capensis* |
| Egyptian Nightjar | *Caprimulgus aegyptius* |
| Common Nighthawk | *Chordeiles minor* |
| Chimney Swift | *Chaetura pelagica* |
| White-throated Needletail | *Hirundapus caudacutus* |
| Pacific Swift | *Apus pacificus* |
| White-rumped Swift | *Apus caffer* |
| Little Swift | *Apus affinis* |
| Pied Kingfisher | *Ceryle rudis* |
| Belted Kingfisher | *Ceryle alcyon* |
| Blue-cheeked Bee-eater | *Merops superciliosus* |
| Northern Flicker | *Colaptes auratus* |
| Yellow-bellied Sapsucker | *Sphyrapicus varius* |
| Acadian Flycatcher | *Empidonax virescens* |
| Eastern Phoebe | *Sayornis phoebe* |
| Tree Swallow | *Tachycineta bicolor* |
| Cliff Swallow | *Hirundo pyrrhonota* |
| Bar-tailed Desert Lark | *Ammomanes cincturus* |
| Bimaculated Lark | *Melanocorypha bimaculata* |
| Dupont's Lark | *Chersophilus duponti* |
| Blyth's Pipit | *Anthus godlewskii* |
| Olive-backed Pipit | *Anthus hodgsoni* |
| Buff-bellied Pipit | *Anthus rubescens* |
| Northern Mockingbird | *Mimus polyglottos* |
| Brown Thrasher | *Toxostoma rufum* |
| Grey Catbird | *Dumetella carolinensis* |
| Black-throated Accentor | *Prunella atrogularis* |
| Siberian Accentor | *Prunella montanella* |
| Siberian Rubythroat | *Luscinia calliope* |
| Siberian Blue Robin | *Irania gutturalis* |
| Moussier's Redstart | *Phoenicurus moussieri* |

**Moussier's Redstart**

| | |
|---|---|
| Desert Wheatear | *Oenanthe deserti* |
| Finsch's Wheatear | *Oenanthe finschii* |
| White-crowned Black Wheatear | *Oenanthe leucopyga* |
| White's Thrush | *Zoothera dauma* |
| Siberian Thrush | *Zoothera sibirica* |
| Varied Thrush | *Zoothera naevia* |
| Wood Thrush | *Hylocichla mustelina* |
| Hermit Thrush | *Catharus guttatus* |
| Swainson's Thrush | *Catharus ustulatus* |
| Grey-cheeked Thrush | *Catharus minimus* |
| Veery | *Catharus fuscescens* |
| Eye-browed Thrush | *Turdus obscurus* |
| Dark-throated Thrush | *Turdus ruficollis* |
| Dusky Thrush | *Turdus naumanni* |
| American Robin | *Turdus migratorius* |
| Pallas's Grasshopper Warbler | *Locustella certhiola* |
| Gray's Grasshopper Warbler | *Locustella fasciolata* |
| Thick-billed Warbler | *Acrocephalus aedon* |
| Desert Warbler | *Sylvia nana* |
| Green Warbler | *Phylloscopus nitidus* |
| Pallas's Warbler | *Phylloscopus proregulus* |
| Two-barred Greenish Warbler | *Phylloscopus plumbeitarsus* |

| | |
|---|---|
| Yellow-browed Warbler | *Phylloscopus inornatus* |
| Hume's Yellow-browed Warbler | *Phylloscopus humei* |
| Radde's Warbler | *Phylloscopus schwarzi* |
| Dusky Warbler | *Phylloscopus fuscatus* |
| Ruby-crowned Kinglet | *Regulus calendula* |
| Brown Flycatcher | *Muscicapa dauurica* |
| Red-breasted Nuthatch | *Sitta canadensis* |
| Brown Shrike | *Lanius cristatus* |
| Isabelline Shrike | *Lanius isabellinus* |
| House Crow | *Corvus splendens* |
| Daurian Jackdaw | *Corvus dauuricus* |
| Yellow-throated Vireo | *Vireo flavifrons* |
| Philadelphia Vireo | *Vireo philadelphicus* |
| Red-eyed Vireo | *Vireo olivaceus* |
| Red-fronted Serin | *Serinus pusillus* |
| Trumpeter Finch | *Bucanetes githagineus* |
| Evening Grosbeak | *Hesperiphona vespertina* |
| Black and white Warbler | *Mniotilta varia* |
| Golden-winged Warbler | *Vermivora chrysoptera* |

**Golden-winged Warbler**

| | |
|---|---|
| Tennessee Warbler | *Vermivora peregrina* |
| Northern Parula | *Parula americana* |
| Yellow Warbler | *Dendroica petechia* |
| Chestnut-sided Warbler | *Dendroica pensylvanica* |
| Black-throated Green Warbler | *Dendroica virens* |
| Blackburnian Warbler | *Dendroica fusca* |
| Cape May Warbler | *Dendroica tigrina* |
| Magnolia Warbler | *Dendroica magnolia* |
| Yellow-rumped Warbler | *Dendroica coronata* |
| Blackpoll Warbler | *Dendroica striata* |
| American Redstart | *Setophaga ruticilla* |
| Ovenbird | *Seiurus aurocapillus* |
| Northern Waterthrush | *Seiurus noveboracensis* |
| Common Yellowthroat | *Geothlypis trichas* |
| Hooded Warbler | *Wilsonia citrina* |
| Wilson's Warbler | *Wilsonia pusilla* |
| Canada Warbler | *Wilsonia canadensis* |
| Summer Tanager | *Piranga rubra* |
| Scarlet Tanager | *Piranga olivacea* |
| Rufous-sided Towhee | *Pipilo erythrophthalmus* |
| Lark Sparrow | *Chondestes grammacus* |
| Savannah Sparrow | *Passerculus sandwichensis* |
| Fox Sparrow | *Passerella iliaca* |
| Song Sparrow | *Melospiza melodia* |
| White-crowned Sparrow | *Zonotrichia leucophrys* |
| White-throated Sparrow | *Zonotrichia albicollis* |
| Dark-eyed Junco | *Junco hyemalis* |
| Black-faced Bunting | *Emberiza spodocephala* |
| Pine Bunting | *Emberiza leucocephalos* |
| Yellow-browed Bunting | *Emberiza chrysophrys* |
| Chestnut Bunting | *Emberiza rutila* |
| Pallas's Reed Bunting | *Emberiza pallasi* |
| Red-headed Bunting | *Emberiza bruniceps* |
| Rose-breasted Grosbeak | *Pheucticus ludovicianus* |
| Blue Grosbeak | *Guiraca caerulea* |
| Indigo Bunting | *Passerina cyanea* |
| Bobolink | *Dolichonyx oryzivorus* |
| Brown-headed Cowbird | *Molothrus ater* |
| Northern Oriole | *Icterus galbula* |

# GLOSSARY

Goshawk

**Accidental:** A species that has appeared in an area only a few times and whose normal range is elsewhere. Also known as a vagrant.

**Altitudinal movement:** The movement of birds from mountains into valleys or lowlands to escape severe winter weather, and back again.

**Aquatic:** Frequenting water.

**Arboreal:** Frequenting trees.

**Axillaries:** The feathers of a bird's 'armpit', where the underside of the wing joins the body.

**Boreal Zone:** The area south of the tundra where climate and soil are suitable for dense coniferous forests.

**Brood:** The number of young in a particular nest.

**Carpal patch:** A patch of feathers at the bend of the wing.

**Cere:** A fleshy, featherless area surrounding the nostrils of birds of prey and a few other groups of birds.

**Circumpolar:** Of or inhabiting the Arctic (or Antarctic) regions in both the eastern and western hemispheres.

**Clutch:** The number of eggs in a particular nest.

**Colonial:** Nesting in groups, rather than in isolated pairs.

**Coniferous trees:** Trees from the conifer family that bear cones.

**Conspecific:** Belonging to the same species.

**Cosmopolitan:** Worldwide in distribution, occurring on all continents except Antarctica.

**Coverts:** Small feathers that overlie or cover the bases of the flight feathers of the wings and tail or that cover an area or structure (e.g. ear coverts).

**Crèche:** A group of young birds from various families that may be nursed and guarded from predators by adults from the same species, which are not necessarily their parents.

**Crepuscular:** Active at dawn and dusk.

**Crest:** A tuft of elongated feathers on the crown.

**Crown:** The top of the head.

**Cryptic:** A jagged or uneven colouring that provides camouflage against a broken background.

**Deciduous trees:** Trees that shed their leaves at the end of the growing season.

**Decurved:** Curved downwards.

**Dimorphic:** Having two plumages, usually male/female or winter/summer plumages.

**Diurnal:** Active during the day.

**Eclipse plumage:** A dull-coloured plumage acquired by most ducks immediately after the breeding season and worn for a few weeks during complete moults.

**Endemic:** Found only in a particular area.

**Eruption:** An irregular, large-scale departure of birds from a particular area.

**Extralimital:** From outside the area under discussion; in this book, a bird not native to Europe.

**Eyestripe:** A stripe of colour that runs horizontally from the base of the bill through the eye and beyond.

**Feral:** A bird that has escaped from captivity, or that is descended from such escapees and is now wild and self-supporting.

**Fieldmark:** A characteristic of colour, pattern, or structure, useful in distinguishing a species in the field.

**Flank:** The area on each side of a bird's body, below the folded wing.

**Fledging:** The point in time when a young bird leaves its nest.

**Flight feathers:** The long, well-developed feathers of the wings and tail, used during flight. The flight feathers of the wings are divided into primaries, secondaries and tertials.

**Frontal shield:** A fleshy, featherless and often brightly-coloured area on the forehead of coots, gallinules and some other birds.

**Fulvous:** Tawny.

**Gape:** The open mouth of a bird.

**Holarctic:** Occurring in both the Palearctic and Nearctic regions, i.e. in northern and north temperate regions of the world.

**Immature:** A young bird in a plumage stage between juvenile and adult.

**Irruption:** An irregular, large-scale arrival of birds in an area.

**Juvenile:** A young bird in its first feathered plumage.

**Lek:** A place where males of some bird species gather to perform courtship displays in a group. Females visit a lek to mate, but build their nests elsewhere.

Azure Tit

**Loafing:** Resting in flocks, on the ground or on the water, usually during the day.

**Lore:** The area between the eye and the base of the bill, sometimes distinctively coloured.

**Mandible:** One of the two parts of the bird's bill, divided into the upper mandible and the lower mandible. The mandibles are joined to the bird's skull, but are able to move independently.

**Mantle:** The back of a bird together with the upper surfaces of the wings; the term is used especially of birds in which these areas are of one colour.

**Migrant:** A bird that regularly passes through an area on its way to or from its normal breeding range.

**Mirrors:** White spots in the black wingtips of gulls.

**Mixed Forest:** A forest consisting of a mixture of coniferous and deciduous trees.

**Montane:** Of, or inhabiting, mountains.

**Moult:** The process of shedding and replacing feathers.

**Moustachial streak, or moustache:** A stripe of colour running from the base of the bill along the side of the throat.

**Nape:** The back of the neck.

**Nearctic:** The region of North America where similar animal and plant groups are found: a zoogeographical region.

**Nocturnal:** Active at night.

**Omnivorous:** Eating both plant and animal food.

**Palearctic:** The region of Eurasia where similar animal and plant groups are found: a zoogeographical region.

**Passage Migrant:** A bird that appears in an area while on migration, but is not a winter visitor to that area and does not breed there.

**Pelagic:** Frequenting the open ocean.

**Phase:** A distinctive plumage colour in certain groups, such as falcons and skuas, that is unrelated to race, age, sex or season.

**Plume:** A long feather, generally used in display.

**Polygamous:** Mating with more than one member of the opposite sex.

**Primaries:** The outermost and longest flight feathers on a bird's wing, numbering 11 in most species.

**Primary Projection:** The extent to which the primary flight feathers project beyond other feathers when the wing is folded.

**Race:** A geographical population of a species, slightly different from other populations of that species; also called a subspecies.

**Raft:** A large number of ducks resting or feeding together on the water surface.

**Range:** The geographical area or areas inhabited by a species.

**Raptor:** A bird of prey.

**Recurved:** Curved upwards.

**Resident:** Remaining in one place all year.

**Ringing:** The marking of birds by rings of metal or coloured plastic on their legs.

**Riparian:** Of or inhabiting the banks of a river or stream.

**Riverine Forest:** An area of woodland alongside a river that floods seasonally.

**Rufous:** A reddish colour.

**Rump:** The area of a bird's body on its back above the tail.

**Sahel (Zone):** An area extending from the south of the Sahara desert into parts of Central Africa that has very severe droughts.

**Scapulars:** A group of feathers on the shoulders of a bird, along the side of the back.

**Scrape:** A shallow depression made by a bird on the ground to serve as a nest.

**Secondaries:** The large flight feathers along the rear edge of the wing, inward from the primaries.

**Sedentary:** Remaining in one place; non-migratory.

**Shearwatering:** Flying on stiff wings, over water.

**Shoulder:** Technically, the point where the wing meets the body, but widely applied to the bend of the wing.

**Spatulate:** Spoon-shaped.

**Speculum:** A distinctively coloured area on the wing of some ducks.

**Subadult:** A bird not in full adult plumage; a term usually used of birds that take more than a year to acquire adult plumage.

Greenish Warbler

**Subspecies:** A geographical population of a species that is slightly different from other populations of that species; also called a race.

**Supercilium:** A conspicuous stripe running above, but not through, the eye. Also known as the eyebrow.

**Superspecies:** A group of closely related species whose ranges do not overlap.

**Tarsus:** The lower, usually featherless, part of a bird's leg above the feet.

**Temperate Zone:** The areas of the Earth that are found between the tropics and the polar circles, where temperatures are moderate.

**Terrestrial:** Frequenting the ground.

**Territory:** Any area that a bird defends against others of the same species.

**Tertials:** The innermost flight feathers on a bird's wing, immediately adjacent to the body. Also called tertiaries.

**Thermals:** Currents of warm, rising air used by hawks and other soaring birds to assist flight.

**Vagrant:** A species that has appeared in a given area only a few times and whose normal range is in another area. Also known as an accidental.

**Vinaceous:** Dark reddish-purple, wine-coloured.

**Western Palearctic:** That part of the Palearctic lying west of the Urals and north of the central Sahara, and including the northwestern Middle East.

**Wingbar:** A bar of colour that runs along or across a bird's wing and is a contrasting colour to the rest of the bird's body.

Common Pochard

# USEFUL ADDRESSES

**ALBANIA**
ALBANIAN SOCIETY FOR THE
PROTECTION AND PRESERVATION OF
BIRDS AND MAMMALS, Faculty of
Natural Sciences, Tirana University,
Al-Tirana
Tel/fax: +355 42 29 028

**AUSTRIA**
BIRDLIFE AUSTRIA (ÖSTERREICHISCHE
GESELLSCHAFT FÜR VOGELKUNDE),
Museumsplatz 1/10/8, A-1070 Wien
Tel: +43 1 523 4651
Fax: +43 1 524 7040

**BELGIUM**
LIGUE ROYALE BELGE POUR LA
PROTECTION DES OISEAUX (LBPO),
Rue de Veeweyde 43,
B-1070 Brussels

**BRITISH ISLES**
BRITISH TRUST FOR ORNITHOLOGY,
National Centre for Ornithology,
The Nunnery, Thetford, Norfolk
IP24 2PU
Tel: +1842 750050
Fax: +1842 750030

ROYAL SOCIETY FOR THE PROTECTION
OF BIRDS (RSPB), The Lodge, Sandy,
Bedfordshire SG19 2DL
Tel: +1767 680551
Fax: +1767 692365

**BULGARIA**
BULGARIAN SOCIETY FOR THE
PROTECTION OF BIRDS, PO Box 114,
Dianabad/Izgrev,
BG-1172 Sofia
Tel/fax: +359 2 689413

**CROATIA**
CROATIAN SOCIETY FOR BIRD AND
NATURE PROTECTION, Ilirski Trg 9,
HR-10000 Zagreb
Tel/fax: +385 1 345 445

**CZECH REPUBLIC**
CZECH SOCIETY FOR ORNITHOLOGY,
Hornoměcholupská 34, CZ-102 00
Praha 10
Tel/fax: +42 2 786 6700

**DENMARK**
DANSK ORNITHOLOGISK FORENING
(DOF), Fuglenes Hus, Vesterbrogade
140, DK-1620 Copenhagen V
Tel: +45 31 314404
Fax: +45 31 312435.

**ESTONIA**
ESTONIAN ORNITHOLOGICAL SOCIETY
(EOÜ), PO Box 227, EE-2400 Tartu
Tel: +372 7 430 198
Fax: +372 7 427 033

**FINLAND**
ASSOCIATION OF ORNITHOLOGICAL
SOCIETIES IN FINLAND, PL 17,
FIN-18101 Heinola

**FRANCE**
LIGUE POUR LA PROTECTION DES
OISEAUX (LPO), La Corderie Royale,
BP 263, F-17305 Rochefort CEDEX
Tel: +33 5 46 821234
Fax: +33 5 46 839586

**GERMANY**
DACHVERBAND DEUTSCHER
AVIFAUNISTEN (DDA), Schafberg 31,
D-96476 Rodach

**GREECE**
HELLENIC ORNITHOLOGICAL SOCIETY,
53 Emm. Benaki Str, GR-10681 Athens
Tel/fax: +301 1 38 11271.

**HUNGARY**
HUNGARIAN ORNITHOLOGICAL &
NATURE CONS SOC (MME),
Költo u. 21, Pf 391,
H-1536 Budapest
Tel/fax: +36 1 175 8327

**ICELAND**
ICELANDIC SOCIETY FOR THE
PROTECTION OF BIRDS, PO Box 5069,
IS-125 Reykjavík

**ITALY**
LEGA ITALIANA PROTEZIONE
UCCELLI (LIPU), Via Trento 49,
I-43100 Parma
Tel: +39 521273043
Fax: +39 521273419

**LUXEMBOURG**
LIGUE LUXEMBOURGEOISE POUR LA
PROTECTION DE LA NATURE ET DES
OISEAUX (LNVL), Kraizhaff, Rue de
Luxembourg, L-1899 Kockelscheuer
Tel: +352 290 404
Fax: +352 290 504

**NETHERLANDS**
DUTCH BIRDING ASSOCIATION, Postbus
75611, 1070 AP Amsterdam

**NORWAY**
NORSK ORNITOLOGISK FORENING
(NOF), BirdLife Norway,
Seminarplassen 5, N-7060 Klæbu
Tel: +47 72 831166
Fax: +47 72 831255

**POLAND**
OGÓLNOPOLSKIE TOWARZYSTWO
OCHRONY PTAKÓW (OTOP), PO Box
335, PL-80-958 Gdańsk 50
Tel/fax: +48 58 412693

**PORTUGAL**
LIGA PARA A PROTEÇÃO DA NATUREZA
(LPN), Estrada do Calhariz de Benfica
187, P-1500 Lisbon

**ROMANIA**
SOCIETATEA ORNITHOLOGICĂ ROMÂNĂ
(SOR), Str Gheorghe Dima 49/2,
RO-3400 Cluj
Tel/fax: +40 64 438086

**SLOVAKIA**
SOCIETY FOR THE PROTECTION OF BIRDS
IN SLOVAKIA (SOVS), PO Box 71,
SK-093 01 Vranov nad Topl'ou
Tel:+421 931 61120
Fax: +421 931 62120

**SLOVENIA**
BIRDWATCHING AND BIRD STUDY
ASSOCIATION OF SLOVENIA (DOPPS),
Langusova 10, SL-61000 Ljubljana
Tel: +386 61 133 9516
Fax: +386 61 133 9516

**SPAIN**
SOCIEDAD ESPAÑOLA DE ORNITOLOGÍA
(SEO), Carretera de Húmera No 63-1,
E-28224 Pozuelo de Alarcón, Madrid
Tel: +34 1 351 1045
Fax: +34 1 351 1386

**SWEDEN**
SVERIGES ORNITOLOGISKA FÖRENING
(SOF), Ekhagsvägen 3, S-10405
Stockholm
Tel: +46 8 612 2530
Fax: +46 8 612 2536

**SWITZERLAND**
SCHWEIZER VOGELSCHUTZ (SVS),
Wiedingstr 78, PO Box 8521,
CH-8036 Zürich
Tel: +41 1 463 7271
Fax: +41 1 461 4778

**EUROPEAN BIRD
ORGANISATIONS**
BIRDLIFE INTERNATIONAL, Wellbrook
Court, Cambridge, England CB3 0NA
Tel: +41 01223 277318
Fax: +41 01223 177200

EUROPEAN ORNITHOLOGICAL UNION,
Istituto Nazional per la Fauna
Selvatica, Via Ca'Fornacetta 9,
40061 Ozzano Emilia (BO), Italy

# INDEX

# ACKNOWLEDGEMENTS

Every effort has been made to trace the copyright holders of the illustrations used in this book. Any person or organization having claims to ownership not identified below is invited to contact the publishers.

**The following abbreviations have been used:** AL = Alfred Limbrunner; GB = Dr Günter Bethge; FH/NF = Frank Hecker/Natur Fotografie; GM = Günter Moosrainer; FLPA = Frank Lane Picture Agency; RV = Richard Vaughan; DT = David Tipling; WP = Windrush Photos; ET = ET Archive; WWI = Woodfall Wild Images

b = bottom, c = centre, l = left, r = right, t = top

2/3 FLPA/W.S. Clark; 3 c Ardea/Z. Tunka; 4/5 c FLPA/M. Withers; 6 WWI/M. Biancarelli; 8 tl Ardea/P. Morris; 9 cr Ardea/P. Morris; 12 tl ET; 12/13 t Archivi di Arte Antica, b ET/V&A Museum, London; 13 tr Ardea/P. Morris, cr Booth Museum of Natural History, Brighton, br ET; 14 tl c ET; 16 bl Ardea/F. Gohier; 16/17 Ardea/P. Steyn; 18 tl WP/ A. & E. Morris, tr Ardea/S. Meyers; 18 bl WP/DT, br Ardea/Z. Tunka; 19 tr WWI/T. Räsänen, c WP/D. Green, br WP/L. Borg; 20 c Ardea/ R.F. Porter, b Ardea/P. Steyn; 21 tl AL, br FLPA; 24 cr Ardea/P. Morris; 24/25 c Ardea/J. Clegg; 25 bc G. Legg/Booth Museum of Natural History, Brighton; 26 b Ardea/W. Weisser; 26/27 ct AL, c Ardea/D. Avon; 28 cr WP/DT; 28/29 t Ardea/F. Gohier, b AL; 30 cr Ardea/Z. Tunka; 30/31 t E. Mestel; 31 cl WP/L. Borg, tr Ardea; 32 tc FH/NF, br WP/DT; 33 tl AL, tr WP/D. Green, bl WP/G. Reszeter, br Oxford Scientific Films/ D. Green; 34 c WP/M. Lander; 35 tl tr Ardea/G.K. Brown, bl Ardea/Bromford & Sadler, br C. Schenk; 37 tl FH/NF, c WP/ H. Nicholls; 38 cr AL, bl Ardea/D. & K. Urry; 40 bl Ardea/M. Iijima; 41 tl FH/NF, tr Ardea/I. Beames; 42 cl FH/NF; 42/43 Ardea/B.L. Sage; 44 tl FH/NF, cl tr AL, bl Ardea/J. Daniels, br WP/J. Roberts; 45 tr WP/G. McCarthy, bl WP/DT; 46 l, r FLPA/E. & D. Hosking; 47 tl Science Photo Library/Planetarium, c Science Photo Library, tr FLPA/H.D. Brandl, bl P. Johansson; 48 tr FLPA/R. Tidman, cr FLPA/ E. & D. Hosking, br Ardea/D. & K. Urry; 50 tr FLPA/A.B. Hamblin, cr FLPA/F. Pölking; 51 bl FLPA/A. Christiansen; 52 cl FH/NF; 52/53 t FLPA/R. Tidman; 53 tr AL; 54/55 t WP/G. McCarthy; 55 tc Ardea/ J.A. Bailey, bl Ardea/RV, br AL; 56 cl WP/R. Tidman, br J. Diedrich; 56/57 t WP/DT; 58 cr WP/J. Roberts, bl AL, br Ardea/G.K. Brown; 59 t AL; 60 br AL; 60/61 t Ardea/C. Knights; 61 cr FH/NF, br Ardea/RV; 62 cr Ardea/G.K. Brown; 62/63 t Ardea/RV, b WP/DT; 63 c J. Diedrich; 64 cl WP/G. Langsbury, br Ardea/B. Gibbons; 64/65 c Ardea/D. & K. Urry; 65 br Ardea/J.A. Bailey; 66 bc WP/DT; 66/67 t FH/NF; 67 tc FLPA/ W. Wisniewski; 68 tr WP/D. Sreen, br WP/D. Mason; 69 cl J. Diedrich; 70 bl Ardea/A. Lindau; 70/71 FLPA/R. Wilmshurst; 72 tl WWI/ D. Woodfall, bl WWI/H. MacKay; 72/73 t Tony Stone Images/ N. Mackenzie, b FLPA/D. Hosking; 73 tr WP/DT, cr Ardea/J. Daniels, br WWI/K. Taylor; 74 tr Ardea/RV, cr WP/DT; 75 cl FH/NF, cr WP/DT, b J. Diedrich; 76 tl Ardea/J. Daniels; 76/77 t b cr br WP/DT; 78 cr WP/ E. Woods, bl Ardea/RV; 80 b FLPA/E. & D. Hosking; 80/81 t FLPA/ C.W. Wisniewski; 81 tr FLPA/R. Wilmshurst, bl Ardea/S. Meyers, br FLPA/Foto Natura/C.W. Meinats; 82 bl Ardea/J.P. Ferrero, br FLPA/ M. Jones; 82/83 t FLPA/R. Wilmshurst; 83 bl Ardea/I. Beames; 84 l WP/L. Borg, r WP/J. Roché; 85 bl WP/R. Tidman, br Ardea/K.W. Fink; 86 b Ardea/F. Gohier; 86/87 WWI/T. Räsänen; 88 tl br FH/NF, tr WP/ D.M. Cotteridge, bl WWI/M. Powles; 89 tl WP/R. Revels, c AL, br WP/A.B. van den Berg; 91 tl E. Mestel, cl Ardea/B.L. Sage, bl Ardea/ J. Daniels; 92 tc Ardea/J.A. Bailey, tr WP/J. Roberts, cr FH/NF, cl Ardea/ S. Roberts, bc Ardea/P. Steyn; 94 tr Ardea/I. Beames, br Ardea/RV; 95 tc Ardea/RV, cl L.E. Lofgren/Natureza Ord & Bild, bc Ardea/R.F. Porter; 96 tc Ardea/RV, bl Ardea/S. Roberts; 97 tl Ardea/J.A. Bailey, bl WP/DT; 98 tr FH/NF, cl AL; 99 tc Ardea/J. Gooders, cl Ardea/R.F. Porter; 100 tl bl GM; 101 tr FH/NF, bc Ardea/F. Labat; 102 tl, c FH/NF, bl AL; 103 tc Ardea/R.T. Smith, br Ardea/C. Haagner; 104 tc Ardea/J.P. Laub, bl Ardea/G. Robbrecht; 105 tl bc FH/NF; 106 tl Ardea/C. Haagner, bl GB; 107 tr bc FH/NF; 108 t cl FH/NF, b Ardea/C. & J. Knights; 109 tc c FH/NF; 110 tc bl FH/NF; 111 c AL, cl Ardea/J.A. Bailey; 112 tr FH/NF, bl Ardea/K. Fink; 113 tr Ardea/I. Beames, bl Ardea/J.A. Bailey; 114 tl AL, cl FH/NF, bl WP/G. McCarthy; 115 tl br FH/NF; 116 tl br FH/NF; 117 tl Ardea/W. Wagner, cl FH/NF; 118 tl Ardea/I. Beames, c FH/NF, bl Ardea/F. Gohier; 119 tc Ardea/J.A. Bailey, cl Ardea/K. Fink, bl FH/NF; 120 tr Ardea/G.K. Brown, bl FLPA/D. Hosking; 121 tl WP, cl FLPA/R. van Nostrand, bl FLPA/T. Whittaker; 122 tl bl FH/NF, cl WP/A. & E. Morris; 123 tl AL, br GB; 124 tl FLPA/M. Withers, cr FH/NF; 125 tl bc AL, cl FLPA/R. Tidman; 126/127 AL; 128 tl Ardea/G.K. Brown, c FH/NF; 129 tl bc AL, cl FH/NF; 130 tl cl Ardea/G.K. Brown, bl AL; 131 tl Ardea/J. Gooders, bl AL;

132 tr bl AL, cl Ardea/G.K. Brown; 133 tl GM, cr AL; 134/135 AL; 136 tl Ardea/G. Roberts, bl AL; 137 tl bl AL; 138 cl Ardea/C. Haagner, bl Ardea/G. Robbrecht; 139 tc bl AL; 140 tr FLPA, cl GB, bl FH/NF; 141 tl AL, br WP/D.M. Cottridge; 142 tc bl AL, c GM; 143 tl, bl FH/NF; 144 tl Ardea/J. Daniels, cr Ardea/D. Avon; 145 tl AL, cl Ardea/ G.K. Brown, bl Ardea/J.A. Bailey; 146 tl AL, cl bl FH/NF; 147 tl Ardea/A. Lindau, br M. Stelzner; 148 tl Ardea/M.D. England, cr bl AL; 149 tc FH/NF, c GM, bl Ardea/C. Knights; 150 tl AL, cr FH/NF; 151 tc cl FH/NF, bl AL; 152 tl Ardea/J.B. & S. Bottomley, bc FH/NF; 153 tl Ardea/G.K. Brown, c FH/NF, bl FLPA/Y. Eshbol; 154 tr AL/ P. Reininger, c FLPA/E. & D. Hosking; 155 tc AL, bl FH/NF; 156 cl Ardea/C. Knights, cr Ardea/J.B. & S. Bottomley; 157 tr Ardea/R.J.C. Blewitt, bl WP/DT; 158 tl FH/NF, bl FLPA/H. Hautala; 159 tl AL, cl Ardea/C. Knights, bl Ardea/R.J.C. Blewitt; 160 cl AL, bc FLPA/G. Moon; 161 tr GM, bl FH/NF; 162 c AL, bl WP/DT; 163 cr Ardea/M.D. England, cr Ardea/J.B. & S. Bottomley; 164 tl AL, cl Ardea/G.K. Brown, bl FH/NF; 165 tr Ardea/ G.K. Brown, cr FH/NF; 166 tl FH/NF, cr AL; 167 tr Ardea/ H. & J. Beste, br FH/NF; 168 tr GB, bl WP/H. Nicholls; 169 cl FH/NF, cr AL; 170 tl FH/NF, bl AL; 171 tr GB, cl FH/NF; 172 tc Ardea/J. Daniels, cl bl FH/NF; 173 tc FH/NF, cr WP/T. Ennis; 174 tl Ardea/RV, bl FH/NF; 175 tc bl AL; 176 tr Ardea/RV, bl AL; 177 tl FH/NF, c Ardea/B. Sage; 178 tl AL, bl Ardea/P. Steyn; 179 tl WP/D. Green, cr FLPA/D. Maslowski; 180 tl Ardea/J. Daniels, br Ardea/P. Morris; 181 tr FH/NF, bl WP/R. Tidman, br FH/NF; 182 tl WP/R. Tidman, br FH/NF; 183 tr bl Ardea/RV; 184 cl AL, cr FH/NF; 185 tl Ardea/G.K. Brown, cl AL, bl FH/NF; 186 tl FH/NF, c AL; 187 tl c AL; 188/189 tl c bl FH/NF; 190 tl P. Johansson, bc FH/NF; 191 c FH/NF, bl WP/DT; 192 tc br FH/NF; 193 tl WP/J.L. Roberts, cr Nature Photographers/P. Sterry; 194 tl bl AL, cl D.M. Cottridge; 195 tc AL, cl FH/NF; 196 tl FH/NF, cl bc WP/DT; 197 tc cl AL, bc GB; 198 tl FH/NF, cl GB, bl R. Schmide; 199 tc FH/NF, cl Ardea/J.A. Bailey, cr Ardea/G. Robbrecht; 200 tl FH/NF, cl T. & I. Loseby, bl Birding World/S. Gantlett; 201 tr AL, br Ardea/A. Greensmith; 202 tl cr FH/NF; 203 tl Ardea/ W. Wersser, c AL, bl Ardea/J.A. Bailey; 204 tl FH/NF; c AL; 205 tc AL; cl FH/NF; bc AL; 206 tr AL, c Ardea/G.K. Brown; 207 cl FH/NF, bl AL; 208 c Ardea/J.P. Laub, bl FH/NF; 209 cl AL, bl FH/NF; 210 t cr Ardea/G. Reszeter, c Ardea/R. Smith; 211 FH/NF; 212 tl FH/NF, bl AL; 213 tr WP/D.M. Cottridge, cr FH/NF; 214 tl Ardea/R. Richter, c Ardea/J.A. Bailey; 215 tc FH/NF, cl Ardea/M.D. England; 216/217 tl bl FH/NF; 218 tc Ardea/ R.T. Smith, cl AL, bl FH/NF; 219 cl Ardea/J.A. Bailey, br AL; 220 cl Ardea/G. Robbrecht, cr FH/NF; 221 cl Ardea/RV, bl FLPA/ R. Wilmshurst; 222 tl Ardea/P. Lamb, bl FH/NF; 223 tl FH/NF, cr Ardea/J.A. Bailey; 224 tl GM, cr Ardea/M.D. England; 225 cl AL, bc Ardea/A. Greensmith; 226 tr Ardea/J.S. Dunning, bl Ardea/D. Avon; 227 c WP/G. Eskström, bl G. Kovars; 228 tl bc AL; 229 tr FH/NF, c Birding World/S. Gantlett; 230 cl WP/F. Ekström, cr WP/P. Doherty; 231 tr Ardea/R. Richter, br FH/NF; 232 tc AL, cl Birding World/S. Gantlett, bc D.M. Cottridge; 233 cl WP/ D.M. Cottridge, bl AL; 234 t Ardea/M.D. England, c Ardea/R.T. Smith; 235 c FH/NF, cl Ardea/M.D. England, bl Ardea/G. Reszeter; 236 tl AL, c Ardea/J.A. Bailey; 237 tl AL, cl FH/NF, bl GM; 238 tl FH/NF, cr Ardea/Z. Tunka; 239 cr Ardea/W. Wagner, cl Ardea/D. Avon; 240 tl Ardea/S. Roberts, cr Birding World/R. Wilson; 241 tl bl Ardea/ R.T. Smith; 242 cr Ardea/J.A. Bailey, cl Ardea/Z. Tunka; 243 tr AL, c D.M. Cottridge, bl Ardea/J.A. Bailey; 244 tl Ardea/C. Knights, cl FLPA/D.A. Robinson, bl FLPA/H.D. Brandl; 245 tl FH/NF, br Ardea/ J.A. Bailey; 246 tl D.M. Cottridge, cr GB; 247 tl E. Tomschi, bl Ardea/J.A. Bailey; 248 tl FH/NF, cl B. Pontinem, bl FH/NF; 249 tl FH/NF, bl AL; 250 tr AL, bl D.M. Cottridge; 251 tl br AL; 252 tc Ardea/I. Beames, c WP/D.M. Cottridge; 253 tr Ardea/A. Weaving, c Ardea/G.K. Brown; 254 tr FH/NF, cl WP/M. Gore; 255 tr FH/NF, bl AL; 256 tl FH/NF, bl FLPA/R. Chittenden; 257 tr AL, bc WP/B.R. Hughes; 258 tl bc AL; 259 cl bc FH/NF; 260 tl FH/NF; cl FH/NF; bc FH/NF; 261 tl FH/NF; cl Ardea/D. Avon; 262 tc FLPA/E. & D. Hosking, c AL; 263 cl FH/NF, cr FLAP/R. Tidman; 264 tl Ardea/J.A. Bailey, cl FLPA/ A.B. Hamblin; 265 cl Ardea/G.K. Brown, c GM; 266 cl FH/NF, cr Ardea/J.A. Bailey; 267 tl Ardea/J.B. & S. Bottomley, c Ardea/R.T. Smith, bl Ardea/S. Roberts; 268 cl FH/NF, c Ardea/S. Roberts; 269 c FH/NF, bl Ardea/S. Roberts; 270 cl WP/D.M. Cottridge, bc H. Hautala; 271 tc WP/R. Tipper, c Ardea/B. Bevan; 272 tl AL, c Ardea/S. Roberts; 273 tc Ardea/R.J.C. Blewitt, c Ardea/RV; 274 tc bl FH/NF; 275 cr Ardea/RV, br FH/NF; 276 cl FH/NF, bl P. Zeimur; 277 tc WP/DT, cl GB; 278 tl WP/DT, bl Ardea/J.A. Bailey; 279 tl WP/R. Brooks, cl FH/NF.